rolling stone the seventies

EDITED BY
Ashley Kahn
Holly George-Warren
Shawn Dahl

DESIGNED BY
Helene Silverman

Little, Brown and Company
BOSTON NEW YORK TORONTO LONDON

A Rolling Stone Press Book

Editor: Holly George-Warren
Senior Editor: Shawn Dahl
Assistant Editor: Ann Abel
Contributing Editors: Ashley Kahn, Alanna Stang

Designer: Helene Silverman
Wenner Media Creative Director: Fred Woodward
Photo Research: Rachel Knepfer, Susan Rubin, Alanna Stang, Brittain Stone

First Edition

ISBN 0-316-75914-7

Library of Congress Catalog Card Number 98-66661

10 9 8 7 6 5 4 3 2 1

Published simultaneously in Canada by Little, Brown & Company (Canada) Limited
Printed in the United States of America

These essays previously appeared in similiar form in the following publications:

"Fact & Fiction & Fear & Loathing" by Hunter S. Thompson in *The Great Shark Hunt* (Summit Books, 1979); "Leaking the Truth" by Jann S. Wenner in ROLLING STONE 147, November 8, 1973; "The Soul Nation Climbs Aboard" by Carol Cooper in *Egg,* November 1990; "Christmas in Hanoi" by Joan Baez as an interview with Tim Cahill in ROLLING STONE 127, February 1, 1973, and in *And a Voice to Sing With* (Summit Books, 1987); "This Precious Right" by Susan Brownmiller in the *Village Voice,* January 27, 1998; "Who's Your Guru?" by Richard Michael Levine in ROLLING STONE 156, March 14, 1974; "Malignant Giant" by Howard Kohn in ROLLING STONE 183, March 27, 1975; "Funky Chic" by Tom Wolfe in ROLLING STONE 151, January 3, 1974; "Deliver Us From Evel" by Joe Eszterhas in ROLLING STONE 173, November 7, 1974; "Live, From New York . . ." by Bill Zehme in ROLLING STONE 562, October 5, 1989; "Leading Country to Rebellion" by Chet Flippo in *Country: The Music and the Musicians* (Country Music Foundation/Abbeville Press, 1988); "Goodbye, Vietnam" by Laura Palmer in ROLLING STONE 188, June 5, 1975; "Tania Got Her Gun" by Howard Kohn & David Weir in ROLLING STONE 198, October 23, 1975 and ROLLING STONE 200, November 20, 1975; "Feverish" by Nik Cohn in *New York,* December 8, 1997; "Destination: Mars" by Tim Ferris in ROLLING STONE 236, April 7, 1977; "A Death in the Family" by Mikal Gilmore in ROLLING STONE 234, March 10, 1977 and ROLLING STONE 632, June 11, 1992; "Hotel California" by Anthony DeCurtis in ROLLING STONE 587, September 20, 1990; "Saint Elvis" by Chet Flippo in *Tennessee Illustrated,* July/August 1989; "Finding Hope in the Middle East" by Joe Klein in ROLLING STONE 267, June 15, 1978; "On the Inside Looking In" by Daisann McLane in ROLLING STONE 632, June 11, 1992; "Paranoia, Panic & Poison" by Tim Cahill in ROLLING STONE 283, January 25, 1979; "Death of the Cincinnati Eleven" by Chet Flippo in ROLLING STONE 309, January 24, 1980.

Picture Credits:

Waring Abbott/Michael Ochs Archives: 95, 97; courtesy American Zoetrope: 276; courtesy Apple Computer, Inc.: 165; AP/Wide World Photos: 19, 99, 187; Archive Photos: 91, 93, 117, 223, 251; Arrow Productions-Las Vegas, NV: 55, 57; Edie Baskin: 173; Peter Beard: 68-69 Howard L. Bingham: 151; Adrian Boot/Retna: 195; courtesy Bowling Green State University: 37, 38, 39; courtesy CBS: 108-109; courtesy the Computer Museum: 167; Fred Conrad/Sygma: 181; Tom Copi/Michael Ochs Archives: 121; Corbis-Bettmann: 31, 80-81, 100, 131, 144, 155, 182, 255, 265, 279; courtesy Stan Cornyn: 249; Jim Cummins/ NBA Photos: 113; Emerson-Loew: 15; Everett Collection: 59; Everett Collection/ 20th Century–Fox 235; John Filo/Archive: 23; David Gahr: 75; Ron Galella: 229; courtesy Mikal Gilmore: 215; Arthur Grace/Sygma: 257-258; Archives of Milton H. Greene: 11; courtesy Ashley Kahn: 261; The Kobal Collection: 207; courtesy Howard Kohn: 123, 125; Tony Korody/Sygma: 199; Gary Krueger: 134-135, 136; J.P. Laffont/Gamma Liaison: 71, 73; J.P. Laffont/Sygma: 41; Annie Leibovitz/ Contact Press Images: 127; Neil Leifer: 147; Laura Levine: 283; Christopher Makos: 161; Mary Ellen Mark: 63, 104-105, 274-275; courtesy Larry Marion: 261; ©Fred W. McDarrah: 88-89; Jack Mitchell/courtesy Patrick Pacheco & After Dark: 219; Michael Ochs Archives: 45, 46, 49, 177, 196; courtesy Dave Otto: 261; Photofest: 29; Robin Platzer/Twin Images: 230-231; Neal Preston: 247-248; Chuck Pulin/Star File: 191; Jamie Putnam: 169; Mick Rock: 143; Raeanne Rubenstein: 203; Sipa Press: 267; Ralph Steadman: 107; Ray Stevenson/Retna: 209; Jay Thompson/Globe Photos: 16; Nik Wheeler/Sipa Press: 158-159; Tom Wolfe: 139; Janet Woolley: 239; Herbert W. Worthington: 227; Michael Zagaris: 51. (Every effort has been made to properly credit every image and to contact every copyright owner.)

preface

ROLLING STONE was to the Seventies what *The New Yorker* was to the Twenties – a signpost and a reflection of a tumultuous decade. Originally published in San Francisco, epicenter of the counterculture, ROLLING STONE heralded the groundswell of change taking place in America. The magazine's in-your-face style and down-and-dirty reportage brought the new frontier to the far-flung corners of the United States (and beyond). Music, politics, film, television, fashion, drugs, sexuality, medical and technological innovations – these components made up the whole of the magazine's beat. For those of us who came of age in the Seventies, ROLLING STONE was the pipeline to the changing times. The events, ideas and trends the magazine covered would eventually become reality in the cultural backwaters of provincial small-town America. And we were ready and waiting for them – thanks to the provocative ideas that sprang forth from ROLLING STONE's pages. As fringe lifestyle and culture mutated into staples of middle-class status quo, the scruffy upstart's role as an underground Pied Piper expanded into that of a New York–based mass-market chronicler, in the process transforming itself into a sophisticated, glossy magazine read by more than a million mainstream Americans every two weeks.

In *Rolling Stone: The Seventies*, we've sought to capture the full gamut of the decade with words and pictures representative of the ROLLING STONE style. Thus, we've called upon a diverse group of movers/shakers and innocent bystanders, participants and spectators. Journalists, musicians, photographers, newscasters, politicians, directors, screenwriters, producers, designers, novelists, artists, impresarios, leaders, followers – all are included here. Our contributors were forever changed by the decade, and within these pages they tell us how their lives were altered, as they report on an event or movement as they saw it or lived it. In addition to the new essays written for this book, we've excerpted several groundbreaking pieces originally published in ROLLING STONE. Throughout, emphasis is on the first-person perspective, and to that end we've provided eyewitness accounts of a number of defining Seventies moments, from the Kent State massacre and the siege of Wounded Knee to the Jimmy Carter presidential campaign and boogie nights at Studio 54.

As the decade unfolds in *Rolling Stone: The Seventies*, we see how America became the country it is today, in the shadow of the millennium. The music, movies, fashion and television programs of the Seventies are more popular now than ever, thanks to CD repackagings, sampling of key Seventies riffs, new films about the decade, rereleases of Seventies blockbusters and classics, reruns of the decade's TV shows on cable networks, and a proliferation of polyester and recycled Seventies style. Many of the decade's crucial issues have returned to the headlines: scandal in the White House and the possibility of impeachment, violent strife between opponents and proponents of the *Roe* v. *Wade* decision, exploration of the possibility of life on Mars, moral questions raised by the death penalty, antiwar protest over continuing conflict in the Middle East. It seems that – as the old maxim goes – the more things change, the more things stay the same.

So, whether you lived the decade its first time around or are living it now vicariously, we hope that *Rolling Stone: The Seventies* enlightens as well as entertains. It is our goal that the truths uncovered and reported herein will serve us all as we venture into the next century.

Holly George-Warren
Editor, Rolling Stone Press
April 1998

contents

rolling stone **the seventies**

the power of ten
by ashley kahn

PEOPLE REALLY DO build their dreams and expectations in ten-year blocks. As those great digital counters in our collective conscious click away, weighty meaning is forever attributed to the sequential turnover from years ending with a nine. Call it the Power of Ten: It has the strength to cast an energizing beam of hope on the brave new decade ahead or an instant shroud over the one recently departed.

For many, the Seventies began with a backward, rueful glance at the Sixties. If we can just hunker down and get through the next ten years, it was thought, maybe the Eighties will fulfill the promise made in some acid-tinged dreamscape when the Beatles and San Francisco were in full flower. "We're just waiting out the Seventies," said Steely Dan's Donald Fagen, voicing a shared, generational case of denial, "waiting for better times."

Pity the poor decade: Even when it was still the Seventies, it didn't stand a chance . . . Consider how that must have been – being pushed onstage immediately after the fabulous, furry, revolutionary Sixties. No intermission, either. Kinda like you're Andy Gibb and Stevie Wonder's your opener. "What? Me follow *him*?"

And check out your act: You've got Nixon at the helm, promising a swing to the right like never before (at least through his mouthpiece, John Mitchell), then the Vietnam War actually escalates (after how many years of protest?) and the billy clubs of Chicago '68 turn into the bullets of Kent State '70. No surprise that by that decade-opening summer, an entire (counter)culture mobilized itself into reverse in the hopes of tripping the clock backward.

But as the decade started rolling, strange times – *better* times, as Mr. Fagen put it – began happening. The stark, well-defined straight-versus-freak world of the Sixties fell out of focus – in favor of the freaks. The social loosening and unbridling and unbuckling for which so many had prayed and marched and shouted and smoked was becoming a reality. "If the goal was to get everybody to have long hair and take drugs," remarked Country Joe McDonald in 1971, "then the revolution is over with, and we've succeeded."

Before the decade was even half gone, the United States was out of Vietnam, Nixon was out of the White House and mainstreamers like Barbra Streisand were showing off the counter part of their personal culture, gettin' real and lightin' up onstage in Vegas.

Most significantly, in the hearts and hearths of Middle America, the wild social experiments incubated at Woodstock and in Haight-Ashbury were being adapted and applied. The partaking – or at least acceptance – of casual sex, recreational drugs and some form of rock & roll was the most visible crest on a tidal wave of informality that was sweeping the Not-So-Silent-Anymore Majority.

But the changes went much deeper than just lifestyle: How we thought (and now think), what we expected (and now demand) from ourselves, our society, our leaders were molded and remain set by events that transpired between 1970 and 1979. The effects are manifest: an innate, widespread political cynicism. A fallible and fallacious White House. A deep-seated reluctance to play the role of the world's policeman. An increased reliance on government policing of our ethnic checkerboard. A powerfully independent (some might say overly so) media.

America had awoken from the Sixties wiser and better prepared for the surprises the next decade would unveil. The litany of the Seventies' defining, hard-news events reveals the origin of so many of the forces still shaping our world:

The Pentagon Papers. The Munich Olympics. Nixon's visit to China. Watergate. The bombing of Hanoi. The Paris Peace Talks. Wounded Knee. The Yom Kippur War. The energy crisis. Busing. The Presidential resignation and pardon. Foreign assassinations and domestic spying by the CIA. Inflation and recession. The fall of Saigon. Mayaguez. The Bicentennial. Three Mile Island. The Camp David Accords. The Iranian hostage crisis. Afghanistan.

In weird and sometimes unsettling ways, today's headline-grabbing issues play out like reruns of Seventies news, begging the question of how much we have really learned from our recent past: Saddam Hussein (Ayatollah Khomeini), Heaven's Gate (Jonestown), Jack Kevorkian (Karen Ann Quinlan), Waco (Wounded Knee), Gulf War Syndrome (Agent Orange), gangsta rap (blaxploitation), goth (glam), Mars landing (Mars landing).

I MYSELF WITNESSED a good chunk of the Seventies as a high schooler in Cincinnati, ending up in New York by the close of the decade. I watched the horror of the Olympics carnage on television, caught the long, drawn-out Watergate hearings, saw the helicopters leaving Saigon, cheered the near-perfect Miami Dolphins dynasty and worshiped Terry Bradshaw, Franco Harris and the Pittsburgh Steelers (over my hometown Bengals, mea culpa).

As a budding "head," Zen-focused on the origamic art of achieving the perfect joint, I was enthralled by lingering rumors of the Sixties, reading about Acid Tests, university takeovers and free love (a well-thumbed copy of the ROLLING STONE coffee-table book *The Sixties* was a favorite – and an inspiration for this endeavor). Like most of my peers, on a cultural plane at least, I had my eyes consistently focused on the rearview. It wasn't until mid-'75 – when I started hanging out at Mole's Record Exchange near the University of Cincinnati campus – that I started to pick up on the here and now: Led Zeppelin, then Marvin Gaye, Hound Dog Taylor, Arthur Blythe. My cultural antennae primed me for *Saturday Night Live* and *Close Encounters* when they hit, and, later, for British punk and new wave when they reached our shores (thank you, *Trouser Press*).

Nowadays, the world remains remarkably comfortable and familiar to me, and it's not just the endless Seventies reruns on cable or inundation of "classic rock" stations on the FM band (though I do admit being tempted, when I hear the neighbor's kids cranking "When the Levee Breaks," to bust in and shout "Yo! That's *my* music!"). Rather, it's the cross-cultural, informal, human, funky way of being that settled in by the close of the Seventies and is still around: presidents blowing saxophone or skydiving, sports icons romping onscreen with cartoon characters, casual Fridays at the office. Sure, some of it's now manipulated "hip" – more a product of spin than sin – but the Jerry Garcia neckties adorning today's Wall Street boomers are displayed as proudly and sincerely as the Deadhead stickers on my high school buddies' Camaros and Gremlins.

To remember and celebrate the Seventies now is not to give in to nostalgia or trendy revisitation. It's a chance to better understand a miscast decade, to get past the disco balls and episodes of *Love Boat* and misguided hairstyles that are too commonly mistaken for the caliber of the decade's advances.

What's most absent now – what seemed to fade as the Eighties arrived with its Teflon presidents, Wall Street hijinks and another British invasion (this one vinyl-suited and videotaped) – is a general trait the Seventies clearly inherited from the Sixties. Call it the Pursuit of the Unbeaten Path, of not giving in to the knee-jerk impulse to limit oneself to a safe, corporate mind-set. Pardon an old-timer's generalizing prattle, but free thinking and chance taking ain't what they used to be.

If there's a lesson within these pages – an essential spirit of the Seventies – that's probably it right there: Keep your eyes open, question all you hear, pick your own path and avoid clichés. So expect no smiley faces, Pet Rocks or trivia quizzes on this tour. Rather, listen to those who witnessed the highs and lows of a redirecting decade, weigh the facts and foibles as the years speak for themselves – and then pass your own judgment.

Meet you at the end of the time line . . .

us versus hem
by mary peacock

NINETEEN SEVENTY was the year I had my picture in *Time* for being the editor of a fashion magazine called *Rags*. My fifteen column-inches of fame. It was an optimistic time, and we had seen no reason why we couldn't launch a national publication from an office that was the equivalent of a garage. Alas, by 1971 *Rags* was as dead as Janis and Jimi, the casualty of a hippie business plan that put more faith in vibes than accounting. But before *Rags* sank, it managed to help modernize fashion reporting by making it (a) entertaining and (b) relevant to many more people by insisting that fashion is defined by personal style, not by imitating the mode of the season.

Of course, nothing succeeds like good timing. The cover story of our best-selling issue, October 1970, was FASHION FASCISM: a report from the retail front on the bombing of the midi skirt.

That fall, every department store in America had dutifully stocked up on the latest style, the midcalf-length skirts that had been shown in Paris for a couple of seasons ("le midi") and were being echoed at the other end of the fashion rainbow by the long gypsy skirts of romantic hippie girls. But this time, when fashion spoke – "Buy Midi" – for the first time, customers answered, "I don't think so."

Young women liked their minis, older women had been tricked into looking like fools one time too many (in *their* minis, for example), and no one saw the point in replacing an entire wardrobe, including overcoats, just because the garment industry wanted them to. *Life* magazine made mini versus midi a cover story (the pundit who told *Life*, "They'll fight like hell but they'll fall into line," had better instincts about his or her own reputation: The quote was anonymous). But just a few weeks into the fall season, the financial press was reporting a "fiasco." The "lower the hem, the lower the sales," noted the *Wall Street Journal*; *Forbes* labeled the midi the Edsel of fashion. In the end, retailers and manufacturers lost millions, and some who bet too much on the long look were taking their last look at their businesses.

The politics of midi permanently changed the way fashion design worked. Stores with floors full of a truly disastrous style clarified to women the fact that fashion was not a democracy. So they voted with their wallets, and from then on, the industry began listening to its customers. Goodbye one-style-fits-all, hello options.

Before the demise of fashion dictatorship, the majority of women wore styles that originated in Paris (the wealthiest wore originals, the rest bought whatever level of knock-off they could afford). The hippies, who rooted through thrift shops and surplus stores for their finery, dressed as wizards, cowboys, pioneers, gypsies, Ruritanian palace guards, you name it. But they all had long hair. In fact, being a freak had just as many rules as being on the best-dressed list. After the Midi Revolt of 1970, the party was open to everyone.

Myself, I favored satin bell-bottom jeans, henley T-shirts (the ones with four-button neck plackets) and hand-painted clogs for the office – of course it *was* the *Rags* office. For serious occasions, like the *Time* photo shoot, I wore a pantsuit with a jacket cut so tight in the armholes (very chic) that I could hardly lift a hand, and cuffed wide-bottomed trousers with a waistline that dipped to the navel in front. My major accessory was a beaded American Indian belt draped around my hips. The other *Rags* writer pictured, Blair Sabol, wore a pair of elaborately custom-studded jeans (rock & roll couture), a skinny shirt with sleeves that got fuller near the cuff, a silver concha belt and a load of silver bracelets. Her curly hair was in a huge Jewish Afro, mine was waist-length, dead straight and parted in the middle.

Someone else's strongest fashion memories of the Seventies might be completely different from mine, because the first half of the decade played out the rest of the Sixties, and after the bicentennial, clothes began looking like what would come in the Eighties. But some fundamental things applied as time went by. The death of fashion despotism made way for profound changes during the Seventies.

The first, of course, was that the industry now paid attention to the consumer. Seventh Avenue designers stopped looking across the ocean and started seeing what was outside their own office windows. This led to some unfortunate fashion moments like "funky chic," mass-market attempts at rock & roll cool: suede and denim combos with fringe and studs. But other commercializations of counterculture clothing, like jeans, leotards and leather jackets, translated well. On the whole, the industry learned to be responsive, which was a good thing.

Another change was the emergence of a new definition of fashion-as-costume. Clothes were no longer simply emblematic of economic, social and cultural status, but also came to be donned by anyone and everyone to create new personas at will. Preppy by day, punk by night? No problem.

The most subtle Seventies fashion alteration was the rise and triumph of American sportswear: softly tailored jackets and pants and skirts. The kinds of mix-and-match separates that are less than dressy but more formal than jeans; the kinds of outfits that now define the words *work clothes* for white-collar women. Halston, Anne Klein, Calvin Klein, Ralph Lauren and many other designers created simple, dignified clothes that women could wear without making a big production of getting dressed. In the process, a unique and important identity for American fashion was established. From then on, the Paris collections were fun for the few; the New York collections were what women were really going to wear the next season.

Fashion-as-costume, the first child of the revolution, was operating on all levels in the Seventies. A subtle change in language both signaled and enabled an enormous shift in attitude. Clothes used to be about clothes themselves; designers and journalists had previously talked a lot about cut, fit and fabric. Around 1970 they shifted to a different jargon: They spoke of the "look." The parts no longer counted so much – it was about the whole image. (The relationship between language and perception is what Gloria Steinem had in mind when she named *Ms.* magazine – my next editorial stop after *Rags* – in 1971, and lobbied other media to use the term *Ms.* rather than *Miss* or *Mrs.*)

Hippies had started the costume ball rolling in 1968, and in the Seventies all kinds of like-minded groups discovered the joy of advertising their subcultures with their outfits. Funk and glam shared platform shoes in the early Seventies – some trends reach everyone – but every tribe had its own uniform as well as its own music and art.

In street culture, you were what you wore, clothes-as-ID. In straight (as opposed to counter) culture, "looks" were "fun," to be tried on, and then changed. Designers encouraged women to put on a persona for a season – or just a night. You could try the Twenties clothes inspired by the 1974 movie version of *The Great Gatsby* or ethnic looks ranging from imperfectly cured Afghan sheepskin coats available in low-rent East Village shops (a few drops of rain and the smell was extremely authentic) to Yves Saint Laurent's famous 1976 Russian-inspired rich-peasant collection of big, jewel-colored taffeta skirts and velvet tops belted with corselets. Or you could go to WASP heaven in Ralph Lauren's upper-class-aspirational tweeds, a look that was brilliantly twisted into yet another look in 1977 by Diane Keaton in *Annie Hall*.

At the same time, all these costumes were having a curiously subversive effect. If you could look like anybody, why not look like yourself? Starting early in the Seventies, an ever-growing number of women quietly left the costume party and began to wear the clothes that worked best for their bodies and lifestyles. They assembled wardrobes that were formal enough for work, practical enough for travel and comfortable enough to wear from morning till night. Ironically, the mini-midi war simply pushed a lot of women out of skirts altogether, and into pants. Soon trouser suits became commonplace in offices.

Fashion editors were pulling their hair out: How could they talk about what everyone should want for fall when everyone could no longer be persuaded to want the same thing? Then the real horror dawned: They didn't necessarily want anything new at all! The coup that enthroned rationality took place in 1973. Grace Mirabella, the champion of real clothes for real women, replaced Diana Vreeland, the legendary creator of fantasy fashion pages, as editor of *Vogue*.

The ascendance of sportswear designers contributed to another Seventies phenomenon: the spread of status logos from their traditional spot on expensive accessories to even the most casual clothes. In 1971, Edward Gorey, creator of slightly weird and very clever, satirical illustrated books, had this idea for a fashion fable: The heroine is run down by a taxi in front of Bergdorf Goodman in New York City. People rush to her assistance, but it's too late. Who is the unfortunate lady? Her bag is initialed LV (Louis Vuitton), but her belt says CC (Chanel). Her umbrella is covered with Fs (Fendi) yet her shoes read GG (Gucci). Her identity remains unknown, and, sadly, she is carried off to be buried in potter's field.

When designers of simple, wearable clothes gained as much status as couture-oriented designers, it triggered an exponential increase in labeling. By the end of the decade, Gorey would have been able to tell the same story even if his protagonist were dressed in jeans, sneakers and a T-shirt. French couturiers had long since discovered how to create cash flow by selling perfume. High-end designers Bill Blass and Halston became the American licensing champions, putting their names on everything from BB chocolates to Halston suitcases. In trying to up the ante of fame and fortune, Halston, arguably the best-known designer of the decade, made a Faustian bargain by selling his name to conglomerate Norton Simon rather than maintaining control of individual licensing deals. Before long, the designer whose name had been synonymous with elegance saw it pasted on a parade of products that diluted the Halston label down to department-store lines of sheets, towels, bras and bathrobes. Designers who started out a little lower on the ladder of chic tried their luck in the label game by putting their names on an ocean of of jeans and T-shirts.

Designer jeans were, in fact, the most durable mass-market contribution of the decade. The whole thing started in 1970. While I was choosing between the Landlubbers (lowest-riding and widest bell-bottomed fashion jeans) and the Levi's (classic Western style exerting a powerful romantic pull), more cutting-edge clothes dogs had discovered Fiorucci, an Italian clothing manufacturer with a hyperhip store on East Fifty-ninth Street in Manhattan. Fiorucci took American denim and cut it with Italian style. The quadrupled price was no object because the fit was fabulous.

In the good old days before preshrunk fabric, the cowboy way to get new Levi's to fit perfectly was to jump in that big water tank by the horse trough and then walk around in the sun (without bending your knees too much) till the jeans dried to your body. In the Seventies, the proper fit for designer jeans was achieved by worming into the smallest possible size while lying down in the dressing room (to counteract the effect of gravity) and pulling up the zipper with a pair of pliers. Those breathless moments on the fitting-room floor were satirized – only a comic genius could have improved on the real thing – in Gilda Radner's "Jewess Jeans" sketch on *Saturday Night Live*.

The late-Seventies designer-jeans explosion was so lucrative that everyone was fighting to jump into tight-fitting denim. Gloria Vanderbilt lent her high-society name to a brand, Sassoon infused theirs with French flavor, Studio 54's famous address appeared on countless denim derrieres and R&B mogul Kenny Gamble developed a style specifically for African-American physiques that cross-promoted his client, singer Teddy Pendergrass. Ta-daa! Teddy Bear jeans.

But in 1978, Calvin Klein seized the upper end of the fashion-jeans market. His original white-label, nothing-comes-between-me-and-my-Calvins jeans were such an icon that contemporary interest in the Seventies inspired the company to reintroduce them for a twentieth-anniversary edition in the fall of 1998.

At the time of this writing, the Seventies have been inspiring fashion all over the place. Take Prada's recent brown/purple and mustard/olive geometric prints – please. The shiny synthetic fabrics and pond-scummy color combinations that were not only decidedly downscale, but totally nerdy in the Seventies came back as haute-design stars. Perhaps Prada, the coolest of fashion houses in the Nineties, is engaged in a premillennial search for meaning, wondering if those ugly, man-made fabrics weren't somehow beautiful after all. Or maybe polyester had lived such a humble yet helpful life by freeing people of the need to iron that it was reborn on a higher plane of existence. Synthetics are just one item on a retro-revival list that includes the skinny shirt-and-pants silhouette, bare midriffs and platform shoes. It's interesting that one of the most

> **Both Tricia and Julie are fortunate that they have the kind of figures that permits them to wear miniskirts, but women should not complain about the new longer lengths, because most don't have the figures for the shorter ones. Don't get me wrong! I appreciate a nice miniskirt tripping down the Champs Elysées, or on the White House staff – there are plenty of minis here. –Richard Nixon**

reviled fashion decades of the century proved so influential in so short a time. Knowing fashion, however, doubtless we'll soon be reliving the Eighties. They're already talking about shoulder pads.

The lasting legacy of the Seventies is fashion democracy – personal style. This victory is best illustrated by envisioning a contemporary cocktail party. There's a group of women talking. The magazine editor has come from her office in a tailored pantsuit, the writer has had the time and inclination to put on a little black dress. Next to them is an actress in cowboy boots, Levi's and a silk shirt, having a word with a lawyer in a fitted dressmaker suit. Coming over to say hello are the host's mother and aunt, one in pearls and a classic silk dress, the other wearing leggings and a big chenille sweater with lots of silver jewelry. An art dealer arrives in the latest outrage from Comme des Garçons. Each one thinks she and everyone else looks . . . just . . . great. ⊕

the ascension of led zeppelin
by dr. donna gaines

MY BLANK PAGES

Cotton balls. By 3:00 a.m. a crusty white gunk has settled in the corners of my mouth. Slink around for zero-hour joints. A year out of high school, I'm an art school dropout, selling beads and candles on the beach. Painting by day, hanging on the corner by night, part of the residue freak population of Rockaway Beach, Queens. Here, high school kids, townies, college dropouts and assorted fuckups pursue sex, drugs and rock & roll as the ends, not the means, to personal liberation. My look: long, sunbleached, stringy Janis hair wrapped in a kerchief, enamel-painted earrings dangling, homespun beads draped over a purple Danskin leotard. Jeans hanging low, almost to the pubes. A strip of embroidery meticulously mapped out down the left leg of my raggy bells, fruit of an all-night Cream-fueled suburban speed ritual. The Sixties are ending, the promise of Utopia is in my next buzz.

The wasted years. Led Zeppelin, live in Central Park. Wall-to-wall people, they play for over three hours. That's what my friend says, I don't really remember. I'm on a date with a hippie fuzzball, a Deadhead with a VW bus. My Archie Bunker parents won't let Fuzzball in the house – hair, odors, politics. He dreams of splitting for the coast, or making the B.T.E. (Big Trip East – to India). He wants me to go. I'm not leaving the corner. Fuzzball hates the crowd. "Grippies," he declares, "greaser hippies!" Imported from the 'burbs and boroughs of New York, tough guys preening in shag haircuts and tank tops, pumped up. "Tinks," he calls them, Brooklyn boys making the scene, loitering with intent narcotic purposes, hitting on the hippie chicks.

Back in high school they would have been the hitters, tough-guy commandos of candy stores and parking lots, culturally stranded, misfit between the doo-wop crews of the early Sixties and flower power. Lumpen-hippie scum, fights, scars, the draft. "Yeah man, 'Nam!" Fuzzball resents their intrusion. This democratization of Woodstock Nation brought an unpleasant influx of working-class kids into the cultural mix. Despite Fuzzball's anarchistic rap and his visions of an egalitarian society, this scene is a *bummer*.

Fuzzball resented the Zeppelin fans on the basis of class difference and subcultural sensibility. He found no transcendence here, no deep meaning or communion. Sure, the music could be melodramatic and dopey, but that's what made it so great. In my aimless wanderings, I had followed the Fuzz to Dead shows. Always feeling slightly detached, restless. By now, reefer made me paranoid, it was impossible to tolerate without the covert aid of central-nervous-system depressants. Led Zeppelin provided shelter by the authority of Marshall (Amp) Law. It was a power much greater than me, one that guided, enveloped and protected me. A place of refuge, a means to exorcise my bad memories, racing impulses and ugly feelings. To feel myself and lose myself.

Justifying my passion for Zep, I told Fuzzball, "Robert Plant gives me orgasms." But that's not what I meant at all. Their music could be tantric, but what did I know about that at eighteen? It was impossible, hopeless, to explain something I knew he'd never get. But this guy next to me is getting it. He winks, grinning, cracked teeth behind a stubble mustache and a weak goatee, a manly man caught in the crossfire of John Paul Jones's strident bass runs and Plant's metallic blues yodel. An unpretty segment of boomer youth was in formation tonight, carving out turf. An amalgam of locals, leftovers, greaser-hippies, bright-eyed flower children, earnest politicos and a majority of marginal young people adrift on an anomic sea, sucked up in the shaman's sway of Jimmy Page's guitar magick. Led Zeppelin's grubby, velvet-ruffled sex-bombast slammed us right into the Seventies. Heavy metal was ascending, claiming psychic space. Nothing could withstand the annihilating assault of John Bonham's thirty-minute, whiskey-soaked, bloody-fisted Armageddon drum solos.

Hair medley "Aquarius/Let the Sunshine In." Harry Nilsson and Peggy Lee receive one each for, respectively, "Everybody's Talkin'" and "Is That All There Is?"

14 The TV special *Switched-On Symphony* airs, featuring Zubin Mehta and the L.A. Philharmonic with Santana, Jethro Tull, the Nice, Ray Charles and last-minute addition Bobby Sherman.

16 Tammi Terrell, hitmaking partner of Marvin Gaye, dies from a brain disorder first detected after she collapsed in Gaye's arms onstage in 1967.

20 David Bowie and Angela Barnett are wed. The two had been introduced by a mutual male lover.

21 Led Zeppelin kicks off a 26-date North American tour in Vancouver, Canada, with an unprecedented $650,000 tour guarantee.

22 A homemade pipe bomb rips through New York City nightclub the Electric Circus, injuring 15. Robbery is believed to be the motive.

24 Jennifer Thomas, a 16-year-old runaway, is severely beaten by Boston police for wearing an American flag she was given at the funeral of her father, a serviceman.

26 On the heels of Peter, Paul & Mary's Grammy win (Best Children's Recording for *Peter, Paul & Mommy*), Peter Yarrow pleads guilty to "taking immoral liberties" with a 14-year-old girl. Eleven years later President Carter will issue him a pardon.

27 South Vietnamese ground forces, with U.S. air support, invade Cambodia, attacking Communist forces there. The American military denies crossing the border.

1970 APRIL

2 ROLLING STONE reports that Joe Cocker has recruited a new band including Leon Russell. The extravaganza promptly hits the road billed as the Mad Dogs and Englishmen Tour.

ROLLING STONE reports that due to increasing litigation incited by musicians' obscene comments, gestures and acts during many rock concerts, performance contracts now often carry anti-obscenity clauses.

ROLLING STONE reports on the rapid rise in cocaine consumption and distribution, noting that in 1967, 22 kilos of the

In Led Zeppelin, I understood my American destiny at once. I hungered for *more*. More volume, higher proof, another hit, a bigger dick, heavier riffs, harder pounding. My love of the holy Zep grew concurrently with my alcoholism. I adored the elixir Jack Daniel's most of all. Jack tempered my reds and reefer till I simulated nirvana – the carbona buzz of my formative years. A space somewhere between childhood-tonsillectomy ether dreams and visions of pirate love. The music, coupled with the chemicals, smashed me up against the brick wall, bounced me around and then sweetly whispered *I love you*. This was passionate music, direct, with great sincerity and drive. Implicitly, I trusted Led Zeppelin. *My* Seventies were delivered, full metal jacket, by four Englishmen who pirated

Led Zeppelin, the harbingers of heavy metal, at the dawn of a new decade at the Chateau Marmont, Los Angeles: John Bonham, John Paul Jones, Robert Plant and Jimmy Page *(from left)*

the blues for the white race once and for all. In time, there would be other contenders – second and third waves of metal bands, and new generations of fans. But none would ever match God Zeppelin, not in the whole history of the world.

BIRTH OF A NATION

A new soundtrack for America's youth culture was gurgling up, a mutant strain out of the belly of Zep, the vulgate of classic rock. Traces had appeared as early as 1967, in Hendrix's "Purple Haze." Heavy-metal thunder was at once menacing and thrilling, like the sound of ten thousand motorcycles ripping the roadways, careening forward. By 1975, ZOSO was painted or carved on every static thing rocker kids could find. It had become a unifying symbol for America's suburban adolescents. The Children of Zoso are Zep's legacy. Mostly white males, nonaffluent American kids mixing up the old-school prole values of their parents, mass culture, pagan yearnings and Sixties hedonism. For the sons and daughters of white rural America and turnpike suburbia, Led Zeppelin marks the beginning of creation. If you ask the Children of Zoso what it is about Led Zeppelin that matters most, they will always say "the songs," not the words, not even the chords. The songs. Majestic tales of olden days, electric gasps of Celtic glory. Alchemy of the first world's decline, a mixture of hard and pretty, of ballistic missiles and tender sentiments. "Zoso" was the common-law title of Zep's untitled fourth and most-revered album. It's the name fans gave to the 1971 masterpiece that included "Stairway to Heaven."

Jimmy Page was the mystic junkie, a dabbler in the black arts, a self-styled disciple of Aleister Crowley. Fanlore held that Led Zeppelin had a pact with the devil. Except for John Paul Jones, the band had sold their souls for rock immortality. Some people thought Page's spells had actually killed people – John Bonham, for instance, and Robert Plant's young son, Karac. Led Zeppelin was followed by a trail of destruction through its twelve years, culminating in Bonzo's alcohol-related death in 1980. These tragedies are as easily explained by the "too much too soon" fate of legendary rock & roll bands as by satanic lore. By all accounts, though, the band was particularly rowdy, vulgar, sadistic and wild. At a time when most rock bands were pretty raunchy and intimidated many adults, Zep always did it better.

Of course, Led Zeppelin could be embarrassing, over-the-top, cheesy, corny. But that made them immortal like suburbia, the family, patriotism, religion and true love. They were at once sweet and decadent, sincere and campy, expressing faith and betrayal, hope and despair. Biographer Stephen Davis places the band somewhere between *Beowulf* and Marvel Comics. This is the foundation of heavy metal – contradictions, folklore as anthem, comic-book-hero theatrics, video-game action, pop satanism and horror-movie gore thrills. Get the Led out, volume and elixir, onward into the orgasmatron.

Upfront, Atlantic Records' Ahmet Ertegun was convinced that Led Zeppelin was the new supergroup. Before he even had the tapes for the eponymously titled first album, he wrote out a $200,000 check and left creative control to the band. To date, this Zep legend is every suburban rocker's prayer. To live large and emerge victorious on the basis of being yourself. When the band was hailed by their label as heirs to the empty thrones of Cream and Hendrix, critics resented the record-company hype, and dismissed the whole enterprise as crass. "Commercial, capitalist, overly promoted group that still needed to prove itself musically," tour-manager-*cum*-biographer Richard Cole reported. Likewise, Stephen Davis chronicles various instances of audience-bashing by the press, who sneered that "Led Zeppelin appealed to Seconal gobblers and Boone's Farmers. To field hippies and speed freaks. Led Zeppelin was déclassé, low-rent, sleazy cock-rock with no redeeming social values."

The band, in turn, was protective of the fans. Plant lovingly referred to them as "my people." Bonham was a model of workingman stamina, while living life in overdrive. Page's dabblings have armed a generation of powerless, voiceless young people with satanic imagery and esoterica. The black arts are good for putting forth an alternative view on pleasure, as well as scaring the piss out of parents. At least, it buys a kid a moment's dignity.

Led Zeppelin communed with their fans through esoteric signs and symbols, creating a secret society that excluded the profane world. The band procured loyalty through the music's implicit sex magick. William Burroughs compared Led Zeppelin's effect on its audience to that of the trance musicians of Morocco and likened the rock stars to priests. After seeing Zeppelin live, Burroughs said, "The result aimed at would seem to be the creation of energy in the performers and the audience. For such magic to succeed, it must tap the sources of magical energy, and this can be dangerous." It was, for these are the elementary forms of religious life.

GRACE

Led Zeppelin orchestrated a world-historic cultural transformation in rock, by altering the critic's role as arbiter and mediator between band and fan. Rock criticism itself was fairly new, and its reaction to Zep and their legions revealed an unspoken class bias: *No Respect.* Disgusted with the media's misunderstandings and relentless trashing of their music, Led Zeppelin instituted a press ban, denied interviews, ultimately undermining the cultural authority of critical acclaim. The aesthetic and sociocultural estrangement between the early rock press and metal bands and fans solidified with the rise of Black Sabbath, Judas Priest and Iron Maiden. Critics' taste is almost always an inverse barometer of popular taste. To this day, heavy-metal fandoms rarely rely on anything outsiders say, preferring word of mouth via fanzines, metal mags and the Internet. Fans defy record-company market manipulations, radio and MTV rotation regimentation and remain loyal to their bands. By now, mainstream coverage is generally regarded as an intrusion, a death knell. Fans drive the narrative of heavy metal.

Heavy metal is simultaneously mass-marketed, commercial, personal and cultish. It is a testimony to our human capacity to draw meaning and truth even from within consumer society, to the power of people to keep what they love alive. I'm almost as old as Plant and Page. I've got the battle scars of Alloy Nation, hearing loss and a herniated disk in my neck – head banger's syndrome. By now, I've divorced Jack Daniel's and joined the club with Ozzy, Aerosmith and Alice. I've parlayed the fine art of hanging out on street corners into a respectable career as a sociologist and journalist. But I still need Led Zeppelin in my life. Like one day I'm walking across West Fifty-seventh Street in Manhattan. It's lunch hour. I want to scream, "White-collar workers unite!!!" Everyone looks so unhappy, so distant, cold, sterile and stiff. It seems so hopeless. This is humanity? "Stairway to Heaven" is rotating on the radio of my Walkman. "To be a rock and not to roll . . ." I've heard the song a million times and I still don't know all the words. But in a split second, it gets me there, soothes and reconnects me to myself, to the world. On a riff I'm reaching up, then out. Pretty soon, the people don't seem so far away. ⊕

one man out
by allen barra

THE FIRST TIME I met Curt Flood, life was simpler for both of us. I was in high school, and he was an All-Star, Gold Glove center fielder for the soon-to-be-World-Champion St. Louis Cardinals. He was autographing a baseball for me, a foul ball he hit into my box seat in Fenway Park just before stroking a single in the Cards' win. Curt Flood wasn't my favorite player; I even resented him a bit because he had supplanted my main man, Willie Mays, as the game's best center fielder. But there was no way not to admire Flood, his fluid grace in the field and the wiry, whiplash power of his line-drive swing. He smiled when he handed the ball back. That was unusual. A ballplayer never looks a fan in the eye. Up close, Flood seemed smaller and slighter than me, and near-ly as young.

The next time I saw him he was in a dark business suit walking up the New York federal courthouse steps where I stood covering the story for my college paper. Life had become a great deal more complicated for both of us. Flood had made it that way. In 1970 Flood was suing Major League Baseball for his right to be a free agent, and I, a junior-grade student activist in college who upheld everyone's right to freedom and the pursuit of happiness, wrote a nasty editorial about him in my college paper. Did this guy think athletes had the same rights as the rest of us?

Flood lost his case, but his stand set in motion a process that changed professional sports forever. He certainly altered the way journalists thought about sports. Because of Flood, sports journalism no longer simply required a writer to be knowledgeable about the subjects of batting averages and ERAs. You had to be a part-time econo-mist, sociologist and labor-relations historian.

The two big changes in sports in the Seventies were the increasing predominance of black athletes and the huge influx of TV money into baseball, football and, by the end of the decade, basketball. By the time the Eighties were under way, the two devel-opments had converged: Athletes won their independence and America had a tiny but highly visible super-rich black upper class.

It's easy to see the effect that Jackie Robinson had on baseball and on all professional sports when he joined the Brooklyn Dodgers in 1947 and became America's first black major-league player. All one had to do was look at a team photo from that year in any pro sport and then compare it to one taken ten years later to see the dramatic difference.

But Curt Flood's impact wasn't quite so easy to discern. At the opening of the Seventies, the most dynamic decade for professional sports in the Twentieth Century, he was the first athlete capable of challenging the power structure at its own game – in the courts and in the boardrooms. A *white* power structure, of course; there wasn't any other kind. The line of individual notoriety and financial inde-pendence that stretches from Curt Flood declaring himself a free agent to O.J. Simpson sharing a rental

St. Louis Cardinal Curt Flood in top form at Wrigley Field, Chicago

car with middle-American icon Arnold Palmer isn't a straight one. But the connection is there, clearing the path for a long line of talented black athletes and allowing a super-star like Michael Jordan to become the most famous sports figure on the planet.

That being said, it must be pointed out that Flood's stand may have been a civil rights issue, but it was not a racial issue; the only color involved was green, as in the money the Lords of Baseball were keeping from the players. Flood's lonely, quixotic mission benefited all baseball players after him. As he explains in his autobiography, *The Way It Is*, Flood was motivated in no small part by what he felt was owner August A. Busch Jr.'s betrayal of his team, the 1967 World Champion St. Louis Cardinals. As Flood tells the story, the Cardinals knew they were a dynasty and had a warrior's pride in the team's greatness, but beer magnate Busch would rather have sabotaged the team than offer appropriate financial rewards to the players. The owners preached loyalty but never offered it themselves; Flood called their bluff.

denying Slick the chance to drop LSD into the communal teapot, as she had suggested she might do.

Chicago blues-piano giant Otis Spann, who recorded with Eric Clapton and members of Fleetwood Mac, dies.

29 "Cambodiazation" of the Vietnam War escalates as a combined force of 20,000 U.S. and South Vietnamese troops crosses Cambodia's border. The next day, President Nixon officially announces his intention to send U.S. forces there. Critical reaction to this widening of the conflict is immediate and severe, as UN General Secretary U Thant warns of its engulfing effect on all of Southeast Asia, and 11 major university newspapers call for a nationwide moratorium in protest.

1970 MAY

1 Elton John's debut U.S. album is released, featuring his and lyricist Bernie Taupin's first Top-10 hit, "Your Song."

2 Mississippi educational television removes *Sesame Street* from its programming schedule because of the show's multiracial nature.

4 At Kent State University in Ohio, four students die from shots fired by the National Guard, which was called in to control an antiwar rally. A yearlong investigation follows. Though President Nixon immediately calls the killings "unfortunate," 37 university presidents blame his policies for having an alienating effect on the nation's youth. A week later, subsequent protests and student boycotts close down over 400 campuses throughout the country.

7 Archaeologist Richard Leakey reports finding bones and tools from the earliest known humanoid to date.

8 In a seventh-game surprise, injured team captain Willis Reed limps onto the court, rallying the New York Knicks to their first NBA title, downing the Los Angeles Lakers, 113–99.

9 An estimated 90,000 antiwar protesters descend on Washington, DC.

11 The live triple-LP set *Woodstock* is released, going gold in two weeks.

14 ROLLING STONE reports on the arrival of a "new [drug] mixture being marketed as 'fairy dust' or 'angel dust.' Not only is it a burn in money terms,

Baseball players were bound to one team by a "reserve" clause in a player's contract that gave management the right to re-sign the player again at the end of the season. In other words, he was the team's property for life unless they chose to trade or release him. The player had no bargaining power in negotiations other than the threat to hold out or quit. (Ty Cobb was one of the first players shrewd enough to understand this, and he invested as much of his salary as possible in Coca-Cola stock, becoming independently wealthy while in his prime. Detroit management had to take his retirement threats seriously.)

What the reserve clause did was work to the owners' advantage by keeping salaries down. If every player had the right to seek out the best offer for his services, he was bound to get a far better deal than any single team would offer him.

A couple of players had legally challenged the reserve clause over the years, but though the court decisions were ambiguous on some points, they pretty much agreed on one thing: Any change in the system would have to come about as a result of collective bargaining. Since the players' union was controlled by the owners, management was pretty safe on that front – until Curt Flood got together with Marvin Miller, a former chief economist from the Steelworkers Union who specialized in collective bargaining and was then the executive director of the Major League Baseball Players Association.

In 1969 the first stirrings of a players' rebellion were felt when infielder/outfielder Ken "Hawk" Harrelson refused to report to work after the Boston Red Sox traded him to the Cleveland Indians, relenting only after being granted a significant pay raise; and first baseman Donn Clendenon refused to go to the Houston Astros when he was traded by the Montreal Expos. He finally ended up with the New York Mets.

In 1970 the Cardinals traded Flood (along with Tim McCarver) to one of the worst teams in major league baseball, the Philadelphia Phillies, for slugger Dick Allen. Flood refused to report, and no pay raise or reassignment would placate him. He maintained he should be able to decide what team he would play for. He was a twelve-year veteran. He was also an intellectual and an artist (he supported himself after his baseball career ended by painting portraits). He came at the tail end of a cycle of controversial, political and social-minded black athletes – Muhammad Ali, of course, and Jim Brown in football and, to a lesser degree, Bill Russell in basketball. Arthur Ashe came later. But Flood was the first to articulate his rebellion against an established sports power structure.

After conferring with his attorney and Miller, Flood wrote a letter to Baseball Commissioner Bowie Kuhn that said, "After twelve years in the major leagues, I do not feel that I am a piece of property to be bought and sold irrespective of my wishes. I believe that any system that produces that result violates my basic rights as a citizen and is inconsistent with the laws of the United States. . . ." Kuhn replied disingenuously that "I certainly agree with you that you . . . are not a piece of property to be bought and sold" but "I cannot see the applicability to the situation at hand." If Flood hadn't already known what to expect, that line would have furnished a clue.

In January 1970 *Flood* v. *Kuhn* went to court. The federal court ruled against Flood, and he decided to sit out the season while his lawyers appealed. In June 1972 the case reached the Supreme Court, which ultimately upheld the lower court's decision by a vote of five to three, with one abstention. The highest court maintained that the reserve clause binding Flood to his team was not in violation of antitrust laws. Incidentally, only three players or former players showed up during the trials to wish Flood well or give testimony that would plead his case: Jackie Robinson, Hank Greenberg and Jim Brosnan.

Even as the courts were deciding Flood's case, the results of his stand against baseball's empire were bearing fruit. During spring training of 1972, before the Supreme Court vote, Miller played the trump card that would break the owners' hegemony forever: Baseball players called a general strike that carried over into the regular season. By the time Miller was finished with the Lords of Baseball, thirteen days and eighty-six games of the regular season had been canceled.

Marvin Miller was able to turn Flood's eventual defeat into a long-term victory for the players' union by following a simple and direct course. The baseball team owners were shaken. They had nearly lost their precious reserve clause in court – to say nothing of their exemption from antitrust laws – and discovered that the players were willing to act as a concerted body for the first time in history, so the owners made a concession to the union in the form of an agreement to submit to binding arbitration on some issues. In 1974, star Oakland A's right-hander Jim "Catfish" Hunter was ruled a free agent due to a contract violation, and in 1975 pitchers Andy Messersmith and Dave McNally were ruled free agents after sitting out their contracts for a season (the reserve clause said a player would be the property of a team for only *one year* after signing his contract).

The Messersmith-McNally deal was significant in terms of shaping future individual contracts and basic agreements between the players' union and the league. But Hunter's was more important in one respect: It showed how deep the owners' pockets really were when they *had* to shell it over. When Hunter pitched for the Oakland A's, he had made $100,000 a year. After attracting the best offers from numerous big-league teams, he signed a $3.75-million, five-year deal with the New York Yankees. Hunter's contract proved that the owners, in effect, could afford to pay their players five, six or even seven times what they had previously maintained they could afford!

Football and basketball unions generally followed the lead of baseball's MLBPA in tactics and strategy, mostly because Miller was the first and only sports union leader to come out of a collective-bargaining background. Any gains made by the baseball union were soon followed by union gains in other sports.

Football and basketball players did not have as far to go as their pinstriped cousins, and it wasn't because the owners were more generous than those in baseball. Pro football and basketball had no reserve clause and conducted business in the free market; they weren't exempt from antitrust laws, and thus were powerless to stop new rivals from cutting into the growing popularity of team sports. In the Sixties, the NFL had to answer the challenge of the newer, hipper American Football League, while the NBA faced off with the funkier American Basketball Association. Both older leagues met the challenge by absorbing franchises from the younger leagues, but not before player salaries received a big boost.

The reason there were new leagues in the first place was television; TV contracts provided lucrative start-up incentives for any entrepreneur looking to cash in on America's favorite pastimes. In fact, TV changed the way all of us not only looked at sports but thought about them. Let's just say it: TV changed the whole nature of what it meant to be a hometown fan. Radio and TV were around, but from the Thirties through most of the Sixties, to *watch* your favorite team was understood to mean buying tickets, driving to the stadium, parking the car and finding your seat.

By the early Seventies, baseball's Game of the Week, the All-Star games, the playoffs and the World Series all aired coast-to-coast; by the latter half of the decade, cable, with its nightly broadcasts of far-flung teams that most fans had never seen before, was on the rise.

But it was football and basketball that benefited more from the TV boom. With their straight-ahead motions and fluid bursts of action, the games of football and basketball seemed designed for TV, and marketed correctly, they began to pick up tens of millions of viewers who might not have become fans otherwise.

By the end of the Seventies, basketball began its dazzling assault on the TV market. Magic Johnson and Larry Bird found each other in the 1979 NCAA championship game and went from there into a long-term pro rivalry that dominated the Eighties. Thanks to TV, players who had extensive national exposure in college went straight to the pros as celebrities, full-formed like Athena from the head of Zeus. Kids who had never made a foul shot in the pros were richer after two or three years of college than Bill Russell and Wilt Chamberlain at the end of fifteen seasons in the NBA.

For us, the fans, the end of the Seventies delivered an uncomfortable paradox. Sports had become more popular than ever before, but more remote as well. The money we paid for tickets, and the ratings we gave the telecasts, all brought in revenues undreamed of as recently as the Sixties. And as the athletes sought to control their own destinies and grab fairer slices of the pro sports pie – a noble and estimable effort in this land of free enterprise – so they became removed from their fans, images on TV rather than ball-signing individuals down at the ballpark.

By the close of the Seventies, sports became modern-day gladiatorial combat, with corporations buying up blocks of tickets for baseball, football and basketball games, making it increasingly difficult for fans, and the families of fans, to get in and enjoy the games. The 1975 film *Rollerball* – in which James Caan stars as a champion in a bloody TV sport created for a futuristic society where violence has been outlawed – proved the perfect metaphor for professional sports. For the average person, TV became the primary, often the only, connection fans had with the players, the team and the game itself.

In 1991 I had the privilege of seeing Marvin Miller in New York City at a party in Mickey Mantle's restaurant. He sat with his old friend Curt Flood at the dinner. At the end of the party, I shook hands with Flood; for a moment I thought about mentioning the autographed ball from 1967. But the look in Flood's eyes indicated he was not in the mood for frivolity. The smile was weak. In fact, in less than six years he would be dead from cancer.

I spent two hours listening to Curt and Marvin reminisce; it was the closest I've ever been to two men who changed the lives of thousands. I remember best Flood's words as they shook hands and said goodbye: "We did it, didn't we?" Curt said. "Yes," replied Marvin, "yes we did." There wasn't a hint that either man remembered the lawsuit as a failure.

What did Curt Flood give up in challenging the most powerful establishment in sports? Maybe a couple of years off his playing career, probably not much more. (Out of shape, he played briefly for the Washington Senators in 1971, then packed it in for good.) He definitely gave up an active post-career, a benefit enjoyed by many of his Cardinal teammates (Joe Torre, McCarver, Bob Gibson, Lou Brock, Bill White, just to name a few). Certainly the strain cost him several years of his life.

But Curt Flood wasn't naive; he knew precisely what he was doing. "I was offended," he wrote in *The Way It Is*. "I wanted reality upgraded, pretension abolished. Baseball was socially relevant, and so was my rebellion against it." Reality upgraded – not a bad thing to have written on your scorecard at the end.

chrissie hynde
on kent state

I WAS A FRESHMAN at Kent State University in Ohio in 1970 and, as I recall, the weekend before the shootings was kind of a blast for us students: The National Guard was shooting tear gas, and we were throwing the canisters back at them. Students were ripping up sheets and dipping them in water, showing us how to put them on our faces for protection. It was like a crash course in how to deal with the military – with tear gas. The Guardsmen had put up big Cyclone fences, and a bunch of guys were jumping against them until they had pushed the stakes over far enough so that the fences were nearly horizontal and you could jump on them like you would a trampoline – people were running up and bouncing off. It was crazy – everyone was out of their heads, and we actually had fun, in a way. I hate to say that, but I was eighteen – just a kid who had been in high school a year earlier.

I don't want to be flippant about it, but I still don't know exactly why the shootings happened at Kent State. I believe they were a horrible, horrible mistake, and I don't think anyone ever really understood why it all turned out the way it did. I still have a pretty good grasp of the proceedings, though, since I saw it all firsthand.

I started going to Kent State in the summer of 1969, when I was seventeen, and I guess you could have called me a little hippie. I had already embraced the freelove, vegetarian, barefoot, flower child sort of thing and had been reading books by Jack Kerouac and on Zen Buddhism before I was even getting drunk or having sex.

That was my generation! We were pot smokers, reading about mystical Eastern religions and taking a stand against anything that was Establishment, rejecting all the values that had come before. The general sentiment on student campuses at the time was extremely anti–Vietnam War. Americans were supposed to be fighting against communism, but, of course, from our point of view capitalism didn't look so great either. Our antiwar attitude was part of a rejection of our parents' values, and the students at Kent State were sincere in this – I don't think anyone was just going along with the trend.

For us, there was a big question mark hanging over the war. No one understood the Vietnam situation – it was shrouded in contradictions. None of us had any faith in anything that was going on over there, and we thought it was wrong for the U.S. to be involved. We harbored a general suspicion of the war's validity, a feeling compounded by our overall sort of peacenik attitude. I remember that I personally thought the Vietnam War was a truly evil thing. We were also all very personally threatened because it was claiming many of our peers – I think the average age of everyone who was fighting was around nineteen. You could avoid being sent over there by going to a university, so ghetto kids would get drafted, but kids with better resources were managing to get out of it. The inequality of it all didn't seem right. Everyone was living in fear of this war. Actually, I don't think most of our generation would have been so reluctant to go off to war if they had known why we were fighting – but nobody did. As a result, there was this large body of American students and kids with no clear way to vent their frustration at a senseless war; student unrest was rife in the United States.

At the time, Kent State University was considered a pretty radical campus by Midwestern standards. It had a very strong cinematography department, and I myself was a fine arts major. I thought we were a pretty sophisticated bunch, but looking back, we were just a bunch of Northeastern Ohio kids. I'm not saying we were all farmers, but we definitely represented Middle America.

Kent was this old, rustic town which had an old train station and a small-town kind of vibe. All the towns surrounding it were small, too, like Ravenna, Ohio, and a lot of the students were from that general area. Kent had a concentrated downtown

May 4, 1970: Moments after the National Guard opened fire, Kent State University sophomore Jeff Miller lay dead in a puddle of blood

area with about twenty-seven off-campus bars and a live-music scene. I remember a lot of bands playing there at the time: Joe Walsh with the James Gang, Eric Carmen and his band and many others. Consequently, in the Northeastern Ohio area, starting Friday night of every weekend, all the hilljacks and bikers and crazies from all over the area would come in to Kent and hang out with the college students in all these bars. There wasn't really much else going on in the area.

I was living off-campus that year, and on May 1 – I remember it was a Friday night – we heard that President Nixon had ordered the invasion of Cambodia, which totally went against what we had been led to believe was going to happen in Vietnam. We were downtown at the time – not all of us students, but predominantly so – feeling this sense of betrayal and anger. A small protest started up: We took these big garbage cans from the side of the road, wheeled them into the middle of the street and set them on fire. It was an awesome sight. It was basically a peaceable protest, albeit attended by a bunch of tripped-out acidheads and drunks who were hanging around at the time. No one could drive through the streets, though there was a bastard who decided to try, but we just jumped on his car and kicked all the windows out to punish the driver for having the gall to interfere with our protest.

A curfew was imposed Saturday night on the whole city. I believe everyone had to be in by 8:00 p.m. if they were in town, and a little later if they were on campus. Consequently, people like me had asked one of their mates living on campus if they could sleep in their dorm room that night in order to stay out the extra time. So there were a lot of students – "anti-students" living off-campus like me – avoiding the curfew and hanging out in the middle of the university grounds that Saturday night. I remember the tone of things: A lot of people were taking acid, and it was a pretty crazy scene. Hey, it was 1970.

So everyone – and when I say everyone, I mean there were thousands of students, though I don't believe there were any outside agitators or anyone like that – had congregated around this hilly area called the Commons, which is where the ROTC (Reserve Officers Training Corps) building was.

The ROTC building was this old wooden shack with other buildings surrounding it. The art building, which was used for the Life Drawing classes I attended, was one of them, so I remember the setting well. The students resented this sort of military aspect of the university very much. Someone had the idea of burning down the ROTC building, and everyone said, "Good idea." Then someone else got some railway flares, lit them, ran down the hill and threw them right into the building. Everyone was thinking, This is fantastic – we're burning down the ROTC building! And it burnt right down to the ground.

As soon as it flamed, the fire trucks arrived, and students started pulling hoses out of the trucks so the firefighters couldn't use them. I was right there in the front line.

At the same time this was happening, we suddenly saw, coming down Main Street from Ravenna, actual military jeeps and tanks. It turned out there had been a trucker's strike in Ravenna, about eleven miles up the road from Kent, and the National Guard had been stationed there. Now their presence added increasing fury to our protest. The Guardsmen tried to disperse the crowd of students, using tear gas, and everyone was cordoned in by Cyclone fences, so thousands of people were running rampant within them. It actually became a riot.

Though we were angry, the whole scene was kind of a gas, too, because it was Saturday night, and a lot of people (myself not included) were tripping. With or without drugs, it was awesome to see the hated ROTC building going up in flames. It was definitely a night to remember.

My recollection of Sunday is that everything around town was completely dead, nothing was happening.

I know that the following Monday was the end of half-term, because I had my portfolio of drawings with me. I had left my apartment and was walking onto campus toward the art building, at around noon or one o'clock. On the way in, my girlfriend had told me there was going to be a peaceful demonstration on the Commons because everyone was very pissed-off that the National Guard was still on campus. What had been the ROTC building was now a pile of about four inches of charcoal, in a huge rectangular area surrounded by National Guardsmen, who were each on one knee pointing a rifle, as if guarding this burnt-down building. It was creating a very bad vibe.

I was strolling down into the Commons area, and just as I caught sight of the art building, I saw at least fifty guys – I don't know the exact number – with rifles. They were surrounding the building, and it looked really scary to me.

As I approached, I heard what I thought were fireworks but actually was, I later realized, gunfire. Since the time was around noon, everyone was on their way to classes. I heard somebody say, "They've killed someone!" and I just stood there in utter disbelief. Suddenly I was aware of a real sense of mayhem – I can remember hiding and running through back gardens and behind buildings to try and get to a friend's house for safety, and to find out who had been killed. All I knew, at the start, was that some students were dead. I heard sirens, and there were ambulances everywhere. The campus was evacuated; there were jeeps on every corner. Kent State became a little war zone.

Apparently what had happened was that a few students had picked up rocks and started throwing them at the National Guard, saying, "Fuck off – get off our campus," and the Guardsmen had just fired into the dense crowd of students. Later I learned that four students had been killed, including Jeff Miller, the boyfriend of the girl who had told me about the demonstration earlier that day.

Everyone I knew was in an utter state of shock. I refused to leave campus but was finally forced to when they cleared everybody off. I think they evacuated the entire city, and certainly they evacuated the whole campus. By that evening there were hundreds of students hitching out of the area to go back to their homes. It was the end of the school year, and that was the end of the debacle as far as I remember.

In the aftermath of the killings Neil Young wrote the song "Ohio," and I thought it was particularly fitting because Jeff Miller had been such a big Crosby, Stills, Nash and Young fan.

I can't remember whether I ever went back to Kent State. I do recall that we were supposed to finish our courses through the mail. If I did go back, I didn't last long, because I started working as a waitress then and started saving my money to leave the country altogether. I don't think my decision was a direct result of the shootings. I was sure I didn't want to live in America, but it wasn't because of the political scene – it went a lot deeper than that. I wanted to see the world; I didn't have a plan.

By today's standards, those killings might not sound that shocking – these days someone can walk into McDonald's and blow away fifteen people and it doesn't surprise us. Of course, Kent State was different because it was the *government* killing students. But I can still remember standing there looking at those poor guys in their uniforms. I think that when the National Guard were called in, they were not highly trained in crowd control or anything like that. They were just young guys; they looked exactly like the students, only they were wearing uniforms. In fact, some of them *were* students!

Of course, at that time in American history, uniforms provoked a very negative response in those of us who were opposed to the war. Today, anyone who was a Green Beret or served in Vietnam back then will tell you about the venomous response they got from civilians when they returned to America. It didn't matter whether they were war heroes or not, they were considered real scumbags just for going over to Vietnam. That sentiment really divided the country.

So I remember looking at these poor guys who thought they had simply obeyed orders by shooting into the crowd, and I can now imagine how stunned they must have been when they realized they had just blown away all those students – students who were their peers.

Kent was a leafy, green, nice suburban place – it was *Ohio*, not Vietnam. That fact just magnified the tragedy. Trying to explain its occurrence is kind of like attempting to figure out the cause of a road accident, you know. Was the driver drunk? Did he lose control? Were there some weird weather conditions? Did something fall in front of the car?

I still don't know whether there was a conspiracy, whether one person was behind the tragedy or whether it was actually provoked by student leaders. I do know that it was a really big fuckup – inexperienced people were put in charge of events they didn't know how to handle.

Because I left the States in 1973, my political sensibilities were kind of arrested, still back in that time. When I came home after living in London, I noticed that Americans had become extremely patriotic. Weird things started happening around America – it reminded me of *Invasion of the Body Snatchers*. Suddenly, instead of putting up an American flag only on Veterans' Day, people everywhere were flying flags all the time. I thought that maybe everyone was afraid there was going to be an alien invasion, and so were reasoning: In case someone lands, let's let them know what country they're in! Then I noticed these patriotic bumper stickers and kick-butt slogans – gung-ho Americana.

Especially around the time of the Gulf War, the media seemed to reflect that sort of gung-ho-ism. When I went to New York at one point, it was such a sensitive issue that I wouldn't dare say anything that related to the war; I didn't feel free to express myself about it. I remember reading the *New York Post* headlines with their kick-butt attitude and thinking that the national mood had shifted into a whole new redneck gear – fierce patriotism – that was way beyond anything I could have fathomed back at Kent State.

I remember that when Sinéad O'Connor came over to the States and said she didn't want the national anthem played before her concert, she was nearly run out of the country. Suddenly the whole idea of freedom of speech in America seemed to be a sick joke, because now if you criticized America, everyone went fucking ape-shit on you – even the so-called hip people! I found it really odd that Sinéad was booed (though she was cheered, too) at the Bob Dylan tribute. She's a very sensitive person who left the stage in tears because of the response she got for being political and for ripping up a picture of the pope on television.

See, back in my day we all believed we were *supposed* to be free to express ourselves, but now, suddenly even Bob Dylan fans were booing Sinéad for doing it. I guess I found it all especially weird because of my long absence, and I really didn't know what to say to her, so I just said, "Hey, when I lived here, we were burning flags." ⊕

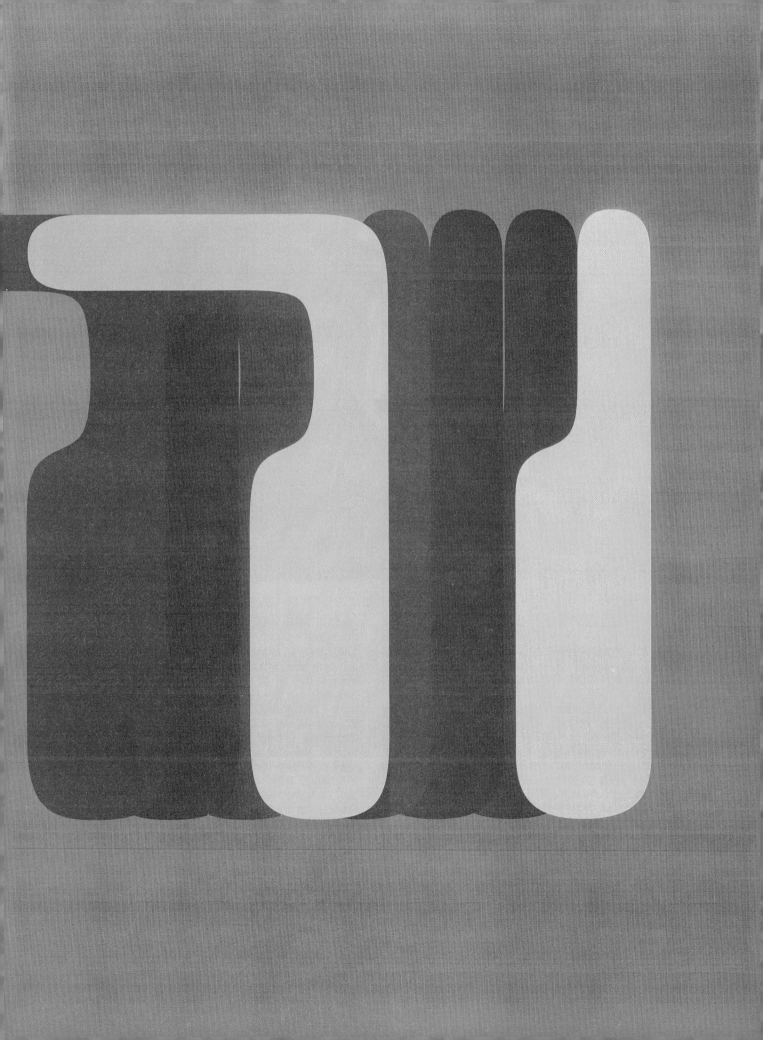

changing the channel
by david wild

FOR ONCE, the revolution *was* televised. At 9:30 p.m. EST on January 12, 1971, *All in the Family* hit the airwaves for the very first time. By the end of that summer, a considerable portion of both the washed and unwashed American masses were hooked, including my own family. Sure, there were a few naysayers. Indeed the noted television critic Richard Nixon – a fellow better remembered for his early groundbreaking work in the field of home taping – apparently had a big problem with the series that would become the single most influential television show of the Seventies.

"Do you know the famous Nixon line?" asked *All in the Family*'s legendary creator and producer Norman Lear. With considerable relish, Lear – a proud, long-standing liberal – recalled, "On one of Nixon's tapes, he said, 'How could they do that to that good man? How could they make that good man such a fool?' "

That "good man" was the one and only Archie Bunker – the world's best-loved armchair reactionary and a key member of *All in the Family*'s fab four. Just as the Beatles forever altered the direction of rock & roll and youth culture in the Sixties, *All in the Family* forever changed the range and vocabulary of the sitcom (and television in general) during the Seventies. *All in the Family* would turn out to be much more than just another hit show; it became a weekly sociopolitical event – so much so that Jimmy Carter told the Associated Press in 1978 that while he was working out a Middle East peace accord at Camp David, "The only thing I was hoping when we signed the agreements was that we didn't interrupt *All in the Family*."

Growing up in a family of longtime F.D.R. liberals, whom Archie would have almost certainly called "pinkos" and perhaps some even less flattering names, I lived in a home that fully embraced but didn't exactly re-enact *All in the Family*. Rather than a blue-collar house divided, ours was a somewhat more luxurious abode full of standard-issue East Coast lefties, even the ten-year-old version of myself, who in 1972 proudly handed out George McGovern bumper stickers to a significant portion of Tenafly, New Jersey, in my own failed attempt to bring Tricky Dick down.

The Family Bunker: Mike Stivic (Rob Reiner) and his wife, Gloria (Sally Struthers); Archie (Carroll O'Connor) and his wife, Edith Bunker (Jean Stapleton) *(clockwise from top left)*

As far as I can recall, none of us assorted Wilds were ever personally touched by other more Bunker-ish political viewpoints until Dad voted for Reagan in 1980, so ending our collective, suburban, socialist innocence. Neither my older brother, Jeff, my little sister, Wendy, nor I were likely to argue over hot-button issues of the day such as Vietnam with our folks, who on the domestic front were then moving toward their own senseless pre-divorce ground war. I do recall my parents insisting Jeff and I flee to Canada if we were ever drafted, not a particularly pressing matter, since back then we were both still holding on to the relatively careless side of adolescence.

What my semi-commie clan and millions of others in every sort of American home responded to about *All in the Family* was the fact that the show captured some of the absurd bite of reality, a funny and true sense of life as it was lived in *any* family. The America that got intimate with *All in the Family* was not exactly Victorian England, and the culture reflected back by episodic television in 1971 generally lagged far behind the real-life tumult of the day. The sitcom format was largely unaffected by the cultural chaos of the late Sixties – the boob tube remained a place where one could still kick back in the bland and often brainless comfort of series like *Petticoat Junction*, *Gomer Pyle, U.S.M.C.*, *Green Acres* and *Bewitched*.

Certainly, the Seventies saw other great shows – like *The Mary Tyler Moore Show*, *The Odd Couple*, *The Bob Newhart Show* and *M*A*S*H* – and plenty of very fine ones – including *All in the Family* spin-offs *Maude* and *The Jeffersons*, and other biting Lear shows like *Mary Hartman, Mary Hartman* and *Fernwood 2-Night* – but ultimately none would convey the shock of the new with the uproarious urgency of *All in the Family*.

4 In the Pennsylvania and New Jersey countrysides, members of Vietnam Veterans Against the War stage a reenactment of a brutal search-and-destroy mission as an antiwar protest.

9 Elvis Presley returns to the road for the first time since 1957, kicking off a six-date tour in Phoenix.

10 A team of geologists introduces the "continental drift" theory, hypothesizing the existence, 225 million years ago, of a continent comprising all the earth's current continents.

14 The publisher of the fashion trade paper *Women's Wear Daily* pushes the new look of the midi skirt, but women refuse to buy into it.

15 The Baltimore Orioles defeat the Cincinnati Reds in five games, to win the 67th World Series.

18 Jimi Hendrix dies after choking on his own vomit, in the London apartment of a girlfriend. Nearly two weeks later, he is buried in his hometown of Seattle, with attending mourners including Miles Davis, Johnny Winter and John Hammond Jr.

1970 OCTOBER

2 The Environmental Protection Agency, proposed by President Nixon in order to oversee most federal pollution-control activity, is established with congressional approval.

4 Janis Joplin dies of a heroin overdose in Hollywood, CA. On Oct. 13, the ashes of the Texas-born singer are scattered in the Pacific Ocean.

13 Charles Reich's *The Greening of America*, an antitechnology examination of American society, is published and later becomes a bestseller.

18 In a report bordering on bureaucratic paranoia, which even the White House calls "overly pessimistic," the CIA contends that 30,000 Communists have infiltrated the South Vietnamese government.

24 In a speech to a White House radio broadcasters' conference, President Nixon appeals for the screening of rock lyrics and the banning of those advocating drug use. Two weeks later, the politically conservative MGM Records president, Mike Curb, drops 18 acts from his roster; among the "drug advocates"

In *All in the Family*, Archie Bunker, his doting wife Edith, his spunky, sexy daughter Gloria and his lefty, ever-hungry son-in-law Mike Stivic together played out the comic drama of the Seventies in all its fractious glory, touching upon previously untouchable topics like abortion, Vietnam, racism, Watergate, wife-swapping, menopause and, lest we forget, Sammy Davis Jr.'s glass eye. Taboo words like "spade," "spic" and "hebe" flew freely from Archie's mouth. In the process the show proved television could, in the right (leftist) hands, become one hell of a hot medium. Finally, American viewers could stop being treated like a bunch of "dingbats" and "meatheads" and find themselves confronted instead with a brilliant, brutally blunt show that never asked its audience to "stifle" themselves in the slightest.

Initially, the events unfolding inside that modest row house at 704 Hauser Street in Queens were considered so potentially offensive that the first episodes came complete with an on-air warning: "The program you are about to see is *All in the Family*. It seeks to throw a humorous light on our frailties, prejudices and concerns. By making them a source of laughter, we hope to show – in a mature fashion – just how absurd we are." As mission statements go, this was truth in advertising. As an official warning, it proved about as effective as the surgeon general's words on a cigarette box.

Suddenly millions spent their evenings gathered around the electronic hearth soaking up the heat of *All in the Family*. Every Saturday night Americans avidly watched a brave new kind of family show that dared to suggest that perhaps father *didn't* know best, after all, about politics, race, sex or pretty much anything else for that matter.

Unsurprisingly, considering the medium's resistance to change, *All in the Family* had an unusually difficult birthing process. TV and film veteran Lear – working with his then-partner Alan "Bud" Yorkin – happened upon an issues-oriented British comedy called *Til Death Us Do Part* in 1968, and bought the American rights. He reworked the material into a more fleshed-out, character-driven show that was, as Lear rightly puts it, "indigenously American." A deal was made with ABC, and a first pilot was produced under the title *Those Were the Days*, starring veteran actors Carroll O'Connor and Jean Stapleton as Archie and Edith Bunker (other actors played the roles that would even-

> Anyone could walk through the front door: Cleavon Little and Demond Williams *(from left)* hold the Bunkers hostage in a robbery gone wrong

tually go to Rob Reiner and Sally Struthers). Unconvinced, ABC ordered another version of the pilot, then decided afterwards to let its option run out anyway.

And that was quite nearly that.

"It took three years to get *All in the Family* on the air because they were afraid of it," recalled Lear, who points out that the script did not change at all during the course of making the different pilots, nor did the two leads.

Fortunately, at the dawn of the Seventies, the then-new president of CBS, Robert Wood, turned out to be more afraid of boring audiences than of shaking up the tubular status quo. "Before *All in the Family* came to his attention, Bob was determined to do some comedy programming that was quite different," Lear said. "He perhaps didn't know what he had in mind, but he *didn't* want to do the *Beverly Hillbillies* kind of show that was the hallmark of CBS at that moment. He deliberately wanted to do *something* different, so when *All in the Family* came to his attention, he said '*That's it*.' "

Undoubtedly, *All in the Family* was something completely different.

Lear is quick to share credit with the show's cast for the success of the series and its strong emotional connection with its audience. O'Connor took a potentially hateful and one-dimensional character like Archie and found the painfully recognizable core of humanity inside him, thus creating the most important blue-collar TV character since Jackie Gleason's Ralph Kramden in *The Honeymooners*. No one ever played dumb as smartly and subtly as Jean Stapleton, the nurturing Mother of all TV Mothers. Sally Struthers brought an earthiness and emotionality to Gloria, while future *auteur* Rob Reiner did the impossible in going toe-to-toe with O'Connor on so many occasions and proving his longhaired equal.

"God was smiling on us," Lear said. "The interesting thing was, three years before, I'd talked to Rob Reiner but I felt he was too young. In Rob and Sally, it was the same sort of miracle that Carroll and Jean represented. It's hard for me to talk about the casting as if *I* did it. Yeah, I found the actors, yeah, I made those decisions, but the

miracle was attendant to all of them being around at the same time, all of them being available and each of them having a kind of chemistry that melded with the other three. *Nobody* can take credit for that. That's sorted out in the heavens."

All in the Family's onscreen dream team gave the show's gifted writers license to let it rip, and soon the show was moving with amazing grace from Swiftian satire to Arthur Miller–like tragedy within a single half-hour.

"It's always appeared to me that laughter and tears follow each other very closely," Lear said. "You laugh till you cry, and you cry until you get hysterical. Treading that line *always* appealed to me. Also, we were a group of writers who wanted to bring an audience to its *knees*. We weren't looking to have a *lightly* funny show or a *somewhat* emotional show. We wanted to *cream* them. And we never lost that. We might have missed, but we never lost the desire to cream 'em."

Part of this televised creaming of America resulted from the way the hyperopinionated Archie and the perennial student Mike hashed out so many of the incendiary issues of the era in a sort of open televised debate that proved even more gripping and entertaining than any Nixon-McGovern grudge match.

"Neither Archie nor Mike *really* took the responsibility to know what they were talking about," Lear explains. "You had people who were arguing out of a deep conviction and passion who didn't have enough information. So they left it to *us* to carry on the conversation."

This conversation would continue until 1978 when Reiner and Struthers left *All in the Family* (soon followed by Stapleton), and the show morphed into *Archie Bunker's Place*, which stayed in business until leaving the air in 1983.

Even with Archie's chair now safe on institutional display at the Smithsonian, *All in the Family*'s edgy legacy continues in the form of any comedy that's tried to push the boundaries – be it an endlessly brilliant show like *Seinfeld* or a more pandering piece of work like *Married . . . With Children*. Any time you see a family show and find convincing human conflict and affection, you can send a thank-you note to Archie's clan.

Asked what he's most proud of about *All in the Family*, Lear says this: "We didn't underestimate the intelligence of the American people. We were vulgar, we were not dealing with characters of great intellect, but we were dealing with the subjects of our times, the culture of the moment. We were dealing with issues of significance even though we were told we shouldn't and we *couldn't* – if we wanted to send a message, use Western Union.

"It wouldn't fly in Des Moines – that was another big network line. I think we simply knew the American people were ready for anything and that they would welcome the challenge, and that no state would secede from the nation because we were on the air. I'm most proud that we did not underestimate anyone." ⊕

fact & fiction & fear & loathing
by dr. hunter s. thompson

THE BOOK BEGAN as a 250-word caption for *Sports Illustrated.* I was down in L.A., working on a very tense and depressing investigation of the allegedly accidental killing of a journalist named Ruben Salazar by the Los Angeles County Sheriff's Dept. – and after a week or so on the story I was a ball of nerves & sleepless paranoia (figuring that *I* might be next) . . . and I needed some excuse to *get away* from the angry vortex of that story & try to make sense of it without people shaking butcher knives in my face all the time.

My main contact on that story was the infamous Chicano lawyer Oscar Acosta – an old friend, who was under bad pressure at the time, from his super-militant constituents, for even *talking* to a gringo/*gabacho* journalist. The pressure was so heavy, in fact, that I found it impossible to talk to Oscar alone. We were always in the midst of a crowd of heavy streetfighters who didn't mind letting me know that they wouldn't need much of an excuse to chop me into hamburger.

This is no way to work on a very volatile & very complex story. So one afternoon I got Oscar in my rented car and drove him over to the Beverly Hills Hotel – away from the bodyguards, etc. – and told him I was getting a bit wiggy from the pressure; it was like being onstage all the time, or maybe in the midst of a prison riot. He agreed, but the nature of his position as "leader of the militants" made it impossible for him to be openly friendly with a *gabacho.*

I understood this . . . and just about then, I remembered that another old friend, now working for *Sports Illustrated,* had asked me if I felt like going out to Vegas for the weekend, at their expense, and writing a few words about a motorcycle race. This seemed like a good excuse to get out of L.A. for a few days, and if I took Oscar along it would also give us time to talk and sort out the evil realities of the Salazar/Murder story.

So I called *Sports Illustrated* – from the patio of the Polo Lounge – and said I was ready to do the "Vegas thing." They agreed . . . and from here on in there is no point in running down details, because they're all in the book.

Caesar's Palace, Las Vegas, 3:00 a.m., April 26, 1971: Hunter S. Thompson and Oscar Zeta Acosta *(from left)* during their infamous "savage journey to the heart of the American Dream"

More or less . . . and this qualifier is the essence of what, for no particular reason, I've decided to call Gonzo Journalism. It is a style of "reporting" based on William Faulkner's idea that the best fiction is far more *true* than any kind of journalism – and the best journalists have always known this.

Which is not to say that Fiction is necessarily "more true" than Journalism – or vice versa – but that both "fiction" and "journalism" are artificial categories; and that both forms, at their best, are only two different means to the same end. This is getting pretty heavy . . . so I should cut back and explain, at this point, that *Fear & Loathing in Las Vegas* is a *failed experiment* in Gonzo Journalism. My idea was to buy a fat notebook and record the whole thing, *as it happened,* then send in the notebook for publication – without editing. That way, I felt, the eye & mind of the journalist would be functioning as a camera. The writing would be selective & necessarily interpretive – but once the image was written, the words would be final; in the same way that a Cartier-Bresson photograph is always (he says) the full-frame negative. No alterations in the darkroom, no cutting or cropping, no spotting . . . no editing.

But this is a hard thing to do, and in the end I found myself imposing an essentially fictional framework on what began as a piece of straight/crazy journalism. True Gonzo reporting needs the talents of a master journalist, the eye of an artist/photographer and the heavy balls of an actor. Because the writer *must* be a participant in the scene, while he's writing it – or at least taping it, or even sketching it. Or all three.

Probably the closest analogy to the ideal would be a film director/producer who writes his own scripts, does his own camera work and somehow manages to film himself in action, as the protagonist or at least a main character.

The American print media were not ready for this kind of thing, yet. ROLLING STONE was probably the only magazine in America where I could get the Vegas book published. I sent *Sports Illustrated* 2,500 – instead of the 250 they asked for – and my manuscript was aggressively rejected. They refused to even pay my minimum expenses . . .

But to hell with all that. I seem to be drifting away from the point – that *Fear & Loathing* is not what I thought it would be. I began writing it during a week of hard typewriter nights in a room at the Ramada Inn – in a place called Arcadia, California – up the road from Pasadena & right across the street from the Santa Anita racetrack. I was there during the first week of the Spring Racing – and the rooms all around me were jammed with people I couldn't quite believe.

Heavy track buffs, horse trainers, ranch owners, jockeys & their women . . . I was lost in that swarm, sleeping most of each day and writing all night on the Salazar article. But each night, around dawn, I would knock off the Salazar work and spend an hour or so, cooling out, by letting my head unwind and my fingers run wild on the big black Selectric . . . jotting down notes about the weird trip to Vegas. It had worked out nicely, in terms of the Salazar piece – plenty of hard straight talk about who was lying and who wasn't, and Oscar had finally relaxed enough to talk to me straight. Flashing across the desert at 110 in a big red convertible with the top down, there is not much danger of being bugged or overheard.

But we stayed in Vegas a bit longer than we'd planned to. Or at least *I* did. Oscar had to get back for a nine o'clock court appearance on Monday. So he took a plane and I was left alone out there – just me and a massive hotel bill that I knew I couldn't pay, and the treacherous reality of that scene caused me to spend about thirty-six straight hours in my room at the Mint Hotel . . . writing feverishly in a notebook about a nasty situation that I thought I might *not* get away from.

These notes were the genesis of *Fear & Loathing.* After my escape from Nevada and all through the tense work week that followed (spending all my afternoons on the grim streets of East L.A. and my nights at the typewriter in that Ramada Inn hideout) . . . my only loose & human moments would come around dawn when I could relax and fuck around with this slow-building, stone-crazy Vegas story.

By the time I got back to the Rolling Stone Hq. in San Francisco, the Salazar story was winding out at around nineteen thousand words, and the strange Vegas "fantasy" was running on its own spaced energy and pushing five thousand words – with no end in sight and no real reason to continue working on it, except the pure pleasure of unwinding on paper. It was sort of an exercise – like *Bolero* – and it might have stayed that way if Jann Wenner, the editor of ROLLING STONE, hadn't liked the first twenty or so jangled pages enough to take it seriously on its own terms and tentatively schedule it for publication – which gave me the push I needed to keep working on it.

So, six months later, the ugly bastard was finished. And I liked it – despite the fact that I failed at what I was trying to do. As true Gonzo Journalism, this doesn't work at all – and even if it did, I couldn't possibly admit it. Only a goddamn lunatic would write a thing like this and then claim it was true. The week the first selection of *Fear & Loathing* appeared in ROLLING STONE I found myself applying for White House press credentials – a plastic pass that would give me the run of the White House, along with at least theoretical access to the big oval room where Nixon hung out, pacing back & forth on those fine thick taxpayers' carpets and pondering Sunday's point spread. (Nixon was a *serious* pro football freak. He and I were old buddies on this front: We once spent a long night together on the Thruway from Boston to Manchester, dissecting the pro & con strategy of the Oakland–Green Bay Super Bowl game. It was the only time I've ever seen the bugger relaxed – laughing, whacking me on the knee as he recalled Max McGee's one-handed catch for the back-breaking touchdown. I was *impressed.* It was like talking to Owsley about Acid.)

The trouble with Nixon was that he was a serious *politics junkie*. He was totally hooked . . . and like any other junkie, he was a bummer to have around: especially as President.

Anyway, the main point I want to make about *Fear & Loathing* is that although it's not what I meant it to be, it's still so *complex* in its failure that I feel I can take the risk of defending it as a first, gimped effort in a direction that Tom Wolfe calls "The New Journalism" and had been flirting with for almost a decade.

Wolfe's problem is that he's too crusty to *participate* in his stories. The people he feels comfortable with are dull as stale dogshit, and the people who seem to fascinate him as a writer are so weird that they make him nervous. The only thing new and unusual about Wolfe's journalism is that he's an abnormally good reporter; he has a fine sense of echo and at least a peripheral understanding of what John Keats was talking about when he said that thing about Truth & Beauty. The only reason Wolfe seems "new" is because William Randolph Hearst bent the spine of American journalism very badly when it was just getting started. All Tom Wolfe did – after he couldn't make it on the *Washington Post* and couldn't even get hired by the *National Observer* – was to figure out that there was really not much percentage in playing the old *Collier's* game, and that if he was ever going to make it in "journalism," his only hope was to make it on his own terms: by being *good* in the classical – rather than the contemporary – sense, and by being the kind of journalist that the American print media honor mainly in the breach. Or, failing that, at the funeral. Like Stephen Crane, who couldn't even get a copyboy's job on today's *New York Times*. The only difference between working for the *Times* and *Time* magazine is the difference between being a third-string All-American fullback at Yale instead of Ohio State.

And again, yes, we seem to be rambling – so perhaps I should close this off.

The only other important thing to be said about *Fear & Loathing* at this time is that it was *fun* to write, and that's rare – for me, at least, because I've always considered writing the most hateful kind of work. I suspect it's a bit like fucking, which is only fun for amateurs. Old whores don't do much giggling.

Nothing is fun when you *have to do it* – over & over, again & again – or else you'll be evicted, and that gets old. So it's a rare goddamn trip for a locked-in rent-paying writer to get into a gig that, even in retrospect, was a kinghell, highlife fuckaround from start to finish . . . and then to actually get *paid* for writing this kind of manic gibberish seems genuinely weird; like getting paid for kicking Agnew in the balls.

So maybe there's hope. Or maybe I'm going mad. These are not easy things to be sure of, either way . . . and in the meantime we have this failed experiment in Gonzo Journalism, the certain truth of which will never be established. That much is definite. *Fear & Loathing in Las Vegas* will have to be chalked off as a frenzied experiment, a fine idea that went crazy about halfway through . . . a victim of its own conceptual schizophrenia, caught and finally crippled in that vain, academic limbo between "journalism" & "fiction." And then hoist on its own petard of multiple felonies and enough flat-out crime to put anybody who'd admit to this kind of stinking behavior in the Nevada State Prison.

So now, in closing, I want to thank everybody who helped me put this happy work of fiction together. Names are not necessary here; they know who they are . . .

In a nation ruled by swine, all pigs are upward-mobile – and the rest of us are fucked until we can put our acts together: Not necessarily to Win, but mainly to keep from Losing Completely. We owe that to ourselves and our crippled self-image as something better than a nation of panicked sheep . . . but we owe it especially to our children, who will have to live with our loss and all its long-term consequences. I don't want my son asking me why his friends are calling me a "Good German."

Which gets down to a final point about *Fear & Loathing in Las Vegas*. I have called it, only half sarcastically, "a vile epitaph for the Drug Culture of the Sixties," and I think it is. This whole twisted saga is a sort of Atavistic Endeavor, a dream-trip into the past – however recent – that was only half successful. I think we both understood, all along, that we were running a hell of a risk by laying a Sixties trip on Las Vegas in 1971 . . . and that neither one of us would ever pass this way again.

So we pushed it as far as we could, and we survived – which means something, I guess, but not much beyond a good story . . . and now, having done it, written it, and humping a reluctant salute to that decade that started so high and then went so brutally sour, I don't see much choice but to lash down the screws and get on with what has to be done. Either that or do nothing at all – fall back on the Good German, Panicked Sheep syndrome, and I don't think *I'm* ready for that. At least not right now.

Because it was nice to be loose and crazy with a good credit card in a time when it was *possible* to run totally wild in Las Vegas and then get paid for writing a book about it . . . and it occurs to me that I probably just made it, just under the wire and the deadline.

So much, then, for The Road – and for the last possibilities of running amok in Las Vegas & living to tell the tale. But maybe we won't really miss it. Maybe Law & Order is really the best way to go, after all.

Yeah . . . maybe so, and if that's the way it happens . . . well, at least I'll know I was *there*, neck deep in the madness, before the deal went down, and I got so high and wild that I felt like a two-ton Manta Ray jumping all the way across the Bay of Bengal.

It was a good way to go, and I recommend it highly – at least for those who can stand the trip. And for those who can't, or won't, there is not much else to say. Not now, and certainly not by me, or Raoul Duke either. *Fear & Loathing in Las Vegas* marks the end of an era . . . and now, on this fantastic Indian summer morning in the Rockies, I want to leave this noisy black machine and sit naked on my porch for a while, in the sun. ⊕

Kantner and Grace Slick, is born. The little girl was originally to be called "god . . . no last name, no capital G, and he can change his name when he feels like it," as Slick had said during her pregnancy.

The Tate–La Bianca murder trial case ends with Charles Manson and three female members of the Manson Family convicted of first-degree murder. Two months later, a jury will recommend the death penalty for all four.

31 On the heels of *Apollo 13's* near disaster, the third lunar mission, *Apollo 14*, lifts off from Cape Kennedy; six days later, Alan Shepard and Edgar Mitchell become the fifth and sixth men to walk on the moon.

1971 FEBRUARY

9 Southern California is hit by a major earthquake (6.6 on the Richter scale), which kills 62 and causes billions of dollars in damage.

13 With American air support, a South Vietnamese force of 5,000 invades Laos. While the Defense Department's March draft call-up reaches 17,000, the White House assures Congress these actions will quicken the end of the war and the return of all U.S. troops. Over the next week, antiwar protests erupt nationwide, with student groups calling for a major antiwar demonstration in Washington, DC. Congressman Paul McCloskey (R-CA) suggests impeachment as a negative incentive for President Nixon to alter his policy on Vietnam.

20 Top of the charts: the Osmonds' "One Bad Apple" (pop single); *Jesus Christ Superstar* (pop album).

21 In Vienna, 21 countries sign an international agreement to end illegal sales of stimulants, tranquilizers and hallucinogens.

23 In a career high point, Charley Pride, country music's first postwar black star (and a former professional baseball player), collects two gold records for his best-selling albums *10th Album* and *Just Plain Charley*.

1971 MARCH

1 A bomb planted in protest of the American invasion of Laos explodes at the Capitol building and destroys a U.S. Senate bathroom, though an early warning ensures no one is hurt. The Weather Underground claims responsibility.

my pop conscience
by robert a. hull

I GREW UP listening to AM radio in Memphis. Through the crackle and hum, the programming was dense – gospel, soul, country and Elvis. In the midst of this musical jungle, there was always something new and mysterious appearing unannounced and seemingly far removed from the sin-and-redemption lifestyle of Elvis's hometown.

Those days, in the world of pop, there was value in the unknown. It was a pivotal time: The Beatles had gone, leaving a swath of harmony and brightness in their wake. Faceless, flawlessly melodious voices abounded on the airwaves, singing brilliantly orchestrated tunes that seemed crafted to appeal to the lingering optimism that splashed into the Seventies – like Gallery, the Marmalade and Pilot.

Who? These names and titles were (and still are) little more than tags on the ends of undyingly familiar song titles or lyrics: "Nice to Be With You"; "Reflections of My Life"; "Ho, *ho, HO* – It's MAGIC!" Indeed, it is the sound and the mystery that survives . . . not the face or the name.

Ultimately, it was a long-forgotten band called Hackamore Brick that taught me about the meaning of pop's meaninglessness. (By 1971, I had abandoned the static of AM, and was busy being cool in the progressive mind-set of FM radio.) I discovered their sole album, *One Kiss Leads to Another*, when I was working as a program director and album reviewer at my college radio station, Brown University's WBRU-FM.

The albums regularly played on the air occupied one side of WBRU's studio (jazz, blues, Fifties oldies, Beatles, Rolling Stones and then-acceptable acts such as Elton John, Rod Stewart, Fleetwood Mac, Pink Floyd), while records considered unworthy were relegated to a section on the opposite side of the studio and branded with a pink Magic Marker X. The demarcation was given for offensiveness – not for violation of FCC rules, but for a violation of the rules of good counterculture taste: a failure to measure up to the new classics of rock by Jefferson Airplane or the Grateful Dead.

Out of curiosity and a youthful sense of rebellion, I began to explore this pink-Xed netherworld. There I found Hackamore Brick's unknown work, buried and defaced. I was drawn to the album because the four kids standing on a New York fire escape on the cover looked like me at the time: drugged, ragged and awkward. When I played the record, it was immediately apparent that no one had even bothered to listen to it before assigning it to pink-cross purgatory. Though ROLLING STONE – the unofficial voice of the counterculture and, by extension, FM radio – actually reviewed *One Kiss Leads to Another*, critic Richard Meltzer dismissed it as "limbo plus filler."

In hindsight, Hackamore Brick's raw garage sound, influenced by Neil Young and the Flamin' Groovies, significantly prefigured rough homegrown New York punk of the late Seventies such as the Ramones. Of course, by 1977, punk style and culture would flip its finger at the rock establishment and get away with it so successfully that it is now hard to imagine popular culture prior to the advent of the Sex Pistols. At that point, WBRU had even moved the Stooges' *Raw Power* out of the pink-cross section and onto the regular playlist.

But back in 1971 Hackamore Brick taught me what the mysterious world of AM radio had become: the home for music banished by Seventies FM stations, rock journalists and the counterculture establishment. This music was pre-1977, overly commercial, somewhat polished pop – hits rock critics ignored. It is the same stuff radio stations now debase with where-are-they-now contests, that hip reissue labels market with a sly wink under cheesy banners of HAVE A NICE DAY and smiley faces. In this age of irony, it's as if no one wants to openly admit to the unjaded joy these songs can still evoke.

In the early Seventies, it was more important to understand the beauty of a James Taylor or Paul Simon recording than to lose oneself in a throwaway pop song. What meaning could there possibly be in the "Ooga-chuka"s that open Blue Swede's amazing and comical version of B.J. Thomas's "Hooked on a Feeling"? And who were these unknown

1971 APRIL

idiots compared to the serious singer/songwriters and inventive rock musicians of the era? Gallery? Skylark? Jigsaw? Their names and faces meant nothing.

Today there is an unspoken cultural agreement that great pop hits must be the work of a personality, an auteur, and cannot be created by anonymous artists. Perhaps this is a genuine consequence of our post-MTV era, a time when images are intrinsically linked with music: The very notion of a "faceless" band cannot exist in such a media-focused age, with interviews, photo opportunities and music videos all waiting to propel the next music star across cable channels and magazine spreads.

The faceless pop music of the early Seventies has not left us, of course; in fact, there seems to be a growing nostalgia for, and rediscovery of, those anonymous productions. Syndicated DJs like Casey Kasem, as well as regional stalwarts like New York's Cousin Brucie and Boston's Barry Scott, continue to spin the one-hit wonders. College and indie bands cover the songs with either tongue-in-cheek irony or academic devotion. Gen-X-targeted commercials and almost every major film release with any indie or hip credibility must now include a sliver of Seventies "cheese" on its soundtrack. (The genius of Quentin Tarantino's use of Stealers Wheel's "Stuck in the Middle With You" in *Reservoir Dogs*' ear-slicing scene is *not* in its devaluation of a hokey song but in the tension created between sunshine pop and torture.)

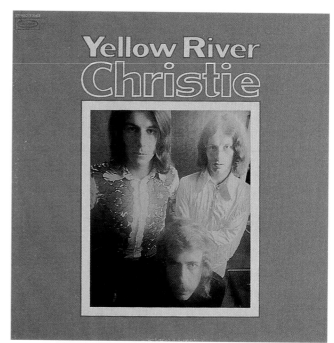

Whether packaged with quaint labels or exploited as oldies, Seventies pop songs and bands, in the breadth of their variety, give testimony to the wide appeal these concise explosions of fun-filled innocence had at the time. They still hold a clear vision of pop's message of urgency and frivolity, practically leaping, even today, out of the radio. The anonymous gestures of Seventies pop carry no hidden agenda, no baggage of personality. They are simply good, silly songs, produced with great craft.

Take Pilot's 1975 hit, "Magic": a hook-filled three and a half minutes overflowing with irrepressibly effervescent spirit. A Scottish trio of studio musicians, Pilot unapologetically combined Hollies-like harmonies with *Sgt. Pepper*'s artful ambition. Building from its falsetto harmonies to its climactic outpouring of good cheer, "Magic" wove together hand claps, plush orchestration, a distorted rock-guitar line and a "la-la-la-la" chorus into a singular anonymous gesture. Magic indeed.

In the late Sixties, however, the crafters of faceless pop magic were still at odds with the self-integrated songwriting bands that had followed in the Beatles' wake, and held fast to the days of matching song with singer and calling in the standby string section. By the early Seventies, as all things countercultural began to take over, pop production happily embraced all of rock's advancements: meticulous studio experimentation, new sounds like distortion, electric piano and wah-wah pedals and the free quoting of youth-music genres. The flowering of faceless magic was nourished directly by this progressive, creative fare, led in particular by one unknown – but certainly not unheard – singer.

No one knew Tony Burrows then, and no one knows him today, but he was the best-known anonymous voice of the Seventies. A professional British session vocalist, he sang with over twenty different studio groups, shaping a sound without revealing his identity. Between 1970 and 1974, his lead vocals were heard on five Top Fifteen hits and countless other non-charting gems.

Burrows's skill lay in an uncanny ability to adapt a specific vocal approach to a wide variety of pop-harmony groups. Whether he was singing a Beach Boys tribute (First Class's "Beach Baby"), a grittier gospel-inspired tune (the Brotherhood of Man's "United We Stand"), a novelty gag (the Pipkins' "Gimme Dat Ding") or any of his blue-eyed-soul numbers (Edison Lighthouse's "Love Grows (Where My Rosemary Goes)," White Plains's "My Baby Loves Lovin'"), Burrows's success was proved by his anonymity. Of course, he wasn't the first. In style and career, Burrows was simply carrying on a tradition begun in the late Sixties by producers Jeff Katz and Jerry Kasenetz, who singlehandedly created the genre known as bubblegum music (Ohio Express, 1910 Fruitgum Company, the Lemon Pipers).

By the Seventies, the sunny innocence of "Yummy, yummy, yummy, I got love in my tummy" matured into the more worldly optimism of "We had joy, we had fun, we had seasons in the sun" (as Terry Jacks had reworked the bittersweet Jacques Brel lyrics). Indeed, sunshine seemed to be dancing from the grooves of singles recorded by a host of inheritors of the bubblegum aesthetic. The Shocking Blue's "Venus," Christie's "Yellow River," Vanity Fare's "Hitchin' a Ride," Daniel Boone's "Beautiful Sunday," Gallery's "Nice to Be With You," Redbone's "Come and Get Your Love," Looking Glass's "Brandy (You're a Fine Girl)," Lighthouse's "One Fine Morning" and Lobo's "Me and You and a Dog Named Boo" are but a handful of pop masterpieces.

The Seventies themselves – the movements and themes

of the decade – are inextricably attached to the musical time capsules that were the top 45s of the day: antiwar protest (Coven's "One Tin Soldier," Bo Donaldson and the Heywoods' "Billy, Don't Be a Hero"), social and racial commentary (Stories' "Brother Louie," Three Dog Night's "Black & White"), looser sexual mores (Sammy Johns's "Chevy Van," Starland Vocal Band's "Afternoon Delight"), new spirituality (Norman Greenbaum's "Spirit in the Sky," Ocean's "Put Your Hand in the Hand"), drugs (Brewer and Shipley's "One Toke Over the Line," America's "A Horse With No Name") and even fads (Ray Stevens's "The Streak," Carl Douglas's "Kung Fu Fighting").

I discovered most of these Seventies recordings, forgotten and abandoned, in the pink-cross section at WBRU. I came to love and appreciate artists like Crabby Appleton and Sugarloaf, who both wore the light-scarlet letter bequeathed them by an overly self-conscious rock establishment. I did not know who these pop artists were, but I cherished them just the same.

I didn't really understand all of this until the late Eighties. In 1989 I was hired as an editor, researcher and producer by Time-Life Music. My task was now a simple one: to package and sell the music that I once experienced as a guilty pleasure to a wide audience that needed to be reminded of its emotional attachment to Gary Glitter and the Poppy Family. I was being paid to research and resurrect those early Seventies days of innocence, discovery and communion with Hackamore Brick, dusting them off for our era of microscopic scrutiny and predictable publicity.

What I began to learn was a truth about all pop music – whether from the Forties or the Nineties – that I had intuitively sensed in the early Seventies while I was working at my college radio station: that the *real* gems are the songs stored in the pink-crossed section of our consciousness. We just don't want to admit it.

the war in Vietnam, President Nixon appears on TV and claims that announcing a complete withdrawal date of U.S. forces would aid Hanoi's war effort.

15 *Patton* marches to the top of the Academy of Motion Pictures heap, claiming seven Oscars, including Best Actor, Picture and Director, while Glenda Jackson grabs Best Actress for *Women in Love*.

20 The Supreme Court upholds the validity of busing and redistricting as means for integrating schools, opening the door for years of protest to follow.

24 Over 200,000 antiwar protesters march through Washington, DC, (and other cities) to rally support for ending the U.S. military presence in Southeast Asia. Protests continue a week later in the nation's capital, as 30,000 people gather on the banks of the Potomac, and a record 7,000 are arrested as they try to disrupt traffic.

27 Baseball player Curt Flood, who sacrificed his career to test the legality of the game's reserve clause, retires after sitting out the 1970 season during his legal battle.

29 The U.S. death toll in Indochina crests at 45,019, a total exceeded only in World Wars I and II.

30 Kareem Abdul-Jabbar leads the Milwaukee Bucks in their domination over the Baltimore Bullets to capture the NBA championship.

1971 MAY

7 Rival basketball leagues the ABA and the NBA seek congressional approval to merge. They will finally join forces in 1976.

9 Emmy wins go to popular TV programs *All in the Family*, *The Flip Wilson Show*, *The David Frost Show* and *Singer Presents Burt Bacharach*.

12 Mick Jagger, living in tax exile in southern France, marries socialite and Nicaraguan shopkeeper's daughter Bianca Rose Perez Moreno de Marcias in an exclusive but highly publicized wedding in St. Tropez. Keith Richards celebrates by chucking an ashtray through a plate-glass window.

13 The long-deadlocked Paris Peace Talks on the Vietnam conflict enter their fourth year; the count of U.S. forces in Indochina reaches 240,000.

15 The creator of the yo-yo and

leaking the truth
by jann s. wenner

On June 13, 1971, the 'New York Times' began publishing excerpts from an exhaustive seven-thousand-page government study officially entitled "History of U.S. Decision-Making Process on Vietnam Policy." It was commissioned by then–Secretary of Defense Robert McNamara in 1967, and only fifteen top-secret copies were originally printed (though McNamara later attempted to have it declassified).

The official announcements, classified memoranda and other sensitive documents constituting what are known as the Pentagon Papers all proved a rare example of government self-reflection: a long, hard, nonpartisan attempt to understand just how the devil the United States ever got so irretrievably embroiled in the Vietnamese conflict.

Were the Pentagon Papers really top secret? Should they have been made available to the public? Was national security at stake? These were the questions that were foisted on the Supreme Court as the White House led a cat-and-mice battle to squelch the unauthorized printing of the Papers by the 'New York Times,' then the 'Washington Post,' 'Boston Globe' and a host of other similarly motivated dailies.

By the end of that summer – for a moment anyway – freedom and truth emerged triumphant. The Pentagon Papers were successfully released with the Supreme Court ruling in favor of the fourth estate. "Only a free and unrestrained press can effectively expose deception in government," wrote Justice Hugo Black in his concurring opinion; clearly, his were prophetic words with the Watergate affair waiting just around the corner.

If there was a hero in the Pentagon Papers affair, he was a former Defense Department middleman and think-tank employee named Daniel Ellsberg. He was the one who stole the truth and set it free. He was prosecuted for his efforts – twice – and, due to prosecutorial improprieties (such as the break-in of his psychiatrist's office by White House agents), was eventually exonerated.

Daniel Ellsberg was perhaps the first highly placed official ever to have left the inner government and then reveal to the public, with top secret documents, its closely guarded secret operations. As befits a man who risks his reputation and ruin to fight a corrupt and unlawful government, he is vain, egocentric and completely convinced of the rightness of his action. But examine this statement: Ellsberg revealed a dark picture of what had been occurring in American government by acting on one of our country's basic democratic beliefs – "a man can make a difference."

June 28, 1971: Daniel Ellsberg stands with his wife, Patricia, outside a Boston federal court

I spoke with Ellsberg in 1973 after his second trial was dismissed, in order to understand the man and his motivations; we originally published the sixty-thousand-word interview in ROLLING STONE in two parts.

THE RELEASE OF THE PENTAGON PAPERS has revealed much more than the tragic outcome of the government's consistently misdirected approach to Vietnam. The incredible information-gathering systems and the willful editing and ignorance of recent history strike an uncanny similarity to Orwell's '1984' – do you find that so?

Yes. Definitely. I was particularly struck when I went back to look at *1984*, in the fall of 1971, to read about a war "on the vague frontiers whose whereabouts the average man could only guess at," which had gone on for twenty-five years when the book opened. December 19, 1971 – six months after I'd given the Pentagon Papers to the press – was the twenty-fifth anniversary of our involvement in the Vietnam War.

The fact is, as you read it, an enormous number of analogies come out. The key theme of the book is the slogan: "Who controls the past, controls the future. . . . And who controls the present controls the past." Now let's consider the fact that the U.S. Executive, this year and last year, lied in writing to the Senate about what we had done four years earlier in Vietnam. How was the lying done? You may remember that Winston Smith, the protagonist in *1984*, had a job that consisted of changing histori-

the parking meter, Donald Duncan, dies.

20 Peter Cetera, bass player and singer for Chicago, undergoes emergency surgery after being beaten and losing four teeth while attending a baseball game between the Los Angeles Dodgers and the Chicago Cubs. He had been attacked by a gang who objected to the length of his hair.

22 A Gallup Poll finds 72% of Americans do not believe Nixon will ever be able to withdraw U.S. forces from South Vietnam and leave it strong enough to defend itself. As well, 69% believe that he has not told the public all it should know about the war.

Top of the charts: Three Dog Night's "Joy to the World" (pop single); the Rolling Stones' *Sticky Fingers* (pop album).

24 Rock's poet laureate Bob Dylan turns 30 (a *Peanuts* comic strip even makes mention of it), and he celebrates at Jerusalem's Wailing Wall.

31 A well-publicized antiwar march by approximately 400 Vietnam veterans takes place in Boston.

1971 JUNE

2 Farm-labor contractor Juan Corona is charged with murder after the bodies of 24 migrant workers are found buried in California.

5 Grand Funk Railroad sells out a concert at New York City's Shea Stadium in less than 72 hours, breaking the Beatles' long-standing record and underscoring Grand Funk's popular -- if not critical – support. Only a month before, their press conference drew just 6 of 150 invited journalists.

6 The Soviet Union's *Soyuz 11* docks with space station *Salyut 1*; it is the first successful manned docking in space. Tragically, the crew perishes when a valve accidentally opens on its return journey.

TV's *Ed Sullivan Show*, which had featured such rock legends as the Beatles, the Rolling Stones, the Supremes and the Doors, broadcasts for the last time, with featured musical guests Gladys Knight & the Pips.

John Lennon performs onstage for the first time since 1969, joining Yoko Ono and Frank Zappa in a Fillmore East jam, which will later be released as part of Lennon's

cal records to make sure there was nothing in writing that would ever give the lie to a current statement by "Big Brother."

We now know that the White House hired a former CIA agent, in part to break into my doctor's office, but also, as Nixon described, to prepare "an accurate history of some of our earlier diplomatic involvements in Vietnam." Meaning? Hunt's work with a razor blade and a Xerox machine to forge cables, to indicate, historically, that the dead brother of one of Nixon's current opponents has cooperated in the assassination of a friendly head of state. So what Nixon describes as historical research is, in fact, direct forgery.

But here is the difference. At one point [in *1984*] Winston Smith holds in his hand a document. It happens to be a photograph giving the lie to a charge of treason against an earlier member of the Inner Party. He holds it for a moment with the notion in his mind "that a single piece of paper could destroy the regime." But he puts it in the burn bag, or down the memory hole, and it's destroyed.

But the Pentagon Papers were one example of a piece of paper that ultimately didn't get destroyed, that did get out. The questions then to face are: Can that make any difference? Can one example lead to any others? Do the people actually care about the difference between truth and falsity? Do they care about the difference between self-defense and murder? I would say that most people I've run into, and most media commentators, give a negative answer to that.

Take us back to the point at which you first turned against U.S. involvement in the Vietnam War.

I called [Assistant Deputy Secretary of Defense for International Security, Morton] Halperin in late June of '69 with a question that was new to me: "What's your estimate of the number of Vietnamese who would rather see peace even under a communist government than see the war continue?"

"Oh, 90 percent," he said.

"Do you think your boss thinks that?" I asked.

"I've never discussed that with him precisely, but I would guess that he did."

"Then how can we justify continuing this a day longer?"

"Well," he said, "that's a good question . . . let me think about it."

That was the moment I began to see the need to end the war most urgently. I began to see that domestic politics couldn't excuse it. I finally saw continuation as immoral, not just mistaken.

What I lacked then was documentary evidence of what I had just been told by Halperin. But I *did* have something unusual. I had the Pentagon Papers. Unfortunately they ended in March of 1968. But the promise they held was that the pattern of 1964–65 was close to what was now a prospect; and if I could show that at least once in the past an administration had acted in a conspiratorial fashion, people should at least consider the possibility that it was happening again.

Moreover, since it was a story about a Democratic administration – several of them, really, including Truman's – releasing these documents would make it tempting for Nixon to throw the responsibility for the war onto Democrats, where it mainly belonged, and bring it to a quick halt.

Then in May of '70, when the Cambodian invasion took place, Halperin resigned as consultant to Kissinger, and three members of Kissinger's staff left in the dispute.

You asked how I could have thought Nixon would change the policy? But really, *everybody* thought that, for what seemed perfectly natural reasons. I think the harder question to answer is, why *didn't* they change the policy? How could they have possibly dreamed of winning the Vietnam War as of 1969?

I think the best answer is that both Nixon and Kissinger have a deep and fundamental belief, an almost mystical faith in the effectiveness of threatening and causing pain or death.

You have stated that you believe the military was not responsible for our Vietnam policy. How did the Pentagon Papers prove this?

The Pentagon Papers show unmistakably that each president pursued policies that were different from ones the military had proposed to him. While military pressure for greater measures was possibly a factor in Nixon's prolonging the war, he *was* taking courses of action that the military consistently said would not work.

I attacked the "quagmire myth" of the Vietnam War – that it was "the politics of inadvertence," the inattention of the president, which allowed the military to drag us into the war. I came to believe from studying the Pentagon Papers that the quagmire myth was quite wrong, that the president *was* responsible.

One of the first people you actually "leaked" the Pentagon Papers to was your former colleague, Henry Kissinger. What was his reaction?

He was as bad as I'd ever imagined he was. My earlier feelings were based on his attitude toward a fairly hypothetical situation toward nuclear war. But now I was confronting a man who was managing the actual destruction of Cambodia.

I thought of leaking information *into* the White House about what was actually visible from the outside, to try to make them understand that their policy *was* foreseeable. The more foreseeable it was, the less viable it might appear to him.

I saw Kissinger for lunch at San Clemente. I asked Kissinger if he knew about the McNamara study on Vietnam and he said he did. (I didn't know then that he had actually been a consultant in the first month of the study.) "Do you have a copy of it in the White House?" He said he did.

"Have you read it?"

"No, should I? Do we really have anything to learn from this study?"

My heart sank. The major lesson of the study was that each person repeated the same patterns in decision-making and pretty much the same policy as his predecessor, without even knowing it. I thought, My God! He's in the same state of mind as all the other makers of decisions in this long process, each of whom thought that history had started with his administration, and had nothing to learn from earlier ones.

Do you remember the first time you actually walked out with some of the Pentagon Papers with the intent to copy them?

I remember the day very well. In fact, I remember the moment I decided to do it. It was September 30, 1969. I'd gotten the *L.A. Times* in the morning, took it back to bed, and was reading the lead story, about the dismissal of charges – "Termination with extreme prejudice" – in the Green Beret murder case, involving the killing of a supposed double agent.

There had been stories about the case, and suddenly it was dropped. There was no doubt the White House had ordered the dropping of the charges.

I remember lying in bed and thinking: This is the system I have been part of, and have been working for, for fifteen years, including three years in the Marine Corps, and it's a system that lies automatically to conceal murders, from top to bottom, from the sergeant up to the commander in chief. I'm not going to be part of that anymore.

I got dressed and went over to see Tony Russo [a likeminded colleague at the Rand Corporation] down the road in Santa Monica; I went in and said, "Tony, can you get a hold of a Xerox machine?" I said I had some studies that I wanted to copy. That night or the next, we started copying.

Tell me about the copying process.

I started with what seemed the most important, most useful material, on the assumption that the whole thing would come out within a matter of weeks. We were just working all night, standing over the machine and running the stuff through. If I'd had one of those fast machines, the kind that just go zip, zip, zip for each copy, that would have been marvelous; I could have given a copy to every member of Congress. But as it was, I had a rather slow machine. In fact, I started out wanting to make four copies, and within an hour, we switched to two because it just took too long – we couldn't afford the time.

I decided not to take it to a commercial place because of the chance that somebody would be suspicious about what the stuff was and tell the police, or the FBI might get wind of what I was doing and come down on it.

We went into a very heavy night-and-day operation making lots of copies which proved to be crucial, because when the *New York Times* was enjoined – which I'd thought was possible but didn't really expect – I had a whole box of other copies and ultimately gave trunkloads of them to nineteen newspapers, including the Knight chain.

What about the legality of what you were doing?

Our first notion was that I had been indicted simply because I'd just given out thousands of pages of information stamped TOP SECRET, so how could they *not* indict me? But the more we looked into precedent and the actual law, the clearer it became that no statute had been violated.

This must have been known to the Justice Department. If there was no way to prove intent to harm the interests of the United States or to help a foreign power, there could be no prosecution under the Espionage Act. And as far as copying was concerned, transferring *information*, not tangible property, is not subject to prosecution as theft.

What do you think of the media's coverage of you?

I'm very puzzled by the press, in a way.

Why?

The media constantly reiterate that not only was my act unprecedented, but that my motives were unique and strange and had to be investigated, because no one had ever seen anything like this before. This was a way of denying the existence of tens of thousands of people who would have done exactly what I did in the same situation.

Do you see this suppression of the political role of the individual as the product of a conscious effort of the government?

I began to see what we had as a political depression in which people felt they had no political role in this country.

Nixon made this perfectly explicit. Back in October 1969 – when I was copying the Pentagon Papers – just before the second Moratorium effort of November, he said no matter how large the demonstrations, they would in no way influence anything that he did. He would not listen.

In a general way, what I did could be seen as a classic Gandhian dream, to suppose that such an act of nonviolent truth-telling – and taking personal responsibility for it, publicly – is precisely what it took to disturb this government profoundly.

Their policy and administrative framework had been based for a whole generation on secrets and lying. The notion that the Ship of State is leaking truth is as frightening and unstabilizing for the government as anything could possibly be. ⊕

the soul nation climbs aboard
by carol cooper

IN THE EARLY Seventies the two newest things in my life were college and *Soul Train*'s refitted theme song. On Saturday mornings a bunch of us African-American types would gather in the room of whichever upperclassman had the biggest color TV, and at the first do-do-do-do-da-dos of "The Sound of Philadelphia" would begin another round of our favorite intramural sport: dishing and dissecting the Dictionary of Hip as crafted by the first American dance show ever controlled, owned and presented by blacks.

Before *Soul Train*'s national debut in 1971, black American music and dance were usually filtered through white hosts and white dancers. *Soul Train* removed that filter. Because so few blacks had been seen anywhere on television (*Julia*, the first prime-time network sitcom to star a black, Diahann Carroll, did not begin until 1968), viewers of all persuasions couldn't help being impressed, and occasionally shocked, by an entire show, commercials and all, filled with and directed at young people who didn't look like Shelley Fabares or Fred MacMurray's Three Sons, and hosted by a man who *never* had the same haircut as Dick Clark.

"At the beginning we were determined that if *American Bandstand* was going right, *Soul Train* would go left," recalls Don Cornelius, the show's founder, franchise owner and the man who can say "Love, peace and soul" more sonorously than anyone else, except maybe Levi Stubbs of the Four Tops. "When we started, *Bandstand* still had a pretty conservative dress code. We let our kids dress almost any way they liked. Instead of something static like the Spotlight Dance, we came up with a more competitive and exhibitionistic idea that came out of our house parties in Chicago: the *Soul Train* Line."

But what made *ST* much more than just song and dance and hair-care products was Cornelius's own on-camera persona. Here was a black elder who, unlike Clark, did not try to be America's second-oldest teenager. Nixing behavioral concessions, never seen dancing – in fact, relishing the distance – Cornelius created and enjoyed a more paternal role. The uniqueness of his appeal was that he presented an image consistently denied black role models on television: a sense of regal, even absolute, authority.

Cornelius gave visual form to the disembodied voice of a traditional leader within the black community, the omniscient black radio jock. And while his suits and hair modified with annual trends, his slow, measured speech, overly precise diction and benevolently autocratic rule over the wild goings-on never did. Late in 1997, he finally ceded his on-air role as host to the younger actor/comedian Mystro Clark. But Cornelius is still heard every week as the show's opening announcer – presiding over the longest-running show in television history still in first-run syndication. For those of us who watched in preparation for an even wilder Saturday night of our own, Cornelius became a lingering specter who, no matter how loose the rhythms became, made us stop just short of losing control.

At right: The Lock, the Robot, the L.A. Hustle: America learns the latest moves on *Soul Train*; following page: "Love, Peace and Sooooul!": Don Cornelius, *Soul Train*'s perfectly coiffed conductor, with Johnny Nash *(from left)*

Not that all our motives for watching *ST* were merely moral. Emerging from the racially turbulent Sixties, *Soul Train* was the first national television hit completely supported by a black advertiser, namely Chicago-based Johnson Hair Care Products.

"For the longest time, what I paid the most attention to were the commercials," said Debra, a former schoolmate. "We were so brainwashed by corporations refusing to use black models that we figured this company must really have no money if it was using them. It took a year or two before we fully realized what we'd been missing."

But it didn't take that long to realize that the show almost immediately became a powerful avenue for breaking new records. The Seventies were a highly transitional time in the music business, and potential mass-market exposure made the major labels take black artists more seriously. Kenny Gamble and Leon Huff's getting together

the right of the *New York Times* to publish the Pentagon Papers. Within two months the Nixon administration releases an edited version of their own secret studies of the Vietnam conflict.

3 The Doors' lead singer Jim Morrison dies of an alleged heart attack while in the bathtub in the Paris apartment where he had been living since March. Four days later he is buried in the Père Lachaise cemetery in Paris; his death is made public on July 9.

6 Legendary trumpeter and first ambassador of jazz, Louis "Satchmo" Armstrong, dies. A week later, thousands attend his traditional jazz funeral in New Orleans.

25 The 26th Amendment to the U.S. Constitution is ratified, expanding the 1970 law lowering the voting age to 18 in all elections.

26 Adding mobility to the moon program, the *Apollo 15* mission blasts off, and five days later, astronauts David Scott and James Irwin are the first to ride across the moon's terrain in the Lunar Rover Vehicle.

1 The Concerts for Bangladesh, featuring performances by George Harrison, Bob Dylan, Ringo Starr, Leon Russell, Badfinger, Ravi Shankar and others, are held in New York City's Madison Square Garden to benefit the starving refugees of the Bangladesh nation. The sold-out event is filmed and recorded for later release.

2 Opening the door to normalized relations with Communist China, the U.S. (after 20 years of opposition) agrees to a United Nations seat for the country separate from and in addition to that of Taiwan.

3 Ex-Beatle Paul McCartney unveils his new group, Wings, which includes his wife, Linda McCartney, Denny Seiwell and former Moody Blue Denny Laine. Though the lineup will change over the years, Wings will remain McCartney's primary working band for the next decade.

10 Country-rock group the Nitty Gritty Dirt Band assembles a cross-generational array of traditional country-music legends including banjoist Earl Scruggs, fiddler Roy Acuff, guitarist Doc Watson and members of the Carter Family to record the triple LP *Will the Circle Be Unbroken.*

with Don Cornelius to write "T.S.O.P." ("The Sound of Philadelphia," a.k.a. the *Soul Train* theme) coincided with CBS's decision to pick up and develop Gamble, Huff and producer Thom Bell's Philadelphia International label. Stax, also a key supplier of performers to the show, was another black label acquired by CBS not long afterward. Throughout the late Seventies, Solar Records owner Dick Griffey as well as other record producers and ad agencies routinely borrowed from *ST*'s stable of dancers.

Saturday mornings, a nationwide army of largely black viewers would sit in front of *Soul Train*, talking into our Princess phones, comparing notes on everything we saw and heard. Then we'd listen for the same song to blast out at our house party later that night and bust our asses trying to imitate dance moves we had imperfectly studied and hurriedly practiced. Bizarre California trends like the Robot and the Bump developed regional variations overnight. Across the country, school recess on Monday became the hottest dance class in town. Fans in Los Angeles were even more ambitious. At *ST*'s once-a-month tapings, fresh waves of career-minded college and high school kids would dress up, sweat and hang out all weekend on the chance they'd be discovered during their brief moments on camera.

Not all those hopefuls were black. But the show's pioneering mix of blacks, Latinos and Asians was purely coincidental. "Cheryl Song and some of the Latin kids who became regulars were part of the racial integration that has always existed on the show," claims Cornelius. "This was something I never went out of my way to affect either way. I know in some circles it was said that we wouldn't allow whites to dance on the show. But whoever showed up is who we picked from. White kids would often come down just to test us, but if they danced well enough for our talent coordinators, we'd put them on. Even so, they seldom came back."

The core dance group, however, was coordinated by a young parks-and-recreation worker from Chicago, Pam Brown. "We had two huge open calls at the local high schools, which attracted five hundred kids just by word of mouth," she recalls. "As the years went by and the show's reputation grew, the average age of the dancers went up. In addition, more semi-professional black dancers turned out." Damita Jo Freeman, a break and electric-boogie dancer credited with teaching Michael Jackson how to moonwalk, went on to do *Bandstand* after *ST*. Jody Watley and Jeffrey Daniels rose to star-dancer status and, along with Gary Mumford, were chosen to form the group Shalamar, whose first single was even released on the short-lived *Soul Train* label. Their later albums went gold on Solar, and Jody and Jeffrey moved on into solo careers.

Soul Train's inside track to instant fame was not lost on us so-called passive viewers. As more black artists crossed over to the pop charts, the show's credibility grew to the extent that much of the *AB* audience found it mandatory to watch

changed little over the years – except for a constantly updated theme song, some computer graphics, new sponsors, better sets and lighting. Cornelius is a firm believer in the credo, "It ain't broken, so I ain't fixing it."

"*Soul Train* will only change as the black music industry changes," he says. "We are the backdrop to whatever is happening there. Because we specialize, we are willing to make concessions to some artists that other shows will not. Several of the stars we wanted most refused to lip-synch, even though dance shows are a lip-synch medium. So in spite of the extra expense, we have done setups for live performances over a dozen times, because of our responsibility to the music and because the best way to appreciate Barry White is with his full orchestra, or James Brown with his sixteen-piece band, Al Green in person, or B.B. King with Lucille.

"The only question I have about rap, which we've supported since it started coming up on charts in the late Seventies, is that I don't see it creating artists with any

One day I got tired of kicking. I held my leg out and soon everybody was holding their leg out – *Soul Train dancer Damita Jo Freeman*

both shows if they were to have the full index of what was hot and not. The shows were usually programmed close enough in major regional markets for easy comparison – except there was no comparison, which is why it wasn't long before *AB* began borrowing *ST*'s look, feel and its better dancers.

Because he ran the show on the tightest possible budget, Cornelius learned to live without certain "luxuries." Those looong pauses between words that characterize his patter reflect not the influence of Robert Wilson, but rather the absence of cue cards and Teleprompters. Cornelius ad-libbed the whole show, an impressive tradition Mystro Clark tries to maintain. Four weeks' worth of programs are filmed once a month over a weekend. Assuming an average of three musical numbers per show, that means orchestrating a dozen performance shoots in a weekend, often with artists so green they haven't gotten the knack of lip-synching down just yet. Four *Soul Train* Lines must be staged. Four *Soul Train* Scramble Contests must be unscrambled, though for the sake of speed and accuracy the answers are leaked to the players before they begin (then why do some of them take so long?). True, it was more fun when the contest was legit and certain dancers' inability to guess or spell a name like Harriet Tubman was the source of an entire week's cafeteria jokes. But otherwise, the show has

staying power or solid stage appeal. I've been able to stay on television for twenty years because the black community has continued to generate performers who are interesting to look at and can deliver live. Rap and dance acts are making lots of money for the moment, but also have some of the shortest careers in the history of show business."

Ask Cornelius which are his favorite *ST* tapings and he hardly hesitates. "When *Soul Train* did a tribute to Minnie Riperton after she died it was to make sure that an incredible talent like hers did not pass away completely unremarked by mass media.

"There are at least two almost opposing standards for greatness in this society, and if black people follow the white standard instead of their own, there will always be black artists who are not paid a lot of attention by the general marketplace and whose true importance will be lost to history. That's why there is still a real need for *Soul Train*, BET (Black Entertainment Television) and other black-controlled programming to help blacks maintain their own standards. Believe it or not, I wish there were more *Soul Train*s, but I also hope that whatever black personality gets the media baton next realizes that there's more to 'walking this way,' as Run-D.M.C. might say, than a song and a dance." ⊕

11 Defense Secretary Melvin
Laird announces that, as part
of the continuing disengagement of American troops,
South Vietnam has assumed
responsibility for all ground
operations in the Vietnam conflict, effective immediately.

13 R&B saxophonist King Curtis
is stabbed to death during an
argument on a New York City
stoop. His funeral draws such
soul and rock stars as Aretha
Franklin, Stevie Wonder,
Cissy Houston, Brook Benton,
Duane Allman and Herbie
Mann.

15 President Nixon suddenly
imposes a 90-day wage, rent
and price freeze. He also ends
the convertablity of dollars into
gold.

1971 SEPTEMBER

2 ROLLING STONE reports Lenny
Hart, father of Grateful Dead
drummer Mickey Hart and
former manager of the group,
is arrested after a lengthy
search initiated when the
Dead discovered he had pil-
fered $70,000 from the band
in 1970. New Dead manager
Jon McIntire says, "You
wouldn't think that he'd fuck
his own son."

3 The body of Eva Perón is
returned to her widower, former Argentine president Juan
Perón, by the Argentine government to curry political favor.

9 Inmates at the Attica
Correctional Facility in upstate
New York begin an uprising
protesting prison conditions.
After four days of negotiations, impassioned speeches
and media focus, Governor
Nelson Rockefeller orders
state agents to storm the
prison, resulting in the deaths
of 43, including 39 inmates.

15 Stan Smith and Billie Jean
King capture U.S. Open
tennis titles.

29 The Vietnam War–era draft is
officially extended through
June 30, 1973.

1971 OCTOBER

1 Disney World, the world's
largest theme park, opens in
Orlando, FL, at a cost of at
least half a billion dollars.

2 The first nationally syndicated
episode of *Soul Train* airs, featuring performances by Gladys
Knight & the Pips, Honey
Cone and Eddie Kendricks.

3 Peter Bogdanovich's
cinematic treatment of Larry
McMurtry's novel *The Last
Picture Show* opens; four
days later the cops-and-
dope thriller *The French*

southern accents
by mark kemp

MY SISTER had just gotten her driver's license and a brand-new 1971 Mustang Mach I. Metallic blue with soot-gray racing stripes, deep bucket seats, a roaring 350 engine – it was a white-trash Cadillac piloted by a pot-smoking, bell-bottomed, blond-haired hippie girl whom I adored unconditionally.

Cheri was taking me for a ride through the rolling hills outside the small North Carolina mill town where we lived when she reached into the glove box, pulled out a new 8-track tape and shoved it into the deck.

"Listen, Mark," she instructed, looking straight ahead at the narrow country road as though she were the keeper of all the world's knowledge. "It's this band; they're called the Allman Brothers." She turned to me and squinted her eyes: "They're from Georgia."

Georgia?

I was eleven years old, and to me, rock & roll was the stuff of modern British mythol-ogy, made by scrawny English guys in frilly shirts, flashy boots and skin-tight pants. Mama had told me that Elvis Presley was somehow connected to the birth of rock, but in 1971, I couldn't see it. Elvis was country – a hayseed from Mississippi. At least, that's how he came off on TV.

In those days, that's how *all* Southerners came off on TV. On the sitcoms you had your Gomers, your Goobers, your Jethro Bodines, and on the nightly news you had your real-life Southern sheriffs spraying high-powered water hoses at black demon-strators and governors blocking college doors to black students. The notion of a promi-nent white, male Southern role model was one mess of a contradiction. What, pray tell, could a rock & roll band from *Georgia* offer that the Rolling Stones couldn't deliver with far more sym-pathy and taste?

We cruised further into the countryside, and the acoustic intro of the Allmans' "Revival" gave way to dueling harmony guitars, a sweet organ part that

High Southern Gothic: The Allman Brothers Band in original form: Duane Allman, Gregg Allman, Jai Johanny Johanson, Berry Oakley, Dickey Betts, Butch Trucks *(clockwise from top left)*

sounded as though it was coming from one of the tiny churches at the side of the road we were traveling and a funky foundation of bass and percussion. Toward the end of the song, the guitars and organ dropped out completely, leaving only bass and drums and a chorus of singers chanting the words: "People can you feel it, love is everywhere." I felt it. I felt it big. It reminded me of the gospel songs I'd heard when passing by the old black tent revivals on Loach Street.

I studied the grainy group shot on the tape's cover. There was Gregg Allman, his long blond hair parted straight down the middle – just like mine. His rapt blue eyes betrayed not the face of Southern stupidity or intolerance, they mirrored the resigna-tion I heard as he moaned the words to the tape's final track: "Think I'll drink up a lit-tle more wine, to ease my worried mind/Walk down on the street, and leeeeave my blues at home."

There were skeletons in this man's closet, and there were skeletons in mine, too, even though I had yet to reach my teens. There were skeletons in the closet of the entire South, a truth that simultaneously fascinated and terrified me. It was too much for me to comprehend totally at eleven, and though I'd share some feelings with my sister, I could not tell her everything. So I let the Allman Brothers Band hold it for me for a while.

The early Seventies was a socially confusing time to be young and Southern. I had begun first grade just as the public schools were being integrated, and I was getting mixed messages. My parents would tell me it wasn't right to denigrate *colored* peo-ple. But at family get-togethers, many of my aunts, uncles and cousins freely tossed out the word *nigger*.

The Allman Brothers Band, a multiracial outfit of hippies *and* rednecks, had risen above all of that: the family legacies of racism, the drudgeries of a rural working-class exis-

tence. Their ambitious mix of blues, rock, jazz and country was sonic integration. Over the next three years I collected most of their albums and each day, after school, retreated to my bedroom to spend hours with their music. The Allmans were revolutionary. They turned the academic, progressive ideals of the Sixties into reality and spawned one of the Seventies' most popular and enduring musical phenomena: Southern rock.

The roots of this musical secession go back to 1968 when, after a nightmare experience in the hands of the L.A. music establishment, brothers Duane and Gregg Allman decided to regroup and reclaim the blues of their black Southern brethren (Muddy Waters, Willie Dixon, Elmore James) and the rock & roll of their pioneering white precursors (Elvis, Jerry Lee Lewis, Johnny Cash). For too long, the roots-based music of the South had been co-opted, not only by British combos like the Stones and the Yardbirds but also by lukewarm California hippie bands who got the words right but lacked the grit and heart to make it grab.

So when the Nashville-born Allmans brought it all back home – or to nearby Macon, Georgia – they conjured the original pain that fueled the blues, and put their own stamp on the music, updating it with extended, jazzlike improvisations, doses of hypnotic psychedelia and a more authentic country moan. And America heard that moan: By 1971, the Allman Brothers Band was the biggest (and busiest) rock act on the road.

Over the next decade, the Allmans' influence, and the Southern-gothic mythos that surrounded them, proved immeasurable. Their big, fat, double–lead guitar and double-percussion sound spread across the South like the kudzu that covers the sides of its highways. From the Carolinas to Texas, groups were either forming in the Allman Brothers' mode or playing variations on the band's American blues-rock sound: the Marshall Tucker Band, ZZ Top, the Atlanta Rhythm Section, the Charlie Daniels Band, Wet Willie and lesser outfits like Black Oak Arkansas, Molly Hatchet and the Outlaws. Daniels got so swept up in Southernmania that, in 1974, the fiddler penned a jaw-jutting jig called "The South's Gonna Do It," wherein he name-checked most of the bands mentioned above. In 1977, when Jimmy Carter strolled into the White House with a push from post-Watergate politics and more than a little help from his Southern-rock friends, the CDB performed its rebel flag-waver at one of the inaugural parties – a fitting capper to the cresting of Southern rock's popularity.

Lynyrd Skynyrd lead singer, Southern gentleman and noted Neil Young fan Ronnie Van Zant

If the Allmans were the harbingers of Southern rock, helping to form a new identity for Southern youth, Lynyrd Skynyrd emerged in 1973 to take that message a step further: They told us we could be our own rowdy selves and still not be forced into the racist stereotype. If you *did* stereotype us, then fuck you, we'd kick your ass.

The Allman Brothers may have opened my mind to how complex being a Southerner was, but to the rest of America, we were still crazy rednecks (see: Neil Young's holier-than-thou "Southern Man"). That's where Lynyrd Skynyrd came in. Their singer, the irascible Ronnie Van Zant, displayed a swaggering anger that stood in stark contrast to the deep, bluesy melancholy of Gregg Allman. And yet Skynyrd sounded very much like the Allman Brothers. In fact, when my friend Bucky first played me the Florida band's 1973 debut, *Pronounced Leh-Nerd Skin-Nerd*, he hid the cover, cued up the last track and told me to guess what band it was. Upon hearing the aching organ-and-slide-guitar intro, and Van Zant's wistful "If I leave here tomorrow, would you still remember me," my response was immediate: "It's the Allmans." At the time, no one else made music that sounded like that. Little did I know then that this song, Skynyrd's epic "Free Bird," would become one of the defining anthems of Seventies rock.

As the music of the decade grew harder and heavier, Skynyrd brought the sound of the New South full circle (and to a wider audience) by adding the crunch of British hard rock to their traditional Southern blend of country, gospel and blues. And Ronnie Van Zant had a self-conscious sense of humor. He would sing "Sweet Home Alabama" (the rebuttal to Young's "Southern Man") in a Neil Young T-shirt, implying that, though we all found Young's chiding simplistic, we had his albums anyway.

Lynyrd Skynyrd were Southern punks, long before "punk" carried the currency it

would in the later Seventies (they even bucked their corporate record label, singing "Workin' for MCA" with the same venom that the Sex Pistols later spat into the letters "EMI"). But as the decade moved on so would I, slightly embarrassed that I'd been a fan of these rabble-rousing homeboys who'd sung of poison whiskey, simple men and Georgia peaches. By then, Skynyrd's legacy had been reduced to one lone song title, shouted out as a rebel yell at every bar band that passed through town: "Freeeeeeeeee Bird!"

The news knocked me out of my stupor. It was a Friday, late October 1977. As usual, my friends and I had gathered at Crystal and Keith's place – a tiny, white clapboard house out on the edge of town – drinking beer, smoking dope and listening to music. Suddenly, Marie burst into the living room, the tears streaming down her face mingling with her blue eyeliner and strands of dirty-blond hair.

"Skynyrd's plane," she began, hyperventilating between words. "It crashed. Ronnie's dead."

The moment of stunned silence was broken by sobs from the girls and curses from the guys, some of whom kicked the walls with their motorcycle boots. I remained seated, in a daze, clutching the red bong positioned between my legs. It was the first rock & roll tragedy that actually affected me.

We weren't thinking about the pop-cultural ramifications of the crash on that dark fall night, but in hindsight, the death of Ronnie Van Zant marked the end of Southern rock's reign. The "Southern" tag had become little more than a marketing tool, used to peddle acts like .38 Special (led by Van Zant's brother Donnie), whose glossy, middle-of-the-road sound blended in all too well with the pervasive corporate-rock sound of the late

Seventies. Even Ronnie Van Zant had expressed concern about the term's ghettoizing effects; five days before the crash he told the *Miami Herald*, "Southern rock's a dead label, a hype thing for the magazines to blow out of proportion. We don't play like the Allmans did, or like Wet Willie. Southern groups are different."

As for me . . . well, I became part of the backlash. As the Eighties approached, I began trading my Skynyrd albums for the latest British punk and new wave infiltrating American shores. I moved to New York and tried hard to lose my Southern accent.

Looking back, I realize that Southern rock may have died as a cultural movement, but its ashes had been scattered across the musical spectrum. You can hear elements of the Southern-rock sound in the hard-rock twang of many post-Seventies country artists – from Hank Williams Jr. to the Kentucky Headhunters to Travis Tritt. Enough time and distance have passed that a younger crop of genuine Southern boogie bands, unashamed of their roots – like Georgia's Gov't Mule, Tennessee's Screamin' Cheetah Wheelies and Missouri's Bottle Rockets – has reclaimed the brash energy and unabashed stance of Southern rock.

Now I'm trying to *regain* my North Carolina drawl. Listening to the Allman Brothers or Lynyrd Skynyrd no longer leaves me embarrassed, only homesick. As for the Allman Brothers Band, well, they've continued to rock and tour and carry the grail of Southern gothic mythology; as Gregg Allman predicted in "Midnight Rider" so long ago, "the road goes on forever." Southern rock may no longer sound as startlingly fresh as it did in 1971. But what does? There's little else that still takes me, like an old, trusted friend – so consistently and so wistfully – home.   ⊕

easy come, easy go
by richard zacks

FOURTH OF JULY, 1972. I was hovering outside a porn theater in New York City's Times Square, trying to summon the courage to buy a ticket to the next showing of *Deep Throat*. I was a sixteen-year-old virgin, and I desperately wanted to see this movie. 'Cause I knew, 'cause my friends had told me, that there, up on the screen, inch by fat inch, this guy's very large erect penis was going to completely disappear into this woman's mouth and then slowly reappear. How could she do that? And, more important, would anyone ever do it for me? No courage was forthcoming and after twenty minutes, I sadly shuffled off.

The great decade of inventive sex had just begun, and in 1972 *Deep Throat* was a *date* movie. It didn't just play to the raincoat/jerk-off crowd, it became a kind of kinky-wink-wink-let's-check-it-out entertainment for heterosexual couples. And it played all over America, the first porn movie ever to gross a million dollars.

The Seventies were an especially great time to have genitals. The so-called "Sexual Revolution" that began in the late Sixties among college-age hippies was reaching mainstream, middle-class – even middle-aged – America. The rock & roll dopers of the Sixties had spread the legs of a generation and now, as the new decade progressed, we could *all* get laid more easily, even if we weren't that cool.

It's hard for those who weren't there to realize how risk-free sex seemed at the time. The Pill was everywhere, abortion was legalized in 1973 and there were no incurable STDs, no AIDS. (A case of syph, you got a penicillin shot from the campus nurse and you were back in action.) Casual sex could be truly casual.

By 1971, more than 75 percent of America thought premarital sex was okay, a threefold increase from the Fifties. And the number of unmarried Americans aged twenty to twenty-four more than doubled from 4.3 million in 1960 to 9.7 million in 1976. Now it was no longer necessary to buy the cow to get the milk, so to speak. In fact, a mind-boggling 35 percent of the country in 1971 thought marriage was obsolete.

Hollywood both reflected and embraced this openly lusty attitude. In the 1975 hit movie *Shampoo*, Warren Beatty grouses to a standoffish Goldie Hawn: "Everybody fucks everybody, grow up, for Christ's sakes. You're an antique, you know that? Look around you – all of 'em, all of these chicks, they're all fucking, they're getting their hair done so they can go and fuck; that's what it's all about. Come into the shop tomorrow and I'll show you – 'I fucked her, and her and her, and her and her – I fucked 'em all!' That's what I do, I fuck. That's why I went to beauty school, to fuck. I can't help that, they're there and I do their hair and sometimes I fuck 'em. I stick it in and I pull it out and that's a fuck; it's not a crime." And Goldie Hawn replies: ". . . Well, I'm glad you told me."

Maybe you're still thinking: Sure, Warren Beatty was getting laid like that in the Seventies but everybody else wasn't. Trust me, you're wrong. I had acne. I had a prematurely receding hairline. I couldn't dance without half a bottle of Jack in me. Yet by the mid-Seventies, I was a pretty happy camper.

America was clearly taking off the sexual blinders. *Playboy* added pubic hair to its girl-next-door centerfolds in 1971 (a startling change at the time), a touring (and very naked) cast for the Broadway rock musical *Hair* barnstormed the country, giving the folks from Des Moines and everywhere else an eyeful. And look at the two books that dominated the nonfiction bestseller list for 1972: *Joy of Sex* by Alex Comfort and *Open Marriage: A New Lifestyle for Couples* by Nena and George O'Neill. If you haven't read *Joy of Sex*, you should know that it's no tame little *Joy of Cooking*.

Scenes from a date movie: Linda Lovelace in Florida; Linda makes a house call to the Blue Cross Man; Linda again; Linda at the end; Dr. Young (Harry Reems) prescribes deep throat; Linda's roommate (Dolly Sharp) and the Orgy Men *(clockwise from top left)*; following page: Post-orgy smoke

DEEP THROAT

THE END

and deep throat to you all

passengers and their baggage go into effect.

NASA begins to focus its efforts on a manned, reusable space-shuttle program, with a target launch date of 1978.

7 President Nixon announces his intention to run for reelection. Spiro Agnew will again be his running mate.

9 Billionaire recluse Howard Hughes reveals in a conference call with the press that his purported autobiography, told to Clifford Irving, is a fraud. Two months later, Irving and his wife plead guilty to defrauding their publisher, McGraw-Hill Inc.

10 According to the U.S. surgeon general, the health of nonsmokers is endangered by secondhand cigarette smoke.

16 Led by star quarterback Roger Staubach, the Dallas Cowboys defeat the Miami Dolphins, 24–3, in Super Bowl VI.

19 The National Commission on Marijuana and Drug Abuse reveals that 24 million Americans have experimented with marijuana and that a third of those are regular users.

22 Top of the charts: Don McLean's "American Pie" (pop single) and *American Pie* (pop album).

23 R&B shouter Big Maybelle Smith dies.

24 Discovered still hiding in the jungles of Guam, Sergeant Shoichi Yokio of Japan's Imperial Army is informed of his country's World War II surrender 27 years earlier.

27 Mahalia Jackson, the preeminent female gospel singer of all time, dies.

28 Carol Feraci, one of the Ray Conniff Singers, holds aloft an antiwar sign reading STOP THE KILLING while performing at the White House for President Nixon and guests.

30 Los Angeles Laker Wilt "the Stilt" Chamberlain grabs the NBA title for most career rebounds, with 21,734. Two weeks later, he becomes the first NBA player to score more than 30,000 career points.

31 Large-print health-risk warnings will now be mandatory on cigarette advertising, according to a Federal Trade Commission report.

1972 FEBRUARY

3 The first Winter Olympics held in Asia are opened by Emperor Hirohito in Sapporo, Japan.

It placed on the night's menu the possibility of a partner performing *feuille-de-rose*, i.e., "tongue stimulation of the anus of either sex," or of asking the woman to assume the "Viennese Oyster" position, i.e., where she lies on her back with her ankles behind her head. For couples, Comfort recommended the "Goldfish." That's when both partners strip naked, have their hands tied behind their backs and use any and all body parts to stimulate each other.

As for the now-forgotten *Open Marriage,* the authors jump right to the point: "To begin with, we would like to lay to rest the idea that sexual jealousy is natural, instinctive and inevitable." (You can almost hear Austin Powers say: "Right, baby!") Chapter titles included: "Why Save Marriage at All?" and "Love and Sex without Jealousy."

The porn industry exploded. As *Deep Throat* traveled around the country, proving in city after city that it was legal to show the film, more and more XXX theaters with screaming marquees started popping up nationwide. The days of stag films in smoky back rooms were gone. John Holmes of the enormous tallywhacker was the big male headliner, while Marilyn Chambers's career rocketed after her remarkably athletic performance in *Behind the Green Door.* On the magazine front, among the one-handed reading material, *Playboy* hit its all-time peak circulation of more than seven million copies in 1972 and lonely men started having more choices: *Penthouse, Hustler* (with its Jackie Onassis nudes), *Gallery, Oui* and others. As for sex with a partner, the communes of the Sixties (sex and organic vegetables) were being replaced by the mate-swapping swinger clubs of the Seventies (sex and cash). About a hundred swinger magazines full of classified ads were launched, and swinger clubs – convening in places ranging from the informal suburban home to disco-sized emporiums – promised a smorgasbord of sexual possibilities and free mouthwash. Bill Goodwin started taking small cash donations for entrance to weekly orgies at his modest Orange County home in Southern California (which he held well into the Nineties). In New York City Larry Levenson opened the 23,000-square-foot Plato's Retreat in 1977, offering such amenities as Jacuzzi, steam, dance floor, swimming pool and complimentary drinks and food. To avoid problems with the state liquor authority, Levenson banned alcohol. One sign read: NO BOOZE, NO BREW. SO WHAT? LET'S SCREW. Plato's was probably the closest heterosexual America has ever gotten to the sexual frenzy of gay bathhouses.

With all those promises of easy promiscuity and sexual experimentation without risk hanging in the air, I finally lost my virginity in 1973. The act, however, wasn't what I'd expected. I got raped. My first sexual experience with someone other than myself was with two men I met in a bus station. I have some bi tendencies, but this was not my idea of a dream date.

It was Thanksgiving of my freshman year at the University of Michigan in Ann Arbor, and I decided I would spend the holiday alone at Niagara Falls instead of shuttling home to Mama. It seemed like a funky thing to do. I missed the last bus back and wound up spending the night in the Detroit bus station, where two black guys approached me and started chatting me up about getting high, getting laid, etc. (Silly me, I thought they meant women.) Wanting to cast off the shackles of virginity, I left with them and wound up getting attacked in a boardinghouse. When I tried to escape, the one named Jimmy almost strangled me to death. (His finger marks, all ten of them, were on my neck for a week.) Don't cry for me, though; many of the moments from that night still fascinate me: the view of the big dangle, the crack of the pain, the rhythm of the slide. And there was no AIDS back then. I didn't catch anything.

About a year later, I hooked up with a woman for the first time. She was a blonde with the softest skin. Finally, at age eighteen, intercourse with a woman, but that wasn't all. I discovered that eating at the Y was heaven, is heaven and always will be heaven. The rest of the Seventies were solid, with twosomes and threesomes and virgins and exotic girlfriends. I remember walking down the road late one night in Raleigh, North Carolina, in the summer of 1975. I was drunk. I was rasping out Dylan's "Lay Lady Lay" lyrics when a Mustang pulled to a stop with two pretty women inside. They asked me if I was some kind of rock star. I told 'em no. They invited me into the car anyhow. I sang a few more songs till they asked me to stop; we drank some bourbon; we parked; we groped; I caught the midnight train out of town.

The end of the decade saw me high on peyote at the Ann Arbor Blues and Jazz Festival, rocking my best friend's Tree of Life medallion against my chest to the beat of Max Roach's drums as I stripped down to just a pair of pants. I was supposed to hook up later with my buddy's girlfriend but the cocaine ran out and so did she.

The party started to sour as the Eighties rolled in. A huge club like Plato's Retreat was getting increasingly hassled by public health authorities, who eventually shut it down in 1985. Crabs and herpes were irritating American genitals in greater numbers. The divorce rate in the United States shot up, topping all the countries of the world with its record of nearly 40 percent of all U.S. marriages ending in divorce. The number of unwed mothers also skyrocketed, bringing all kinds of new social problems as society tried to figure out how to support these kids. Then, in 1981, most devastatingly, a strange pneumonia was detected in five otherwise healthy gay men. AIDS was just around the corner.

The Seventies, in hindsight, seem like some kind of dream, some fluky alignment of the planets. For multipartner, no-one-paying-for-it, consensual, no-death-risk sex, the Seventies can be judged as the best decade ever – that is, until a cure for AIDS is found and the big party starts all over again. ⊕

fools, suckas & baadasssss brothers by nelson george

ON A WARM SUMMER SATURDAY in 1972, my friends and I – resembling Fat Albert and the Cosby Kids – gather in front of 315 Livonia Avenue, a sixteen-story building in the Tilden housing projects. We're smack in the middle of Brownsville, Brooklyn, a ghetto with all the credentials: junkies, gangs and lazy cops. It's the age of suede Pumas and red canvas Converses; red-black-and-green sweatbands and street-scraping bell-bottoms; elaborate cornrows and bushy, uneven Afros.

It was an age without giants – King and Malcolm were dead, Ali was great but no longer the greatest and the let's-march-and-change-the-world optimism I remembered from my childhood was already a memory. Nowadays, from my sixth-floor window, I would watch police cruisers receive brown paper bags from passersby; I'd peer into crowded, ugly tenement apartments and see junkies clustered by candy stores. It didn't seem that bad, really, but by '72 no one in Brownsville was singing "We Shall Overcome."

We hop the IRT to the Deuce (Times Square, that is), and on the hour-and-fifteen-minute subway ride we compare notes on fly-ass *Soul Train* dancers and relate the latest tale of somebody's mom being mugged in a project stairwell. The deeper into Manhattan the iron horse rides, the fewer black passengers come aboard. Four loud, boisterous, black adolescent males, my friends and I draw anxious glances and steely glares from riders in the grip of urban paranoia.

We emerge from the damp subterranean station into Forty-second Street's urban blightscape: the tawdry glow of crumbling old theaters, noisy-clanging-beeping pinball arcades, greasy luncheonettes and cheap-looking hookers. Invisible from the street, the Kings of Forty-second Street loom larger than life inside their movie-house palaces – the Harris, the Selwyn, the Amsterdam – where we pay weekly homage to a new generation of heroes for a new black age: Richard "Shaft" Roundtree, Fred "the Hammer" Williamson, Jim "Slaughter" Brown, Jim "Black Belt Jones" Kelly and, of course, that royal Queen, Pam "Coffy" Grier.

From our $3.50 balcony seats – a better vantage point for scouting girls – we spend the afternoon cheering car chases, ogling busty women in distress and savoring dialogue laced with "fools," "suckas" and "muthafuckas." Unlike Sidney Poitier – the Sixties' embodiment of noble striving in his white shirt, dark suit and tie – the blaxploitation guys and gals are as funky as their multicolored bell-bottoms and

> **Richard Roundtree is Shaft – one of the Kings of Forty-second Street**

two-toned platform shoes. Their state-of-the-art threads seem to free them to live as large and insolent as we all dream we might.

In their depictions of aggressive black heroism, the stars of *Shaft*, *Hammer*, *Trouble Man* and *Slaughter* show us attributes that comprise another facet of black power: tough, no-nonsense and cool as the underside of a pillow. Like Western sheriffs and Mafia dons, our cinematic heroes make, and live by, their own rules; their worldviews and attitudes are the same as those of film-noir private detectives – the irony being these really are "black" films. Even the antisocial coke dealer, Priest, in *Superfly* and the pimp, Goldie, in *The Mack* are elevated to heroic stature, filling their films with a sly cinematic presence objectionable only to church ladies and NAACP spokespeople.

Underscoring the cursing and the revenge-fixated plots are the chicken scratch of guitars, the percolating polyrhythms of congas and bongos and the wailing of soul singers about "a bad brother" ready to "take down the man." Sometimes, when the movie is really bad (as in not good) and the scent of cheeba has induced a contact high, I close my eyes and let the soundtracks fill me up. After the credits roll, it's back on the street for hot dogs at Nedick's (cool 'cause Shaft ate there, too) before we board the train again. On the way home, we reenact our favorite scenes, quote choice dialogue and hope that next Saturday we'll have the bank for another day on the Deuce.

Admittedly predictable, cheap and disposable, the sensationalistic black-oriented genre that the Hollywood trades dubbed "blaxploitation" wasn't built to last. But now, almost two generations removed from their first-run double-feature glory, blaxploitation films fill the collections of teenagers and flow into the iconography of hip-hop and R&B. Why? Whereas, back then, my friends and I were experiencing for the first time the heady exhilaration of commercially viable aggression, today's hip-hop generation has embraced "in-your-face" as a guiding principle. Viewed today, blaxploitation movies seem crudely made and haphazardly conceived, yet the brashness of their characterizations remains vividly compelling. Shaft and Coffy don't look back on a past filled with public humiliations but at a present where a cocky attitude, a sullen face and gaudy materialism are not only celebrated, but essential to street survival in the early Seventies.

From where we sat in the balcony, the appeal was visceral and direct. Never had there been so many aggressive, I-don't-give-a-damn black folks on screen, and that aspect is so crucial. Blaxploitation movies reserved little space for turning the other cheek, singing Negro spirituals or chaste kissing. In fact, characters who engaged in those activities bore the brunt of the hero's much-applauded derision. In blaxploitation, black people shot back with big guns, strutted to bold jams and had sweaty, bed-rocking sex. Whatever stories the often loopy plots told, they were usually secondary to the rejection of passivity they dramatized and glorified.

Take *Shaft*, for instance. Seems the daughter of a Harlem ganglord has been kidnapped, and Shaft – a "spade dick" (as he sarcastically calls himself) with an office in Times Square and a pad in the Village – is the man to find her. But the plot is frequently backseated as Shaft's exploits and explosions take the wheel. Along the film's circuitous, ninety-eight-minute, uptown-downtown path, he throws a brother out of his office window, saves a black revolutionary from a hail of bullets, cracks a bottle over the head of a mob henchman and continually sasses a long-suffering white police detective. His attitude is less about being cool than it is about just plain simmering; the movie opens with him walking past the marquees of Forty-second Street and then directly into swollen traffic. As a taxi screeches to a halt and honks, it's Shaft who flips the bird: "Up yours!" is his first line of the film.

Shaft also proves to be an adroit lover who drives his women to nails-digging-into-the-small-of-his-back ecstasy;

settlement of a government antitrust action against the conglomerate and a large ITT contribution to the Republican party. In the bizarre two-month Senate investigation that follows, a battle over the validity of the memo erupts, with ITT lobbyist Dita Beard – author of the memo – being declared mentally disordered by her physician, ITT claiming the "original" memo contained no mention of antitrust actions, the FBI confirming the authenticity of the published memo, Beard suffering severe chest pains during her testimony to the Senate Judiciary Committee while in a hospital bed and cardiologists testifying against any evidence of Beard's alleged heart condition. Further efforts are stonewalled as the Nixon administration invokes executive privilege, refusing to participate in the investigation.

John Lennon's immigration visa expires, leading to his three-and-a-half-year battle to remain in the U.S., which at times draws negative action and comment from officials as high up as the White House. Lennon's trouble stems from a 1968 marijuana-possession conviction in the U.K.

1972MARCH

2 Carrying a peace-offering plaque adorned with figures of a man and a woman, *Pioneer 10* is launched on its multiyear mission and becomes the first man-made object to fly past Mars. In Dec. 1973 it reaches Jupiter, sending back the first-ever close-up images of the planet. Ten years later, still broadcasting signals back to Earth, *Pioneer 10* becomes the first spacecraft to exit the solar system.

Superjockey Bill Shoemaker marks his 555th trip to the winner's circle, a new horse-racing record.

3 West Germany discloses that 398 East Germans have escaped to the West in the preceding year.

6 Jack Nicklaus becomes professional golf's leading money-winner with the Doral Eastern Open title, bringing his career earnings to $1,427,200.

A Gallup Poll reveals that 69% of Americans oppose busing as a means of integrating public schools.

7 In the New Hampshire primary, President Nixon soundly

the white girl he picks up in a bar is just another conquest he can't be bothered with the next morning. Shaft not only gave it to the man, but to his woman too; with his black-leather battle gear and ever-ready sneer, Shaft was our black id unleashed, realizing the worst nightmares of both the NAACP and the KKK.

Shaft's prowess – on the streets and between the sheets – caused much trepidation on both sides of the race line not because it broke any new ground, but because it seemed to embody and even amplify black stereotypes. Because blaxploitation glorified blacks in the very terms racists had long used to malign the race, mainstream civil rights leaders such as CORE and the NAACP railed against it, warning of its long-term negative effects on black youth. The words of Junius Griffin, head of the NAACP's Beverly Hills–Hollywood branch in 1972, were typical of the black establishment view: "We must insist that our children are not constantly exposed to a steady diet of so-called black movies that glorify black males as pimps, dope pushers, gangsters, and super males with vast physical prowess but no cognitive skills."

But there was always more to it than that. The film that inspired blaxploitation, Melvin Van Peebles's *Sweet Sweetback's Baadasssss Song* (1971), was a gritty X-rated venture made outside the studio system. Essentially the tale of a stud on the run, it had a distinctly revolutionary flavor. Like the films that followed, it took a very cynical view of all types of politics – black and white, civil rights and radical – and in doing so, reflected a nation that was generally exhausted, weary from the battles of the Sixties. In the ensuing years, this jaundiced view of politics and political leaders threatened to undermine the nonviolent, work-within-the-system principles of the civil rights movement, which explains why many blacks found the subtext of blaxploitation so alarming.

After decades of striving to depict a positive image of blacks, the African-American artistic community was surprisingly ambivalent toward blaxploitation. Despite a few late-Sixties breakthroughs in television and the success of the aforementioned Mr. Poitier, black actors remained grievously underrepresented in all visual media, especially film. Individual actors and, on occasion, groups of actors would protest blaxploitation's negative stereotypes, but many of these same performers continued to audition for roles in them. It was the only game in town.

The parallels between blaxploitation and hip-hop run close and deep. The attacks on blaxploitation foreshadow the later criticism of gangsta rap, and both incurred the black establishment's wrath for their failure to present blacks in "positive" terms. Because hip-hop has remained stubbornly grassroots and its creative energy still flows directly from the black community, it has grown despite this criticism. Blaxploitation, on the other hand, was produced – and abandoned – by Hollywood. Lacking hip-hop's intimate link to its audience and the resulting ability to continually reinvent itself from within, blaxploitation was thematically and commercially doomed.

And yet blaxploitation lives on. Samples of its in-your-face dialogue have been popping up on hip-hop records for years (e.g., a sound bite from *The Mack* intros "Rat-Tat-Tat-Tat" on Dr. Dre's *The Chronic*). The Players' Ball scene in *The Mack*, where the story's pimp protagonist is crowned "Mack of the Year," has been referenced in several music videos. And female rapper Foxy Brown owes her handle to a Pam Grier vehicle.

Video-store geek turned gritty auteur Quentin Tarantino injected blaxploitation's potboiler story lines and "nigga"-driven language into his peripatetic soul: Ving Rhames's gangster Marsellus Wallace and Samuel L. Jackson's Jheri-curled, Bible-quoting hit man in *Pulp Fiction* are bloody cousins of the uptown kingpins who stride the blaxploitation landscape. And, of course, there is no *Jackie Brown* without the busty, bullet-blasting canon of Ms. Grier.

The youth culture of aggression that hip-hop codified (and commodified) also has roots in another early-Seventies exploitation genre – kung-fu flicks. While the submerged key to blaxploitation's appeal was naked black aggression, kung fu provided an exotic, nonwhite, non-Western template for a seemingly more disciplined, time-honored expression of justified violence. Though kung-fu movies were becoming passé by the time of "Rapper's Delight" in 1979, they continue to leave their mark on hip-hop culture. These "chop-socky" flicks gave Joseph Saddler the "Grandmaster" in the moniker Grandmaster Flash. And the "Furious" title his five rapping cohorts adopted to describe their antic delivery harks back to kung-fu movie titles. In the Nineties, the vogue for the more sophisticated contemporary Hong Kong action movies that blend Seventies martial-arts attitude with more elaborate special effects (as in the popular *Chinese Ghost Story* series) informs the rhymes, names and cosmology of the Wu-Tang Clan. Hailing from Shao Lin (the group's faux-Chinese name for their native Staten Island),. its nine members view themselves as members of a secret sect in search of the thirty-sixth chamber of martial-arts wisdom. While far from projecting a coherent vision, the Wu-Tang have nonetheless injected a tinge of Asian mysticism into hip-hop.

The final and certainly most crucial link between my Forty-second Street Saturdays and current turn-of-the-century youth culture is the persistent influence of blaxploitation soundtracks. The best blaxploitation music – the albums *Shaft* and *Superfly*, Marvin Gaye's *Trouble Man*, Willie Hutch's tune "Brother's Gonna Work It Out" from *The Mack*, James Brown's "Down and Out in New York City" from *Black Caesar* – retains a theatricality and sense of place that no succeeding genre of African-American pop, including hip-hop, has consistently matched.

No one can dispute the enduring quality of Isaac Hayes's *Shaft* and Curtis Mayfield's *Superfly*, both Number One pop albums in their time. Hayes and Mayfield, Sixties soul producers, writers and singers, used these scores to expand the sonic scope of their work beyond the limits of crafting three-and-a-half-minute hit singles. Jammed with wah-wah guitars, sensuous Latin percussion, blaring horns, supple flutes and vocal choruses, these albums continue to inspire current music makers. In a nod to those classic tracks, Dr. Dre, the dominant hip-hop producer of the early Nineties, has extensively used freshly created flute, keyboard and bass lines to add cinematic sweep to his famous tales of drive-bys and machismo. It's quite appropriate that Dr. Dre, as the definitive gangsta-rap producer, has consistently paid homage to blaxploitation in his provocative immorality plays.

Likewise, Lenny Kravitz, fan of vintage amplifiers and all sounds retro, often uses blaxploitation soundtrack clichés – especially the wah-wah pedal and righteous string arrangements – to spice up his more soulful material. In fact, his cover of "Billy Jack," on a 1994 Curtis Mayfield tribute album, sounds more of the period than the 1975 original. D'Angelo, a son of soul with a hip-hop pedigree, opens his live show with the "Theme from *Shaft*." In so doing, the singer isn't in search of postmodern irony or nostalgia but an affirmation of his own baadness, which his fans happily co-sign.

From its inception, hip-hop embraced the rhythmic underpinning of the blaxploitation scores. Beats and bits of rhythm from those records were utilized by early hip-hop DJs. I remember that in the late Seventies the soundtrack from *Shaft in Africa* was prized by party throwers not for the Four Tops' hit "Are You Man Enough," but for a percussion break on an obscure instrumental. Other Forty-second Street

exploitation genres – the spaghetti Western, the white urban detective movie starring Clint Eastwood, Charles Bronson, et al. – contributed to hip-hop as well. The three pioneering hip-hop DJs – Flash, Afrika Bambaataa and Kool DJ Herc – were relentless vinyl archaeologists who combed the aisles of Downstairs Records, a cluttered Times Square shop on Forty-third Street, for the unknown, the awful and the ignored.

Today's Deuce is a very different place from the one where my homies and I chilled. Disney's theatrical version of *The Lion King* rules the (New) Amsterdam, and a Disney store sits at Seventh Avenue and Forty-second, where Shaft (and I) ate hot dogs. Nearly all the familiar aspects of the Deuce we knew back in the day are in the process of being multiplexed, reconstructed and cleaned up. Except the memories.

As a once young, impressionable connoisseur of blaxploitation, I admit its effects have lingered, both on me and on our culture. My wardrobe has always had more than its share of turtlenecks and leather jackets because of Roundtree's gear in *Shaft*. The roots of my (sometime) swagger and street-strut can be pinned on *Slaughter*. And I still cherish and file those blaxploitation soundtracks in my music collection – *Superfly* and *Trouble Man* especially – under "A" for attitude, right next to N.W.A and Wu-Tang Clan.

Culturally, the period from 1970 to 1974 was amazingly fertile in terms of African-American music and imagery.

It's not that the ghetto is thriving with pimps and pushermen, it's just that they are the most visible part of the ghetto. –Curtis Mayfield

The creation of larger-than-life black heroes in films coincided with the electrified jazz of Miles Davis, Sly Stone's cross-racial appeal, the comedic maturation of Richard Pryor, the surreal satire of Ishmael Reed and other funky expressions too numerous to list.

All this stuff washed over me and fueled my ambition to contribute somehow, in whatever way I could, to this dark, rich continuum. However, with the possible exception of the late Eighties, when Spike Lee and Public Enemy gave an Afrocentric charge to the general pop imagination, no time since the Seventies has felt quite as flavorful or fun. Maybe it was some kind of trashy, flashy cultural high point. Or maybe I was just a kid with very sweet dreams of being a King of Forty-second Street.

So, if you ever see me striding purposefully across Forty-second Street in a leather jacket with the collar up, wearing a neatly-rolled turtleneck and an intense scowl on my face, don't doubt that somewhere, deep in the folds of my soul, amid guitars, french horns and the low-pitched punch of a Fender bass, sassy women are singing "*They say this cat Nelson is a baad . . .*" ⊕

defeats his sole challenger for the Republican nomination, Congressman Paul McCloskey, 68% to 20%. McCloskey bows out of the race three days later, leaving Nixon to run uncontested. On the Democratic side, Edmund Muskie leads the pack with 46.4%, trailed by second-runner George McGovern with 37%.

9 In the kind of trendsetting marriage of music and politics that will become common-place in the Seventies, rock and pop heavyweights Carole King, James Taylor and Barbra Streisand lend their talents to support McGovern's cam-paign in a well-attended concert at the L.A. Forum.

10 After months of bombing of North Vietnamese targets and a seesaw series of battles along the DMZ, 5,000 South Vietnamese forces invade Cambodia, with U.S. air sup-port, in search of Communist forces. Within three weeks, the North Vietnamese will in turn launch the largest coun-terassault since the 1968 Tet offensive.

14 Singer/songwriter Carole King is the big Grammy win-ner, collecting four major awards, including Record of the Year ("It's Too Late"), Album of the Year and Best Pop Vocal Performance, Female (*Tapestry*) and Song of the Year ("You've Got a Friend").

George Wallace pulls ahead of other Democratic hopefuls, winning the Florida primary with 42% of the vote.

15 Francis Ford Coppola's screen adaptation of Mario Puzo's best-selling epic, *The Godfather* – filmed with the caveat that the word "Mafia" never be mentioned – is released, starring Al Pacino, Robert Duvall, James Caan and Marlon Brando.

In a publicity stunt and com-ment on current pop-music standards, Los Angeles DJ Robert W. Morgan plays Donny Osmond's "Puppy Love" non-stop for 90 minutes. Fearing subversion of some sort, scared listeners call the police, who raid the radio station.

21 Adding fuel to the ITT fire, columnist Jack Anderson releases company memoranda stating that the U.S. ambas-sador to Chile assured ITT representatives the U.S. would attempt to block elec-tion of Chilean president Salvador Allende. The Senate

radical feminism reaches the suburbs by barbara o'dair

THE PERSONAL IS POLITICAL

In 1972, when I was twelve, my family moved from a town that had tutored me in Earth Days, moratoriums and black armbands to a town of country-club commuters. I'd been wearing overalls and pocket T-shirts to school. I didn't own a dress. In my old town, they were protesting apartheid in South Africa, exploitation of migrant workers in California vineyards, union-busting in Southern cotton mills. My old town had sent busloads to the March on Washington protesting the Vietnam War. Whole families went.

In my new town, seventh-grade girls were trying out for cheerleading, buying make-up and learning ever more ways of becoming charming and beautiful. Whole families went to the club to swim and play tennis on the weekends.

Freak: a word that came in at the time, distinguishing a type from the beaming, milder-mannered *hippie* and the more socially integrated, intellectual *leftie*. There was a smattering of each in my new community; pooled, still a minority, they stood out. Freaks, however, had more aggressive hair, wore nastier bell-bottoms, had a harder edge. "Let your freak flag fly high": Post-Woodstock, while the Vietnam War wore on, freaks were cynical but proud. A few girls belonged to each group, variations on earth mother, student leader, bad-ass druggie slut. But feminists? They were too few in my junior high and high school to form a happening cabal, despite the fact that historically, nationally, 1972 was a banner year for feminists. It was challenging enough to make the periphery the place to be.

I befriended Katrina. She was a little older than me, a little wiser, a little wilder. In addi-tion to chasing a fast crowd, we read Doris Lessing and Sylvia Plath and listened to Joni and Jimi. She had a wicked and sophisticated sense of humor. Still, we threw the *I Ching* anxiously for clues in dealing with the various foxy menchildren in a semi-commune up the hill. On that same hill was the Unitarian Church, the local magnet, it seemed, for all things alternative, bohemian, rock & roll. We hung around the church's weekend "coffeehouses," where teenage couples bonded in blankets amid the strumming of local folk rockers or smoked hash on the lawn. It was on one of those evenings, I suppose, that we saw the sign announcing the all-women get-together of what we would come to call our CR group (for consciousness-raising). We steered our way there without a second thought. Sisterhood was powerful.

In that brief, shining moment, women's liberation seemed downright reasonable and actually inevitable, as radical feminism reached its arm even into our privileged suburb. Although I didn't recognize my budding feminism as radical at the time, that peri-od permanently changed me. It's taken me more than two decades since to untangle the valid expectations radical feminism – and consciousness-raising – had formed in me from the disappointments that followed: that more people weren't similarly changed, that it didn't stick. Still, I'd rather have the bar raised that high again than lose the oppor-tunity to look over it and gauge the distance.

RAISING THE BAR

By 1972 consciousness-raising had gone nearly mainstream, to the extent, anyway, that the National Organization for Women, which had initially shunned the concept as too far-out (or too petty), had started groups in community centers and private homes throughout the cities and suburbs of America. (Come to think of it, NOW initiated our group, offering guidelines to each of us on how to run a CR group successfully.) Then, all sorts of women were attracted to the opportunity to open up to a group of people for whom the only common denominator was the possession of female genitals.

Before the democratization of therapy, before the onslaught of twelve-step pro-grams, before the "Me Decade" was anointed, but after sexual liberation and the

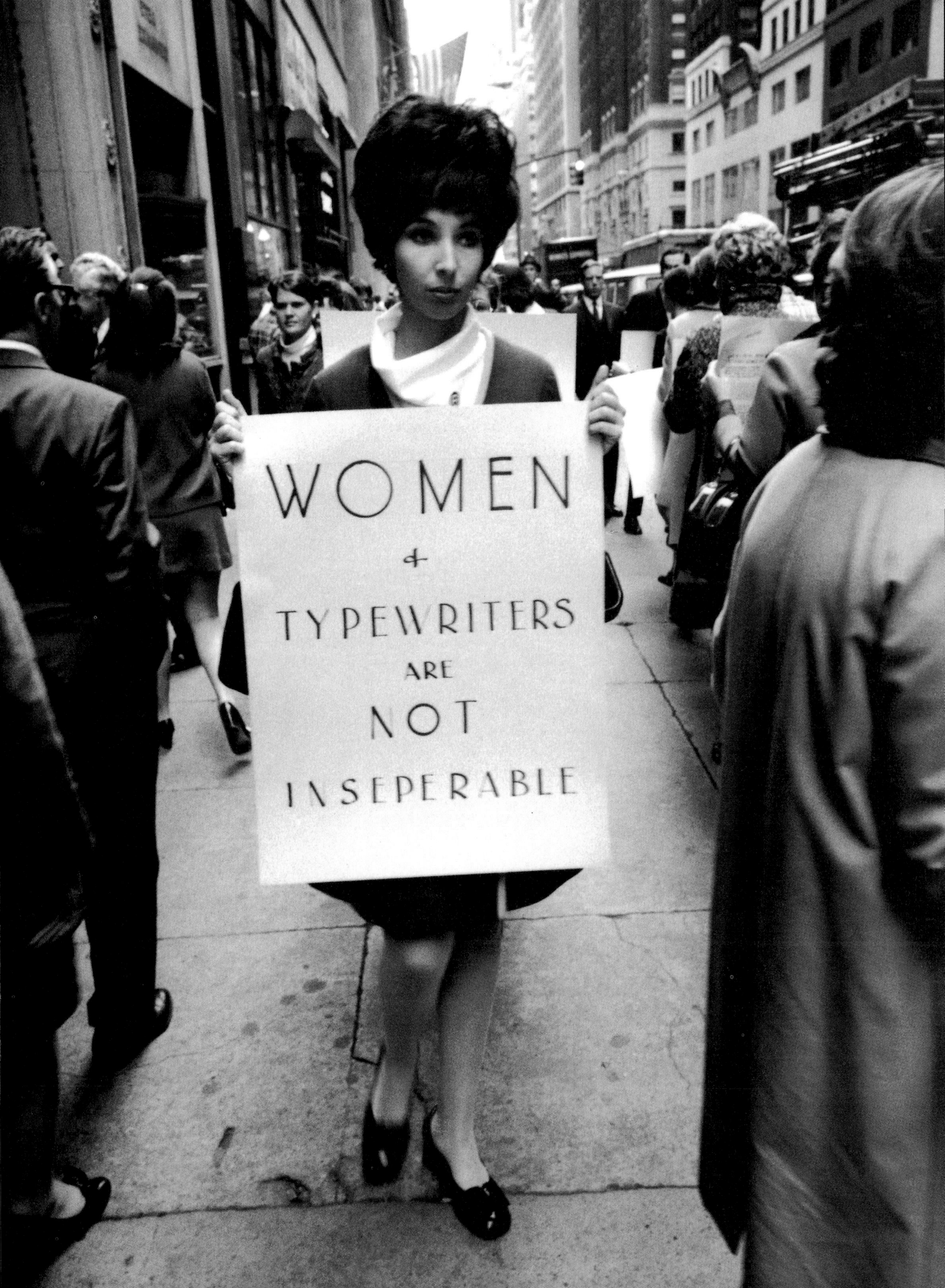
WOMEN
&
TYPEWRITERS
ARE
NOT
INSEPERABLE

civil rights movement shook up the early Sixties, idle outsiders confused consciousness-raising with inveterate navel-gazing. In truth, CR was the boldest Sixties-rooted attempt – and perhaps the last concerted effort – to fuse self-examination with political action, and to identify and understand the relationship between the political and the personal.

To feminists working toward a mass movement of women, the idea of CR was fundamental. CR's purpose, said Kathie Sarachild, an original member of the radical feminist group Redstockings, was "never to be nice or tolerant or to develop speaking skill or the 'ability to listen.' It was to get closer to the truth" – that is, to share information about the real way women lived their lives. A new and deeper understanding would evolve from this process and inform our activism, which without study could bear only superficial solutions. This is what is meant by "the personal is political," although outside this time period, the phrase has often been misunderstood (as has CR) as a kind of group therapy.

My CR group: A moon-faced graduate-student violinist; her flirtatious cellist roommate; a small knot each of educated homemakers and working mothers; a couple of oddballs, maladjusted and a little spooky; some older women, community organizers, big mouths. And us, me and Katrina, with bravado, ideas and anger to burn. We were almost all white and middle to upper-middle class, a reflection both of the cliché and the reality of the typical American suburb. Though not locked in a death struggle with racism or poverty, we were still in serious confrontation with the status quo.

We told personal tales helter-skelter. We furiously compiled bibliographies of important books – Shulamith Firestone's *The Dialectic of Sex*, Kate Millett's *Sexual Politics* (both 1970) – and circulated mimeographs of groundbreaking essays – Anne Koedt's "The Myth of the Vaginal Orgasm," Pat Mainardi's "The Politics of Housework," Carol Hanisch's "The Personal Is Political." Each text prompted contemplation and discussion, to which we contributed pieces of our life stories.

We had large purpose and were bent on excavation. While we didn't go so far as to conduct internal self-exams with mirrors and speculums, as other groups had done, we nevertheless thrashed out, ever so tentatively, issues around work, family, friendship and sex – including lesbianism, a topic that fully flowered *entre nous* as the aforementioned violinist declared her love for the aforementioned cellist, who kept a boyfriend on the side.

Although I was ready to get closer to it, I'm certain I was not fully capable of accepting the whole truth of my life at twelve. But when I looked at my world, this is what I saw: My mother was a nurse who'd given up working to raise my sister and me; by 1970 or so, she was restless. Although a tennis player, she didn't fit into the suburban world herself, she later told me – "not a socializer," as she put it. As a girl, she had thought of being a doctor. Her father, a fireman, encouraged her, but she had reservations about her abilities. And, like many women of her generation, she wanted to get married and be taken care of. Later, when she realized that these ideals were not being fulfilled – "My marriage was less than ideal" – she felt her only recourse was to "learn more."

So, she went back to school for a degree, and then to another in preparation for teaching. While my father, a Wall Street lawyer, did not vocally oppose her move toward independence, she was still expected to come home to make supper for us every night. She had to borrow money from her own father for a used car to take her to and from school. The lack of support "disturbed me but didn't stop me," she says. "I had an idea of being a role model for my daughters."

Twenty-three years younger than my mother, I was luckier. I walked right into the women's liberation movement and took a seat. I followed a sign that read CONSCIOUSNESS-RAISING GROUP and went downstairs and into the basement of our local Unitarian Church. It felt more like home than home.

For a while anyway. Six months in, our free-ranging and often flammable personal testimony was compromised by *Robert's Rules of Order*. When the group unraveled, it was also due partly to our impatience, an uncertainty about the position sexuality held in feminist activism, even perhaps, a fear of alienating men. Not coincidentally, these were among the same reasons why radical feminism as a movement lost its momentum and was overtaken by mid-decade.

A BRIEF HISTORY OF SECOND-WAVE FEMINISM

Before I discovered CR, I knew as much about feminism as a twelve-year-old could. Alongside my copies of *Vogue* and ROLLING STONE, I had begun receiving the new *Ms.* magazine, which Gloria Steinem had launched in 1971 in response to a need for "a new kind of women's magazine, one about making change, not 101 kinds of hamburger." I'd volunteered to sell buttons at an ERA function. I'd even gone to a talk that Betty Friedan – the first president of NOW, in 1966 – had given in 1971. Women's liberation, largely born out of the Sixties radical movement, had divided by this time into three basic camps. Socialist feminists (offshoots of Students for a Democratic Society and largely dominating the seminal New York Radical Women) believed that women's liberation would naturally arise out of socialism. Radical feminists (Redstockings was perhaps the most influential group of this ilk) were unified in their position that, as Redstockings member Ellen Willis put it, "men have *power* over women and that we can only liberate ourselves by uniting to combat that power." And then there were the liberal feminists, institutionally personified by NOW. The organization's Statement of Purpose described itself as a "civil rights" group made up of women *and* men.

According to Veronica Geng, who chronicled the feminist movement(s) in *Harper's* magazine in 1976, "Friedan founded a new women's rights movement, which emphasized lobbying, electoral politics, and education for women, and the benefit of the doubt for men." (In fact, Geng wrote, NOW's "reiteration of the phrase 'partnership with men' verged on the obsessive.")

Although radicals and liberals had their own agendas, they both eventually rallied around the Equal Rights Amendment. Even I, as a junior high school student with no immediate need for workplace equality, recognized the ERA's symbolic power. Its proponents argued that economic injustice to women could be corrected constitutionally, homemakers' work should be recognized as having economic value, and lower-income women would be ERA's prime beneficiaries, because those women were more likely to hold sex-discriminatory jobs. The arguments made sense, but the existence of a proposed amendment to the Constitution galvanized antifeminists and conservatives in a way that took most feminists by surprise. It also helped to distort the distinctions between radicals and liberals, for even though the ERA found its initial support in the NOW contingent, the ERA collapse was construed by many as the failure of radical feminisim.

Nevertheless, the wrangling over and ultimate defeat of the ERA in 1982 dealt a crippling blow to organized mainstream feminism, marking the beginning of a new, "postfeminist" age.

THE F WORD: POSTFEMINISM IN OUR TIME

Susan Faludi popularized the notion of the backslide on feminism in her 1991 book, *Backlash: The Undeclared War Against American Women*, in which she detailed the assault on women's liberation by men and interests in the media establishment, academy and politics. Ever since the word *liberation* was conveniently dropped from the term "women's movement," the combination of liberal feminists' promotion of one image of the liberated woman – middle class or more, careerist, usually white and married with children – with the entrenchment of male power helped to create a backlash among women as well.

The rise of "cultural feminism," which, in its many manifestations – from the belief in innate gender differences to all-out separatism – also helped to contribute handsomely to the great confusion around the original goals of radical feminism.

"Most fundamentally, radical feminism was a political movement dedicated to eliminating the sex-class system," wrote social historian Alice Echols in *Daring to Be Bad: Radical Feminism in America, 1967–1975*, "whereas cultural feminism was a countercultural movement aimed at reversing the cultural valuation of the male and the devaluation of the female." If radical feminists were "typically social constructionists who wanted to render gender irrelevant, cultural feminists were generally essentialists who sought to celebrate femaleness."

Celebrating femaleness might seem like a terribly worthy goal in a world in which women were and are still the second sex. But it's hardly the point. The upsurge of visibility of women of color and lesbians in the Seventies highlighted the shortcomings of this approach. Radical feminists always maintained that their notion of sisterhood didn't mean that women should transcend their differences in order to bond.

Feminism has prevailed in several important ways over the decades: Abortion is still legal. Rape and domestic violence have received some serious attention in and out of the courts. Women's studies is an established academic discipline. And debate rages on: Last decade's culture wars over sexually explicit material, which manifested in the pro-sex, anticensorship vs. antiporn struggle, and the recent imbroglios over the definition of sexual harassment show that feminist work is far from done.

The important theoretical work contributed on pornography and sexuality and collected in Eighties feminist texts such as *Powers of Desire: The Politics of Sexuality, Pleasure and Danger*, and *Caught Looking: Women, Pornography and Censorship* (which I helped to edit), has been supplanted by groundbreaking "queer theory" and gay and lesbian studies in general in the Nineties, or by catchy postfems or antifeminists Camille Paglia and Katie Roiphe.

I'm still waiting for a new generation of feminists to materialize who are not embarrassed or ashamed of the F word, who don't contort themselves explaining its antiquation. As the backslide into essentialism and cultural feminism is challenged by everyday examples of women's power, as science and technology continue – albeit slowly – to alter women's reproductive functioning and capabilities, as more and more women head households and demand equality in the workplace, it's impossible not to imagine the dawn of the new millennium in which feminism, again, causes the kind of excitement that spawned Redstockings, CR – hey, even the ERA. ⊕

tours de force
by ben fong-torres

IN 1972, the Rolling Stones flew around North America in a customized four-engine plane nicknamed the "Lapping Tongue." Onboard, playing to a documentary filmmaker's camera, a member of the Stones' entourage lifted a naked young woman over his shoulder and proceeded to do the wild thing.

The Stones were hosting a string of celebrity-studded parties and pausing, on occasion, to perform a concert. Every night in Chicago, the Stones were guests at the Playboy mansion, where lapping tongues met willing bunnies. In Los Angeles, the crowd at the Fabulous Forum included Jack Nicholson, Britt Ekland, Karen Black and Ike and Tina Turner. In Washington, Robert F. Kennedy Jr. caught the Stones. In New York, Bob Dylan, Princess Lee Radziwill, Andy Warhol, Muddy Waters and Zsa Zsa Gabor helped Mick Jagger celebrate his twenty-ninth birthday. Even the reporters on the tour were superstars. "Hey, there's Terry Southern – and, look, he's hanging out with Truman Capote."

It was their first American tour since 1969's, which had concluded in a hastily planned, open-air concert at the Altamont Speedway near San Francisco – a concert most memorable for having ended in mayhem and a murder. This time around, things were different: Security was tighter, ticket prices were higher and everything had been moved indoors.

Over eight weeks, the Stones delivered fifty-four concerts in twenty-nine cities, invariably in large arenas and stadiums designed for professional sports – and invariably sold out. Chip Monck, the staging mastermind of Woodstock fame, filled the sterile, concrete-and-steel facilities with state-of-the-art technology and showmanship: A twelve-foot-high stage fronted by a sixteen-by-forty-foot mirror made of Mylar panels allowed the band to be backlit and spotlit all at once. Ensuring that all eyes and ears in the back row would be reached, five-ton hydraulic lifts flanked the stage and bore loads of eighteen-foot-high Tychobrahe speakers, blasting the music out through 16,000 watts of amplifiers.

Supersensory, high-decibel arena rock spilled off the stage into the general-admission seats (a ticketing policy that allows promoters to charge the same price to all concertgoers) and reverberated through the parking lot. The Rolling Stones American Tour 1972 set the tone of concert tours for the rest of the decade. Gate-crashers and other troublemakers triggered arrests in at least eight cities. In Montreal, a flying bottle hit Jagger onstage. Outside Boston, a scuffle with a photographer resulted in assault charges against Keith Richards, while Jagger was accused of obstructing a police officer. Their concert was delayed by two hours, nearly causing a riot. No wonder the Stones resorted to private planes and parties. At its highest, most glamorous levels, this was the state of the rock scene in the Seventies.

I was one of the lucky ones. As a reporter for ROLLING STONE, I had a job that put me not only backstage, in the dressing rooms with all the beer, buffets and properly separated M&M's, but also onstage to witness the explosive flowering of arena rock.

By the time we got to Woodstock, we were half a million strong . . ." sang Joni Mitchell in 1969. However many there were at the various festivals and benefits that proliferated, it was clear that rock had outgrown the psychedelic-era ballrooms and auditoriums of the Sixties. Artists – along with managers and promoters – were now looking for bigger stages.

And so, as the decade turned the corner, sporting arenas became the churches, the chosen gathering places, of rock. From Joe Cocker's Mad Dogs and Englishmen tour in 1970 to George Harrison's 1971 Concert for Bangladesh to the Stones' trendsetting 1972 tour, rock roared into a decade of one-upmanship. Fog machines and lasers replaced flashing lights; hanging, quadraphonic sound systems upgraded the stacks-of-speakers approach; and look: a huge video screen! (the Stones), five grand pianos!! (Elton John), a full orchestra!!! (Emerson, Lake and Palmer), a Texas-shaped stage with a real live buffalo, buzzard and armadillo? (ZZ Top, of course). By mid-decade, high-tech wizardry and Vegas-style extravagances became as *de rigueur* (and predictable) as the preordained three-song encore.

Along with the rising number of blown minds, eardrums and egos, ticket prices rocketed, and artists, promoters and merchandisers got rich. Leading the charge to indoor sports facilities was Bill Graham, who, after closing the legendary Fillmores on both coasts and moving his bigger concerts into an ice-skating arena called Winterland, explained: "It had gotten to the point where the demand was greater than the supply. . . . Unless the band was willing to give us three dates, we could not satisfy the demand. Bands began to realize that if they could make as much in one date as they could in three, they wouldn't have to stay on the road as long . . . the conclusion they reached was, 'I want to make more money in less time.' Result? Stadiums."

The business thrived in the larger venues, and Graham became as much a part of the Barnum & Bailey syndrome as any of the concert producers or stage designers. He erected an extravagant fantasy world backstage at his annual Day on the Green at the Oakland Coliseum (a baseball park), including a catered restaurant, a kiddie amusement center, potted palm trees and his ubiquitous basketball court. When the Band

Despite having to stand in line for hours for higher-priced tickets or having to pay scalpers' prices, fans expanded their expectations, which were regularly met. Though their favorite groups gave less spontaneity, they delivered more spectacle. Now, instead of being surrounded by psychedelic lights, the audience got timed explosions, levitating drum kits and flying guitar players. The idyllic nights at outdoor festivals, where one could lie back, stretch out and will the stars – the ones up in the sky – to dance along to the music, became few.

By the end of the Seventies, arena rock was parodied (intentionally or not) in Kiss's comic-book, blood-and-brimstone assault, rebelled against in the back-to-the-bars backlash of punk and pub rock, and turned inside out in the "everybody-is-a-star, that's-me-on-the-stage-under-the-colored-lights" participatory aesthetic of disco.

Meanwhile, the concert business – firmly forged into a coast-to-coast chain of arenas, amphitheaters and stadiums – became one of rock's solid financial pillars. To this day, Pearl Jam, U2, packaged tours, once- or twice-in-a-lifetime reunions and assorted Seventies chestnuts still sell seats. But it should be noted that the Stones are counted upon –

Gone is the age of doing a 72-bar guitar solo with your back to the audience. –Peter Frampton

disbanded in 1976, and agreed to a final stand at Winterland, Graham rose to the occasion and transformed the stage of the arena into a grand opera house for the legendary Last Waltz.

Mick Jagger, too, saw the writing on the coliseum wall in 1971. "Either we're going to play in a club with five hundred people and actually play, or we're going to play really big crowds," he reasoned. "Playing to five thousand is really nonsensical; it's not intimate." Not surprisingly, by 1978 the Stones were making headlines by popping up at various nightclubs and bashing out rock & roll and blues standards like in their good old pub-crawling days.

Bruce Springsteen, who later proved that an artist could achieve intimacy even in the largest facilities, hated playing them early on, when he and his E Street Band were an opening act in 1973. "They just won't listen to you," he said. "Some groups just go out and plow through it. But I can't do it. And it showed. We played thirteen or fourteen gigs in them big halls and we sold no records. We didn't start sellin' records until we started playin' smaller places."

As the decade proceeded, most artists were listening to their managers (and accountants) and reasoning that, if they were going to play for uncountable thousands in a succession of fields of dreams, they might as well make a show of it. In the Seventies, a full-charged arena tour – replete with explosive sound and lights, black tour T-shirts and eager (if at times hard-bitten) opening bands – was the pinnacle to be reached.

usually every three years – to push the financial and creative limits of the Great Rock Tour. Who will take over their pacesetting duties when they permanently park their steel wheels remains to be seen.

While some bands defy gravity and sanity and continue to soar in luxury jets, others have wisely downsized. Personally, I cannot deny the fun of flying in the Starship, a 707 retrofitted for rockers, with Elton John; of hanging backstage with an unusually jocular Bob Dylan; and of seemingly endless postconcert parties with stars and their always noteworthy satellites. But, looking at my own back pages and backstage passes, I note that a few of my favorite tours were on buses with the likes of Linda Ronstadt, Bonnie Raitt, Tom Waits and John Prine, and one of my all-time favorite shows was at a nightclub in Redondo Beach, California, where Gary Busey, who'd portrayed Buddy Holly in *The Buddy Holly Story*, hopped tabletops and rocked the joint with "Rave On." Another fave rave, circa then: Van Morrison sizzling through a set at a low-ceilinged San Francisco nightclub called the Old Waldorf. And Delbert McClinton at the Lone Star in lower Manhattan, where, if memory serves, one had to walk past the band before elbowing into a spot from which to watch them. Up close and sweaty. And that, in the end, is the way to rock & roll.

Sure, I go back to stadiums on occasion. But it's usually to see a ball game. ⊕

the peace candidate
by bob greene

IT HAPPENED one October day during the 1972 presidential campaign. You ask yourself whether anything quite like it could happen now.

At first it didn't seem to be an unusual moment. We were on our way from Boston to Minnesota, aboard George McGovern's campaign plane, the *Dakota Queen II*, when McGovern came walking toward the back compartment.

I was twenty-five, a columnist for the Chicago *Sun-Times*, assigned to my first presidential campaign. We who were traveling with McGovern saw him and spoke with him all the time; as the Democratic candidate, McGovern's style was dramatically different from that of his opponent, the Republican incumbent, Richard Nixon.

With the war in Vietnam raging, Nixon was spending most of the campaign at the White House, well ahead in the polls, answering few questions, waiting out the days until the November election. McGovern – fervently against the war, quiet and subdued by nature, knowing that his message was not getting across to the electorate – traveled day and night, campaigned to the point of exhaustion and often seemed to know that he was going nowhere.

In the eyes of much of the public, McGovern – a liberal senator from South Dakota, in the conservative center of the country – had been categorized as almost a fringe candidate. Part of this was the result of very effective attacks by President Nixon's political team; they relentlessly portrayed McGovern as being sympathetic to draft evaders, as being too forgiving of drug use by young people, of generally being much more radical in his beliefs than Nixon. McGovern's supporters in the primaries had unseated the traditional Democratic power brokers, including Mayor Richard J. Daley of Chicago; because of that, he had few real friends among the longtime established leaders of his own party.

What upset McGovern most, on a personal level, was that the Nixon campaign had somehow been able to plant in the minds of many people that he was unpatriotic. McGovern had been a B-24 pilot in World War II, flying thirty-five missions over enemy lines and winning the Distinguished Flying Cross. Yet the attacks by his opponents seemed to be sticking; as he campaigned across the country, it was evident every day that people believed much of the worst of what his political adversaries were implying about him.

On this day, aboard his airplane, he said a few hellos to those of us riding in the press section as he moved toward the work area in the back. We were eating lunch, and those who weren't eating were writing stories for our newspapers, or sleeping, or talking.

It wasn't until a few minutes later, when McGovern hadn't returned, that it occurred to any of us to see what he was up to. He was sitting on a table in the back area, his feet lifted up off the airline carpeting. There was a Sony stereo tape player in the cramped workspace, its twin speakers taped to the wall of the plane. A tape was playing, and McGovern was staring at the revolving reels of the recorder. He was crying.

The tape had been given to McGovern a few hours earlier, in Boston. McGovern had been the guest on a radio talk show hosted by a man named Jerry Williams. Williams had told McGovern about a young man who had called the show on Labor Day. Williams had asked McGovern to listen to a tape he had made of the show.

McGovern had been behind schedule and hadn't had time, but he took a copy of the tape with him. Now, on the plane, tears in his eyes, he was listening. The young man's voice was soft and shaky. Several times, as he spoke, he had to stop to try to compose himself:

Yeah, I am a Vietnam veteran, and I was over there in March, and I am a little nervous. I heard the program tonight and heard quite a few people call up about the war in Vietnam. I don't think the American people really, really understand the war and what's going on. . . .

1972 JULY

We went into villages after they dropped napalm, and the human beings were fused together like pieces of metal that had been soldered. Sometimes you couldn't tell if they were people or animals. We have jets that drop rockets, and in the shells they have penny nails and those nails – one nail per square inch for about the size of a football field – you can't believe what they do to a human being.

I was there for a year, and I never had the courage to say that was wrong. I condoned that. I watched it go on. Now I'm home. Sometimes I – my heart – it bothers me inside because I remember all that, and I didn't have the courage to say it was wrong. And I see people call up and talk about killing and they wouldn't mind their sons going over there and doing that to other human beings. It doesn't matter what the Viet Cong – the Viet Cong are bad. But that doesn't make it right for me to be bad or for someone to say that we should send their son or their husband or their brother to go over there and to be just as vicious. . . .

And what bothers me is when you're there, you accept it. You rationalize it. You condone it. You say it's right because they are the enemy, and then when you come home you can't believe that you didn't have the courage to open your mouth against that kind of murder, that kind of devastation over people, over animals. You don't know they are Viet Cong. You can't tell . . . Napalm – there's no way people in this country can understand what napalm is. . . .

And you have to come home and live because you didn't have the guts to say it was wrong. . . . Guys like me . . . we condoned it. We rationalized it. That is all I have to say. . . .

When the tape ended, McGovern came out of the work space. No one knew what to say. We all looked at each other, and after a few minutes McGovern started to talk with us about other matters, and in a while he went up to be by himself.

But for the rest of the flight it was hard to think about anything except the tape. For all the months of his campaign against Richard Nixon, McGovern had been trying to explain to people why the war was slicing him up inside but hadn't been able to get it across. His shy voice and manner had served to hide the seething he felt. This tape, though – in the voice of the young veteran was everything that McGovern had been feeling about the war.

There was a rally at the University of Minnesota scheduled for that afternoon. It was the usual McGovern rally: happy and easy and full of good feeling. It was a chilly day, and fifteen thousand students stood on the grass as McGovern made his speech. The rally ended with noise and laughter.

But then McGovern asked the students to wait for a few minutes. He said he had something he wanted them to hear, and the tape-recorded voice of the young veteran began to come over the loudspeakers, and the man's tortured words filled the campus green.

No one moved. No one spoke. McGovern stood with his hands in his pockets, staring straight ahead. People in the crowd began to weep, to bite their lips, to breathe through their mouths and look down at the ground.

You wonder, today, if such a moment could happen during a presidential campaign. The most effective campaigns are pre-planned down to the minute, and there is a specific message to be gotten out in a specific way each day – if a candidate is permitted to stray from the day's plan, then the day has been a failure.

On this day, McGovern stood there and listened along with the students – listened to the tape that had been handed to him, that had moved him to tears and that, on his own, he had decided to share with the people who had come to see him. Within weeks, he would be defeated in a landslide of historic proportions; within weeks, the American people would tell him, as loudly as a man can be told, that they preferred Nixon to him. Within weeks, his country would send him home a loser.

On this day in Minnesota, though, he stood at the front of the crowd, yet a part of the crowd, listening to the young man's voice. It took about six minutes for the tape to play. When it was over, McGovern told the students that there was not much else to say. They began to drift away. A guitar player went to his microphone and hit the first chords of "This Land Is Your Land," the song that traditionally ended McGovern rallies. But this time, on this day, the people were not singing along. This time no one was making a sound.

working-class hero
by robert santelli

IF YOU STOOD outside the Student Prince when a stiff onshore wind was blowing, and the surf was up, you could smell salt in the night air and hear the waves, big and angry, breaking on the beach. The Kingsley Avenue club stood just a couple of blocks from the boardwalk, and during the winter of 1972, Asbury Park, New Jersey, was a cold, lonely place.

Inside was a different story. The Student Prince was just another gin mill in a dying resort town, with a cramped bar, cropped stage, warping pool table and the smelly scent of stale beer and smoke. But on this particular night, it was packed to capacity with about 180 people, so staying warm was not a problem. Most of us were students from nearby Monmouth College, a school where a twenty-two-year-old guitarist and songwriter named Bruce Springsteen had performed frequently, cultivating a sizable portion of his Jersey Shore support.

Finding it impossible to stay afloat financially with so many musicians in its fold, the ten-piece Bruce Springsteen Band was playing its farewell to the Student Prince. (They had held residency there for several months – playing every Friday, Saturday and Sunday – and though they would play a few scattered gigs through the spring, this amounted to their swan song.) Crammed onto the club's tiny stage, backed by a blaring horn section and black backup singers, Springsteen promised his fans that he would make the show a memorable one. He kept his word, lobbing hot volleys of soul rock into the crowd. Just about anywhere else, such a sound would have seemed out of place in 1972 – Springsteen neither wore glitter or makeup like the glam stars of the day nor offered the sensational, classically inspired bombast of prog-rock bands like Yes and King Crimson. But in Asbury Park his particular brand of rock & roll – a solid mix of blues covers and original songs – sounded as natural and as right as the calliope in the nearby penny arcade.

Opening with a slow, sleazy version of the old chestnut "C.C. Rider" that medleyed into Chuck Berry's "Down the Road Apiece," Springsteen then carved his initials into "Route 66," "Walking the Dog" and "Bright Lights Big City" before launching into horn-driven originals like "You Mean So Much to Me" (a song Southside Johnny and the Asbury Jukes would later record), and "Goin' Back to Georgia," a showstopper from his old power-rock band, Steel Mill.

The 1971 collapse of Steel Mill, a band with Led Zeppelin and Cream roots featuring bassist and guitarist "Miami" Steve Van Zandt, had followed the collapse of Asbury Park, the onetime vacation place for North Jersey and New York City blue-collar families. Long-simmering racial discord had erupted into riots, leaving Asbury Park's once-busy downtown a war zone with boarded-up windows, empty streets and an ugly tension that floated ominously in the air. White flight took its toll: FOR SALE and FOR RENT signs popped up on a large number of streets all over town.

Springsteen then created Dr. Zoom and the Sonic Boom, a Mad Dogs and Englishmen–inspired experiment that featured twirlers and a Monopoly game onstage to complement the music performance. Three performances later (including a gig opening for the Allman Brothers), what started as a goof ended just as offhandedly.

By spring 1972, everyone seemed to be leaving Asbury Park; it was surprising that the Student Prince was still there. Even the musicians started drifting away – getting married or enrolling in college to avoid Vietnam. Except Springsteen. He chose to remain within bus-commuting distance of New York City, where he was playing the Greenwich Village club Kenny's Castaways as a solo act, and was unwilling to leave the inspiration and good times of the Shore. He wound up sleeping on the floor of a friend's house after his rent money ran out. But with no band to front, the young king of Asbury Park rock traded in his electric guitar for an acoustic one, and turning inward, began to transform himself into a singer/songwriter in the mold of Bob Dylan and Van Morrison.

Clive Davis signs Aerosmith.

11 Apparently unaware of the duo's sex-and-drugs focus, the mayor of San Antonio declares August 11, 1972, Cheech & Chong Day.

12 Following weeks of intense bombing of military and non-military targets in North Vietnam (including admitted "accidental" damage to important irrigation dikes), the U.S. deactivates its last ground-combat forces in South Vietnam, leaving 43,500 mostly service personnel behind. National Security Adviser Kissinger is now involved in secret negotiations with North Vietnamese officials in Paris, though massive U.S. air strikes continue.

22 Richard Nixon is almost unanimously renominated as the Republican candidate for president with Spiro Agnew as his running mate at the Republican National Convention; the sole dissenting vote is cast for antiwar candidate Congressman Paul McCloskey. Six members of Vietnam Veterans Against the War, including wheelchair-bound Ron Kovic, will be charged with planning to violently disrupt the convention.

26 The XX Olympic Games open in Munich, Germany. Highlights will include U.S. swimmer Mark Spitz's earning of seven gold medals, and the Soviet Union's diminutive gymnast Olga Korbut's winning of two golds and one silver medal and countless hearts around the world. These victories will be overshadowed on Sept. 5, when the Palestinian terrorist group Black September breaks into the lodgings of the Israeli athletic team, killing two and taking nine hostages. As the games are suspended and the world watches in horror, a gun battle erupts the following night between West German police and the terrorists, leaving four Palestinians, all nine captives and one policeman dead.

A money trail leads to the White House, as certain unreported donations to the Committee to Re-elect the President (CREEP) are linked to one of the five Watergate burglars. Three days after this finding, President Nixon states that his own internal investigation revealed no link between any of his staff and this "very bizarre incident." Three days later, Nixon promises that the first six months of his second term

But as the Bruce Springsteen Band belted out its swan songs that night in 1972, spirits were high and the magic of rock & roll was in the smoky air. By the time he jumped into his rollicking version of "Jambalaya," all of us at the Student Prince were wedged between the stage and the few tables and chairs on the perimeter of the dance floor, demanding that the sweat-soaked Springsteen push the energy higher and higher. With a fury of horns and soul shouts that would have impressed Wilson Pickett or even James Brown, the band climaxed with a twin-guitar solo shootout – Springsteen versus Miami Steve – that temporarily transformed the Student Prince into the center of the rock & roll universe, with Springsteen its ruler.

I had seen Springsteen perform as early as 1969, had remained a fan and had since become an aspiring rock journalist, writing about him in the Monmouth College student newspaper, the *Outlook*. On this bittersweet night – as the band and Springsteen said their (so we thought) last goodbyes – I witnessed a show like no other up until then, and it was all the proof I needed to understand what critic and future manager Jon Landau would prophetically write in 1974: Bruce Springsteen was "rock & roll future." It would take the rest of the world a bit longer to embrace what Springsteen brought to the music. First, they had to hear his songs, then they would have to see him perform. Finally, they would have to wade through all the hype. But ultimately the sheer integrity of his music, the apoplectic intensity of his concerts, would reinvigorate Seventies rock & roll and carry it through the oftentimes theatrical excesses and pretentious conceits of that decade.

Springsteen's inward journey – his retreat from rock foppery and affectation and his maturation from a bar-band leader to a songwriter of clear and universal vision – was one that mirrored the lost and searching spirit of the early Seventies. I myself was trying to decide whether to run down the newly established rock-critic path or to continue pursuing my American history degree and plans to become a high school teacher.

Springsteen had spent less than a year at a Jersey Shore community college, so his searching took place in the everyday. As with John Steinbeck, whose works he would later read, admire and draw inspiration from, Asbury Park was Springsteen's Cannery Row, providing greasy boardwalk settings and idiosyncratic characters, such as Madam Marie the fortune-teller, that populated the lyrics and music of his first two albums: "4th of July, Asbury Park (Sandy)," "Spirit in the Night," "For You" and "Blinded by the Light." Few rock songwriters at the time were so linked to a specific geographical space as was Springsteen.

Springsteen spent his mornings writing songs and his afternoons wandering the boardwalk. In the evening, whenever he got a gig and had the money to get there, he took a bus to New York to play various clubs as a solo act. These were hard days, but good days, too. Tunes were flowing out of Springsteen.

The story of Springsteen being discovered, managed (by Mike Appel) and signed to Columbia (by legendary A&R man John Hammond) is an oft-told one; part of his audition was the now-classic "It's Hard to Be a Saint in the City," written on that long bus ride from the Shore to the city. Hammond thought he had signed a solo singer/songwriter, another street poet like Bob Dylan. But Springsteen had no plans to be a strumming troubadour forever; he took his folk-rock songs and gave them a Jersey backbeat, using some of the musicians who had helped him say farewell earlier that year at the Student Prince.

One day, back on the boardwalk, Springsteen had come upon a tourist postcard from his faded resort city and decided it would provide the title and cover of his first album. He liked the idea of being an outsider, of celebrating his Jersey Shore roots, not only in his music, but in his manner of speech (heavy street slang, nicknames) and dress (torn T-shirt, black leather jacket, newsboy cap).

Greetings From Asbury Park, N.J. was released in early 1973, and later that year its followup, *The Wild, the Innocent, and the E Street Shuffle,* further explored Asbury Park in song. Neither album sold well. But Springsteen's artistic growth was only beginning. His quest for meaningful rock & roll now extended far beyond the horizons of early-Seventies Jersey Shore; he was stretching his imagination and musical gifts to take in all of America and use it as his canvas.

Springsteen's self-education, with friendly encouragement from then-producer Jon

Landau, reached back into American history and culture. He discovered and absorbed gothic Americana through the literature of writers like Steinbeck and Flannery O'Connor; the Western films of John Ford and John Huston; and the Everyman-as-hero songs of Woody Guthrie, Pete Seeger and Hank Williams.

The unlikely heroes that Springsteen began to celebrate in song were the disgruntled and disenfranchised struggling to make ends meet, to find meaning in a world that was cold and cruel, to retain a personal dignity and to triumph in small ways. Teenagers and hot rods. Street gangs and hustlers. Dead-end jobs and open roads. His songs were like Edward Hopper paintings – never had rock seemed so stark and austere and romantic and hot-blooded all at the same time.

In 1975, Springsteen painted his masterpiece. *Born to*

Fleetwood Mac floated balloons of pigs and penguins in rock's stratosphere during the latter part of the decade, Springsteen's notoriety helped keep the rock & roll spirit grounded, close to its roots. Indirectly, he held the door open for like-minded, up-from-the-bar bands like the Iron City Houserockers and homies Southside Johnny and the Asbury Jukes, while the stateside success of British pub rockers – like Graham Parker, Dave Edmunds and even the Clash – owes a tip of the pint glass to Springsteen. He was also a champion of New York undergrounders Lou Reed and Patti Smith (cowriting her only Top-Twenty hit "Because the Night"); American punk rock certainly drew its sound, fury and "Born to Die" worldview from the same wellspring that powered *Born to Run*.

On a grander, more far-reaching scale, Springsteen's

It's Moses's fault. He was so scared after ten, he said this is enough. You shoulda seen it – great show, the burning bush, thunder, lightning. You see, there was supposed to be an Eleventh Commandment. All it said was: *Let it Rock! –Bruce Springsteen*

Run unveiled the artist in full maturity, capturing America in all its glory and contradictions in eight songs. Musically, Springsteen turned back the clock for the album's joyous title track, reviving his Student Prince formula of repeatedly building a song's energy and then letting it all go in explosions of rollicking euphoria. With all its roots showing, *Born to Run* reinvented and exulted in an earlier period of rock & roll, drawing sounds and inspiration from Roy Orbison, Phil Spector, the Rolling Stones, Bo Diddley, Dylan and others.

The unexpected magnitude of success reached by *Born to Run* heralded "Rock's New Messiah" (as *Newsweek* trumpeted), but overshadowed his universal message. The unprecedented simultaneous *Time* and *Newsweek* cover stories in October of that year, engineered by the publicity current from Columbia Records, nearly swept away Springsteen in a wave of hype. By the time he made it to London's famed Hammersmith Odeon theater that year, he was personally tearing down posters that (mis)quoted the famous Landau praise.

But the starmakers' machinery could not and would not detract from what became one of the Seventies' most distinctive, clear-eyed and rocking voices. As Pink Floyd and

populist vision can also be credited for inspiring a family tree of songwriters, all working in and helping give rise to the late Seventies/early Eighties phenomenon of Heartland rock. John Cougar Mellencamp cultivated the Midwest as his personal song garden, while Tom Petty focused on Southern heritage and accents. Steve Forbert kept it acoustic, and, later, Steve Earle came along and infused Nashville with the same rocking, blue-collar perspective Springsteen had first designed.

Though Springsteen's legend now places him aloft in the same star-filled ether that holds other icons who achieved prominence in the Seventies, there remains no rocker whose public image is so close to his private self: There's practically no distance between the singer and the songs. Springsteen can still fill stadiums with his sincerity, his lyrics of sympathy and courage and his tireless, eager-to-please onstage energy. And in front of tens of thousands, he can still successfully reach out, touch each individual and make them feel like they are one of a select, 180 lucky people enjoying the spirit of rock & roll in a small, crowded bar on an otherwise cold, lonely night.   ⊕

christmas in hanoi
by joan baez

THIS IS THE STORY of my thirteen days in Hanoi, eleven of which were the days of the Christmas bombing, the result of the "most difficult decision" President Nixon had to make during his term in office. That Christmas bombing was, as it turned out, the heaviest bombing in the history of the world.

In December 1972 I received a call from a group that had been sending a steady flow of American visitors to North Vietnam to try to keep up some kind of friendly relations with the Vietnamese people even as our country continued to bomb the hell out of them, burn their villages and napalm their children. Before Watergate, anyone who talked or wrote about the atrocities committed by the U.S. military or who performed in Vietnam was looked upon skeptically, or with great annoyance and anger, by a high percentage of the American population. I decided to go nonetheless.

I was the guest of a North Vietnamese group called the Committee for Solidarity with the American People. Four Americans were invited, including myself. I traveled with a conservative lawyer, ex–Brigadier General Telford Taylor; a liberal Episcopalian minister, Michael Allen; and Maoist Vietnam Veteran Against the War, Barry Romo. No serious fighting had taken place in the north for many months. Among other services, we were to be delivering Christmas mail to the POWs in Hanoi. My son, Gabriel, was with his dad at the time, and I had been told I would be able to return home by Christmas Day.

I remember landing in Hanoi on a short runway, piling out of the plane and being met by a group of the loveliest people one could imagine. Quat was the leader of the group; he was lively and intelligent and full of jokes. During the time we were there, Quat's wife would give birth to their baby during a bomb raid; one member of the committee would lose his wife and eight children; another would lose track of his wife's whereabouts and spend all of the time he wasn't with us trying to track her down, not knowing whether she was alive or dead. Throughout, they looked after us as though they were our personally assigned guardian angels and had nothing else in the world to do.

Following pages: Mike Allen, Joan Baez and Barry Romo *(from left)* walk through the rubble of Gialam International Airport in Hanoi after it had been bombed by American B-52s

On the third night after our arrival I cleaned up and went down to dinner. From that point on, my mind has retained only vivid flashbacks of what took place. The electricity in the building failed, leaving us sitting in the dark. Everyone stiffened, the Americans uneasy, the Vietnamese speaking rapidly to each other in quiet tones. Then I heard a siren coming from the distance, starting at zero bass and rising evenly to a solid, steady high note, where it stayed for a second or two and then slid back down through all the notes like a glider. All I could think of were the civil defense drills from grammar school. I sat still, aware that my heartbeat had doubled in pace, and waited for instructions from the Vietnamese. By the time the siren began its second wail, one of our hosts had lit a candle and said to us in English, calmly and with a smile, "Please excuse me. Alert."

"What's going on?" I asked a Cuban man.

"They don't know. Maybe planes. I don't hear them. We'll just wait. Hasn't been any bombing for a long time."

Bombing? I heard the word, and I had surely suspected that was what the sirens were all about, but hearing this man say it as he looked so matter-of-factly at the sky was something different.

A tall Indian held up his forefinger and said, "Shhh." In the distance I heard them – the planes. Everyone went on standing there in the moonlight, but now we were talking. The sound faded into the distance and the voices came back, only much softer. People let out sighs. There were a few jokes, the voices almost back to normal.

And then it hit.

The planes were coming fast, and they were loud. The group jumped as a unit, heading for the door of the shelter down the narrow stairs. A big boom happened somewhere, and it shook the shelter walls and sent a wave of adrenaline through all of us. People hurried down the steps. The Cuban sat me down at the end of a long narrow bench. I had to go to the bathroom. There was another blast.

My ears were fluttering and popping as if I was on a plane gaining altitude quickly. I didn't know what was happening. The Cuban was telling me to lean away from the wall, to keep swallowing and pop my ears. I grabbed his arm with both hands. For a while all I could think of were my straining sphincter muscles. The bombs were coming down continuously. The Cuban was shouting in my ear. "It will be all right. They are not as close as they sound. Don't worry." I introduced myself to the Cuban. His name was Monti. I told him that I was trying to stop shaking and thanked him for the loan of his arm.

CRACK-BOOM! This time the bomb exploded before any of us heard the planes. I took a deep breath and felt like vomiting. I took Monti's hand again, breathed deeply and waited. This time I made a conscious effort to keep my head up. I was only partially successful. Monti explained that we were hearing carpet bombing. It was like thunder, the kind of thunder that rolls and rolls when you see purple lightning like strobe-lit twigs hurled into the air at the edge of a desert horizon. The intermittent cracking of antiaircraft seemed to be coming from the hotel patio. I didn't understand that it was ground-to-air, and its volume added to my panic.

Carpet bombing is relentless. I realized with shame and horror that to pray for the planes to go away was to pray that they would drop their bombs somewhere else. I was kneading Monti's hand and sweating all over, my body shaking again as badly as before. But I was beginning to get a grip on myself. As soon as the noise became less than deafening, I felt like making a joke.

"I wonder if Macy's is open till nine this evening."

"What is Macy's?" asked the big Indian.

"It's a department store in the States. There's some last-minute Christmas shopping I have to do." They began to laugh. The bombing was in the distance now.

"Oh yes, Christmas. Your country has an amusing way of celebrating." It was not said bitterly.

The first day of the bombing I had been mentally saying goodbye to my son, to my sisters, to everything. On the second day of the bombing . . . the first raid of the second day . . . I remember I was getting something to eat and someone slammed a door. I dropped my plate. By the fourth or fifth day I would walk nonchalantly to the shelter.

I played my guitar and sang in the shelter sometimes. The best song was "Don't Let Nobody Turn You Around." It's short and easy to translate. The people clapped along and sang, "Ain't going to let no Pentagon turn me around." It was something we needed after an hour in those shelters.

There were about four or five raids a night, lasting an hour or an hour and a half apiece. We'd get up and go to the shelters. Some nights there were nine or ten raids and we'd just sleep there. We went to sleep and got up whenever we heard the siren.

During one of the raids I talked to a reporter for the French Communist news service. He was talking about packing away his typewriter and getting out a rifle to fight the Americans. He asked me if I didn't like the sound of antiaircraft fire and I had to tell him I did. The next question was, "Don't you like to see the planes explode in the sky?"

I said, "Yes, if I know the pilot has bailed out." I cannot enjoy the idea of anyone being blown up. That is on the moral side. On the human side I was glad there was ground-to-air fire. It meant that the planes were going to go away and that someone else below wasn't going to be killed. If my pacifism was ever put to a test, this had to have been the time. I don't like to see war and I don't like killing, on any side. I'm not a fake pacifist.

Aside from that, I could visualize every man in every one of those planes as a future Vietnam Vet Against the War.

We never heard about a Christmas Day halt in the bombing so we all went to sleep and didn't get up for fourteen hours on Christmas Day. Mike Allen and I had planned a small holiday service to take place in the lobby for the hotel guests and for our hosts, who I thought would be amused. There had been a lull in the raids, and I was hoping that a twenty-four-hour cease-fire had begun. I don't know what Christmas was to the United States president and secretary of state in 1972, but some of the true spirit escaped them.

During the service, my head was stuffed up with a cold, but my voice was coming out fine. *Our Father who art in heaven, hallowed be Thy name.* What a strange and pitiful Christmas. *Give us this day our daily bread. Hallowed be Thy name.* Perhaps Quat would eventually get to his islands. That will be my prayer for him. *Forgive us all our trespasses. Hallowed be Thy name.* God, bless and keep Gabriel. Give him a good Christmas. And keep his daddy well. *As we forgive those who trespass against us. Hallowed be Thy name.* I wondered if my family got the last telegram we sent out. It told them we were all right, and wished them a merry Christmas. Best not to think of home. *And lead us not to the devil to be tempted. Hallowed be* – a bomb exploded somewhere in the city. I went on singing – *Thy name. But deliver us from all that is evil.* The lights went out. I stopped my song. The French were telling me to keep going, and the Vietnamese were asking us to go to the shelter. The siren commenced. Mike was swearing. People lit candles and I tried to go on singing. My voice came out so weak that I thought it was someone else's. I realized later that I was trying to keep quiet so that the bombs wouldn't know where we were. I strummed on the guitar, waiting for the hotel to be blown to bits or my voice to return. Either would have been a relief. I cut a verse, and amidst the shuffling of feet, encouragement from the French and the closing notes of the siren, finished the Lord's Prayer. *Amen, Amen, Amen, Amen, Hallowed be Thy name.*

the novelty song "My Ding-a-Ling."

22 In a full seven games, the Oakland A's, with the aid of four home runs from Gene Tenace, derail the Big Red Machine of Cincinnati to clinch the World Series. Two days later, baseball legend Jackie Robinson dies of an apparent heart attack.

26 Kissinger publicly announces that after weeks of "shuttle diplomacy" among Paris, Saigon and Washington, a final political agreement and cessation of hostilities in Indochina is expected soon. The election polls predictably tilt even further in Nixon's favor, though a missed deadline on Oct. 31 will rekindle North Vietnamese attacks in November.

1972 NOVEMBER

2 At the end of the cross-country Trail of Broken Treaties Caravan protest march, a large group of Native American activists arrives in Washington, DC, and occupies the Bureau of Indian Affairs building. The 500 protesters will remain there until Nov. 8.

3 Singer/songwriters James Taylor and Carly Simon are married in Simon's New York City apartment, then travel downtown, where Taylor performs a concert at Radio City Music Hall.

5 Two weeks of bizarre rock deaths begin with Miss Christine, a member of Frank Zappa's GTOs, dying of a heroin overdose. Then, on Nov. 6, New York Dolls drummer Billy Murcia dies in London from accidental suffocation as friends attempt to revive him; on Nov. 11, Allman Brothers bassist Berry Oakley dies in a motorcycle accident three blocks from the site of Duane Allman's fatal accident just a year before; and on Nov. 18, Crazy Horse guitarist Danny Whitten dies of a heroin overdose.

7 In the largest landslide since the election of 1936, President Nixon is reelected. He carries every state except one – Massachusetts – to defeat George McGovern, claiming more than 60% of the popular vote.

Andrew Young of Georgia becomes the first black from the South elected to Congress since Reconstruction.

16 Pepsico reveals its agreement with the Soviet Union to

One morning after a particularly bad night we were taken to a business district called Kan Thiem that had been devastated by carpet bombing. It shook us all more severely than anything else had so far. Even our hosts seemed shocked.

Kan Thiem Street is a district in downtown Hanoi where the houses are very small – mud and brick, jammed close together. As we toured the district, a North Vietnamese war crimes commissioner stood behind us and told us all the figures: the dead, the wounded, the number of raids.

The first thing I noticed was everyone carrying their bicycles, because there was no way to walk them through the rubble. There was an old man who was trying to walk through the mud and brick, but he was hobbling and having a great deal of trouble moving through the wreckage. I reached over and took his hand. He looked up at me with his exquisite old man's face, those lines, the little white wispy chin beard, and I could feel he was trembling. We held on to each other for some seconds, and both our eyes filled with tears. He mumbled some things in Vietnamese that I couldn't understand, then he looked up at me and said, *"Danke schön."*

The next thing that made a deep impression on me was a woman sitting on the rubble and sobbing hysterically. They don't cry very much, Vietnamese women. They cover their faces with their hands or a veil if they do; but this woman was at the point where she would stand and clench and unclench her fists for several minutes, then sit on the rubble and just wail. Her face was bloated from crying and her husband was trying to get her to calm down and stop weeping. I sat next to her and she took my hand. There was a girl sitting next to her holding her other hand and she was crying too, only she wasn't making any sound. The woman squeezed my hand. Behind us the war crimes commissioner was just droning on and on: "215 killed, 257 wounded . . ."

Nearby there was a bomb shelter that had taken a direct hit. Everyone died.

We picked our way across the craters and the debris. It was like a moonscape with all the craters – except for the wreckage. I saw a woman in the distance chanting, but I couldn't see her face. I thought she and her family had survived because sometimes when there is devastation that people survive they get very giddy and actually celebrate. When we got closer, I saw her face wasn't happy. It was twisted in some kind of awful shock and agony. While chanting, dazed, she picked through the rubble. She would pick up a brick and put it down, pick up another brick from someplace else and put it down.

We asked the interpreter what it was she was chanting, and he said it was an old song that went, "Where are you now, my sons, where are you now?" Both her young sons were buried under the bricks. She would never see them again.

I couldn't go on after that. Someone took me back to the car. The others told me that a couple of craters further on a family of four had been killed: They were lying with their arms around one another. After that Mike couldn't stomach any food for forty-eight hours.

Our visit to the POW camp began with the same red tape I'd been through at prisons everywhere, except I was never before given tea in the warden's office. The sun was going down, which meant that the evening raids could start at any minute. I had my guitar, Mike had his Bible, Telford had his notepad and Barry had a stomachache. It didn't really matter what we had with us or what we planned to say or do. In this prison, as in all others I've ever seen, the main issue was boredom and loneliness for home and one's friends and family. We were closely supervised as the pilots showed us around their barracks.

We saw about thirteen POWs. The camp was near a bomb site and flying shrapnel had severely damaged their bunkhouse the night before. Four of them were slightly injured. All the windows were blasted in and there were pieces of shrapnel on the floor. We were going to hold a Christmas service but the big room we wanted to do it in had caved in. The walls and ceiling were up but everything else was rubble. Mike Allen gave a sermon and I was all set to sing the Lord's Prayer, but they said they'd rather hear "The Night They Drove Old Dixie Down."

Most of them, I think, were terrified. They had never been under the bombs before and they didn't know what was going on. The last thing they had heard, peace was at hand.

One of them held up a large piece of shrapnel. "This thing came right through the ceiling. We was hiding under the beds. We've kinda made our own shelters, but they don't amount to much. I don't understand."

"What don't you understand?" I asked.

"This," he said, holding up the deadly looking piece of steel again. "I mean, I don't understand what's happening." He was absolutely serious.

"Well," I ventured. "There are these planes flying over here every night carrying bombs."

"I know that. But I don't understand what's happening," he repeated for the third time.

"Well, it's really very simple," I explained. "These people drop the bombs out of the planes and the bombs fall to the earth where they explode and cause tremendous damage to people and things. Apparently one or several of these bombs landed close enough to send that piece of metal flying through your roof."

"But what I mean is," he persisted, "Kissinger said peace was at hand, isn't that what he said?" The sarcasm drained out of me like milk pouring from the tipped cup of a child. I wanted to cry.

"That's what he said," I told the expectant pilot. "Maybe he didn't mean it. They lie a lot." ⊕

REFLECTIONS

On Tour	(me) "What do you think of this skirt?"
in a mall	(the girl, tilting her head) "Are you a TV star?"
the sales person	(me) "No."
in a generic clothing shop	(the manager to the girl) "You should know
a beautiful Vietnamese girl	her!"
maybe twenty	(the girl) "Oh, I'm sorry . . ."
so beautiful	(me) "When did your parents come to
(I remember	Cincinnati?"
I remember	"In 1981. I was real young. You wanna try
those faces	anything else?"
delicate hands fine skin	"Yes. How did they get here, if I'm not being
I remember)	too pushy."
"What do you think of this skirt?"	"Um, they came in a boat, I don't remember
"Oh it's real neat, it looks real good on you"	much."
who cares	(the manager shakes her head)
"Where are you from?"	I want to take the girl's face in my hands
She is wearing blue nail polish	and kiss her on the forehead
"Cincinnati"	I am in another world
"I mean your parents"	from this American teenager
"Oh. Vietnam"	She has her agenda
A silent slow motion bomb goes off in my head	which includes chewing gum
I want to cry.	maroon lipstick
the fortyish woman store manager flies over to us	and a look of distraction
"Oh my god are you who I think you are?"	the years pass

these are my feelings . . .

– J.B., 1998

manufacture and distribute Pepsi-Cola in the U.S.S.R. The following April, this deal will be expanded into a soda-for-vodka swap, bringing Stolichnaya vodka to American drinkers.

22 The U.S. Navy reveals it has spent over $375,000 studying the aerodynamic qualities of the Frisbee.

24 One of the Seventies' first rock TV series, *In Concert*, produced by impresario Don Kirshner, premieres on ABC, with a lineup including the Allman Brothers Band, Chuck Berry, Alice Cooper and Poco.

1972 DECEMBER

4 Judge John Sirica begins hearing pretrial motions on the Watergate criminal trial, stating that the political aspect of the break-in will be germane.

7 *Apollo 17* blasts off, carrying the last two men to walk on the moon: Capt. Eugene Cernan and Dr. Harrison Schmitt.

8 Citing an inexcusable delay between the seating of the jury and the start of actual court proceedings, the judge in the Pentagon Papers trial in Los Angeles declares a mistrial.

9 Top of the charts: Helen Reddy's "I Am Woman" (pop single); the Moody Blues' *Seventh Sojourn* (pop album).

The first attempt at staging the Who's rock opera *Tommy*, featuring various roles played by all four members of the band plus Rod Stewart, Steve Winwood, Peter Sellers, Ringo Starr and others, is critically panned.

12 The existence of a White House operation known as "the Plumbers," of which the Watergate break-in may have been a part, is confirmed by an administration spokesperson, though E. Howard Hunt's involvement is denied.

Producer Irwin Allen brings *The Poseidon Adventure* to the big screen, establishing the Seventies' successful disaster-movie formula.

16 A day after the heaviest bombing raids of the war, Kissinger admits that his attempts at the Paris Peace Talks have failed, blaming North Vietnam for the stalled negotiation process.

Becoming the first-ever NFL team to remain undefeated and untied through a regular season, the Miami Dolphins shut out the Baltimore Colts, 16–0.

this precious right
by susan brownmiller

SOME OF US remember exactly where we were on January 22, 1973, when the *Roe* v. *Wade* decision came down. Sarah Weddington, in Austin, took an urgent call from a Washington reporter. Stunned by the enormous breadth of the Supreme Court ruling, *Roe*'s lead counsel, a few years out of law school, exclaimed that it was "a great victory for women in Texas." Norma McCorvey, her hard-luck plaintiff, read the news in Dallas. Two decades away from her religious conversion, she pridefully boasted to her female lover, "How would you like to meet Jane Roe?"

Madeline Schwenk, a Chicago housewife and mother of three children, repaired to a Magic Pan and got smashed on crepes and champagne. Arrested the previous May, Schwenk was awaiting trial with six friends for performing illegal abortions in "Jane," the feminist underground service. "I was laughing and crying," she recalls. "*Roe* meant I wouldn't be going to jail." At Mother Courage, the feminist restaurant in Greenwich Village, we uncorked some bottles and had a party.

"The future looked so bright," recalls Camille Gargiso, then a student at City College. "Everything seemed possible after the *Roe* decision."

And though *Roe*'s affirmation of a woman's right to reproductive freedom is as significant to justice and equality as *Brown* v. *Board of Education* in 1954, it has been hotly debated and systematically chipped away at ever since 1973, the voodoo doll of right-wing religious fanatics waving their cynical "family values" banner, while the uneven march toward human equality remains unfinished business for the Twenty-first Century.

My abortions, numbering three, were in the pre-*Roe* Sixties; that is, they were secret criminal acts driven by desperation and a reckless trust in the unknown. One image will suffice: A solitary young woman with not enough money in her pocket clutches a scrap of paper. She is in a Spanish-speaking city, in an unfamiliar neighborhood, and she does not know the language. When the gringa finds the shuttered house she is looking for she pounds on the door and cries, for this address is her last hope. A window opens and slams shut. Somebody opens the door. Ten minutes later she breathes deeply into the anesthetic, her life becomes her own again, and she will never learn her savior's name.

In September 1968, after the third of my secret trips, I walked into a meeting of Women's Liberation in New York and listened to women in blue jeans speak openly and bravely of their attempts to end unwanted pregnancies. Not every story concluded, as mine had, with an expert practitioner and a sound medical success. That transforming evening, the kind that makes you a feminist forever, was repeated in public at the Washington Square Methodist Church on March 21, 1969. The sponsoring group was called Redstockings, and my report on the speak-out appeared on page one of the *Village Voice*.

The feminist campaign to legalize abortion was built around a simple, breathtaking principle: "A woman has a right to control her own body." It was a slogan first employed by Patricia Maginnis, who ran a pioneering illegal referral service in California. Simultaneously with the feminist mobilization, a cautious movement of concerned doctors, lawyers and clergy coalesced into NARAL, then the National Association for Repeal of Abortion Laws, but it was the young feminists' creative juggernaut of impudent actions that set the campaign afire. Public speak-outs. Disruptions of legislative hearings. Mass rallies and marches. KEEP YOUR HANDS OFF MY UTERUS. FREE ABORTION ON DEMAND. Counseling hot lines and referral services not only flouted the law, but a few of the "Jane" women in Chicago actually became trained practitioners, ably performing low-cost abortions themselves. Elsewhere, small groups experimented with "menstrual extraction," a technique developed in Los Angeles by

Lorraine Rothman and Carole Downer that could clean out the uterus in the first month of conception with a small plastic cannula, drip pot and syringe.

On the legal front the most innovative approach began with Nancy Stearns, a lawyer with the Center for Constitutional Rights in New York. In October 1969 Stearns filed a class-action suit in federal district court that sought to overturn New York's antiabortion statutes on behalf of the state's women. (Her co-attorneys were Diane Schulder and Flo Kennedy.) Feminists in New Jersey, Connecticut, Pennsylvania and Michigan quickly adopted the class-action strategy, gathering thousands of named plaintiffs and engaging the media by conducting public depositions and courthouse rallies.

Numerous political strategies were employed during the four hectic years prior to *Roe*, and no one could say at the outset which approach would triumph. With hindsight, I believe a combination of strategies led to the court's decision. The Clergy Consultation Service, begun by Howard Moody at the Judson Memorial Church in Greenwich Village, added tremendous moral stature to the illegal referral networks. The lobby-the-state-legislature approach favored by Larry Lader of NARAL achieved some early, impressive victories – until elected representatives learned the hard way that a vote for abortion rights could end a politician's career.

In April 1970 New York became the second state, after Hawaii, to go legal. Two weeks later Alaska came through. Voters going to the polls in Washington State that November overwhelmingly endorsed a proabortion referendum. Initially proposed as a humanitarian health-care issue, Referendum 20 gathered its energy and positive force after Seattle Women's Liberation reframed the campaign as "Abortion Is a Woman's Right." Barbara Winslow, a historian, believes the wire coat hanger signifying a botched illegal abortion first appeared on placards in Washington State.

Roe in Texas, Sarah Weddington's case, was an early starter, a single-plaintiff suit filed in March 1970 and later amended to be a class action. The idea began percolating at the University of Texas in Austin when the Women's Liberation Birth Control Center proposed to sue the state for driving its activists into illegal work. Linda Coffee, the Dallas lawyer Weddington brought in as cocounsel, gave the Texas statutes a close reading and scotched that first plan. In order to have "legal standing," the plaintiff, in Coffee's opinion, needed to be a pregnant woman who had tried unsuccessfully to get an abortion via a legal route. A friend of hers who handled adoptions came up with McCorvey. Four months pregnant and living the hippie life on the streets when she met the two lawyers at a Dallas pizza parlor, Norma "Pixie" McCorvey, age twenty-one, had brought two unwanted children into the world already. She was too far gone for a first-trimester termination, the standard recourse on the illegal circuit.

Along with *Doe* in Georgia, another single-plaintiff suit, *Roe* moved swiftly through the appellate process, faring better than the multiple-plaintiff class actions, which were foundering on the shoals of "legal standing," just as Linda Coffee had predicted. The lower courts did not look favorably on a mixed bag of claimants – women who had been unable to secure abortions, women who had resorted to illegal abortions, women who were not pregnant but were claiming the right to obtain an abortion at some future time.

In 1972 the *Women's Rights Law Reporter* compiled a list of suits in twenty-nine states and the District of Columbia. Many were slowly climbing the appellate ladder. In addition to the outright feminist cases with their thousands of named plaintiffs, the *Reporter* noted the appeals of doctors convicted of performing illegal abortions, the challenges by doctors claiming their medical, humanitarian and privacy rights to perform abortions, and the suits by referral services run by clergy and some YWCAs claiming their moral and humanitarian right to function within the law.

Faced with a cornucopia of diverse cases clamoring for review, the Supreme Court could pick with care. Judicially speaking, the *Roe* and *Doe* suits were uncomplicated, clean. Each rested on one unfortunate pregnant woman with limited resources and a hard-luck story who had tried but failed to obtain a medical remedy under her state's laws. (The Georgia law was considered more liberal than the one in Texas, but a hospital quota system hadn't helped "Mary Doe.")

If Justice William O. Douglas had gotten his way, the *Roe* decision would have come thirteen months earlier than it did, after Sarah Weddington's first go-round on the oral arguments in December 1971. Douglas had the votes and was itching to write the majority opinion, but Chief Justice Warren Burger threw the assignment to Harry Blackmun, a slow writer who did not relish charting new paths for the law. Blackmun asked for more time. *Roe* and *Doe* were held over and reargued in the next calendar term. An additional year of the national groundswell not only stiffened Blackmun's spine, it tipped Lewis Powell, a new Nixon appointee, into the affirmative column. At the eleventh hour the Chief joined the majority, making the monumental decision seven to two.

Roe was astonishing news, even though it was eclipsed in the headlines by the death of Lyndon Baines Johnson. A militant four-year campaign had altered public perceptions to such an extent that a medical procedure the law had defined as a crime for more than a century was transformed by court dictum into a woman's constitutional right.

Precious rights do not come like diamonds with guarantees of "forever." Few celebrants of *Roe* could have imagined the next quarter-century of constant vigilance and depressing retreat. The defensive actions required to maintain reproductive freedom have worn down many of the original militants, while younger women often take their given rights for granted. A personal stake in the outcome breathes urgency into any political struggle. Hey there, my sisters of reproductive age, the next century's battle is yours. ⊕

the war comes home
by david harris

AS FAR AS I'M CONCERNED, the Seventies didn't really begin until 1973, when the Paris peace agreement was signed and the last American military forces were withdrawn from Vietnam. The war there amounted to a decade unto itself, and no new decade could truly begin until the war ended. Even in 1973, more than two years of carnage was still to come, a period in which the United States would arm and finance its Vietnamese surrogates. But henceforth, Americans would stay behind the scenes in Saigon and do no more of the dying out in the tall grass – an arrangement that passed for "peace at hand" back in the United States. I was in California and heard the news from Paris on the radio. My response was a state of numb anticlimax. The longest decade in American history was finally over, and there wasn't much left to feel about it. It had been that kind of war.

Most of the war's survivors fled into the Seventies and didn't look back, hoping to forget the previous decade. Avoidance was not, however, a universal option. I began the Seventies by giving up political organizing after ten years of doing nothing else and looked for a job in journalism. By the time the last prisoners of war were passed back into American hands, I was on my first assignment for ROLLING STONE, interviewing former Marine Sergeant Ron Kovic, who'd returned home five years earlier, bound to a wheelchair for the rest of his life, his spinal cord having been severed by an AK-47 round. I'd sold the story to ROLLING STONE as my chance for a last word on the vets' homecoming. Kovic said, "A war ain't over until you don't have to live with it anymore," providing not only a last word but, perhaps, the first mantra of the new decade.

More than two thousand Vietnam veterans participate in nonviolent demonstrations at the U.S. Capitol, April 21, 1971: At right: VVAW members carry toy guns; following page: Vets gather on the Mall while Congressmen address their efforts to bring all the soldiers home

These warriors, whose final return jump-started the Seventies, went on to spend the new decade as the ongoing symbols of the nightmare in our immediate past, though it took a while for that stereotype to stick. At first, they were simply ignored. Soldiers were coming home from 1964 on, but no one threw them any parades, and few paid them much regard. They just dribbled in, one by one, full of stories no one wanted to hear, fresh from a conflict that fewer and fewer of their peers wanted anything to do with.

Initially their dissent was personal and largely isolated, often linked to a sense of obligation to their buddies who had never made it home. But as more and more disgruntled veterans found each other, many now scruffy-looking and hirsute, together they became a public voice under the banner of Vietnam Veterans Against the War.

In April 1971, members of VVAW seized the leading edge of the antiwar movement when they returned their medals, marching through Washington and flinging their combat ribbons on the steps of Congress in an act of collective disgust. I listened to live coverage of the event on the radio, driving along the old Nimitz Freeway by the San Francisco Bay. I had been released from prison two weeks earlier, after twenty months of incarceration for refusing to obey orders to report for the war. When the medals flew, I started crying and had to pull onto the shoulder for a while.

The VVAW march finally broke the government's exclusive claim that its administration represented and spoke for soldiers. For the rest of the war, VVAW carried on its case against the government. Sergeant Ron Kovic gained brief national attention when he invaded the 1972 Republican convention in Miami Beach, but by then Richard Nixon had long since concluded that veterans posed a political threat he had to counteract. One of the White House's numerous covert "dirty tricks" teams (a practice that would help bring about Nixon's resignation) was first used to spy on and disrupt the VVAW. A number of the veterans who had organized the demonstrations around the

of heroin addiction; performances feature Townshend, Ron Wood, Steve Winwood and Rick Grech.

14 The Miami Dolphins defeat the Washington Redskins, 14–7, in Super Bowl VII, after a perfect 16–0 season.

Elvis Presley's live performance at the Honolulu International Center Arena captures the largest TV audience to date; the concert is later released as a double LP and becomes his last #1 album.

Glam star Gary Glitter celebrates six months of success with his new moniker by discarding photos, records, tapes and other mementos of his past stage personae – skiffle bandleader Paul Russell and rocker Paul Raven – into the Thames River in London.

16 The Soviet eight-wheeled remote lunar probe *Lunokhod 2* lands and explores the moon's surface.

Steve Carlton signs a one-year, $167,000 contract with the Philadelphia Phillies and becomes professional baseball's highest-paid pitcher.

17 Daniel Ellsberg and Anthony Russo again face charges for leaking state secrets as the second Pentagon Papers trial opens.

18 The Rolling Stones raise more than $400,000 for Nicaraguan earthquake victims with a special benefit concert at the L.A. Forum. Nearly 19,000 fans catch the Stones and openers Cheech & Chong and Santana.

22 In the landmark *Roe* v. *Wade* decision, the Supreme Court rules that no state may prevent a woman from having an abortion during the first three months of pregnancy. Within three weeks, the National Council of Catholic Bishops warns that any Catholic woman undergoing an abortion will immediately face excommunication.

Heavyweight champion Joe Frazier loses the title to George Foreman in a second-round TKO in Kingston, Jamaica.

Former president Lyndon B. Johnson dies of a heart attack in Johnson City, TX.

23 Legendary New Orleans jazz trombonist Edward "Kid" Ory dies.

President Nixon announces that the Paris Peace Talks have yielded an agreement between Henry Kissinger and

convention Kovic invaded were arrested by the federal government and booked on conspiracy-to-riot charges. I covered their August 1973 trial for ROLLING STONE as well. The alleged VVAW ringleader, former Marine Sergeant Scott Camil, talked with me about the crimes the government was *not* charging him with: From atop a railroad trestle, his platoon had shot everyone who moved in the village below; on another occasion, he had personally blown an unarmed woman's brains out when she tried to conceal a fleeing Viet Cong. He said he would willingly plead guilty to those war crimes, but he couldn't find any court willing to charge him. As for the conspiracy, the jury acquitted Camil and the seven other defendants.

Despite their peacemaking role, Vietnam veterans began the new decade subsumed under the sway of dark images attached to the war itself. The public at large knew few veterans, but they knew all about the war itself and were largely unable to separate it from the warriors who had been sent to carry it out. Hollywood did little to dispel the cloudy, threatening image of the returning veteran. In 1974 alone, TV detectives on *Mannix, Cannon, Columbo, The Streets of San Francisco* and *Hawaii Five-0* had their hands full in at least one episode with the "good boy gone bad," twisted by battle and/or drugs.

In truth, the war had been a bloody enterprise and its veterans were often assumed to be dangerous, but such character traits were hardly widespread among the soldiers once they returned stateside. Most of the more than three million men and women posted in Southeast Asia during the previous decade had disappeared into the larger social morass with hardly a ripple.

According to a *Washington Post*–ABC News poll taken on the tenth anniversary of the war's end, 30 percent of veterans of the Vietnam theater, combat and otherwise, had gone on to college, 78 percent owned their own homes, 43 percent considered themselves middle class and 70 percent voted Republican. Little of that America informed the veterans' Seventies stereotype, though – largely because of some veterans' very visible association with two of the decade's flagship issues. And in the light that those issues cast, the young men who returned from fighting among the rice paddies by the South China Sea seemed both the ghosts of an unwelcome past and the harbingers of a future far scarier than that for which we had hoped.

The first issue was drug abuse. The trickle that became a tidal wave of hard-core addiction inundating American neighborhoods, schools and social institutions began in Vietnam, before the troops even came home. In 'Nam, the drug of choice was heroin: grown as opium in the "Golden Triangle" where Thailand, Laos and Burma came together; flown south by the Central Intelligence Agency–fronted airline Air America; refined in Laos by a general in the army of America's principal Laotian allies and distributed in Vietnam by high-ranking members of the Army of the Republic of Vietnam. For the last two years before the American Army withdrew, 80 to 99 percent pure number-four-grade smack was available from dozens of outlets around every permanent American base or along the roads connecting bases. Soldiers used it to treat the pain of having their lives dangled over an abyss ten thousand miles from home with nothing to show for those who fell in. In 1971, army medical officers estimated that 10 to 15 percent of lower-ranking soldiers – 25,000 to 37,000 people – were consuming number four on a regular basis. When those soldiers went home to the streets of America to chase their habit, they were the Seventies' first clear signal that what constituted pursuing "drugs" had escalated from a relatively harmless use of psychedelics to a far more heavy-metal social tryst.

The other Seventies issue attached to the returning veterans was a new, more pernicious from of shell shock, the twisted public reenactment of a past that would not go away when they were confronted by a present they could not master. Just as Kovic had predicted, the war was not easy to end. Early in the decade, several very visible incidents occurred featuring armed and disoriented veterans set off by such commonplace stimuli as car backfires (that sounded like AK-47 rounds) or Caterpillar trucks (that sounded like armored personnel carriers advancing over Vietnamese red dirt, hard as concrete during those last weeks before the monsoon set in). The echo would send a vet reeling back in time, to a firefight somewhere out in the rice paddies, while he was actually standing in a strip mall or housing project. I reported on one former sniper who went up on a hill in Los Angeles's Griffith Park with a rifle and was finally forced to surrender to the police after

a standoff of several hours. The media coverage of this incident and similar segments on the evening news effectively strapped signs that read DANGEROUS around Vietnam veterans' necks for the rest of the decade.

Ironically, the eventual diagnosis of those freak-outs, and a far larger number of similar but less dramatic regressions, led to a psychiatric breakthrough that was perhaps the closest thing to American self-realization the Seventies ever achieved. This condition was labeled post-traumatic stress disorder. It assumes that some experiences are far too intense to be assimilated when they occur, and that one's need to survive the immediate traumatic moment forces a suppression of an inevitable need to come to grips with the experience. If that intense experience remains unassimilated after the fact, obstructed by avoidance and denial, it often breaks to the surface again as a spontaneous recurrence of the emotions of the original circumstance, if not as a full-blown hallucination.

PTSD not only provided a framework for treating those men stuck in time, but also served as a metaphor for the era. Despite widespread avoidance, our trauma was inescapable, and the Seventies were shadowed throughout by the war

America had just managed to survive. Its emblem was always those poor boys who had grown old too soon and come home too late to do anything about it. Now, of course, they are no longer boys, and the traits the Seventies credited to them have long since become commonplace among all the constituencies of American life. But their trauma – and America's – still echoes.

For most of that new decade, I lived in a house in Menlo Park, California, around the corner from a Veterans Administration psychiatric treatment facility. I often crossed paths with the outpatients at the neighborhood grocery store, where both they and I would stop to buy cigarettes. Occasionally, one of them would bum a smoke off me. I got to know Leroy that way. He was at the store a lot. He'd been a Spec. 4 with the 1st Air Cavalry, liked $1.50-a-quart burgundy and smoked Camels. We got so we would banter whenever we encountered each other, always in more or less the same way.

"What's up, Leroy my man?"

"Same old same old."

"Sing me a few bars," I said.

"Jes' like always," Leroy answered. "They's somewhere out there in the trees and we's stuck out here in the middle with no motherfuckin' place to hide." ⊕

discotheque to discomania
by david ritz

I MARK 1973 as the year when the music came into its own. I walked into the Plantation, a gay disco in Dallas, and heard three Barry White songs within a half hour – "I'm Gonna Love You Just a Little More Baby," "I've Got So Much to Give" and "Never, Never Gonna Give You Up." That was enough; disco had a name, beat and attitude all its own. The swirling strings and busy bass, the desperate demand to go higher and higher, the stress on celebration, the breakdown of boundaries – it all seemed too good to be true. And it was. Except no one knew that then. Or wanted to know. If political liberation was a theme of the Sixties, sexual freedom was a cry of the Seventies in the glib lyrics of songs that became simpler and simpler, songs to get you dancing and songs to get you fucking. Dancing and fucking were never so closely aligned. With its humping and bumping, basses and booties, the moment of Dionysiac glory had arrived.

Two other moments linger in my mind – one anticipating the start of the era, the other signaling its end.

Rome, the winter of 1967. My fiancée and I lived in the shadow of the Roman ruins on a cobblestone street called Via Baccina. Walking home at midnight, I was transported back in time. This was the heart of the ancient empire. Suddenly the mood was broken by the sound of a boogie from below. The groove was hot, the bass pumping. I looked around, didn't see the source, but followed the beat until it brought me to a window that looked into a basement. Now the music was in my face, Gladys Knight and the Pips' recording of "I Heard It Through the Grapevine." I saw a small room filled with dancers drenched in sweat, booty-to-booty, frantic, ecstatic. The place smacked of exclusivity; the revelers were elegantly attired. Someone threw a bucket of water on them, and they screamed appreciatively. The exuberance was irresistible. When one of the dancers left, I asked what kind of place this was. *"Una discoteca,"* he said. When I tried to get in, some lug stopped me. Welcome to the Disco Era.

San Francisco, the summer of 1979. I was assisting Marvin Gaye with an autobiography that would never be written. After one of his concerts, we wound up in a disco. Michael Jackson's just-released "Off the Wall" was booming from the speakers. When Marvin's presence was noticed, the DJ switched to "Got to Give It Up," Gaye's 1977 hit and his only nod to disco. "Call it antidisco," said Marvin. "I wrote it as a joke because I wanted to make my disco statement before disco died out. I wanted to tell the world I'm afraid of dancing because I'm a lousy dancer. I say fuck disco; long live art."

Marvin articulated the terms of the argument that rages on whenever disco is discussed. Was it artful entertainment or artless crap? It's tough coming up with an answer outside the context of the Seventies. But it's tougher still when you consider disco in relation to the Seventies, that decade of confusing, exhilarating, heartbreaking hedonism. The Seventies' instant gratification, of course, was a reaction to the Sixties' flowering idealism, which, in turn, was a reaction to the Fifties' stifling conformity. American culture, driven by the genius of populism and the machinery of hype, produces a peculiar mix of junk and jewels. Never was that truer than during the decade of discomania, when everyone from Ray Charles to the Rolling Stones tried jumping on the disco bandwagon. The range of quality was startling. From the heights of Alicia Bridges's "I Love the Nightlife" to the depths of Rick Dees's "Disco Duck," disco defined the pop culture of the decade.

In the Seventies, when soul, thanks to Isaac Hayes and Sly and the Family Stone, went symphonic as well as psychedelic, the stage was set for disco. In some basic sense, disco can be seen as souped-up rhythm & blues. Like all dance music, disco was born in the rhythm section. Back in the Sixties, the musical rapport between Motown drummer Benny Benjamin and bassist Jamie Jamerson generated an intoxicatingly soaring dance beat (listen to the Four Tops). A half-generation later, the Sigma Sound Studios house band in Philadelphia, employed by producers Kenny Gamble and Leon Huff

and featuring drummer Earl Young, bassist Ronnie Baker and guitarist Norman Harris, raised the stakes (listen to the O'Jays). The Detroit string sections seem modest compared to the setup in Philly, where forty-two-piece orchestras were far from uncommon. Philly got the message around the same time Barry White was blasting off in L.A.: The funk had to fly.

Disco might have been flighty, but it was rooted in something real, in a place more than a sound. Some credit film director Roger Vadim for coining the term *discotheque* (a spin on *cinematheque*) to characterize a club where dancers dance to records, not live bands. The absence of living musicians and the dominance of a machine contributed to disco's edgy character. Mechanization was sexy. When James Brown, Godfather of Soul, took on disco, he rerecorded his "Sex Machine." The metaphor was apt. The hump-and-bump, generated by inexhaustible electricity, was now superhuman.

The fact that disco describes a place also explains why the music is visual, why we see it as clearly as we hear it. Listen to Barry White's Love Unlimited Orchestra playing "Love's Theme" and you'll probably start seeing scenes like the one I saw in Rome. White himself explained it a few years back. "Disco was beautiful," he told me, "because it made the consumer beautiful. The consumer was the star. Disco was about elegance. The consumer was superelegant and that's how I wanted the music. The elegant people wanted to dance to elegant music."

That note of idealism in Maestro White's delineation is especially telling; disco, after all, was the most idealized expression of our pop culture. Disco replaced the antimaterialistic stance of the hippies with the hypermaterialistic attitude of show business. Sly said it first: "Everybody Is a Star," and stars never die. The dance never ends; there exist only beautiful dancers dancing themselves into a frenzy on a dance floor, where reality and even (or especially) death is drowned out by the reassurance of a party that lives forever.

If disco synthesized the soul of the Sixties, it also sexualized that same soul (listen to Musique's "In the Bush" or Peaches and Herb's "Shake Your Groove Thing"). Sixties Motown was characterized by a certain innocence – think of the Supremes and Smokey Robinson. And Sixties Stax-Volt/Atlantic records were often marked by racial-political undertones – think of Aretha's "Respect" and Sam and Dave's "Soul Man." But the disco was a place where innocence was lost and politics were strictly sexual. You could say gay liberation was born in the discos and/or that the discos gave birth to gay liberation.

Flights of romantic fancy on the dance floor hark back to the Jazz Age of the Twenties, when liberation, exemplified by the Charleston, was also expressed by kicking up your feet. The big difference, of course, is that those kicking up their feet in the trendy discos of the Seventies included blacks and gays. Groups on the margins of society were boogying their way into the mainstream, a horny media hot on their heels. The fullest expression of that mainstreaming came in 1977 with the phenomenal success of the film *Saturday Night Fever*, the subject matter and soundtrack of which were devoted to disco. The distinction here is that our disco hero was neither gay nor black; he was John Travolta playing Tony Manero, a working-class white boy from Brooklyn. The message was clear: Real men disco, too. Thanks to the charm of Travolta's performance and the irresistibility of the Bee Gees' fabulous suite of songs, disco was suddenly as American as Mickey Mouse.

Like the decade it mirrored, disco could be illuminating and obnoxious all at once. It was as formulaic as it was creative. Often a droning drum machine was the star of the song, not the singer. Yet disco produced a wealth of wonderful singers – most notably Donna Summer, whose powerful voice and singular style rank her among the most divine divas of any decade. Others, like Sylvester, who dressed like a woman and sang like an angel, were able to infuse the form with the spirit of good-news gospel. Hedonism was sometimes offset by optimism – witness Gloria Gaynor's "I Will Survive" and McFadden and Whitehead's "Ain't No Stopping Us Now." Certain dance ditties ignited full-blown crazes, like Van McCoy's "The Hustle." And several enduring disco hits – Thelma Houston's "Don't Leave Me This Way" and Candi Staton's "Young Hearts Run Free" – carried messages that deepened the genre.

The genre also enjoyed a number of master producers. Donna Summer's team of Giorgio Moroder and Pete Bellotte employed an arranging style that was basically baroque; their brilliant orchestrations were little symphonies. Nile Rodgers and Bernard Edwards went the other way, introducing a unique brand of minimalism. Their most effective instrument was their own group, Chic, whose elegant, easy-loping grooves, along with streamlined lyrics, copped a mock-aristocratic attitude. "Le Freak" and "Good Times" displayed rhythmic subtlety that propelled the duo into the vanguard of disco innovators.

By the time the Village People hit in 1978, disco was ripe for parody. The fact that they packaged themselves as homo-

culture absorbs and profits from the radical. In the process, the radical becomes routine. That's the frustrating genius of the American Way. Disco began as a dangerous threat to the status quo, only to become the status quo.

They say disco died, but I don't see it that way. Disco songs, with disco grooves and disco lyrics, are still in the air. Disco-only radio stations prosper in the major markets. And starting with the Sugar Hill Gang's "Rapper's Delight" (which was founded on the grooves of Chic's "Good Times"), rap has borrowed disco's energy and rhythms from the get-go.

erotic comic book heroes only added to their appeal. Their put-on productions like "Y.M.C.A." became monster hits. At virtually the same moment some publicity-hungry DJ was burning disco records at Comiskey Park in Chicago, the Village People were selling their self-mocking humor to Main Street, USA. From forbidden fruit to the ultimate in family entertainment – this is the path traveled by disco.

This is the path traveled by virtually all outside elements of American pop, so why should disco be different? Our culture embraces rather than rejects the rebellious. Our

The Age of Disco expired, but disco itself was transmogrified into a half-dozen other genres – house and hip-hop, trip-hop and, most obviously, pure pop. Just as surely as disco borrowed from our pop-culture past, disco continues to inform our pop-culture future. Disco did its job: It delighted dancers. And disco brought the nation's attention to revelers who had been previously shut out of the national party. That party has been permanently enlarged, with no small thanks to the persuasive charm of a music fueled by the passion of the human spirit to sing, to soar, to dance our cares away. ⊕

russell means on the siege of wounded knee

AS PEDRO BISSONETTE, vice president of the Oglala Sioux Civil Rights Organization, and I drove into the village of Wounded Knee on the Sioux Indian Pine Ridge Reservation in South Dakota on the night of February 27, 1973, we were at the end of a long line of almost two hundred automobiles. On a clear, starlit night that seemed unusually warm, we drove around the line of cars and went straight for the trading post. We were both lost in our thoughts. During those moments, I could still hear the words of the tradi-tional chiefs of my Oglala Lakota (Sioux) Nation, spoken earlier that fateful day.

Chief Fools Crow had told us, "Go to Wounded Knee. There you will be protected." I knew what he meant. In the frigid winter of 1890, the U.S. Army had brutally mur-dered Chief Big Foot and over three hundred of my people. Now that ground was con-secrated, and the spirits of our ancestors would protect us as we made our stand against the U.S. government once again.

I remembered how the Oglala chiefs had recently listened to their people's anguished pleas and descriptions of oppression, repression and suppression at the hands of the fed-eral government's puppet tribal government. Women and girls had been raped. Men jailed. Money and valuables extorted. Homes firebombed. I now realized a critical mass had been achieved. The Lakotas were ready to die, if necessary, to end nearly one hundred years of deceit and abuse at the hands of the U.S. government. We were tak-ing back our freedom one foot at a time, one community at a time, one reservation at a time, and it was going to start right now.

Arriving in darkness, the three hundred Lakotas and the two dozen veterans of the American Indian Movement (AIM) began to dig in around the Wounded Knee museum and general store. I started to direct the defense from the high point at the Catholic church, asking those who were Vietnam veterans to take charge of our defenses and establish roadblocks and patrols in the hills around us. All we had were a few hunting rifles and the integri-ty and moral force of a thousand generations of our ancestors. The cavalry would be arriving again momentarily, and we needed to be ready for them.

Day Four of the siege of Wounded Knee, South Dakota, on March 3, 1973: Oglala Sioux Indians fly the American flag upside-down on the spot where cavalry guns massacred their ancestors in 1890

Our goals were threefold: enforcement of the 1868 Fort Laramie Treaty, which guaranteed our nation's territories and sovereignty; Senate investigations of corruption within the Bureau of Indian Affairs; and free, honest elections on the local Pine Ridge Reservation.

We were also hoping that our stand would inspire other American Indians and other Americans in general to continue their struggles for freedom. For the past decade, led by the black liberation struggle, a wide range of movements – the youth at UC-Berkeley, the peace movement, the women's liberation struggle, the environmentalists – were demonstrating for their respective causes. It had been an exhilarating time in America, but a time that had been totally misunderstood by the people who considered themselves the guardians of freedom, the conservatives on the right of the political spectrum.

I failed to sleep much that first night, knowing what awaited us. As dawn approached, the radio began to report what was happening. We had taken white people hostage, and one had escaped (in reality, one of the local merchants had abandoned his wife and small children when he realized the Indians were coming to repossess their community, so he invented the hostage story to conceal his cowardice). The radio also reported – accurately – that the Feds were mobilizing, and would soon surround Wounded Knee.

Our breath could be seen in the freezing dawn light while I stood with Severt Young Bear and Edgar Bear Runner and said, "We probably won't get out of this alive." Edgar agreed and Severt added, "Just like our ancestors."

At that moment, I realized we would be forced to defend Wounded Knee to the death. Judging by their past actions, we were convinced the U.S. government would not

BATTERY
HOTCHKISS GUNS
Bet. 1st Field Artillery
Capt. Allyn Capron

Wounded Knee demonstrators and in protest of Hollywood's portrayal of Indians.

29 North Vietnam completes U.S. POW repatriation, and the last U.S. combat forces depart South Vietnam; bombing of Communist positions in Cambodia and skirmishes between North and South Vietnam continue. From Jan. 1, 1961, through March 1973, 45,997 U.S. forces were killed in combat in Vietnam, 303,640 were wounded and 10,928 lost their lives in noncombatant incidents.

Dr. Hook and the Medicine Show realize their dream to appear on "the cover of the Rolling Stone" and, true to the lyrics of their Top-10 hit, send five copies to their mothers.

31 Muhammad Ali is defeated by unknown Ken Norton in 12 rounds in San Diego.

1973 APRIL

3 Soviet scientists launch space lab *Salyut 2* into orbit; the U.S. deep-space probe *Pioneer 11* blasts off for Jupiter two days later.

6 The Smothers Brothers win their much-watched four-year legal battle with CBS over their canceled variety show, and are awarded $776,300 in damages.

7 Wounded Knee fighters reach a cease-fire, as Russell Means and Sioux representatives meet with White House officials in Washington, DC. Unfortunately, the talks produce no significant results: The siege continues until May 8, with two men – an American Indian and a Vietnam Veteran – becoming fatalities of the 71-day standoff.

8 Pablo Picasso, the most influential artist of the modern era, dies.

23 President Nixon allows his staff to testify before the Watergate Committee, and former attorney general John Mitchell admits that he knew of political espionage, but not specific bugging operations. The *Washington Post* reveals Nixon's knowledge of his staff's involvement from as early as Dec. 1972.

26 ROLLING STONE reports that Roberta Flack's chart-topper "Killing Me Softly With His Song" was inspired by a live performance by folk-rocker Don McLean. A few weeks earlier, ROLLING STONE had revealed the man behind Carly Simon's less-than-

negotiate our demands. As we stood there, lost in our emotions of the moment, I began to pray to die a good death for my children and my people.

Soon the FBI's agent in charge arrived at one of our roadblocks. Pedro Bissonette, Vern Long, president of the Oglala Sioux Civil Rights Organization, and I took our demands to him. As we walked back toward our forces at Wounded Knee, he yelled, "Who do you think you are? You're in a fishbowl. Don't you understand? We can wipe you out!" With that hard-line response began the most protracted and intense confrontation between American Indians and the United States government since the end of the Indian Wars in 1890.

For seventy-one days, through three blizzards and more than five million rounds of ammunition expended by the Feds, we experienced a freedom we had not known for a century and have not known since. This wasn't the pseudo-freedom of America that gets bandied about every Fourth of July or during political campaign sloganeering. This was the real, no-holds-barred freedom my ancestors had known before we were corralled into the U.S.-run concentration camps known as Indian reservations.

The media came from all over the globe to report on this armed insurrection by a group of people the U.S. government would have the world believe were safely pacified and out of sight, out of mind. All three major broadcast networks arrived, at times with three entire crews each, to cover the events outside and inside Wounded Knee. The added impact of the print media inside the "Knee" and the intense media coverage in general were some of the major reasons we did not suffer the same fate as our ancestors.

During the Seventies, Wounded Knee proved to be the third most photographed event of that era, surpassed only by the Vietnam War and Watergate. In a poll taken among Americans during the siege, 93 percent were aware of the events at Wounded Knee while only 78 percent knew Spiro Agnew was the vice president of the country.

The siege lasted until May 8. Firefights and skirmishes abounded during that time. To make our limited firepower appear more impressive, we would take our one Kalashnikov AK-47 – with its distinctive and respected bark – and periodically run it from bunker to bunker, shooting off a quick burst at each spot. Then we would paint a length of stovepipe and allow the press to stumble across what appeared to be a rocket launcher or bazooka.

Heroes were made, and discoveries, too. Oscar Bear Runner, a World War II veteran in his mid-fifties, backpacked through the federal lines to bring in needed supplies. Two brave pilots – Bill Zimmerman and Rocky Madrid – flew planes with painted-over identification numbers, dodging sniper bullets to bring in medicine, food and ammunition.

The local Wounded Knee museum – which became our security headquarters – was filled with dug-up remnants from the 1890 Indian massacre and held an accounting record of livestock delivered by the cavalry. The book, written by the captain in charge of the deliveries, had made up the most racist, disgusting, vile names for the Indians – "Shits in His Food," "She Comes Nine Times," "Maggot Dick." We burnt the book.

We emerged from the siege at Wounded Knee with two American Indian patriots dead by sniper fire – Frank Clearwater and Buddy Lamont, a Vietnam vet – and fifteen wounded. More than six hundred were arrested in Wounded Knee – or en route to the siege – and faced multiple federal charges. In the end, not one person, black, brown, red, yellow or white, was convicted on any of the original charges.

At Wounded Knee, just as our ancestors had done, we decided to end the siege by putting our faith and trust in the words and documents of the United States government. And once again, the promises given to end the siege were never honored. How could we have foreseen that those we demanded to negotiate with in the White House – Domestic Council Chief John Ehrlichman, White House Chief of Staff H.R. Haldeman, Presidential Counsel John W. Dean III and Attorney General John Mitchell – would end up in prison and the hundreds of fighters at Wounded Knee would not? Now *that* is spiritual power!

Within three years of the siege and the ensuing court trials, AIM and our Chicano support organizations suffered from dozens and dozens of assassinations, with sixty-three deaths (including that of Pedro Bissonette) on the Pine Ridge Reservation alone. No arrests, no convictions and only cursory investigations, if any, were conducted by the FBI, our national police. In *Incident at Oglala: The Leonard Peltier Story*, a Robert Redford–produced documentary shown worldwide in theaters and on television, a former Bureau of Indian Affairs police officer who served during the siege at Wounded Knee admitted the U.S. Department of Justice had trained, supplied and funded an "Indian" death squad to terrorize the people of the Pine Ridge Reservation. When it was exposed later, this proved to be the same brutal tactic employed by the CIA during the Seventies in Chile and El Salvador.

In 1973, AIM and the Black Panther Party were ideological pariahs and labeled the most dangerous groups in America by the FBI. We were the "thought criminals" of the day. The FBI had targeted the Black Panthers and the American Indian Movement for destruction through their infamous counterintelligence program COINTELPRO. We were the ones, along with all the other movements, who dared to envision a different America. Ultimately many people came to see the wisdom of our critique.

We hoped America would remember the advice of legal scholar Felix Cohen, who said the American Indian is the miner's canary for the United States and the general condition of freedom and liberty for America as a whole could be measured by its treatment of Indians. That reflection by Americans has not happened. Instead, American Indian policy has now become general American policy. Look around you.

Today, as I look across the landscape of the United States of America, the opposite of freedom prevails. Just as we had battled for freedom for our lands, we had hoped farmers and ranchers would realize they were next on America's sacrificial chopping block. Over the past three decades, family farm after family farm and ranch after ranch has been auctioned off or sharecropped out to corporations. Self-sufficiency has been replaced by dependency on a malevolent federal government, and the peoples' love of the land has been replaced by personal desperation and self-interest.

Freedom of thought has been replaced by a state-run educational system that produces docile, self-absorbed automatons that would make Orwell blush. War is peace, freedom is slavery and ignorance is strength. Instead of learning to be critical thinkers, America's youth are conditioned into an ethic of mass consumerism and corporate careerism.

Even during the siege at Wounded Knee, when I had left to meet with federal officials and then to speak at a few university campuses, I still remember the same complacency. I was making a speech at UCLA. The students were lounging about the green lawn, taking in the sun and talking among themselves, paying no attention to my words. I walked off without finishing.

Today, the thought criminals are the Branch Davidians or the Montana Freemen. In the Seventies, members of different liberation movements were called "commies," "pinkos," "kooks," "criminals" and the "fringe element." Now these same labels, along with "cultists," are freely used to isolate, marginalize and silence the modern-day thought criminals who dare to express ideas that deviate from the U.S. government's corporate mind-set.

During the siege at Wounded Knee the American Indians of North America began feeling a resurgence of dignity and pride – an immeasurable benefit that continues to this very day. Not only in North America but throughout Central and South America as well, the tiny spark of ancestral pride grew into a flame that has now spread through the entire hemisphere. American Indian people – from virtually every Indian nation in the Americas – now are demanding that the only color of people in the human race currently not allowed to sit at the table of the family of nations be recognized and respected.

American Indian peoples are walking down the corridors of the international community and have brought the rest of our indigenous families from all around our sacred Grandmother, the Earth, to join in the struggle for human dignity and peace on Earth. It's sad that the United Nations recognizes legitimate Indian organizations while the United States will not listen to any Indian voices but its puppet tribal governments.

I continue to struggle for freedom, and my people continue to revolve back toward the realities of our ancestors. But what of America? If the Indians at Wounded Knee represented Cohen's canary, then the federal-government attack on the Waco compound in 1993 proves the canary has died. One does not have to embrace the ideologies of the Branch Davidians or those of the Freemen to realize the willingness of the U.S. government to kill its own dissenting citizens, and to see a society operating without a moral compass.

Our aim at Wounded Knee was to force the U.S. government to live up to its own laws. From that, one can draw the real lesson of our stand there: It is the duty of every responsible American to ensure that their government upholds the spirit and the laws of the United States Constitution.

After all, what freedom really means is that you are free to be responsible. ⊕

who's your guru?
by richard michael levine

In the Sixties, pop icons were the leaders of the spiritual pack, the would-be answer-bearers to whom all seemed to flock. Lyrics were pondered and drugs were taken as young America began its spiritual quest. "I asked Bobby Dylan, I asked the Beatles," sang the Who in 1970's "The Seeker." "I asked Timothy Leary, but he couldn't help me either." As the Seventies arrived and the cultural stars themselves sought self-knowledge from various gurus and along Eastern, mystical paths, it became clear that if one truly wanted the truth, if one wanted answers to a decade's worth of questions, one might have to ask the specialists.

The Seventies certainly offered many possible ministers of the Way, ready to offer solace and succor to the great spiritual hunger in America. There were twists on established traditions (Jews for Jesus, various Christian communes), homegrown mystics leading extended "families" (Mel Lyman, Victor Baranco) and new (and not-so-new) arrivals from the East (Hare Krishnas, Sri Chinmoy, Meher Baba). Later in the decade, spiritual leaders would dress Buddhist practices in three-piece suits (Werner Erhard's est) and reintroduce Christianity in a mass-market, Asian manner (Reverend Sun Myung Moon).

As chanting, robed flower-givers and other proselytizers jockeyed for space on street corners, in airports and in other public places during the Seventies, the pages of ROLLING STONE filled with tales of these new messengers and prophets. This was but one of those stories.

IN THE DAMP, late autumn of 1973 it did not take a religious fanatic in a tattered overcoat to sense that the real Kingdom lay within, things being as rotten as they were without. Corruption in Washington. Mass murders in Texas and California. UFO sightings across the South. An energy crisis that threatened to turn off the Christmas lights and slow Americans down to fifty-five miles per hour. Reports that the brightest comet ever would soon trail orange clouds of cosmic dust over the whole land.

In the coffeehouses and laundromats of the North Beach section of San Francisco, where I live, aging beatniks still write *vers libre* hymns to other false endings/beginnings, and the walls are decorated with posters of the latest jet-setting gurus to arrive in town.

By far the most incongruous of those coffeehouse posters on Grant Avenue began to crop up last summer, advertising a chubby young Indian in a well-tailored, wide-lapelled suit, a sheeny Pierre Cardin tie and a huge gold wristwatch. *He* didn't look at all like the illustration on my childhood copy of the *Golden Picture Book of the Bible*. He looked like a precocious third-world account executive on the make. The banner on the poster asked, WHO IS GURU MAHARAJ JI? and who he is, according to a courteous young man tacking up one of the posters, turned out, in fact, to be the same fellow who appeared on the cover of my childhood book – although the Guru himself (good account executives knowing when to lay back) merely claimed to be the Perfect Master of our time.

The young man, a "premie," as the followers of the Guru call themselves (loosely translated from the Hindi as "lover of truth"), explained to me that Maharaj Ji was indeed a sixteen-year-old Indian kid "this time around."

Sometime during the next several months the WHO IS GURU MAHARAJ JI? posters along Grant Avenue were replaced with posters reading GURU MAHARAJ JI IS HERE AND NOW.

It was around this time that I received a press notice in the mail from the Divine Light Mission announcing – "for immediate release" – the Millennium. The rest of the flyer was equally forthright, explaining that during the three-day "world assemblage to save humanity" at the Houston Astrodome, Maharaj Ji would reveal a "practical plan" to save mankind and would kick off a thousand years of peace on Earth ("for people who want peace" – a small cop-out I ignored at the time). I could be one of tens of thousands of people attending "the most holy and significant event in human history," bearing witness to "the dawn of a New Age." Some invitations are hard to refuse, and this is why I found myself in Houston in early November, feeling a bit like a tourist lured into a shady nightclub, but sustained in some deep recess of my professional ego by the tiniest particle of hope that I was in for, well, the Perfect Scoop.

He is coming! And a couple of thousand exultant premies are waiting to receive him at William Hobby Airport outside Houston on an unseasonably muggy Texas afternoon. The crowd is uniformly young, bright-eyed and clean-cut, the men in ties and jackets, the women in long dresses, everyone wearing some kind of button depicting the Guru. I have been in Houston long enough to know that a good portion of the premies in attendance are former freaks who have only recently made the move from crash pad to ashram, that most of them have been on the usual Sixties trips and consider themselves to have arrived at the Final Destination, where they were unwittingly headed all along. When I ask one of them what he'd been up to before receiving Knowledge, he tells me he had "done a little bit of college, a little bit of revolution, a little bit of acid" – an admittedly sketchy life history that may fit 98 percent of the crowd here today.

Most of the premies are seated on the tarmac in front of an improvised stage loaded down with baskets of flowers and two thronelike stuffed chairs, the larger one for the Guru and the smaller one for his Holy Mother, Mata Ji, who is flying in with him from Los Angeles. The stage is ringed by members of the World Peace Corps, the security arm of the DLM, who are constantly pushing overzealous premies away from the immediate area, a finger-in-the-dike operation. "Please move your physical bodies back," one WPC guard coaxes. "Merge into one."

To the side, a group of girls is decorating the hood of the Guru's emerald-green Rolls-Royce with a heart-shaped floral arrangement of red and white carnations. It is the most blissful of devotional services, and they are singing, "Maharaj Ji, Maharaj Ji/We love you, we love you/Satguru, Satguru . . ." to the tune of "Frère Jacques." Inside the Holy Limo one secretly glimpses a telephone, a framed picture of the Guru on the dashboard and a stereophonic tape deck loaded with a cassette recording of *Your Saving Grace* by the Steve Miller Band.

Someone announces "the moment of moments" is fast approaching, sending a ripple of excitement through the crowd.

The band strikes up "The Lord of the Universe" (sample verse: "Well, we've seen Maharaj Ji coming in glory/Moving like lightning from the East to the West/So rise up my brothers and lay down before Him/Just give Him your love and give Him your minds"), a revamped Methodist hymn that has become a kind of theme song for the Guru. In the middle of the song the Perfect Master walks briskly out from the hangar and takes his seat on the stage. A moment of absolute stillness – of two thousand inhaled breaths – precedes a collective sigh: "Aah!" goes the crowd. "Aaahhh." The premies take up the "*Bolie Shri*" chant while mahatmas place leis around the Guru's neck and kneel down at his feet in a palms-together pose, adoring Magi from the East. He seems

an unlikely figure of reverence, with his adolescent peach-fuzz mustache, his oversized face and the gap between his front teeth, but if there is an aura of power about him, it comes from a sure sense of his place above the world, the total nonchalance with which he accepts the homage paid him.

After the Hindi cheer subsides, Maharaj Ji speaks a few welcoming words. They are not particularly well-chosen ones, for he is no oratorical spellbinder. "It's just something really fantastic and really beautiful to see you here," he says in a flat, imitation American accent that comes from Dehra Dun by way of Kansas. "I guess there have been too many of these mess-ups like Watergate and things like that going on. It's not just here, it's right around the world. So I guess it's just about time when everybody gets together and understand who is God, because it's important that people know that by now at least." More cheers from the crowd as the Guru heads quickly toward his car, with Mata Ji and the mahatmas in tow, for a drive to the Celestial Suite (rented at the celestial rate of $2,500 a day) of the Astroworld Hotel.

It all might seem a bit anticlimactic after a three-hour wait in the hot sun, but not to the premies, who have not come so much to hear him speak as to receive the gift of his holy presence, called *darshan*. They are blissed out, smiling in a manner at once utterly peaceful and childlike and a touch demented, the kind of smile I have seen only on the faces of autistic children.

Later I learn that the reception had been staged. The Guru actually flew into Houston Intercontinental Airport thirty miles across town, but since officials there would have nothing to do with two thousand premies welcoming the Lord Incarnate on their runways, he was driven to the little-used Hobby Airport for the ceremony.

It is Millennium eve and, in the Astrohall, the cavernous convention center adjacent to the Astrodome, last-minute preparations are being made. Although there are several hundred premies scurrying about in a frenzy of activity, they are dwarfed by the sheer size of the place, which does indeed seem more suited to the small-crafts, home-furnishing and livestock shows pictured in the Astrodome's promotional booklet.

In truth, nothing very intriguing is happening inside the Astrohall. Over in one corner premies from Divine Sales are unpacking cartons of souvenirs that will be sold at Astrodome concession stands during the event. Piled on the floor and on tables are stacks of Guru Maharaj Ji stationery sets, Holy Family posters, MILLENNIUM '73 bumper stickers and pennants, "yoga whites," a recently issued Bantam paperback titled *Who Is Guru Maharaj Ji?* and an LP by the Guru's brother's rock band, Blue Aquarius, that the soul-oriented record company Stax has just released on its Gospel Truth label.

On the morning of the second day, the Guru holds a press conference at the Astroworld Hotel. Maharaj Ji, who is clearly accustomed to more respectful attention than he has been getting from the press, appears tense and hostile throughout the questioning. He comes out dressed in yoga whites and sits on an armchair in the front of the room, his expression deadly serious and his arms folded in a manner that makes him resemble the crown prince of some puppet Himalayan kingdom. His opening remarks seem to be deliberately taunting: "The thing is, if you write an article, maybe the credit goes to you or not; but if peace is established in the world, definitely there will be a credit for you. And this is the most important point that press reporters usually look for, 'Will we get credit out of this or not?'" Then the Guru calls for questions:

Reporter: Maharaj Ji, are you the Messiah foretold in the Bible?

Maharaj Ji: Please do not presume me as that. Respect me as a humble servant of God trying to establish peace in this world.

Reporter: Why is there such a great contradiction between what you say about yourself and what your followers say about you?

Maharaj Ji: Well, why don't you do me a favor . . . why don't you go to the devotees and ask their explanation about it?

Reporter: Guru, is it possible to have two Perfect Masters living on the earth at the same time?

Maharaj Ji: Well, I think the best thing for us to do right now is to find out one Perfect Master and be satisfied with that.

Reporter: Do you think that the comet that is coming has any relationship to the Millennium?

Maharaj Ji: Oh, I guess you just better wait and watch.

Reporter: It's hard for some people to understand how you personally can live so luxuriously in your several homes and Rolls-Royces.

Maharaj Ji: That life that you call luxurious ain't luxurious at all, because if any other person gets the same life I get, he's gonna blow apart in a million pieces in a split of a second. . . . People have made Rolls-Royce a heck of a car, only it's a piece of tin with a V-8 engine, which probably a Chevelle Concourse has.

Reporter: Why don't you sell it and give food to people?

Maharaj Ji: What good would it do? All that's gonna happen is they will need more and I don't have other Rolls-Royces. I will sell everything and I'll walk and still they will be hungry.

Reporter: Would you respond to those who say you cannot be a Perfect Master if you have an ulcer?

Maharaj Ji: If an ulcer is the only imperfectness, then people who don't have ulcers are perfect. . . . Perfectness has got nothing to do with an ulcer and a broken leg and things like that. Perfectness is perfectness. When Jesus Christ was nailed to the cross, He bleeded. People could have said, He's not a Perfect Master.

Reporter: Guru, what happened to the reporter in Detroit who was badly beaten by your followers?

Maharaj Ji: I think you ought to find out what happened to everything.

As abruptly as he entered, the Guru suddenly gets up from his chair and heads for the door along a path cleared by a few WPC guards moving before him like a snowplow. Bob Hallowitz, a thirty-year-old neurophysiologist – and premie – with whom I had discussed his receiving Knowledge, struggles unsuccessfully to push his way toward him, then at the last minute drives through a hole in the crowd, stretches out his arm and manages to touch the Guru's foot. "I touched his foot! I touched his foot!" he tells me, beaming. Later he confides: "I couldn't help myself. A premie before his Lord has no control over his actions."

After dinner on the third day, I hurry over to catch the Guru's last show, which, as

usual, opens with a rock set by Blue Aquarius.

As the concert is about to wind up, Maharaj Ji makes his way down a ramp connecting the stage with one of the stadium's upper tiers, wearing a kind of red-velvet smoking jacket and gold pants. The band strikes up a chorus of "Lord of the Universe" while mahatmas place floral leis around his neck and the Astrodome's electronic wizardry goes into full gear, lighting him with powerful spots and projecting his image on the two color video screens adjacent to the stage. The stadium scoreboard begins to peel off a hodgepodge of scriptural citations like Times Square ticker tape reporting the Second Coming. Maharaj Ji then begins his hour-long *satsang*, full of the American youth-culture slang he has recently acquired, spoken in a high-pitched voice that echoes irritatingly off the stadium's Lucite dome.

He repeats the same few notions over and over again: The Knowledge can bring peace, love and harmony to the world. It is "beautiful," "fantastic," "far-out" but cannot really be described in words. Every human being possesses the "primordial vibration" within himself. However, our minds trap us into mistaking the external world for the "real reality." We are all One. Everything is perfect. He is the Perfect Master because he teaches perfection. Other religious leaders say they can bring peace to the world but look at the results. He ends by imploring the audience to experience the Knowledge, alternating a cutely cajoling manner ("Try it, you'll like it") with a vaguely threatening one ("You *better* get hold of it quick, you see").

After the event is over I stay around the Astrodome to catch a crew of premies cleaning up the field. It must be done in a matter of hours in preparation for tomorrow's football game between the Houston Oilers and the Cleveland Browns. The premies sit silently meditating on the sidelines until they are called upon to roll up the tarp protecting the AstroTurf or carry away the plastic modules of the stage or dismantle the sound system. They work smoothly, efficiently, happily into the early morning hours, without a word of complaint or a note of friction.   ⊕

Watergate Committee that all Oval Office conversations since 1971 have been recorded. The next day, the committee asks the White House for all tapes concerning the affair, provoking a yearlong battle as President Nixon vows that only a Supreme Court decision will convince him to release the tapes, and the committee begins legal action to that end.

22A Gallup Poll shows President Nixon's approval rating plummeting from 68% at the beginning of the year to 40%.

25In the first and most effective action of its kind during the Vietnamese conflict, a U.S. District Court upholds the congressional decision to halt all bombing in Cambodia. The decision is reversed on Aug. 8.

28Skylab 2 and its crew are launched to test human ability to survive long periods in space; they stay 59 days.

A record 600,000 concert-goers flock to Watkins Glen, NY, for a one-day festival featuring the Grateful Dead, the Band and the Allman Brothers.

29In one of the largest hotel cash thefts in New York history, between $180,000 and $203,000 – profits from the first two of three sold-out Led Zeppelin concerts at Madison Square Garden – mysteriously disappear from an apparently secure safety deposit box in the Drake Hotel. Neither the culprit nor the money is found.

1973 AUGUST

1 ABA basketball star Julius "Dr. J" Erving signs with the New York Nets, bringing his flamboyant dunking style to a major city.

4 Jazz guitarist and bandleader Eddie Condon dies.

6 Strident blues guitarist and singer Memphis Minnie dies.

Stevie Wonder suffers life-threatening head injuries in a car accident in North Carolina and spends four days in a coma. He survives (minus his sense of smell) and resumes performing the following March.

17 Police find singer Paul Williams, the original Temptations' baritone, dead in an apparent suicide.

29 U.S. district judge John Sirica demands to be allowed to listen privately to White House tapes concerning Watergate; President Nixon refuses to comply, saying he will appeal.

the quitter
by harry shearer

LIKE ALL GREAT TALES, the Watergate saga has at its heart a great character. Without the comic grandeur that was Richard Nixon, the story would have fascinated, but it could not have mesmerized. Nixon was the Twentieth Century's answer to Horatio Alger, an ambitious man from humble beginnings who strove mightily to succeed and strove even more mightily to destroy that success. He never let the fact that he had reached the pinnacle of his aspirations distract him from his mission of vindictive resentment against those who failed (not for lack of trying) to stand in his way.

Nixon was a man who abhorred small talk, yet he chose to enter and scramble his way through a profession that requires an endless stream of amiable banter directed at nearly perfect strangers. (And, in his penultimate moment on the big stage, just before resigning the presidency, he engaged the TV crew gathered in the Oval Office in painfully jocular chitchat, kidding the White House photographer about wanting to get a picture of the president picking his nose. The moment has been preserved on videotape, and the awkwardness is world class.) The only way Nixon could have made himself a more uncomfortable public person would have been to show up for a summit conference dressed as RuPaul.

Watergate was Nixon's Waterloo, a cascade of events that began with what his press secretary, Ron Ziegler, described as a "third-rate burglary attempt" by some Cuban veterans of the aborted Bay of Pigs invasion. A first-rate burglary attempt probably wouldn't have left a stairwell door taped open, and the discovery of that tape – by security guard Frank Wills – opened the door to the revelation of what then–Attorney General John Mitchell described as the "White House horrors": the burglary of the office of Daniel Ellsberg's psychiatrist (Ellsberg had purloined and caused to be published the secret history of the Vietnam War, the Pentagon Papers); the compiling of enemies lists and the use of Internal Revenue Service audits to make people on those lists weep; and the laundering of Republican campaign funds through Mexico in order to keep the Watergate burglars, once apprehended, from talking.

All of it trickled out in painfully slow doses, administered first by two young metro reporters at the *Washington Post*, Bob Woodward and Carl Bernstein, and later by a set of congressional hearings. Even decades later, what came to be known as Watergate (for the name of the building being burglarized) stands as the Mount Everest of contemporary American political scandals. And at its peak, directing the activities in minute detail and commanding it all to be secretly documented on audiotape for the sake of "history," was Richard Nixon.

I had the advantage of growing up in California, where Nixon lore was absorbed right along with the fluoride in the water. The "Pink Lady" campaign, the Checkers speech, the last press conference – we had long since been set up to savor the spectacle of Nixon in the big tent. And it never disappointed. A detail always emerged that made you so very glad you had tuned in: Nixon, while engaging in what then seemed to be (and the tapes later proved to be) a mendacious campaign to prove he wasn't obsessed by the growing scandal, greeting the chief executive of Washington State as "Governor Evidence"; the president, fresh from participating in a yo-yo exhibition at the Grand Ole Opry, declaring on television in a hurt and defiant tone of voice, "I am not a crook." Of course, nobody had ever accused him of being a crook. A plotter against the Constitution, yes, but not a crook.

The hearings – both the original Watergate hearings and the later impeachment hearings – were quintessential Twentieth-Century mass-media experiences. As happened two decades later when a certain ex–football player went on trial for double mur-

der, you could go virtually anywhere in the evening and discuss the minutest wonderments of the day's proceedings with whomever you encountered. Everyone was paying attention. As network executives now lament with regularity, this is an experience rapidly being rendered obsolete by the expansion toward an infinity of the universe of electronic choices. Only Super Bowls, wars and the final episodes of beloved sitcoms can bring us together, to use a Nixonian phrase, in the way that Watergate television did. On the West Coast, you had to wake up early to catch the start of the hearings, but public television reran them each night at the dinner hour. Many people I know watched both airings. I was one of them.

Not only that. Since, at the time, I shared with a couple of partners (David L. Lander and Michael McKean) the occupation of underemployed satirist, I was able to put this material to evil use almost every night. Our group, known in L.A. as the Credibility Gap and unknown elsewhere on the globe, had a running gig at a local nightclub, and rare was the night we didn't incorporate the day's events into a new piece of material. Nothing, either written or taped, survives from those performances – we didn't have Nixon's preoccupation with history – but each day's news came wrapped as a gift that we just had to open and boil down for humorous consumption.

Everybody in the comedy business had his own Nixon: David Frye's waggling arms raised in paired V-for-victory signs and waggling jowls, Rip Torn's sullen mistrust, Dan Aykroyd's oiliness. What I glommed onto in fashioning my Nixon were his eyes. You had to get your eyes really slitty to make them Nixonian; it was as if he used his eyelids as a place behind which to hide, peering out only occasionally. When he did, another important character tic emerged: the telltale flutter of the lids, usually at moments of stress, as if he were saying, "I'm not here. I'm not here. I'm not here."

The mouth had to be drawn tight. The tongue did strange things, darting out and licking the lips to denote the odd flashes of humor. The entire upper body was hunched and crunched; to do Nixon for more than a few minutes was to risk shoul-

der cramps. Finally, there were his arm movements. For a man so determined to project strength as a rebuke to the war protesters and others who tormented him, Nixon had a bizarre tendency to make flailing, almost girlish arm gestures to punctuate and accentuate his comments. Watch the footage of his farewell to Washington. Standing at the entrance to the helicopter, he begins one of these flailings, then remembers only at the last moment to stiffen it into a salute, and, finally, his signature two-handed victory/peace wave.

The temptation, surrendered to in full by the Important Meaning Crowd, is to layer Watergate with great significance for future generations. But the wonderful irony of the Clinton presidency, its first lady a staff member of the Nixon impeachment committee, is that it has brought into question and may hasten the demise of the only two serious initiatives to grow from Watergate: the independent counsel statute, passed to avoid another Saturday Night Massacre, in which Nixon fired the prosecutor (Archibald Cox) who was closing in on the incriminating tapes; and the campaign-finance reforms meant to open the system to the kind of scrutiny the Nixonians, with their money-laundering trail meandering through Mexico, studiously avoided. Both "reforms" have caused or allowed more mischief than they cured and will surely be succeeded by even more wrongheaded improvements.

Watergate had another supposed impact: It enhanced the respect the American people felt for journalists. That change, too, has not stood the test of time, the heroic image of Woodward/Redford and Bernstein/Hoffman having been trashed by two decades of fraudulent I-Team reports on local TV news and by Simpson-Diana-Monica mania.

No, the true value of Watergate, as of so much else in modern America, was as entertainment that put the fictionalizers to shame. Nobody could invent a character as blithely colorful as Anthony Ulasewicz, the New York bagman who left cash money in a paper bag for the Watergate burglars and later testified that it sure was "quite a bit of lettuce." Hard, too, to match G. Gordon Liddy – the former FBI agent who held his hand over a flame to demonstrate his toughness and went to jail for not talking, after which he embarked on a career in talk radio.

The story still fascinates because it still contains mysteries: What were the burglars after when they bugged and ransacked the offices of the Democratic National Committee? Who (if anyone) was Deep Throat, the anonymous source named after a then-popular porno flick, who kept steering Woodward and Bernstein toward the heart of the scandal?

What's best about Watergate, though, is that it has only begun. Thanks to the stubbornness of Nixon and his attorneys in resisting the release of the magnificent tapes – your only opportunity ever to hunker beneath the desk in the Oval Office and listen in – they will continue to be released in small chunks, the better to amaze and delight us with fresh details of presidential scheming and anti-Semitism far into the future.

Take the kids. ⊕

of less than an ounce of pot.

6 The Yom Kippur War erupts as Israel battles Syria on the Golan Heights and Egypt along the Suez Canal. Within days, Israeli forces will come within 20 miles of Damascus, engaging Iraqi and Syrian forces, and will encircle Egyptian units on the far side of the canal. Jordan and Saudi Arabia will contribute forces to the Arab effort; the U.S. will counter Soviet and North Korean aid to Arab states with a large airlift of arms to Israel and a boycott of Arab oil. By Oct. 24, hostilities abate as Israel and Syria, but not Egypt, accept a UN cease-fire. A day later, responding to reports of Soviet plans to send forces into the region, President Nixon orders a worldwide alert, and a tense stalemate ensues. Most U.S. forces return to normal status on Oct. 31 as Nixon and Kissinger negotiate with Israeli and Egyptian officials.

9 Elvis and Priscilla Presley divorce amicably in California; the former Miss Beaulieu is awarded just under $1.5 million, a year of generous monthly alimony, half the couple's Los Angeles home and 5% of Elvis's two publishing companies.

10 After two weeks of hearings before a Baltimore grand jury, Vice President Spiro Agnew pleads no contest to one count of tax evasion during his terms as Maryland governor and resigns from office. His replacement, Congressman Gerald Ford of Michigan, receives congressional approval on Nov. 27.

15 The Supreme Court refuses, 7–2, to review an FCC directive that broadcasters censor drug-oriented songs.

16 Legendary jazz drummer Gene Krupa dies.

20 President Nixon fires Special Prosecutor Archibald Cox and Deputy Attorney General William Ruckelshaus (and accepts the subsequent resignation of Attorney General Elliot Richardson) for not supporting his refusal to submit any White House tapes to the Watergate investigations. Within days of this "Saturday Night Massacre," the House introduces eight impeachment resolutions, and Nixon finally agrees to give the tapes to Judge Sirica.

21 The Oakland A's defeat the New York Mets in seven games and win their second

the doctor of dunk
by al trautwig

I SELECTED THE LIME-GREEN Jethro Tull 8-track from the flimsy black-vinyl shoe box–like tray. Then I wedged a matchbook into the space between it and the player and turned it up loud. Presto – "matchbook magic"! It was either that or suffer through a painful mix of half "Aqualung," half "Locomotive Breath" bleeding together in the grip of bad technology that wouldn't last long.

This was all happening in my 1969 Mercury Cougar, license plate 32 ACT, the one with the cool hidden headlights and the sequentially blinking rear directionals. The purchase had just been made for a bank-account-emptying $1,250. I was entering my senior year at Carey High School in Franklin Square, Long Island, and not too many kids had wheels. Not too many members of the class of '74 had worked full-time since they were thirteen, either, but I had, and it was the greatest job in the world as I knew it. I was called a ball boy, but this job of mine had little to do with balls.

The hot new Sand Knit polyester uniforms of the New York Nets professional basketball team had to be kept clean. The locker room, too. I also handled tickets, treated player injuries, forged a few signatures and yes, took care of the balls. Five years before, the pay had been one dollar a game, then five dollars, and at this point I probably cleared fifty dollars a week. In case you're wondering how much you earn over five years at that pay scale, the total is roughly $1,250.

On this day I was driving myself to the Nassau Coliseum in Uniondale, Long Island, for the very first time. This story is about what went on in that coliseum, and specifically in the basketball locker room, where, for me, the Seventies lived.

Wendell Ladner grabbed a hair dryer – there were always at least six on the counter. Wendell was a basketball player for the Nets. Six feet seven inches and an absolute muscle-bound rock.

"To get your hair to look this good," he said with a rich New Orleans tone, "you flip and dry the piece the way you don't want it to go. That way, in the beautiful end, it goes exactly the way you want."

I was still months away from the big college thing, and to this day I dry my hair (what there is) exactly the way he told me. The crazy thing was that it worked.

Ladner was Burt Reynolds. Looked like him. Sounded like him. Womanized like him. Scored better than him, though, from all over the court. He used to sit in the front row at the coliseum and with a two-hand set shot sink six out of ten, from about forty-five feet. *Sitting down!* All that was missing was Sally Field and a black Trans Am, because this dude was as close to Hollywood as I had ever been.

He looked at himself in the mirror, smoothed out his mustache and looked, with pimpish pleasure, some more. "I'm ready for her now, young Al."

He grabbed his blue-and-red-vinyl Nets bag and turned toward the door, looking perfect in his bright-red plaid suit, with a black fur coat over his arm. I have always believed, and will forever, that sports is society looking in the mirror.

IT WAS 1974 and the New York Nets played in the ABA. The American Basketball Association. Born in 1967, the ABA had an inferiority complex, and with good reason: the NBA. The establishment. This league was born for the same reason the American Football League was formed, and the soon-to-come World Hockey Association, USFL, and so on: money (and the belief that something can always be done a better way, a more entertaining way).

These rebels used a red-white-and-blue ball. The NBA laughed. The ABA teams tried wacky things, like the Miami Floridians with bikini-clad ball girls. The snickers got louder. They had a three-point shot. More chuckles. The ABA had Julius Winfield Erving. The NBA went lawyer, but the ABA won the right to keep him.

consecutive World Series.

What happened was, Julius starred at the University of Massachusetts and was good enough to play professionally before his senior year. The only problem: The NBA didn't draft players who still had college eligibility. The ABA had no such qualms, and the Virginia Squires gobbled him up. Bikinis and three-pointers aside, the ABA knew that the only thing that could guarantee success was good players. The league was comprised of NBA players who were mostly past their prime and players not good enough for the NBA but who turned out to make solid reputations in the ABA.

Erving averaged twenty-seven points a game in 1971, his rookie year in the ABA, and became an All-Star and a sensation. The talk of his abilities included words like *poet, artist, magician*. Because of the almost nonexistent TV exposure of the ABA, the exploits of Erving became almost mythical. The ABA broke through, and a handful of games were televised by CBS. I was at one of those in Hampton Roads, Virginia, and owner Earl Foreman filled the seats on the side of the arena facing the TV cameras. The place looked packed, even if it was half empty.

In the summer of 1973 Julius Erving was acquired by the Nets so that the ABA could rub him in the face of the NBA in the world's biggest market. As a result, he shared the same locker room as Wendell Ladner, and me.

I had seen Dr. J play many times and, while I hated the fact that he so often had found some ridiculously glorious way to beat my beloved Nets, I loved him. He was from Long Island. I was too. I felt some strong connection to him, having played on some of the same playgrounds growing up as he had. The difference was that he had taken the playground game and refined it into cognac – very smooth, but with impact. He wore number 32. I still use 32 for every lucky number choice I have to make (remember the license plate on the Cougar?).

He was called "Doc" because he operated with precision – but not every operation was a success. Critics said he had no outside shot, but we worked on that for endless hours after practice to make sure those critics were wrong, which they eventually proved to be. Those days when I fed him pass after pass in the darkness of the coliseum were some of my most cherished moments. Just me and the Doctor.

The year before Doc arrived I learned that race relations in the Seventies reflected a carryover of emotions stirred up by the civil rights movement of the Sixties. There were a lot more white players in pro basketball when I was a ball boy than there are now, and the racial mix was often volatile. Looking back on it, I don't think the two leagues' racial makeups differed much – neither was more "white" or more "black" than the other. The Nets, though, in 1971 and 1972, were wracked with racial dissension and were destined to fail because of it. The locker room, my domain, was a very tense place – I couldn't believe the things some of the players told me in confidence, both blacks and whites. But certainly a palpable strain existed in that room.

To the best of my knowledge, Doc was one player who cut through all that. His presence on the Nets was pure charm, and his attitude brought him the respect every player dreamed of. That, and the professional way he went about his job, rubbed off on everyone.

There was so much more to this man, though – so much more that made him cool. The Afro: It rose high off his head, and it was perfectly round. Cool. Wendell used to tell me how jealous he was that Doc could come over with his "pick," look in the mirror ". . . and get that sucker perfect in five seconds." Doc had a big contract – I remember four hundred thousand dollars per season being the number. With it he bought a car called an Avanti that was white with turquoise leather. Turquoise was his wife's name. Cool.

I once asked Doc if he would give me the jersey that he was going to wear in the upcoming All-Star Game. Two weeks later, after the game and a long road trip, he walked into the locker room holding it in his huge hands. I still have it. Very cool.

I witnessed so many of Doc's powers and their effect for the first time: his grace and fluidity on the court; the sound of the crowd when he blurred through an entire team, softly rolling the ball off his fingertips into the hoop; the sight of him dunking after soaring to a height from which he was looking down at the basket.

Then there was his business side. There had never been an agent in the locker room as prominent as Doc's: Irwin Weiner. With "Dr. J" at his side, there were always papers to sign, deals to discuss, hands to shake. Looking back on it, these were just some of the things that Julius did to change the game. The player conglomerate was born.

During this time, kids were seeing more and more basketball on television and trying to copy what they saw. That meant attempting to emulate the Doctor's moves. And then there were the agents, the endorsements for big money. What you see today in pro basketball can't all be traced to Julius Erving. That would do a disservice to Bird, Magic and, of course, Michael Jordan, who took the sport and expanded upon it to make it the game we know today. However, any time you see a moment of free expression or financial freedom in basketball, know that Julius Erving played a role in its creation. Its family tree goes back to the Seventies, and to him.

By 1973, with Dr. J in the lead, the business of basketball was reaching critical mass. The ABA style of play was still flamboyant, wide open and appealing, but the league was reaching respectability. For the past couple of seasons many preseason games had taken place between ABA and NBA teams, even an NBA-ABA All-Star "Super Game" at the Nassau Coliseum. I remember them as bitter encounters because of the rivalry between leagues and the ABA players' efforts to prove they were good enough to play in any league. ABA teams started winning those games. Meanwhile, many of the great NBA stars who had fueled the game's play were fading or gone. And still the NBA desperately wanted Julius Erving.

The Nets' 1973–74 season moved along successfully. They had a new coach, former NBA player Kevin Loughery, and many good players, including Larry Kenon, "Mr. K" (the Doctor title was taken). Kenon had been drafted by both leagues, but the Nets' recruitment drive had included a Deep Purple concert with the blue-suit-wearing owner of the team, Roy Boe. I remember seeing the two emerge from the coliseum, enveloped by smoke, nodding their heads in agreement. How "Smoke on the Water" convinced Kenon to pick New York, I'll never know.

Speaking of music at the coliseum: I always chose the nights of the big gigs to go down and do the laundry. Led Zeppelin. Chicago. Elton John. Wings. Loggins and Messina. I actually got the chance to see Elvis leave the building. Theirs was the music of the locker room, too, except when Doc turned on the 8-track player. That's when Isaac Hayes took over.

One Seventies phenomenon that has not taken over is Roller Derby. Maybe you remember Charlie O'Connell on the jam. Joanie Weston. Mike Gammon. Ann Calvello. Round and round they went. The Bay Area Bombers. The Los Angeles Thunderbirds. Los Angeles Thunderbirds? They never had a home that I knew of. Once in a while they would blow through town, and there were always big crowds. Things got thrown. Curses were yelled. Tawdry stuff. Players would leave their jobs at the gas station, then come to the arena and change out of their Texaco duds and into uniform. One night after working a Roller Derby game at the Nassau Coliseum, I went into the locker room to collect the dirty towels, and on the wet linoleum floor I found the evidence generations have sought – a script for how the Derby game was going to go. I was crushed to find out that all those last-second seven-point

comebacks were not real, but I got over it. There was a time, when it was first born, that the ABA had had that same carnival-like feel, but it was gone now.

By the time the seventh ABA season reached its championship stage, the Nets played the Utah Stars in a best-of-seven series. The team took me on the road, so I got to see every game of that series. In what became the clinching game, things were close. Late in the game a furious scramble for the red-white-and-blue ball was won by Doc. As he charged up the floor, only one thing stood in his way: Zelmo Beaty, the six-feet-nine-inch one-time NBA star. The Doctor began to rise at the foul lane fifteen feet from the hoop. Beaty timed his jump to meet him. The next moment, he lay on the floor. Erving had come crashing down in a vicious fury, holding the ball in one hand, windmilling his arm in one momentous dunk. Later, with five seconds to play, the Nets had the ball, up 111–100. The championship was assured, and my mission was to get the ball and make sure some fan did not. The court was surrounded by people, and the ball was put into play. It was a full-court pass, and thinking that would be the end of it, I ran onto the court and caught the ball. Behind me, there was a scream. Larry Kenon stood there in agony. I had stolen his dunk – what would have been a perfect ending to a championship season.

Two years later, at the 1976 ABA All-Star Game, the league would inaugurate something called the slam-dunk contest. That's when Julius repeated his foul-line dunk, to easily win the competition. Later that season, the Nets won another championship, beating the Denver Nuggets, and shortly after, the NBA and ABA "merged." Indiana, San Antonio, Denver and the Nets were accepted. Players from the other teams were spread throughout the NBA. Roy Boe, the owner of the Nets, had to pay the New York Knicks $4.8 million in indemnity money because his team was in their "franchise area." To cover that cost, he sold Julius Erving to the Philadelphia 76ers, where he went on to win another title and have his number retired.

Today, the NBA allows the three-point field goal, remembers fondly its first years of slam-dunk contests, regularly signs teenagers and underclassmen and produced a commemorative red-white-and-blue basketball for use in exhibition games for the 1997–98 season. The greatness of the Doctor is the reason why. (And that All-Star jersey he gave me? Today it's worth $15,000. Still cool.)

What of Wendell Ladner? After the 1974–75 season, he went back to New Orleans. Then, returning to New York to prepare for the next season, he was on an Eastern Airlines jetliner that disintegrated in a field near JFK Airport. The trainer of the team, Fritz Massmann, a second father to all his players, noticed Ladner's red-and-blue-vinyl Nets bag in the wreckage on TV. A huge part of the Seventies died that day.

I prefer to remember this time in freeze-frame: the Doctor in midflight, Afro swept back by his speed, about to deliver another unstoppable dunk, and Wendell Ladner the same way: midflight, looking perfect, sitting in first class, flirting with the stewardess. ⊕

1973 DECEMBER

jazz-funk junction
by martin johnson

BACK IN 1974, when I was in the eighth grade, it wasn't uncommon for public schools on Chicago's South Side to have pianos in many classrooms. That meant at Louis Wirth Middle School, you didn't register high on the cool meter merely by singing the latest pop hits (despite the fact that a young singer now known as Chaka Khan had attended the neighboring high school). You were truly cool if you could play hip music on the piano. It seemed like everyone knew the themes from *Mission: Impossible* and *The Man from U.N.C.L.E.*, and some kids could play the intro to Sly Stone's "If You Want Me to Stay."

But one afternoon, before science class commenced, Chris McGoldrick sat down and launched into the bass line from Herbie Hancock's "Chameleon," the hit single from his *Headhunters* record.

Time stopped. All the commotion typical of a roomful of rowdy fourteen-year-olds came to a crashing halt. Since he had our attention, he played the theme again. The teacher, Robert Wright, walked in and said, "Ah, it's nice to hear some jazz in here."

That puzzled us. Those of us who knew the tune didn't think of it as jazz. Jazz was our parents' music: the Ellington, Basie and Lambert, Hendricks and Ross LPs that got heavy rotation whenever company came over. This wasn't jazz; this was *our* music. But if Mr. Wright wanted to call it jazz, that was cool too. He had a drop-dead-perfect 'fro; girls did not cut his class. And guys loved him too; he coached the basketball team, and if the spirit moved him, he set aside discussions about biology, chemistry and physics to talk about the Norm Van Lier–Jerry Sloan Chicago Bulls. So hey, it was 1974, and we were groovin' to jazz.

> "Miles Davis *[at right]* is the father and we are the sons, and even when you are small and you stand upon the shoulders of the father, you are going to see further than he." – Joe Zawinul

We weren't alone. Jazz or funk, we didn't have a distinct term for it yet, but *Headhunters* was the apex of a trend that integrated jazz into the musical lingua franca of the streets. With a funky bass line that could make any class nerd do the bump, layered with intense synthesizer figures and choppy rhythm-guitar licks, "Chameleon" helped push the album to the status of jazz's best-selling record to date, with more than a million copies sold. Hancock's reputation as an inventive jazz composer with a flair for a catchy, rhythmic hook had been established in the Sixties with "Watermelon Man" and "Canteloupe Island" (the former another hit, but for Mongo Santamaria).

Hancock had taken his synthesizer and soul rhythm section into the studio to create a simpler, beat-based record applying the varied lessons of his jazz club years with the on-the-one jams of James Brown and Sly Stone (one of the tracks is called "Sly"). Other musicians had previously struck the same motherlode, stretching their jazz chops over funk rhythms, like trumpeter Donald Byrd (who, with his Howard University jazz students, the Blackbyrds, placed "Black Byrd" on the R&B charts in 1973), but with "Chameleon" Hancock established himself as the premier exponent of this new electronic style. He would return to the idiom ten years later, fusing it with hip-hop rhythms to create "Rockit," another pop hit.

Hancock's visionary thinking stemmed from his solid grasp of jazz history. His ability to merge jazz and popular dance rhythms benefited from and continued the work of Horace Silver, one of Hancock's key influences. Silver combined blues, gospel and Caribbean musical dialects with post–be-bop jazz to create a powerful synthesis. Although his music became known as "hard bop" and later "soul jazz," Silver proposed another name: His 1953 composition "Opus de Funk" featured starkly synco-pated left-hand figures on the keyboard and an infectious rhythm, and was a direct precursor to "Chameleon." Silver spearheaded a movement that later saw alto saxo-

and film – 1973: Roberta Flack's "Killing Me Softly With His Song" (pop single); Elton John's *Goodbye Yellow Brick Road* (pop album); Marvin Gaye's "Let's Get It On" (R&B single); Merle Haggard's "If We Make It Through December" (C&W single); Richard Bach's *Jonathan Livingston Seagull* (fiction); Thomas Harris's *I'm OK– You're OK* (nonfiction); *The Exorcist* (film).

1974 JANUARY

3 Bob Dylan kicks off a six-week retrospective tour – his first tour in nearly eight years – with the Band at Chicago Stadium. The $9.50 ticket price sets a record. When the tour hits Atlanta on Jan. 21, Georgia Governor Jimmy Carter will host a postconcert party. (Carter will quote Dylan's lyrics in future speeches.) After the last show at the Los Angeles Forum, Ringo Starr, Carole King, Neil Young, Jack Nicholson and Warren Beatty will attend the closing gala. The tour will yield the gold, live double LP *Before the Flood*.

13 The Miami Dolphins win their second consecutive Super Bowl, defeating the Minnesota Vikings, 24–7.

15 Technicians determine that the 18-minute gap in Nixon's White House tapes, evidence in the Watergate investigation, is the result of several intentional erasures, not a single accidental rerecording as claimed.

The first modern telephone answering machine is made available to the American public by Dictaphone, introducing to common usage the apparent contradiction: "Hello, I'm not here . . ."

18 Maine ratifies the ERA, becoming the 32nd state to do so; Ohio follows suit on Feb. 7.

23 Oil company representatives testify before a Senate committee that the oil shortage has not been contrived. Within a week, Hawaii becomes the first state to institute gas rationing, and all major oil companies reveal record-breaking profits for 1973.

24 Ex–White House aide Egil Krogh Jr. receives a six-month sentence for his part in breaking into Daniel Ellsberg's psychiatrist's office.

27 As fighting continues between South Vietnamese and Communist forces, the U.S. admits providing more than

phonist Cannonball Adderley score a pop hit in 1967 with "Mercy, Mercy, Mercy."

The cultural ferment of the Sixties produced an amazingly wide range of musical innovation and cross-genre exchange. The soul-jazz titans were paralleled by another group of blues-rooted players like Ornette Coleman and Albert Ayler, who were looking for a means to amplify the emotional expression in their music and found it in the unfettered architecture of free jazz. Miles Davis took blues in another direction with the hypnotic grooves of *Kind of Blue*. Adderley and John Coltrane were the two saxophonists on that album, but Coltrane went on to further explorations, using drone techniques from Eastern music to expand into microtonal playing. The Sun Ra Arkestra was combining all of these elements with traditional New Orleans music, Fletcher Henderson arrangements, ring shouts, marches and electronic music in what amounted to a recapitulation of the entire history of jazz. In addition, the Afro-Cuban and bolero influences on Sixties jazz were energetically engineered by radio hits like Cal Tjader's "Soul Sauce" and Ray Barretto's "El Watusi."

Meanwhile, rock & roll was poised to take all this dynamic music to another technological level. As electric guitars became more commonplace in jazz lineups and rhythm sections got louder, horns had to plug in just to keep up. By the end of the decade, jazz and rock collided with electric blues and the new post-soul R&B to create the sounds played by Sly, James Brown and an ex–Isley Brothers guitarist named Jimi Hendrix. The Free Spirits, Charles Lloyd and others were now playing this new music to rock audiences.

Suddenly, pop music was no longer bound to simple verse-chorus-verse forms and opaque textures. Extended improvisations or jams became a regular part of songs, and the level of musicianship rose in all genres. The loose-limbed feel of jazz funk – the sense that the music could dart off in any direction at any moment – combined with the sensual elegance of the music to create an appealing sound. Using riffs that were often inspired by Sly Stone's brand of rock, the bassist laid down solid grooves that ordered you out of your seat; then the other instruments let you flow.

Hancock's jazz funk was part of this larger movement, which included the R&B of Kool and the Gang and Earth, Wind and Fire, as well as the rhythmically shifting jazz-rock amalgam known as fusion. The most important figure in establishing fusion was Miles Davis, who had already changed the face of jazz several times in his career. Hancock, along with Chick Corea, Joe Zawinul, Wayne Shorter and John McLaughlin, had proved their mettle within Miles's various (and varied) Sixties aggregations, and taken off to lead a phalanx of fusion-defining groups in the Seventies. Corea melded Latin, Brazilian and rock influences into a group called Return to Forever. Zawinul joined with fellow Davis alumnus and saxophonist Wayne Shorter to form Weather Report, whose music ranged from ethereal to funky with an accent on ensemble playing. Guitarist McLaughlin developed the fiery Mahavishnu Orchestra after having made excursions with Tony Williams's Lifetime.

All of these musicians – save for Hancock and Williams – contributed to Davis's landmark fusion recording, *Bitches Brew*. Recorded in 1969 during the week after Woodstock (Davis was to have played the festival), *Bitches Brew* set the stage for fusion to become the dominant sound of Seventies jazz. Loud and searching, angry and elegant, *Bitches Brew* announced that a new world was at hand. It won a Grammy award and went gold.

With *Headhunters*, Hancock took the idea a step further by coercing the parallel lineages of funk and small-unit jazz to overlap, get down and blare from transistor radios four years later. Call it jazz, funk and fusion. Even eighth-graders could jam to it.

Funk and fusion helped open other doors, as well, for jazz in the Seventies. Davis's band began touring auditoriums and concert halls, often opening for rock bands and airing out jazz that had been kept in smoky clubs by a colony of cognoscenti.

In the early Seventies this kind of cultural egalitarianism ruled onstage and in studios. Bands like the Allman Brothers and Traffic featured extended improvisations in their work, absorbing jazz feeling and instrumentation with the same ease that Miles had plugged in, a few years earlier. Jeff Beck, a former Yardbirds guitarist and one of rock's most respected axemen, did a series of jazz recordings with keyboardist Jan Hammer. And cryptic songcrafters Steely Dan demanded – and got – a dizzyingly talented array of musicians together to help them make pop tunes that swung.

Through fusion, the Seventies introduced the idea of the consummate musician to rock audiences by featuring artists known more for their all-around instrumental prowess than for specific tunes or performances: guitarist Larry Coryell; drummer Billy Cobham; keyboardists Jeff Lorber, Jan Hammer and George Duke; violinist Jean-Luc Ponty; saxophonists Tom Scott and David Sanborn. In studio and onstage, as leaders or sidemen, suddenly instrumentalists were valued as much for their jazz chops as for their standard rock riffs.

Combining and separating into a fertile genealogy of styles, fusion – and its umbrella classification of jazz – became big business by the mid-Seventies. *Headhunters*' top-selling status became short-lived when saxophonist Grover Washington Jr. followed it a year later with 1975's "Mister Magic," a mammoth hit that received pop-radio airplay. In 1976, guitarist George Benson reached the upper echelons of the pop album charts, buoyed by both the crossover pop instrumental track "Breezin'" and the vocal hit "This Masquerade."

But the story behind Weather Report's "Birdland" – the second-biggest jazz hit of that era – is perhaps the best example of the successful intertwining of jazz, rock and funk. The group was co-led by Shorter and Zawinul, two players with solid jazz roots, both with Miles and separately – the former as principal composer with Art Blakey, and the latter, likewise, with Cannonball Adderley (Zawinul wrote "Mercy, Mercy, Mercy" and "Country Preacher" while in Adderley's band).

By 1976, Weather Report had evolved its lineup through various permutations and now had a harder-driving rhythm section in the persons of electric-bass prodigy Jaco Pastorius and drummer Alejandro Acuna. With an incredible match-up of technique, experience and feeling now intact, the group welcomed 1977 with *Heavy Weather*; "Birdland" was reborn.

Dedicated to the legendary club that was itself dedicated to be-bop pioneer Charlie Parker, "Birdland" proved a huge hit, with its infectious progression, danceworthy rhythms and scat-along melody, osterizing the strongest elements of pop, jazz and R&B into one irresistible track.

Heavy Weather went gold. Meanwhile, Shorter and Pastorius ended up touring and recording with Joni Mitchell, who had spent most of the decade doing the same with saxophonist Tom Scott and the L.A. Express. Thus the jazz-rock family tree continued to grow.

After 1974, Davis and Hancock pursued divergent paths, with the former releasing three records, *Dark Magus* (1974), *Pangaea* (1975) and *Agharta* (1976), that sounded like the band that Jimi Hendrix and John Coltrane never got a chance to co-lead. Then Davis gave up public performance and recording until 1981, when he did a series of recordings on which even Miles completists are divided in opinion, before delving into jazz–hip-hop fusion just before his death in 1991.

Ever the chameleon – comfortably moving back and forth between acoustic jazz and electric funk – Hancock returned to his grand piano bench in 1976. He toured with the VSOP ensemble (featuring fellow Davis colleagues Williams, Shorter and bassist Ron Carter, plus trumpeter Freddie Hubbard, who participated in many proto–jazz-funk sessions) and recorded and toured in piano-duo format with Corea.

As the decade closed, fusion as a freestanding, creative format had lost most of its jazz connection. Under the influence of record-industry A&R operatives looking to reproduce a successful formula, it became more pop-based, typified by studio-musicians-*cum*-artists like Lee Ritenour, Spyro Gyra and Earl Klugh, whose music displayed little connection to the earlier, rootsy, ear-challenging tradition.

Rock and pop may share a debt to the Seventies infusion of fusion for having forever raised the ante on the general state of pop-music musicianship. But long live the funk! Hancock's stay-phat melodies continue to feed a hip-hop scene hungry for the freshest bass lines: Us3 filled countless dance floors with their recut "Cantaloop," while a throwaway Hancock riff from the *Blow-Up* soundtrack was the hook behind Deee-Lite's mammoth "Groove Is in the Heart." The spirit of jazz funk lives in the music of almost every R&B act that makes use of live instruments as well as in that of the entire school of hip-hop DJs and groups who make use of lighter, more fluid textures. Acts as diverse as Mary J. Blige, Jamiroquai, Gang Starr, Beck and Luscious Jackson reflect a strong sense of jazz funk. The idiom also inspired a club music, scene and style still known by its odd moniker "acid jazz" (psychedelia has little to do with this rootsy form) and boosting such jazz-funk torch-bearing acts as Groove Collective and Incognito to current prominence.

Many of today's polyglot dance-music styles, like drum and bass and trip-hop, take their nuanced sound from jazz funk as well. Portishead even sampled Weather Report's "Elegant People" on their song "Strangers." It's not unusual to find vinyl copies of Miles Davis's early Seventies releases at DJ-oriented record boutiques. Hancock, Davis and others created a fertile genre from which thousands of musicians – many who weren't even born until the Seventies – are still reaping bountiful harvests.

Most of the new generation of young jazz players dote on the hard bop of the late Fifties and Sixties. However, there are signs of change. Recently, guitarist Mark Whitfield, trumpeter Nicholas Payton and bassist Christian McBride, three of the best young cats on the jazz scene, performed for a week at Birdland in New York doing the music of Herbie Hancock. Their repertoire was mostly drawn from Hancock's acoustic material; however, for their closing number they launched into a raucous version of "Chameleon." The prim formality of the jazz club disappeared as they tore the roof off the sucker. It was as if they'd been playing the tune together since the eighth grade. ⊕

herbie hancock
on headhunters

WHEN THE HEADHUNTERS first played the Berlin Philharmonia, where I had performed several times when I was with Miles Davis, our record wasn't out in Europe yet. The audience booed us. They threw eggs! They threw water and tomatoes! They were outraged. But you know what? The band was hot and burning.

In that audience's opinion, Herbie Hancock wasn't supposed to play funk; he was supposed to play only jazz. That's ridiculous. I never signed a contract saying I was supposed to play anything other than exactly whatever the heck I wanted. Funk is part of my heritage and part of my roots. It's not something from outside my background.

But again, thanks to Miles's influence, I had the courage to stick with my convictions. I knew we had done an excellent job, and I knew we had played excellent music – the solos were all there. The jazz stuff was there. They just hadn't heard our new style. So even with the booing and loud whistling and flying food, we took our bows when we finished. I remember saying under my breath to them, "You'll find out."

A year later we came back and played the same hall, and the audience was dancing in the aisles. It was a complete turnaround.

The early Seventies were a period of time that represented the end of an era, of the Sixties, when there had been so many different revolutions. African-Americans were becoming concerned about their identities and their connection to their African roots. At that time, I took the name Mwandishi, which was my way of saying I supported the black movement, you know. But I didn't stop using the name Herbie Hancock, I just added Mwandishi. Anyway, that was happening, and Afros, platform shoes.

For me, it was a period in which I started establishing my own identity. I was separating from the influences that had come from Miles Davis, and doing something a little bit different from the late-Sixties style of jazz funk. The only group I knew that was delving into anything similar at that time was Donald Byrd and the Blackbyrds. Other jazz artists were playing something more rock-influenced that was at the time called jazz rock, which became fusion – like Tony Williams's "Emergency" and the Mahavishnu Orchestra's music.

In the Seventies, jazz musicians, in general, were looking at rock & roll and saying, "Well, let's see. These records are really selling, so a lot of people must be turned on to rock. And there must be a reason they're interested in it." I don't think, however, that any jazz musicians got into it just to make hit records. It was a whole unexplored territory, and they were just trying to develop something new and fresh.

But I went the funk route, you know. I had started practicing Buddhism in the Seventies, and that was a key element motivating me to do *Headhunters*. After I broke up the Mwandishi band, I didn't know what kind of music I wanted to do. I just didn't want to play music that was so far removed from the earth anymore. I wanted to feel a little more attached to other people, and play music that was more fun *and*, at the same time, demanding. I didn't want it to be so heavy.

It was through that desire that the idea of combining funk and jazz came up. I started thinking about Sly Stone, imagining him playing in my band and me playing in his. I remembered R&B that I'd listened to when I was a kid. Tony Williams and those others came up in a different period – it was more of a rock & roll era. So I listened to Sly Stone and James Brown, and through chanting and practicing Buddhism, I made the decision that I had to pursue this new direction. It became a very strong urge.

I chanted for the name Headhunters, too! I didn't know what I wanted to call the music, I just knew that I wanted the name to sound primitive and have a primal nature to it plus a mental, intellectual aspect – and I wanted a name that had a sexual level to it as well. Suddenly it just popped into my head – "Headhunters." Sexuality was still a big number back then, we had just left the Sixties: free love, flower children and all that.

When I put the band together with the help of David Rubinson (he was my manager and record producer at the time), we rehearsed for a week or two. We wrote music together, and in general inspired each other. And then we set about the business of producing the record.

For the *Headhunters* sessions, we tried something I had never done before. Before we recorded, we went out and played the music in Bay Area clubs for about three weeks. It was something I'd always wanted to do – take something and work it out in front of people first, and then bring it back into the studio after it's found its own center and had the chance to develop. It's a great way to record.

The success of *Headhunters* came as a total shock. I had only been hoping that the record would be viable enough in its own right that nobody would say that it was stupid or primitive or dumb: that it wasn't happening musically. I was also hoping that I wouldn't lose the jazz audience that I already had, although, for the sake of my own integrity, I was willing to put everything that I had done before on the line. So I took the double risk of failing to gain a new audience and of losing an old one.

But it all worked out. A lot of critics were up in arms about *Headhunters*, and what I read in the newspapers made it seem as though the record was extremely controversial. In reality, the controversy was mostly among the media, not really so much with the audience. Some of them liked the record and some didn't. But there's a tendency to take the opinions of music critics as representative of the way the jazz community "voted" on a particular record. In the case of *Headhunters*, I don't believe that the critics' opinions reflected those of our peers.

I hadn't known before what it was like to have a hit record. I remember one of the first concerts we did, we played a show with Santana somewhere on the East Coast. The house was packed. I remember saying to my manager, "Wow, Santana sure draws a lot of people!" He said, "Herbie, they didn't come to see Santana; they came to see you. You have a huge hit record!" I was kind of dumbfounded by the whole thing. So we played, and they loved it.

The attention took some getting used to, but it just blew me away to get that kind of a reaction. I didn't have to restrict

or filter anything and could still sell lots of records and draw lots of people. It was a great show.

One thing that was a little awkward, though: The Headhunters became headliners, and Miles was going to open for us on this short tour. I felt a little embarrassed by the idea, and I never expected Miles to do it. But even after he did, I still, of course, could never think of him as an opening act.

When I was part of Miles's band in the Sixties, I had learned so many valuable things from him: a greater awareness and ability to function as a team player; a greater ability to open my ears to hear what other players are playing, whether I was soloing or accompanying; a heightened awareness of the provocative elements in a composition for improvisation; how to reduce a composition to its lean parts, take the fat off and use space, use time. Another technique that I learned, primarily from Tony Williams, was how to apply rhythm, counter-rhythms and polyrhythms to my keyboard work.

Miles's playing was always interesting and provocative. By 1974 he was using the wah-wah pedal a lot, and the former Motown sessionman Michael Henderson was playing bass with him. Great bass lines! It was definitely a fresh kind of sound.

And then there was the great and constant support I got from Miles for just exercising my creativity in general. Miles always wanted his musicians to be working on something; he would say he paid us to *practice* onstage, not to sound perfect.

I don't think I ever could have done that *Headhunters* album and other subsequent albums of that ilk had I not had my experiences with Miles.

I'm aware now of the scope of my influence because artists who sample or use my music have got to get my permission to do it. I have to listen to how they've used parts in order to make a deal with them. Many musicians have sampled parts of "Chameleon" and "Watermelon Man." And then Us3 did the hit tune "Cantaloop (Flip Fantasia)," in which they sampled "Cantaloupe Island," so of course I'm pleased! It's young people finding a sound that they feel is powerful and putting it into a form that speaks to their generation. ⊕

malignant giant
by howard kohn

It was the autumn of 1974. I was a young freelancer just scraping by. Nothing about the assignment led me to foresee that it would change my life or anything else. It appeared to be nothing more than a whodunit. A woman, en route to a rendezvous to deliver secret documents, is killed when her car goes off the road and hits a culvert wall. The documents are surreptitiously removed from her wrecked car, and there is physical evidence indicating foul play. Her name is Karen Silkwood. She had been employed as a lab technician at a plutonium factory, Kerr-McGee.

This last part, seemingly so incidental, proved to be the heart of the matter. I soon realized the story of Karen Silkwood was not as much a question of vehicular homicide as a plunge into the dark side of atomic fission.

Though it was never determined whether Karen Silkwood's death was the result of foul play, the public's confidence in nuclear power would be so undermined by its aftermath that the industry would become a shadow of its former self.

RAPIDLY, as if no time were left on the clock, Karen Silkwood jammed the dime in its slot and dialed long distance. Washington. Steve Wodka. "Hello." An uncertain trickle started down her face. Her voice tottered. "Please come to Oklahoma," she said. "Something very weird is happening here."

Three times in the past three days Silkwood had been contaminated with plutonium, and no one knew where it was coming from. A monitoring device had first discovered flecks of plutonium on her skin and clothing shortly after she reported for work on November 5, 1974. She had quickly stepped under a brisk shower. But the next day the monitor flashed on again. On the third day the mystery repeated itself – and a nasal smear indicated she was contaminated internally.

At left: Karen Silkwood; following pages: Her car after the crash

How much plutonium, she wanted to know, could a person ingest before it burned out her insides?

Wodka tried to assure her and promised to fly in. Silkwood hung up and sought her old lover. "She was damn near incoherent," says Drew Stephens. "She was crying and shaking like a leaf; she kept saying she was going to die."

Again Silkwood picked up the phone and called long distance. Minneapolis. Dr. Dean Abrahamson. She told him that somehow, somewhere, she had gotten plutonium all over her, inside and out. "She knew what the medical implications were," recalls Abrahamson, "and she was worried."

A team of Kerr-McGee inspectors armed with alpha counters, full-face respirators, special galoshes, taped-up gloves and white overalls were meanwhile hunting the source of the plutonium. There had been no recent accident at the plant to account for her contamination. So, at Silkwood's request, they had trekked to her apartment. There the alpha counters commenced eerie gibberings. Plutonium, in small quantities, was everywhere. Outside on the lawn inspectors filled a 55-gallon drum with alarm clocks, cosmetics, record albums, drapes, pots and pans, shampoo, bedsheets. Alongside they stacked chairs, bed, stove, refrigerator, television, items to be trucked to the Kerr-McGee plant for later burial in a site approved by the Atomic Energy Commission (AEC).

The plutonium trail turned hottest in the kitchen, inside the refrigerator. A package of bologna and a package of cheese were the two most contaminated items in the apartment. Apparently, the plutonium had been tracked around the apartment from the refrigerator. But no one could explain how two sandwich foods had become the source of contamination.

The apartment was sealed off and the AEC called in.

Silkwood, however, was more worried about the plutonium inside her than on the

cheese and bologna. She kept popping the Quaaludes that had been prescribed a few weeks before. "The Quaaludes were just supposed to be taken for sleeping at nights," Stephens says. "But she was using them during the day, just to calm down. I'd never seen her so scared."

Wodka – a legislative assistant for the Oil, Chemical and Atomic Workers Interna-tional Union (OCAW) – had jetted in from Washington and, after talking to Kerr-McGee and AEC officials, had helped arrange for Silkwood to fly to an AEC laboratory in New Mexico to be checked out for poisoning. On Sunday, November 10, five days after her first contamination, she boarded a Braniff airliner.

That same morning a front-page *New York Times* story reported that, according to the AEC's own internal documents, the AEC had "repeatedly sought to suppress studies by its own scientists that found nuclear reactors were more dangerous than officially acknowl-edged or that raised questions about reactor safety devices." One AEC study, kept confi-dential for seven years, predicted that a major nuclear accident could kill up to forty-five thousand people and pollute an area the size of Pennsylvania. *Times* reporter David Burnham had sifted through hundreds of memos and letters and learned the AEC had a ten-year record of blue-penciling alarming data, soft-soaping test failures and glad-handing an industry that increasingly appeared not to know what it was doing.

The report gave scant comfort to Silkwood as she flew to Los Alamos, New Mexico. With her were Stephens and Sherri "Dusty" Ellis, her roommate of the past few months, who also worked at the plant but had refused to get involved in Silkwood's efforts to unmask the company.

Now all three shared the same fears; all had been contaminated in the apartment.

For two days they underwent a "whole body count," a meticulous probing of skin, orifices, intestines and lungs, urinating at intervals into plastic bottles and defecating into Freezette box containers.

After the first day, the three had cause for relief. Dr. George Voelz, the health-division leader, assured them they had suffered no immediate damage.

On Tuesday, November 12, Silkwood called her mother to announce the good news about the tests but added: "I'm still a little scared. I still don't know how I got con-taminated. I feel like someone's using me as a guinea pig."

"I told her to come home," her mother recalls. "And she said she was ready for a vacation. She just had to do a couple of things first."

After more body-prying tests at Los Alamos, the three travelers flew back to Oklahoma City, landing at about 10:30 Tuesday night. Because the women's apartment had been gutted of furniture, they checked in at Stephens's bungalow. Silkwood went to bed early. She had a busy day ahead. She had told Wodka she would give him the evi-dence she was collecting as soon as she returned from Los Alamos, and Wodka had set up a meeting with her and David Burnham, the *Times* reporter, who was winging in from the East Coast. The meeting was scheduled for Wednesday night at the Holiday Inn Northwest in Oklahoma City.

Wednesday morning Silkwood drove to work. Contract negotiations between Local 5-283 and Kerr-McGee had begun the week before and, as a commit-teewoman, she was supposed to take part in the bargaining. She spent the morning in negotiations, arguing union demands for better safety training and higher injury benefits. In the afternoon she met for several hours with AEC inspectors who were trying to unravel the mystery of her contamination.

At 5:15 p.m. she drove to Crescent, about five miles from the plant, and stopped at the Hub Café for a supper meeting, sans supper, to discuss negotiation strategy with Local 5-283. Jack Tice, who headed the negotiating team, told the assembled union mem-bers that, as expected, Kerr-McGee was not budging off its hard line.

Silkwood excused herself at about 6:00 p.m. to telephone Stephens, reminding him to pick up Wodka and Burnham at the airport and to expect her at the motel at about 8:00 p.m. She sounded normal, Stephens remembers, perhaps a bit excited about having an audience with the *New York Times*. At 7:15 p.m. Silkwood left the Hub Café and headed for Highway 74 and the Holiday Inn Northwest. A fellow union man would later swear in an affidavit that Silkwood, minutes before she left the restaurant, was carrying a manila folder an inch thick with papers. The folder, Silkwood told the union member, contained proof that quality-control records were being falsified.

Thirty miles away, Wodka, Burnham and Stephens waited for that proof until 8:45 p.m. Then they picked up the phone; but for some reason the Holiday Inn lines were out of order, and another hour passed before they could get through.

At 8:05 p.m., a truck driver, sitting high up in his cab and rolling along the two-lane highway, spotted the white Honda which was almost hidden in the muddy culvert. Silkwood had traveled about seven miles from the Hub Café, a ten-minute drive.

By the time Stephens, Wodka and Burnham learned the news from a local union member, the 1,638-pound Civic hatchback had already been towed to Ted Sebring's garage in Crescent. And Silkwood had been pronounced dead on arrival at Guthrie Hospital, the victim of multiple and compound fractures.

The three men raced to the culvert, only a mile from the plutonium plant, and prowled about, stepping gingerly through the mud, which in Oklahoma is the color of dried blood. All they could find were shards of aluminum trim, the orange roadside reflectors that had been trampled by the bouncing car and Silkwood's uncashed paycheck.

The explanation the state highway patrol offered was that Karen Silkwood, exhausted after driving six hundred miles from Los Alamos to Oklahoma City, had fallen asleep and drifted off the road to an accidental death. Almost immediately, the police had to alter their original version when they were told Silkwood had flown from Los Alamos and had gotten a full night's sleep only twelve hours before the crash.

The second official version was somewhat more convincing. Sometime during the afternoon of November 13, Silkwood had gulped down at least one of the pasty white Quaaludes from the vial in her coat pocket. Richard W. Prouty – the chief forensic toxicologist at the state morgue in Oklahoma City – discovered .35 milligrams of methaqualone in her bloodstream, conceivably enough to lull her to sleep on the highway.

But that was not sufficient for Steve Wodka.

Silkwood had swallowed several Quaaludes in the past week without nodding out. Why would she fall into a trance on her way to an extremely crucial meeting? And the proof of fraud she was supposedly carrying had disappeared. Her personal effects, listed by the medical examiner, included an ID badge, an electronic security key (for the plant), two marijuana cigarettes, a Kotex pad, two used Kleenexes, a Bradley Mickey Mouse pocket watch, a small notebook, her

clothes, $7 in bills and $1.69 in change. But there was no manila folder heavy with Kerr-McGee documents.

Trooper Rick Fagen, however, had mentioned finding dozens of loose papers blowing about the accident scene when he first arrived. Fagen had plucked up the papers, told his superiors and shoved them into the Honda. According to the highway patrol's information officer, Lieutenant Kenneth Vanhoy, the papers were in the Honda when Ted Sebring hauled the car away.

Presumably they were still there at 12:30 a.m. – five hours after the accident – when Sebring unlocked his garage for a group of Kerr-McGee and AEC representatives who said they wanted to check out Silkwood's car for plutonium contamination.

By the next afternoon, when Stephens, Wodka and Burnham claimed Silkwood's car from Sebring, no papers were inside.

Wodka called in Tony Mazzocchi at OCAW International. Mazzocchi agreed: An outside expert was needed to investigate the crash.

Three days after Silkwood's death, an auto-crash expert arrived in Oklahoma City from the Accident Reconstruction Lab of Dallas. A.O. Pipkin Jr., an ex-cop, was by that time a veteran of two thousand accidents and three hundred court trials, a no-nonsense pro considered the best man around for piecing together an accident scenario.

Dressed in a Day-Glo orange jumpsuit, Pipkin examined the Honda and found two curious dents, one in the rear bumper and another in the rear fender. They were fresh; there was no road dirt in them. And they appeared to have been made by a car bumper.

At the scene Pipkin noted that the Honda had crossed over the yellow lines and hit the culvert on the left side of the highway. If Silkwood had nodded into a stupor, he reasoned, she would have drifted to the right. In the red clay, Pipkin found something else the police had apparently disregarded: tire tracks indicating that the car had been out of control before it left the highway.

Pipkin's disconcerting conclusion: Karen Silkwood's Honda had been hit from the rear by another vehicle . . .

All her old clothes were under quarantine, suspected of plutonium contamination, so Karen Silkwood was buried in a new dress.

"Karen was a very unusual person," Wodka says. "She stood up to the company. She was outspoken. She was very brave, now that we look back on it; in many ways she was a lone voice."

the press & the presidency
by dan rather

IT WAS AUGUST 8, 1974. Still dazed by the events of the past few days, reporters from around the world gathered in Washington to await the announcement that Richard M. Nixon would resign the presidency.

It was a gut-wrenching time, and no one was unmoved. That evening, as I stood across the street from the White House and prepared to broadcast President Nixon's address to the nation, a figure darted out of the shadows and threw something at my chest: a black felt-tipped pen, staining my shirt just over the pocket. The park police rushed up and led the man responsible away. He was a member of the Nixon press staff, half out of his head with emotion.

He wasn't the first Nixon loyalist to blame the press for the president's predicament. Yet, although some of Watergate's questions may never be answered, this much we know: The press, print and broadcast, didn't bring down the president. He was brought down by his own actions and those of associates under his direct command.

For years, he had led what was proven to be a widespread criminal conspiracy, the purpose of which was not just to beat Richard Nixon's personal, political and ideological opponents at the polls – but to destroy them. He had led what amounted to his own secret police in a long, sustained series of illegal operations. In order to maintain this web of crime and to keep it covered up, he sought to subvert the Constitution.

And he very nearly succeeded.

Watergate changed me as a newsman. It changed Americans as a people, and it altered the way we think about politics. I am far less likely now to give any official spokesman the benefit of every doubt. Cynicism as an approach to reporting is wrong. But skepticism is essential.

A mood of intrigue and suspense dominated Washington during Watergate. The case was like a huge oil spill, running in every direction. Two former Cabinet members and several of the president's closest associates were being indicted by a federal grand jury. People were choosing sides, and I was aware – I would've been a fool not to be – that I had become part of that division. Not by design but as a consequence of my job. It wasn't an easy feeling. There was a sense of having traveled a bad road too long. Along the way I had acquired a reputation, as *New York* magazine had put it, as "The Reporter the White House Hates." (Given the time and temper, some people saw that label as a compliment.)

August 9, 1974: CBS News White House correspondent Dan Rather awaits President Nixon's last farewell

Yet, in such controversy-laden times, it becomes even more important to double-check your standards. At all times a reporter must try to be nothing more or less than an honest broker of information: "Just look 'em in the eye and tell 'em what you know," my father used to advise me. Nobody then or now wanted my opinion of the president on the air. What they wanted were facts, answers or at least the right questions. Who did what, when? Had criminal acts been committed? Was the presidency in peril?

By asking one such question, I dove headlong into the maelstrom that developed between the president and the press. The question arose in Smithville, Texas, my wife's hometown. The Pentagon Papers case was underway, and Smithville followed the reports with as much interest, and as many questions, as the rest of the country. According to my father-in-law, Martin Goebel, one question kept coming up in the post office and down at the barber shop: "Did they try to bribe that judge?" Did the president's men try to bribe Matthew Byrne Jr., the judge in the Pentagon Papers case?

I got the chance to ask that question on August 22, 1973.

After keeping a low profile for five and a half months while the country had become obsessed with Watergate, President Nixon decided to hold a press conference at the

Western White House, the first time he'd risk facing the press in a series of carefully orchestrated public appearances.

As the press conference began, the president grew more visibly irritated with each question. He'd prepared himself on a wide range of topics – half a year's worth of hard news had gone by – but almost all the questions pertained to Watergate. Actually, that suited the White House strategy. Pat Buchanan, Ken Clawson and other White House aides had been playing the expectations game for days: The president is going to face a press corps as hostile as a pack of wild dogs out there. With this setup, the president could launch a counterattack.

I'd had all summer to work and rework my question. "Mr. President," I began, "I want to state this question with due respect to your office, but also as directly as –"

"That would be unusual," he broke in.

Startled, but trying not to show it, I said, "I would like to think not."

His flash of annoyance was covered quickly. "You are always respectful, Mr. Rather," he said. "You know that."

I said, "Thank you, Mr. President." Then I went on. "It concerns the events surrounding your contact with the judge in the Pentagon Papers case, Judge Byrne. Now, you are a lawyer, and given the state of the situation and what you knew, could you give us some reason why the American people should not believe that there was at least a subtle attempt to bribe the judge in that case?"

The president reacted sharply to the question. "Well," he said, "I would say the only part of your statement that is perhaps accurate is that I am a lawyer." But his answer rambled and never really dealt with the question. There was little doubt in my mind that he wanted to come across as combative, fighting back. But he evaded the key questions. (Nevertheless, the truth became clear: The president's men had tried to bribe the judge with an offer of the directorship of the FBI.)

Before this news conference, I wasn't convinced there was any special tension between the president and me. Yet, months earlier, before anyone else had brought it up, my wife, Jean, said to me one night, "What is it between you and the president?"

And the answer was, I didn't know. Today it seems obvious. He was going to try to keep anyone off-balance who regularly asked questions he didn't want to answer. CBS News ran harder with the Watergate story than anyone else in television; I was frequently the face of that coverage as the network's chief White House correspondent.

Nixon knew how much he had to hide. We in the press and the public at large were finding out only in bits and pieces. He wanted to discourage any questions designed to ferret out tough truths – especially in public forums such as televised press conferences. Often Bob Pierpoint and I would team up at press conferences, one of us following up on the other's question. This gave us more opportunities to ask about Watergate, with special emphasis on statements by the president that didn't match the record. The president didn't like that, any of it.

Whatever feelings I had about Richard Nixon as a person were shaded by the fact that I never knew him very well and didn't know anyone who did. Some of his allies were sure I had some long-standing animus toward Nixon. They were wrong; I never understood their reasons for that belief. But Nixon seemed to view most of the Washington press, even those he didn't know, as enemies. And he surrounded himself with like-minded assistants.

If questioning and scrutiny by the press counted as enmity in the eyes of the president and his men, then outright opposition by political groups (whether Democrats, liberal Republicans, independents or others) must have been viewed as openly hostile, to be punished or put down with force. I believe that such thinking led to the Watergate burglary.

On June 17, 1972, a team of seven Nixon operatives broke into the offices of the Democratic National Committee in a high-rise complex called the Watergate. They wiretapped the phones. And they didn't take much. But they left a piece of tape on the lock of the stairwell door.

If the night watchman hadn't noticed that piece of tape, the entire Watergate story might have been missed. If a routine police car had answered the call at the Watergate offices, instead of an unmarked cruiser filled with a "Serpico" team (working undercover in hippie disguise), then White House functionaries might have been able to keep the break-in off the blotter altogether. And without that official notation, *Washington Post* reporters Carl Bernstein and Bob Woodward might never have known of the event. Instead, within twenty-four hours, they ran a small story.

That story alerted some of us who covered the White House regularly. For a while no one could begin matching what the *Washington Post* was able to accomplish with its head start, its network of both local and national government sources and the leadership of editor Ben Bradlee. But some of us were suspicious enough after that first story to begin digging and asking questions.

At first, the White House Press Secretary, Ron Ziegler, dismissed the break-in as "a third-rate burglary attempt. This is something that should not fall into the political process." Behind the scenes, White House sources offered "guidance" to key journalists, denying any political connection to the crime. Many print and broadcast outfits wound up dropping the story eventually, if not immediately.

Bill Small, CBS News Washington bureau chief, was an exception. When the first *Washington Post* story appeared, Small told me and my partner on the White House beat, Bob Pierpoint, "Get on it. And stay on it."

And we did – to the bitter end.

Living with a story every day is like trolling on the beach for coins that have fallen out of people's bathing trunks. You have to keep working your sources. During Watergate, the White House hierarchy sought to shut down all access there, but many people on Capitol Hill, from midlevel aides in the executive branch to secretaries, chauffeurs, waiters and cleaning people, knew a lot and talked a lot, once trust was established. Out of this might come a tip or a small break for that night's newscast.

By the waning days of summer 1974, proof abounded that the burglary was part of something much bigger, a sweeping program of political espionage financed with illegal money and directed by the president's closest associates – perhaps by the president himself. Believing Nixon's repeated denials of complicity, Ziegler had dutifully related them for two years. Now, suddenly, he declared all of the president's previous statements "inoperative." Proof positive against the president himself was still lacking. But the evidence was mounting. Week by week, President Nixon's support drained away. Nixon's desperation, and the country's anguish, kept growing.

Vice President Spiro Agnew fell from power, hastened by a push from Nixon himself. Agnew was caught taking money in a bribery deal he'd struck when he was still governor of Maryland. Nixon seemed to believe that sacrificing Agnew might somehow deflect some of the heat off of him.

In the wake of Agnew's disgrace, the White House staff was torn and panicky. First lower, then higher aides marched off to face the grand jury and, some of them, to prison. Much of the most damning testimony came from conversations captured on White House tape recordings – one of which contained a mysterious eighteen-minute gap.

Then, on July 24, 1974, the Supreme Court forced Nixon to release sixty-four White House tapes to the special prosecutor. Among them was one dated June 23, 1972, six days after the break-in at the Watergate. In three conversations that day with chief aide Bob Haldeman, Richard Nixon could be heard conspiring to commit perjury and bribery, to obstruct justice and to subvert the powers of the CIA and the FBI. This was "the smoking gun," proof of the president's guilt. A transcript of that tape was made public on the afternoon of August 5, 1974.

The country had been struck by a thunderbolt. Gamblers quit quoting odds on whether Nixon would be impeached. The ten Republican members of the House Judiciary Committee who had voted against the articles of impeachment now called on him to resign. The Republican leadership of the Senate, where any impeachment trial would be held, came as a group to the White House. They told Nixon he had only two options: to quit or to be impeached.

The president had withheld the truth from his own family. Even now, with his end assured and near, he allowed his daughter, Tricia, to gather a group of reporters and tell them her father had committed no crime, told no lies. It was one of the most poignant scenes in the history of the White House. Standing under the magnolia trees near the Rose Garden, Tricia spoke – with breaks in her voice and in her heart.

Three days later, Richard Nixon went on national television to announce his resignation.

During his first four years in office, I was often puzzled by how Nixon handled himself and allowed himself to be handled. He seemed like a man wounded and angry. It was in his eyes. Yet the few times I was ever actually near him for any length of time and got past the protective armor of the presidency, I can say truthfully that I didn't feel uncomfortable.

I remember an evening spent with him in January 1972. I'd joined him in the Oval Office for a rare, hour-long, one-on-one interview televised live over CBS. He told me later that he'd been surprised when the network assigned me to conduct the interview, but said he hadn't objected. The interview was intense, but he came off as being well prepared.

The time went by in track shoes. My last question had to do with the then-novel use of "Ms." as a salutation on White House correspondence. An attempt on my part to end the interview on a light note, the question was asked with a smile. But it seemed to throw him. He fumbled and never quite addressed the question.

The moment the camera lights went off and the telecast was over, he said, "I didn't understand that last question and I know I didn't handle it well." He didn't say it in an uptight way. As a matter of fact, he reached over from the chair and placed his hand on my arm. Very un-Nixonesque, I remember thinking at the time. It came across as a gesture of lament.

When we had finished, he rose and said, "I wish we could do that part over again." Then he smiled and added, "But that's the way it is with live television, isn't it?"

In no hurry, he moved around the room, posed for pictures and shook hands with every person there. Finally, after twenty-three minutes on the clock – I checked it – he said good night, and rather jauntily, I thought. And one didn't often have reason to describe him as doing much of anything "jauntily." He walked out of the office, through the French doors and across the south portico. No one was around him, not to his left or right. The nearest Secret Service agent stood twenty or thirty paces behind him. And as he walked past the magnolia tree that Andrew Jackson had planted and disappeared into the mansion, he began whistling.

I'd never heard him whistle. I came away from that night thinking, If people were ever permitted to see this open and unguarded side of Richard Nixon, he'd be vastly better off. So would we all.

Many of the recollections above were written much closer to the events they describe than to the day this book was published. Many things that seemed common knowledge a quarter-century ago have slipped into the dark corners of our consciousness: Nobody in Smithville asks about Judge Byrne nowadays, and we've all become so accustomed to the salutation "Ms." that the passage is bound to raise a smile.

Yet, all these years later, many questions from that era endure.

Did the press really deserve the reputation, good and bad, it received? Almost since the day of the break-in, politicians and reporters alike have tried to use the example of coverage of the Watergate crimes to illustrate various points about the role and limits of the press. The trouble with all these arguments, on all sides, is that these circumstances were so precise, indeed unique. Yes, you can draw lessons from Watergate, but it's hard to apply them to other situations. Nevertheless, people keep drawing parallels.

Political factions, especially those loyal to Richard Nixon, also add their voice to critics of the media, portraying Watergate and the president's resignation as "the press's fault." They aren't the first to learn that blaming the press can prove a useful diversion, and politicians from both parties have borrowed that page from Nixon's script. They describe the press as intrusive and abusive, as self-appointed, unaccountable judges, as biased. In the main, these charges are unwarranted – and blatantly politicized. Too often, journalists play right into their critics' hands.

They have the idea that they're going to be the next Bob Woodward and Carl Bernstein. But they're not emulating Woodward and Bernstein as they really were: tired, rumpled, doggedly pursuing musty documents and equally tired and rumpled sources. Too many reporters think there's something glamorous about bringing down a presidency, as if that were the best purpose of the press, as if that were what really happened in Watergate. They see

> The president bids the White House, the Watergate affair and the nation goodbye as his family watches: First Lady Pat Nixon, daughter Tricia Cox and son-in-law Ed Cox *(from left)*

their job as being a movie – starring Robert Redford and Dustin Hoffman – a good-looking, intensely dramatic package. They see *my* job as though it were simply to star on a TV show – also pretty exciting – and ignore the often tedious work that I do (searching out the same kind of musty documents and rumpled sources).

In the years since, reporters have covered subsequent scandals with the attitude that each might be a new Watergate. They apply the suffix "-gate" to anything they can think of: Iran-contra-gate, Iraq-gate, Whitewater-gate, Intern-gate. Some do this for outright ideological and partisan political reasons. Some do this because they're hungry for notoriety, or sky-high circulation figures and ratings. But most reporters do it simply because they're looking for a big score – a story they can sink their teeth into.

To this reporter's way of thinking, Watergate is more important for what it says about our government than for what it says about our press. It was the American people, after all, who decided Nixon's guilt and forced him from office. And how Americans respond when confronted with proof of criminal behavior from our presidents remains the most compelling question.

Watergate wasn't a glamorous time – it was a dangerous and frightening time. Fear of repeating such an episode was foremost in the minds of investigators during the 1980s' Iran-contra debacle. Again there were charges that the president's

top aides had subverted the Constitution by secretly sell-ing advanced weapons to an enemy nation and by con-ducting a clandestine war in Central America. With the Nixon chapter in mind, investigators made a conscious choice not to pursue tips that might have led to the impeachment of Ronald Reagan.

Reagan's vice president and successor, George Bush, also took part in covert actions at the scandal's heart. But Bush profited by the failure of the press to explain the seri-ous Constitutional questions involved. By the time he par-doned the officials whose testimony was believed most damaging to him, there was no outcry, and no threat of impeachment: Bush was hours away from leaving office, hav-ing lost to Bill Clinton.

As this is written, President Clinton is facing yet anoth-er year of intensive scrutiny of his conduct in and out of office. A battery of special prosecutors (along with some private attorneys and much of the press) has pried into

his business dealings and his administration of government, even his private life. Some of the charges leveled against Bill Clinton have appeared legitimate, serious enough to drive him from office, then diminished on closer inspec-tion. Others have appeared frivolous, prurient, tawdry – yet they don't go away.

It bears repeating: The destruction of a presidency isn't a process that should be entered into lightly. Every American must hope that each president is aware of that and so will avoid any action that might lead to his or her being driven from office.

But every reporter needs to be aware, too. Driving a pres-ident from office is not the proper purpose of American jour-nalism. It isn't something that we should look for opportunities to do. It isn't something we're really capable of anyway. All we can do, all we should do and all we *did* do, is find the facts and expose the evidence of wrongdoing where it exists – to help the people decide.   ⊕

deliver us from evel
by joe eszterhas

History will record that on Sunday, September 8, 1974, Evel Knievel, an American Folk Hero, risked death to conquer the Snake River Canyon as millions around the world cheered him on. But History, like the Qualls Park Ranch near Twin Falls, Idaho, where the event took place, is often piled with horseshit.

OUR FATHER WHO ART IN HEAVEN . . .
Weeks have passed since I left the canyons of the Snake. My pores have finally been freed of that foul dust and my sun-broken lips have finally shed their dead-man's crust. Goddamnit, though, I can still hear the howls behind that kiddyland picket fence; a jiggling Jell-O-like wall of flesh is strung around rocks, cottonwoods and sagebrush. Thousands of fists flail the desert-dry air. Thousands of voices, obsessed, howl at the sun.

"Eeeeeeeeeevel! Eeeeeeeeeevel! Knieeeeeeeeeevel!" Then with a whoosh that beer-bottle-shaped rocket zooms the blue sky and the cheap picket fences come creaking down and swarms of shrieking bodies are hurtling wildly through the dust storms of their own demented creation toward . . . the abyss, a few hundred feet from them, where the earth stops and there is nothingness, a headlong suicidal swan dive into the vomit-green waters of the forsaken Snake.

I remember that in the feverish moments before they played the national anthem and "The Ballad of Evel Knievel," I stood watching a girl with doe-soft eyes and layers of baby fat as she stripped her T-shirt away (obeying the scrawled sign that said, CHICKS, SHOW YOUR TITS!) and was then lifted by hundreds of inflamed and horny hands into the scorched air. The hands moved over her, scratching and squeezing and twisting her nipples, and the hands moved down, tearing away her jeans, and the hands grabbed and mauled her buttocks, ripping away her panties and the girl ascended on high into the swelter again. More and more hands wriggled in for yet unsullied pieces of her pale skin until, a human fleshball, her nakedness debauched, her tongue lolling, she was discarded – thrown over the fence and into the press compound. I was a few feet from her, and I will always remember the bleeding and bruised wounds that were her breasts.

In the moments after the jump . . . after he had been rescued from the depths of that void and after he had pranced and paraded before his fawning faithful and after he had mumbled a few grudging pietisms to his own peculiar god . . . I remember that Knievel hurled his legendary cane into a still-hungry crowd. Oh, how they battled for it! That was it, wasn't it? The gold-tipped and diamond-studded magic wand worth thousands of dollars? So a group of men fought wild-eyed over it, clenched their fists and threw their elbows, and the guy who finally won stood with blood shooting from a cut over his eye and with the world's biggest grin on his face. Jesus, he couldn't believe it! And then he looked at it. And Jesus, he couldn't believe it again! It wasn't the magic wand. It wasn't gold. There were no diamonds in it. It was a substitute. A cold piece of steel thrown from that red-white-and-blue Erector-set mountaintop for the sheer showbiz of it. And the guy had fought bravely for his treasured souvenir and had been given nothing but a cheap prop. He was himself nothing more than an extra.

HALLOWED BE THY NAME . . .
On the day I arrive in the Magic Valley I drive out to the canyon and inspect the abyss – 1,600 feet from rim to rim and 540 feet deep, a place Lewis and Clark never discovered, too deep and too steep for most pioneers to have explored, within sight of Shoshone Falls, which is higher than Niagara. The south rim of the canyon, I discover, has some trees and pigeons, while the north side – barren and stark – is a forbidding no-man's-land. The Snake is down there, as still and bilious as a giant oil slick, named for Indians who were so poor they had to dig the earth for food with their bare hands. I stare down

into that moonscape nothingness for a long time and then hurry back to Twin Falls, Idaho.

Evel Knievel's jump was, of course, on a lot of people's minds, but as August ended it was as though no one could ignore it any longer. Knievel himself was running around the country drumming up his show, and a record album he released set a scenario that put two hundred thousand people on that canyon rim. Two hundred thousand people in a town of twenty thousand!

The new Skycycle X-2 squats at the bottom of a 108-foot triangular steel ramp aimed at a 56-degree angle into the sky and anchored in cement atop a pyramid mound of dust. It is bedecked with Mack truck, Harley-Davidson and Chuckles insignias, painted in a stars-and-stripes pattern and bears the words EVEL KNIEVEL and COLOR ME LUCKY.

But staring at the launch ramp, I can't find a motorcycle. I am reminded of the words of Bill Wiseman, a Twin Falls County commissioner, who keeps insisting: "This thing's a phony, if you ask me. It's not a motorcycle jump, it's a rocket jump."

My dilemma is cleared up later that afternoon when I discover that the 13-foot-long and 1,300-pound vehicle is, according to the state of Idaho, an airplane – and has been registered with the state as such. According to the FAA, it is an unmanned rocket – since the star will have little control over it. According to Evel Knievel, it is neither an airplane nor a rocket but a "Skycycle." Well, what the hell kind of animal is a Skycycle? I ask one of the star's aides. "There's never been one before," he muses, "so it's anything Evel says it is."

This beer-bottle-shaped watertank/rocket/cycle at the site is quickly being hemmed in, I notice, by concession stands. While there is a lot of doubt about the exact nature of the beast itself, there is no doubt at all about who is going to cash in on the concessions around it. "I'll own the peanut and popcorn concession out there, too," the star once said, and he has kept his word. Evel Knievel gets a cut of everything here. Nothing, nothing, is sold without his written approval. He gets 60 percent of the gate – and it costs $25 per person to get in here – plus camping permission, which ranges from $7.50 per night for a pickup truck to $2 per for a motorcycle. He gets 30 percent of the profit from the T-shirts sold here, as well as the corn on the cob and beer and 7-Up and the hotdogs, hamburgers and pizzas.

The mind boggles. Will the Star of stars become the Millionaire of millionaires?

At the site Friday, the scene seems more worn-out than ever. The sun beats down from a pitiless sky and the dust is like thin smoke in the air and the abyss is wreathed in a gauzy haze.

By 2:00 p.m., the star's disciples are very restless and the most hot-blooded of them have formed a derelict corner of their own by the gate that is the entrance to the launch ramp. There are perhaps 250 of them in this pack, including a bare-breasted girl. The girl is yellow-haired, in her twenties and pretty, wearing only a pair of cut-off Levi's. But it is her eyes I notice – as empty as a skull's turned inward in contemplation of some drug-induced vision. And she rides on the shoulders of a young man whose belly is so big it seems like a wound. He is hogheaded and repulsive, a walking trophy head, a symbol of the triumph of his piggery, maybe.

The Hollow Lady and the Goiter lead the crowd at the gate to increasing levels of bedlam and chaos. They are beating at the fence and now they are pulling at it and – Jesus! they look like they're coming through, screaming: "Eeeeeeeeeevel Knieeeeeeeeeeevel!"

The star himself has finally arrived and he is in a shit-stomping, fist-fucking mood. His eyes are ice and there is a waxiness to his face and he is stomping and swaggering. Why? Why not? He is the star, the center of this particular universe, the Lord of the Abyss. He is a flesh-and-blood dazzle. He's got his diamond-studded cane and he's wearing his white Old Glory jumpsuit with the red and blue stripes and the white stars spreading in a V across his chest. He's wearing blue leather gloves and red-and-white sneakers and, as an army of musclemen move in lockstep around him, he hustles up the anthill toward the Skycycle with a condescending behind-the-back wave at the Hollow Lady and the Goiter.

The Goiter strains himself as the star rockets by and pushes the Hollow Lady higher into the heat. She stretches up there holding her breasts up and out and whinnying: "Oooooh, Eeeeeeeevel! Ooooooooh, over here!" The Goiter starts the chant again – "We want Eeeeeeeevel! We want in! We want in right now! We're going crazy! We're going crazy!" The star comes down the anthill, revved-up and overheated, sees them, and says to a shotgunned deputy: "If those goddamned sonsobitches come up here, blow their goddamn heads off!" The gunman nods and says nothing. The look in his eyes says he won't have to be told again.

As he heads toward his trailer, event promoter Bob Arum tries to soothe him and the star yells: "Look at this! Sunday is the greatest day of my life and it's being run by a bunch of goddamn Jews!" And Arum backs away from him, laughs, tries to make a joke of it – "It's hot up there, he's tired and he probably needs his salt tablets." Arum grasps for his manhood and adds softly with the ever-present smile: "If there's one thing I can't stand, it's a longhaired loudmouth cowboy."

The star is in his trailer next to the launch ramp and his press conference will begin any minute now. Newsmen swoop around the steps outside the trailer door.

Jim Watt, an NBC cameraman from Los Angeles, a little man with a monstrous camera slung over his shoulder, tells the producer he would appreciate it if the star stood during his press conference.

But the star has overheard Watt. He explodes through the trailer door: "If I wanna siddown, I'm gonna siddown!" Watt stands there bearing the cross of his heavy camera, his mouth open, as though kicked in the gut. "Out!" the star yells.

For eighteen seconds, nothing happens . . . Boom! Here he comes again, as he-man a hero as you will ever see, his face splotched with color and exuding a hellbent ferocity – and all of this, I suddenly realize, is aimed at the stupefied Watt.

"Tell him the next time he looks at me to have a smile on his face!" Evel Knievel yells. "I'm not an actor, Mr. Cameraman, do you understand that?"

Then the scene speeds up and lurches wildly because Watt, an ordinary man with an ordinary man's sense of dignity, suddenly shows the world that he will not be pushed around.

"I don't smile for anybody," Watt says.

conversation (six days after the Watergate break-in) that clearly reveals Nixon's knowledge of the incident and his desire to stop the FBI investigation. Congressional opposition to impeachment all but disappears.

6 Jazz saxophone legend Gene "Jug" Ammons dies.

7 J. Geils Band frontman Peter Wolf and actress Faye Dunaway marry in Beverly Hills; they'll divorce in 1979.

8 Nixon announces that, effective the next day, he will resign the presidency, the first time a U.S. president has ever done so. His successor, Vice President Ford, assures the country that there will be no change in foreign policy, and that Secretary of State Kissinger will remain in office.

9 Nixon resigns and Ford is sworn in as the 38th president of the United States of America. Five days later, private citizen Richard Nixon is served papers to appear at John Ehrlichman's Watergate trial.

16 The Ramones play their CBGB debut; the club will become New York's punk-rock mecca.

20 President Ford nominates former New York governor Nelson Rockefeller for vice president, shortly after requesting $850,000 from Congress for "administration transition expenses" and to help former President Nixon through the next fiscal year. Ford had also announced that the White House would retain control of all of Nixon's Watergate-related documents and tapes until their legal ownership is determined.

24 Paul Anka's "(You're) Having My Baby" tops the pop singles chart despite denunciations from feminists (who object to the term "my" baby instead of "our") and government officials (who claim the lyrics are unclear as to the parents' marital status).

1974 SEPTEMBER

8 President Ford grants Nixon a full pardon for all federal crimes he may have committed, although he has yet to be charged with any.

Daredevil Evel Knievel fails to complete his much-publicized 1,600-foot jump over the Snake River Canyon in Idaho when the parachute on his steam-powered "Skycycle" opens prematurely.

The star comes at him. Evel Knievel stands inches taller than Watt and he has that damned cane in his hands and he is using it now on Watt's camera and on Watt's shoulders. The little man tries to defend himself, which is not easy with that cross over his shoulder.

"Get him out!" the star yells. "I don't need any crap from any cameraman like you!" and then Evel Knievel jams the camera into Watt's face and hits him with the cane and Watt is on the ground, the camera smashed out of his hands.

THY KINGDOM COME . . .

Whenever some occasional stray fool questions the star about the risks involved, casting aspersions, really, on his very *machohood*, the star has the proof. Risks? Shit, man, two Skycycles have gone down already – "the only two tests have been failures that would have killed me."

Late Saturday afternoon, sitting on the Holiday Inn floor, I am waiting for Evel Knievel, and so are some four hundred other reporters.

"Are you going to apologize to that cameraman for roughing him up?" I ask Knievel.

It goes off like a shotgun blast in a tunnel. My colleagues' silence is the silence of the dead. Evel Knievel stares at me and a voice inside me warns: Watch your ass, pal.

"I wouldn't apologize," Evel Knievel growls. "And if I see the little sonofabitch again I'll throw him out of here. How's that?" My colleagues cheer.

One of them begins a question. Knievel and I still have our eyes locked.

"Why should I apologize to him, is he a friend of yours?"

"No," I say, "I don't even know him." The reporters laugh. Knievel looks off into the back of the room and smirks.

"However," I say, my finger jabbing the air, "I think you should apologize to him."

He can't believe it. He clenches his cane so hard his fingers are like snow. The silence in the room is very loud.

"What?" he says.

Knievel gives me a look that a reporter for the *New Mexico Independent* will describe as "seeming on the verge of ordering the offending newsman dismembered on the spot."

"I think you should apologize to him," I repeat.

"I wanna straighten you out right now!" he yells. "Number one, I was in the Skycycle all day. Number two, you were a guest of mine in a press area, do you understand that? And so was he! Number three, when I've been up there all day and the blood's coming from my hands and my feet into my head and I come down to wanna get some rest and get along with you people – don't tell me to come out and stand up. If I wanna come out and try to get along with you, you should at least allow me to sit down! So tell him I said to" – he bellows the words – "kiss my ass! And you too!"

THY WILL BE DONE . . .

On the day of the Event of the Century, the temperature is in the high eighties and a twenty-miles-per-hour wind is blowing. The dust is so thick that some people look gray. Photographers are covering their equipment with plastic bags, crying about the cost of ruin.

New security guards have been hired to replace those who've abandoned the site. They are standing in a group near the Skycycle, the brave men who will keep the horde from going over into the abyss. They are being paid exactly nothing – except the chance to get a close-up look at the jump and at the abyss. They are led by . . . the Goiter! The Goiter waves his fat arms a lot and shouts a lot of commands. He has been legitimized.

The swarm has little to do and not much to see. It has but one thing to do and it throws itself militantly into this task. The swarm screams and tugs at the fence.

The star is up on the anthill in his Old Glory jumpsuit talking to David Frost. "If I have to hit that wall over there on the other side," he says, "I think that I would rather do that than become the victim of a senseless tragedy. I'd rather be busted into the wind like a meteorite and not become just dust."

A kid watches them outside the fence but can't hear what they are saying. "Cut the shit!" he yells. "Get it the hell on!"

The swarm is really crunching into the fence now and screaming at the newsmen. "You cocksuckers! Let us in there!" one kid yells. "Get the press!" says another. "Kill the goddamn press!" Some of the reporters are becoming very . . . concerned . . . and flee inside the big top.

Father Jerry Sullivan, wearing a rumpled suit, solemnly says the benediction. "We all pray that he'll have a successful landing," Father Sullivan prays, "whether that may be on Earth or in heaven." Linda, a woman with size-46 double-D breasts, wears a T-shirt that says: BUILT LIKE A MACK TRUCK. Linda says she camped out here all night with some guys representing Mack trucks. "Boy," she says, "after all this heavy foreplay this thing better have a juicy ending."

The preliminary acts are over now. The moment has come. The star begins ascending toward the Skycycle in his Freedom Crane. The swarm howls.

A guy outside the fence grabs his girl by the hair, forces her on her knees and unzips his fly. He is hanging out there in the hot air at the very moment Evel is ascending and she is sucking his cock. The guy yells: "For you, Evel! For you, man!" The girl stops resisting and gets into it.

The teenage ladies of the Butte High School Marching Band play "The Star-Spangled Banner." The star waves to his wife, then flips a thumbs-up salute to his masses.

"Bob," the star says to Truax, his engineer, "you and your men have done every single thing that you could do. The rest is up to me."

"Cut the shit!" a kid screams. "Get it on!"

He's strapped into his Skycycle. There is a long silence, then a whoooooooooooosh!, orange smoke and the rocket/water-tank/cycle is off.

The moment it goes up, the Goiter and his deputies abandon their fence. Fuck the security! They can't see from here! They turn from the fence and start running across the press compound toward the fence in front of them only a few feet from the rim. The Goiter leads. His outlaws follow. The swarm knocks down the abandoned fence and follows the outlaws. The Goiter is the king of the swarm once again.

But something is very wrong up there in the sky. The drogue parachute on the Skycycle opens when it is not yet two-thirds of the way up the ramp. The rocket goes up too slowly and then, as it heads toward the sun, the main parachute opens and the rocket stops dead. It is like a ball that has come to the end of a rubber band . . . turns upside down, and drifts slowly into the abyss.

ON EARTH AS IT IS IN HEAVEN.

As I listen to those unending "Eeeeeeeeeeeevel! Knieeeeeeeeeevel!" screams, I realize it is time for a final tally. So I check my list.

The test-failures weren't test-failures.

The Skycycle wasn't a cycle.

The two hundred thousand people expected to attend turned into fifty thousand people.

The fifty thousand people turned into fifteen thousand people.

Invited guest Elvis Presley turned into an invisible being. So did John Wayne. So did Steve McQueen.

The Evel Knievel Security turned into Goiter and his outlaws.

The VIP bleachers turned into the Hollow Lady's perch.

The public-relations men turned into misinformation men.

The reporters turned into public-relations men.

The jump turned into a nosedive.

The abyss turned out to be harmless.

The Event of the Century turned into a farce.

Monday morning, the day after the Event of the Century, the headlines are splashed over the top of the front page of every newspaper of every city in the land. The headlines are the focus of much of the world's attention. FORD PARDONS NIXON, the headlines say. ⊕

10 St. Louis Cardinals infielder Lou Brock sets a professional-baseball record when he steals his 105th base of the season.

12 Violence erupts as white students and families opposed to integrated busing boycott classes in South Boston. Schools call in police protection, but fighting continues for weeks, peaking Oct. 15. Gang wars ignite, several students are hospitalized and the presence of the Massachusetts National Guard is requested.

15 Soviet authorities use bulldozers and antiriot gear to crush an open-air "unofficial art" show in Moscow.

16 Strongly criticizing the prosecutor of the case, a federal judge dismisses all charges relating to the Wounded Knee occupation against AIM leaders Russell Means and Dennis Banks.

President Ford signs a Vietnam War clemency act offering repatriation and pardons to all draft resisters and military deserters in exchange for two years of public service and an oath of allegiance. When the program period ends the following Mar. 31, only 22,500 of the 124,400 eligible will have acted on the offer.

17 After repeated *New York Times* reports of U.S. involvement in the overthrow of Salvador Allende Gossens's Chilean government, the Senate Foreign Relations Committee initiates an investigation. On Oct. 3, Chile's military junta admits to holding more than 700 political prisoners, though press reports give numbers as high as 60,000.

18 A sell-out crowd of followers of Korean preacher Rev. Sun Myung Moon flocks to New York City's Madison Square Garden; approximately half of the "Moonies" depart before the end of his speech.

23 Average White Band drummer Robbie McIntosh dies after inhaling white powder procured from a Los Angeles scene-maker, believing it to be cocaine. It turns out to be strychnine-based heroin.

24 A three-day music festival opens in Kinshasa, Zaire, heralding the upcoming George Foreman–Muhammad Ali fight. It features 31 musical acts, including event coproducer Lloyd Price, James Brown, the Staple Singers, the Spinners, B.B. King, Miriam Makeba, Hugh Masekela and

funky chic
by tom wolfe

BY OCTOBER OF 1969, Funky Chic was flying through London like an infected bat, which is to say silently, blindly, insanely and at night, fangs afoam – but with an infallible aim for the main vein. Funky Chic, as I say, came skipping and screaming into the United States the following year in the form of such marvelous figures as the Debutante in Blue Jeans. She was to be found on the fashion pages in every city of any size in the country. There she is . . . wearing her blue jeans and her blue work shirt, open to the sternum, with her long pre-Raphaelite hair parted on top of the skull, uncoiffed but recently washed and blown dry with a Continental Pro Style dryer (the word of mouth that year said the Continental gave her more "body") . . . and she is telling her interviewer:

"We're not having any 'coming-out balls' this year or any 'deb parties' or any of that. We're fed up with doing the same old things, which are so useless, and seeing the same old faces and dancing to so-called 'society bands' while a lot of old ladies in orange-juice-colored dresses stand around the edges talking to our parents.

"We're tired of cotillions and hunt cups and weekends. You want to know what I did last weekend? I spent last weekend at the day-care center, looking after the most beautiful black children . . . and learning from them!"

Or, as a well-known, full-grown socialite, Amanda Burden, said at that time: "The sophistication of the baby blacks has made me rethink my attitudes." Whereupon she described herself as "anti-fashion."

Anti-fashion! Terrific. Right away anti-fashion itself became the most raving fashion imaginable . . . also known as Funky Chic. Everybody had sworn off fashion, but somehow nobody moved to Cincinnati to work among the poor. Instead, everyone stayed put and imported the poor to the fashion pages. That's the way it happened!

Today, in 1974, the age of Funky Chic Égalité, fashion is a much more devious, sly and convoluted business than anything that was ever dreamed of at Versailles. At Versailles, where Louis XIV was installed in suites full of silver furniture (later melted down to finance a war), one could scarcely be *too* obvious. Versailles was, above all, the City of the Rich. Hundreds of well-to-do upward-hustling families had quarters there. The only proper way to move about the place was in sedan chairs borne by hackmen with straining trapeziuses. Anytime a notable of high social wattage gave a party there, there would be a sedan-chair traffic jam of a half hour or more outside his entryway as the true and original *jeunesse dorée*, in actual golden threads and golden slippers, waited to make the proper drop-dead entrance.

One has only to compare such a scene with any involving the golden youth of our own day. I recommend to anyone interested in the subject, the long block, or concourse, in New Haven, Connecticut, known as Broadway, where Elm and York Streets and Whalley and Dixwell Avenues come together. This is near the heart of Yale University. Twenty years ago, at Elm and York, there was a concentration of men's custom-tailoring shops that seemed to outnumber all the tailors on Fifth Avenue and Fifty-seventh Street put together. They were jammed in like pearls in a box. Yale was, after all, the place where the *jeunesse dorée* of America were being groomed, in every sense of the word, to inherit the world; the world, of course, being Wall Street and Madison Avenue. Five out of every seven Yale undergraduates could tell whether the button-down Oxford-cloth shirt you had on was from Fenn-Feinstein, J. Press or Brooks Brothers from a single glance at your shirtfront – Fenn-Feinstein: plain breast pocket; J. Press: breast pocket with buttoned flap; Brooks Brothers: no breast pocket at all. Today J. Press is still on the case, but others of the heavenly host are shipping out. Today, a sane businessman would sooner open a souvlaki takeout counter at Elm and York than a tailor shop, for reasons any fool could see. On the other side of the grand concourse, lollygagging up against Brooks Health and Beauty Aids, Whitlock's and the Yale Co-op, are the new Sons of Eli. They are from the same families as before, averaging about $37,500

17 Zairian groups.

26 John Lennon's last album of original music released in the Seventies, *Walls and Bridges*, is released; with the help of Elton John's backing vocals, it becomes his first #1 LP. On Nov. 16 the album's lead single, "Whatever Gets You Through the Night," hits the top of the charts as well. Twelve days later, Lennon fulfills a promise and joins Elton John onstage at Madison Square Garden, singing "Whatever . . .," "Lucy in the Sky With Diamonds" and "I Saw Her Standing There."

1974 OCTOBER

1 One of professional basketball's highest-scoring players (on and off the court), Wilt Chamberlain announces his retirement.

5 Top of the charts: Olivia Newton-John's "I Honestly Love You" (pop single); the Beach Boys' *Endless Summer* (pop album).

8 Wearing a button that reads WIN, President Ford explains the acronym by stating that his economic reform program intends to "Whip Inflation Now."

13 TV's legendary variety-show host Ed Sullivan dies.

17 The Oakland A's defeat the Los Angeles Dodgers in five games and win their third consecutive World Series.

18 *The Odessa File*, a film based on the best-selling novel about a reporter investigating neo-Nazis and starring Jon Voight, opens.

25 Singer Al Green suffers severe burns when his girlfriend Mary Woodson (who suffered from depression) throws a pot of boiling grits on him. She then shoots herself in Green's Memphis home. The former gospel singer will soon return to the church, adopt a sacred-music-only repertoire and become a minister.

29 Following surgery for phlebitis, former President Nixon suffers postoperative shock and falls into critical condition in California. Judge Sirica will excuse him from two ongoing Watergate trials until Feb. 1975. He will not testify at either.

30 In a moonlit championship bout that begins at 4:00 a.m. local time, Muhammad Ali regains the heavyweight boxing title in Kinshasa, Zaire, defeating George Foreman in eight rounds.

gross income per annum among the scholarship students. But there is nobody out there checking out breast pockets or jacket vents or any of the rest of it. The unvarying style at Yale today is best described as Late Army Surplus. Broadway Army & Navy enters Heaven! Sons in Levis, break through that line! That is the sign we hail! Visible at Elm and York today are more olive-green ponchos, clodhoppers and parachute boots, more leaky-dye-blue turtlenecks, pea jackets, ski hats, long-distance-trucker warms, sheepherder's coats, fisherman's slickers, down-home tenant-farmer bib overalls, coal-stocker strap undershirts, fringed cowpoke jerkins, strike-ball-blue work shirts, lumberjack plaids, forest-ranger mackinaws, Australian-bushrider mackintoshes, Cong saddles, bike leathers and more jeans, jeans, jeans, jeans, jeans, more prole gear of every description than you ever saw or read of in a hundred novels by Jack London, Jack Conroy, Maxim Gorky, Clara Weatherwax and any who came before or after.

Of course, this happens to be precisely what America's most favored young men are wearing at every other college in the country, so that you scarcely detect the significance of it all until you look down to the opposite end of the concourse, to the north, where Dixwell Avenue is the main drag of one of New Haven's black slums. There, on any likely corner, one can see congregations of young men the same age as the Yalies but . . . from the bottom end of the great greased pole of life, as it were, from families whose gross incomes no one but the eligibility worker ever bothered to tote up. All the young aces and dudes are out there lollygagging around the front of the Monterey Club, wearing their two-tone patent Pyramids with the five-inch heels that swell out at the bottom to match the Pierre Chareau Art Deco plaid bell-bottom baggies they have on with the three-inch-deep elephant cuffs tapering upward toward that "spray-can fit" in the seat, as it is known, and the peg-top waistband with self-covered buttons and the beagle-collar pattern-on-pattern Walt Frazier shirt, all of it surmounted by the mid-length leather piece with the welted waist-seam and the Prince Albert pockets and the black pimpmobile hat with the four-inch turn-down brim and the six-inch pop-up crown with the golden chain-belt hatband . . . and all of them, every ace, every dude out there just *getting over* in the baddest possible way, come to play and dressed to slay . . . so that somehow the sons of the slums have become the Brummels and Gentlemen of Leisure, the true fashion plates of 1973, and the Sons of Eli dress like the working class of 1934 . . .

. . . a style note that I mention not merely for the sake of irony. In 1968, 1969 and 1970 the term *counterculture* actually meant something. In those wild, spitting hot-bacon days on the campus, counterculture referred to what seemed to be a fast-rising unity of spirit among all the youth of the nation, black and white, a new consciousness (to use a favorite word from that time) that was mobilizing half the country, the half that was now under twenty-five years old (to use a favorite statistic from that time), under the banner of revolution or something not far from it. Yet at that very moment the youth of the country were becoming bitterly divided along lines of class and status. The more the New Left tried to merge them in a united front, the more chaotic and out-of-the-question the would-be coalition became.

Fashion was hardly one of the root causes of this division – that is another, longer story. But fashion was in many cases the cutting edge. Fashion brought out hopeless status conflict where there was no ideological conflict whatsoever. Groups who were unified ideologically remained split along a sheerly dividing line, an instinctive status line, a line that might even be described by the accursed word itself, *fashion*. This was multiplied endlessly, through every instance in which the New Left tried to enlist the youth of the working class or of the slums. There never was a counterculture in the sense of any broad unity among the young – and this curious, uncomfortable matter of fashion played a part, over and over. I never talked to a group of black militants, or Latin militants, for that matter, who didn't eventually comment derisively about the poor-boy outfits their middle-class white student allies insisted on wearing or the way they tried to use black street argot, all the *mans* and *cats* and *babys* and *brothers* and *baddests*. From the very first, fashion tipped them off to something that was not demonstrated on the level of logic until much later: Namely, that most of the white New Lefters of the period from 1968 to 1970 were neither soldiers nor politicians but simply actors.

The tip-off was not the fact that the middle-class whites were dressing *down* in order to join their slum-bound brethren. The issue was not merely condescension. The tip-off was that when the whites dressed down, went Funky Chic, they did it *wrong!* They did it *lame!* They never bothered to look at what the brothers on the streets were actually wearing! They needed to have their coats pulled! The New Left had a strictly old-fashioned conception of life on the street; a romantic and nostalgic one somehow derived from literary images of proletarian life from before World War II or even World War I. A lot of those white college boys, for example, would go for those checkered lumberjack shirts that are so heavy and woolly that you can wear them like a jacket. It was as if all the little Lord Byrons had a hopeless nostalgia for the proletariat of about 1910, the Miners With Dirty Faces era, and never mind the realities, because the realities were that by 1968 the real hard-core street youth in the slums were not into lumberjack shirts, Can't-Bust-'Ems and army-surplus socks. They were into ruffled shirts and black-belted leather pieces and bell-cuff herringbones, all that stuff, macking around, getting over, looking sharp . . . heading toward the

was utterly lost on black or any other-colored street aces and scarlet creepers. Jeans were associated with funk in its miserable aspects, with Down-and-Out, bib overalls, Down-home and I'm Gonna Send You Back to Georgia. Recently jeans have just begun to be incorporated in the Ace or Pimp look thanks to certain dramatic changes in jeans couture, such as the addition of metal-stud work, bias-cut two-tone swirl mosaic patterns and the rising value of used denim fabric, now highly prized for its "velvet hand" (and highly priced, just as a used Tabriz rug is worth more than a new one). In other words, the aces will now tolerate jeans precisely because they have lost much of their funk.

Well-to-do white youths still associate jeans in any form and at any price with funk, however, and Funky Chic still flies and bites the main vein and foams and reigns. The current talk of a Return to Elegance or the Gatsby Look among the young immediately becomes a laugh and a half (or, more precisely, the latest clothing industry shuck) to anyone who

Everybody wears clown suits these days. Denim jackets and leisure suits. Bellbottoms! Everybody wants to look like a lifestyle now. –R. Crumb

high-heeled pimpmobile *got to get over* look of Dixwell Avenue 1973. If you tried to put one of those lumpy mildewed mothball lumberjack shirts on them – those aces – they'd *vomit.*

For years the sheerly dividing line was the single item of clothing that is practically synonymous with Funky Chic: blue jeans. Well-to-do Europeans appreciated the chic of jeans – that primitive rawness! that delicious grip on the gourd and the moist skinny slither up into all the cracks and folds and fissures! – long before Americans. Even in the early Fifties, such special styles as the London S.W.5 New Wave Habitat Bentwood Movie-Producer Chic and South-of-France Young Jade Chic and Jardins du Luxembourg Post-*Breathless* Chic all had at their core: blue jeans. Cowboy Chic, involving blue jeans and walking around as if you have an aluminum beer keg between your thighs, has been popular among young Parisian lollygaggers for at least fifteen years. Well-to-do whites in America began to discover the raw-vital reverse-spin funk thrill of jeans in the early Sixties. But until very recently any such appeal

sets foot on a mainly white American campus, whether Yale or the University of California at San Diego. A minor matter perhaps; but today, as always, the authentic language of fashion is worth listening to. For fashion, to put it most simply, is the code of the language of status. We are in an age when people will sooner confess their sexual secrets – much sooner, in many cases – than their status secrets, whether in the sense of longings and triumphs or humiliations and defeats. And yet we make broad status confessions every day in our response to fashion.

Goethe once noted that in the last year of his reign, Louis XVI took to sleeping on the floor beside his enormous royal bed, because he had begun to feel that the monarchy was an abomination. Down there on the floor he felt closer to the people. How very . . . funky . . . Well, I won't attempt any broad analogies. Nevertheless, it demonstrates one thing. Even when so miserable a fashion as Funky Chic crops up . . . stay alert! Use your bean! ⊕

the androgynous mirror
by jim farber

ON A SWAMPY July night in 1974, I left my suburban home bound for David Bowie's Diamond Dogs concert, dressed in midnight-blue eyeliner, hepatitis-yellow platforms and a lollipop-green jacket poofed at the shoulder and bustled at the back.

Somehow I was not killed. Done up to this degree – and joined by a male friend bedecked in a banana-cream suit with strawberry-puff platforms – I made it down the long street where I lived, onto the Metro-North train, through the sweep of Grand Central Station, between the clanking doors of a downtown subway and up to Madison Square Garden, all the while drawing no more than a few affectionate snickers and a string of raised eyebrows – mainly from the old or the clueless.

At perhaps no other time in history could two sixteen-year-old boys have made such a trip and not been slandered, beaten or worse. Yet here we were, graced by a time (the mid-Seventies) and buoyed by a trend (glitter rock) that turned out to be golden – a time when the relationship between flouncy affectation and sexual orientation seemed tenuous at best. The glam revolution, which took Bowie as its hermaphroditic patron saint, promised to forever sever the bonds between prissy finery and what you did down there, to fuck with gender like it has never been fucked with before. How lucky for me to be going through a sexual identity crisis at the precise moment that pop culture was having one too!

At its commercial zenith (1974–75), glitter shone through nearly every genre of pop. It dictated fashion and loosened behavior: The more fey an act, the more media play it got, affecting everyone from hard-rock acts like Blue Öyster Cult to R&B groups like Labelle. By '73, the movement had become common enough to make then-trendy fops like Rod Stewart claim to have created it. "Shit, I'm sure we must have been one of the first with glitter," the straight star told ROLLING STONE at the time.

In such a topsy-turvy sliver of time, no one had to know that I was precisely as gay as my clothes might inform anyone from a later – or earlier – generation. In fact, with my attachment to glitter, as a nervous, virginal midteen, I wasn't announcing my coming out but insuring my staying in. Pledging allegiance to glitter rock awarded me a safety zone in which I could both sidestep old definitions of what it meant to be a boy and stave off a commitment to what it would eventually mean for me to be a gay man.

At right: David Bowie assumes his Ziggy persona at home, 1972; following page: Lance Loud (*top left*) with his family

In terms of the larger culture, several factors drove rock to put on the pumps and pencil in the eyeliner. In part, the sexual revolution of the Sixties upped the stakes from hetero promiscuity to an omnisexual free-for-all. Glitter also served as a nifty PR gimmick, injecting fresh shock into rock. The focus on flash came as something of a theatrical necessity, too. As rock shows started to be staged in increasingly large halls – moving from 3,500-seat theaters to 20,000-seat arenas – rock stars had to concoct a sense of spectacle to reach the last row. The new glam stars didn't just plunk out songs like their psychedelic predecessors. They offered complete shows, enlivened by sets, props and costume changes.

Seventies rockers could hardly be credited as the first pop stars to take an androgynous turn. In the Fifties, the very tutti-frutti Little Richard became a flamboyant star. The Stones did themselves up in frumpy drag to promote their 1966 single "Have You Seen Your Mother Baby." But neither antecedent mothered a movement.

You could start an international incident trying to name precisely where and when glam rock first glistened. Stateside, the trend snakes back to Alice Cooper, the first male rocker loopy and press-starved enough to take a girl's name, in late 1968. Overseas, the equally-hungry-for-attention David Bowie rouged his cheeks and wore a billowing dress for the cover of the 1971 U.K. version of *The Man Who Sold the World*. Using their androgynous images to create strikingly different characters, Cooper and Bowie

bassist.

Francis Ford Coppola's film *The Godfather, Part II*, starring Al Pacino, Robert De Niro, Robert Duvall and Diane Keaton, premieres.

15An arbitration panel invalidates Oakland A's pitcher Jim "Catfish" Hunter's contract, making him professional baseball's first free agent. Five days later, a federal judge rules the NFL's long-standing indefinite-length contract system illegal.

16After five and a half years together, glam pioneers Mott the Hoople disband.

19Nelson Rockefeller becomes vice president after a lengthy approval process, and President Ford signs a bill authorizing the federal government to take custody of Watergate-related documents.

21Comedian and violinist Jack Benny dies.

The *New York Times* reveals CIA surveillance of antiwar activists – in direct defiance of the agency's charter banning spying on American citizens – during Nixon's presidency. Five days later, after a perfunctory self-investigation, CIA director William Colby admits agency wrongdoing. On Jan. 5, Ford will empower Vice President Rockefeller to investigate CIA domestic espionage.

23George Harrison releases his Christmas rock song "Ding Dong, Ding Dong." The next day, James Taylor, Carly Simon, Linda Ronstadt and Joni Mitchell are heard caroling through the snowless streets of L.A.

27As antibusing violence subsides, Federal District Judge Arthur Garrity charges and fines three Boston school officials for refusing to enforce steps to integrate public schools.

31Most popular music, books and film – 1974: Barbra Streisand's "The Way We Were" (pop single); Elton John's *Greatest Hits* (pop album); Roberta Flack's "Feel Like Makin' Love" (R&B single); Charlie Rich's "A Very Special Love Song" (C&W single); Peter Benchley's *Jaws* (fiction); Alex Comfort's *The Joy of Sex* (nonfiction); *The Towering Inferno* (film).

1975 JANUARY

1The Watergate criminal trial ends with H.R. Haldeman, John Ehrlichman, Robert Mardian and John Mitchell

epitomized a schism between much of the American and British glam to come. For the most part, the Americans arrived through the more garish realm of TV-bred shock value, whereas the English came to their glitter via the upscale influence of theatrical affectation. America's most popular glitter czar distanced himself from his antics by claiming to be playing a character. In his off-hours, Alice indulged in such ultra-straight activities as playing golf and drinking beer. To him, glitter was just a gig. Bowie treated it like a lifestyle. Eagerly labeling himself "bisexual," he cemented glam's tone of hedging provocation.

In 1971, it was the cherubic Marc Bolan who became the style's first star with his outrageously swaggering singles, "Jeepster" and "Bang a Gong (Get It On)," establishing the glam sound and one of the style's alternate names. Bolan's use of glitter on his face and hair inspired the English press to name the emerging trend after the sparkling stuff. Yet his pretty-boy looks still conformed to an unthreatening world of teen idols. Once again Bowie pushed glam to a more daring and avant-garde level with his seminal work *The Rise and Fall of Ziggy Stardust and the Spiders From Mars* in 1972.

That was the year glam seized the United Kingdom. It's no surprise that the trend took a firm hold there before it did in America. Not only did the British lack the more confining definitions of masculinity rooted in America's cowboy culture, they boasted a smaller, trendier and more pop-saturated media, allowing their crazes to fester faster.

But only in media-saturated America would a glitter-style icon arise from the verities of real life rather than the PR-manipulated world of showbiz. Decades before MTV began regularly featuring young gay people in its semidocumentary series *The Real World,* public television filmed a real American family that included a gay son. For seven months in 1971, a film crew lived with the Bill and Pat Loud family of Santa Barbara, California. The twelve-part series debuted January 11, 1973, presenting the dark (and true!) side of the Brady Bunch. The parents got divorced in full view of the American public, while their teenage kids ran around smoking pot and playing in a rock band. Their alienated eldest son Lance lazed around New York City's Chelsea Hotel in the company of obvious homosexuals on the fringe of the Warhol underground. A role model was born! Lance seemed the ultimate figure of freedom and defiance to an incubating gay boy of fifteen, suffocating in the suburbs. America had never seen anything like it. PBS advertised the show with the tag line: "Are You Ready for the Louds?"

I could barely wait! To cement my identification, Lance's record collection, featured on the show's soundtrack, seemed always to include the latest glitter music from London. Even those who expressed horror tuned in often enough to make the show a smash, generating a *Newsweek* cover and endless grumbling op-eds.

Similarly, even those resistant to the larger glitter trend couldn't deny its role as the era's cutting-edge sound. A sound with a retro appeal, glam gave rock & roll its balls back. While the previous psychedelic trend encouraged decadent solos and haughty musicianship, glam revived the hard, mean chords of Chuck Berry and the Rolling Stones in the Fifties to mid-Sixties. Contradictions in the music abounded: Bowie's "Rebel Rebel" floated lyrics like "Got your mother in a whirl/She's not sure if you're a boy or a girl" over the most virile rock riffs since those in "Jumpin' Jack Flash." The New York Dolls rolled their eyes and whistled to sailors over Johnny Thunders's unforgiving guitar crunch in "Looking for a Kiss."

By '73, English glam mushroomed into a commercial mandate. You could surf glitter's wave all the way from lowbrow rock groups (like Slade and Sweet), to campy teenybopper acts (Gary Glitter and Suzi Quatro), to the snooty art act Roxy Music. A year later, glitter proved such a market force on both sides of the Atlantic that performers from every genre – save that last bastion of butchness, Southern rock – had to apply some blush to stay current. The range of variations on the style proved dizzying: from Kiss, who used makeup as a circus sideshow, to George Clinton's Funkadelic, who used glittering space clothes as a metaphor for the black man as alien in a funk-free America.

Within this ever-broadening glam world, however, actual homosexuality remained veiled. In the mix of male and female friends making up my glitter coterie, I was the only one who was gay (and the only one who knew that I was gay). My sit-

uation mirrored the drama existing within one of the new glam bands of '74: Queen. Only their singer/frontman, Freddie Mercury, was "of the faith." Yet his band's early music drew from the straightest of pop audience segments – young hard-rock fans. It used to amaze me no end that, before Queen broke through to pop fans with "Bohemian Rhapsody," Freddie could come flouncing to the front of the stage and address all the hard young boys in the crowd as "my little bathing beauties," *and get away with it!*

He was protected by the band's music; the harder you banged your guitars, the more you could camouflage bent desires. Once glam rock went mainstream in the U.S. – once its shock value was diffused by sheer popularity – its days as rock's cutting edge were numbered. Soon glitter's covertly gay concerns were overshadowed by a form ready to deal with homosexuality more openly: disco.

The fading of glitter hardly halted rock's infatuation with gender-fuck. Rock had always questioned conventional masculinity – if only as part of a general mandate of outrage and rebellion. But by the Eighties, more forthright gay images came along to confuse matters. While "outrageous" new stars like Boy George, Dead or Alive and Pet Shop Boys didn't literally "come out" at first, any gay kid could tell they weren't just pretending like the earlier crew.

In the Nineties, the flirty old tease of sexual ambiguity transformed into a kind of wan sexual ambivalence. Michael Stipe of R.E.M. offered a chaste kind of implicit gayness, established more by his righteous rejection of macho conventions than by an embrace of anything sensuously bisexual. Likewise, rock's spiritual leader, Kurt Cobain, used his famous declaration, "Everyone is gay," more to critique masculine conformity than to promote open sex play. At the same time, the campy shock value of Alice Cooper's glam coarsened into the creepy violence of Marilyn Manson's goth. The humor and adventure of the Seventies has turned to self-righteousness or depression today.

No matter. By this time, crucial changes in gay life have wound up making rock's sexual critiques more useful to straight listeners than to gay ones. Real gay people are coming out in full view of the media like never before. Many kinds of pop stars can speak their love's name and suffer no material consequences, from Elton John to k.d. lang.

Unlike the teens of the Seventies, today's kids no longer need to rely on older straight stars to serve as mock role models. Neither does modern gay culture require the androgynous code of camp as its signal. Current queer kids can see handsome, young, openly gay men on *The Real World* or represented on any soap opera in need of easy PR.

Yet modern kids lack what I had. They can't call on glitter's zone of ambiguity that defended me against my own fears and sheltered me from the world's judgment. As a confident adult, I'm thrilled with the ever-increasing honesty about sexual orientation. But I'm sure gay kids still have to suffer many of the same old internal fears and external hostilities. Only now, in a less naive world, queer kids have to face the truth sooner. Shorn of glitter's use as a cunning decoy, modern kids lose a whole world of freedom that made the style such a gift to my generation of the stumbling young. ⊕

convicted of obstructing justice. On Feb. 21, Judge Sirica will sentence all four to prison terms of lengths ranging from ten months to eight years.

President Ford signs the Freedom of Information Act, giving, for the first time, individuals access to federal files on themselves, excepting law enforcement and security information.

2 Secretary of State Kissinger allows that U.S. military intervention in the Middle East is possible if another Arab economic boycott is initiated.

A federal judge rules that John Lennon's lawyers may have access to Immigration Department files concerning his case in order to determine the real reasons for the government's actions against him. By June 19, Lennon will file suit against specific Nixon administration officials, contending that he is the victim of selective persecution based on his political beliefs.

6 Ticket-buying hysteria greets the news of Led Zeppelin's upcoming tour: Fans wreak $30,000 worth of damage on Boston Garden while waiting for the box office to open and thereby cause the concert's cancellation; two days later, three Madison Square Garden shows sell out in a record four hours.

7 In a major victory on South Vietnamese soil, North Vietnam captures the capital of the Phuoc Long province. Ten days later, South Vietnam counterattacks along the Cambodian border to halt a Communist takeover of the Kien Tuong province.

12 The Pittsburgh Steelers rise to football prominence as they defeat the Minnesota Vikings in Super Bowl IX, 16–6.

Warner Bros. Records boldly sponsors an 18-show European tour by their lesser-known artists: Little Feat, Tower of Power, the Doobie Brothers, Montrose, Graham Central Station and Bonaroo. The Warner Brothers Music Show will prove a wise investment, establishing overseas cult audiences for Little Feat.

14 Former CIA agent Philip Agee's *Inside the Company: CIA Diary* is published, offering a detailed look at agency activities in various Central American countries. CIA director William Colby later states that the book has compromised CIA operations and put some operatives under the threat of death.

leon gast
on the rumble

I BELIEVE the Rumble in the Jungle was the high point of Muhammad Ali's career: He felt very strongly about returning to Africa and winning back his championship title. First Ali had been the champ, then Frazier was, and then Foreman – but Ali had never lost his title in the ring. He had lost it as a result of a court decision, and was then arbitrarily stripped of his championship belt by various boxing commissions that refused to allow him to fight. As an African-American, he loved the idea of going to Africa and winning back his title outside the country that had taken it away.

It was a time when black Americans were feeling a strong pride in their African heritage; they were wearing their hair in Afros, wearing beads and dashikis – expressing an intense African consciousness. Ali's fight in Zaire certainly added to the spirit of the time.

The Rumble in the Jungle was one of the greatest fights in heavyweight history. Ali was able to withstand the full force of Foreman's best punches, while he landed some very heavy combinations of his own. If you view only edited films of the fight, like *When We Were Kings* and others, you will see Ali's "rope-a-dope" strategy and the knockout in the eighth round highlighted. But the second, fifth and seventh rounds were just incredible, with a lot of nonstop, toe-to-toe combat.

In June 1974 I first heard about the project: a boxing match and music festival in Zaire. Don King called it "the Rumble in the Jungle – plus a music festival so big and monumental it'll make Woodstock look like a kindergarten picnic." Or something like that. It would be a spiritual commitment, "from the slave ship to the championship." He said that the concerts were going to feature performances by James Brown, B.B. King, the Pointer Sisters, Marvin Gaye, Stevie Wonder, Aretha Franklin, Hugh Masekela and the Fania All-Stars with Jerry Masucci. All the music would be wrapped around the George Foreman–Muhammad Ali heavyweight championship bout scheduled for September 25 in Kinshasa, Zaire.

> Zaire, October 30, 1974: George Foreman faces the referee's count moments after being knocked out by Muhammad Ali in the eighth round.

So I met with Don King, Hank Schwartz, Lloyd Price, Stuart Levine – all the producers and promoters – and applied for the job of directing the filming of the event. At first, Price and King didn't want me. As the date of the fight approached, I had another meeting with King and showed him some Hell's Angels film I was editing, which contained some extremely controversial footage that didn't make the final cut of the movie *Hell's Angels Forever*. King was impressed: "If you can work with those crazy motherfucking Hell's Angels . . ." he said. Eventually it got so close to the event that King finally approved me, with the stipulation that there would be at least forty black faces in my eighty-man crew. I told King I didn't know that many blacks in the film business, but he was insistent. "Look around and find 'em, but we're going to Africa, and at least half the crew should be black."

As soon as I got the job I began visiting Ali's camp with a camera crew, in mid-August. He was training in Deer Lake, Pennsylvania, where he had a sprawling hilltop camp with a crude log cabin which he slept in and trained right outside. Ali was always on, talking about big, bad clumsy George Foreman, about Africa, Sonny Liston, Vietnam, music, Negro culture, politics, women, Islam, but mostly the honorable Elijah Muhammad. In contrast, Foreman was training out in San Francisco and pretty much keeping to himself and not saying much.

SOON EVERYBODY started leaving for Africa. A few performers – such as Marvin Gaye and Aretha Franklin – wouldn't fly, so they canceled, but James Brown, B.B. King, the Staple Singers and many others did make it. I traveled with Ali from Deer Lake to New York, where he did a press conference, and then on to Paris – just following him everywhere with a camera crew, shooting everything. Then we arrived in Zaire.

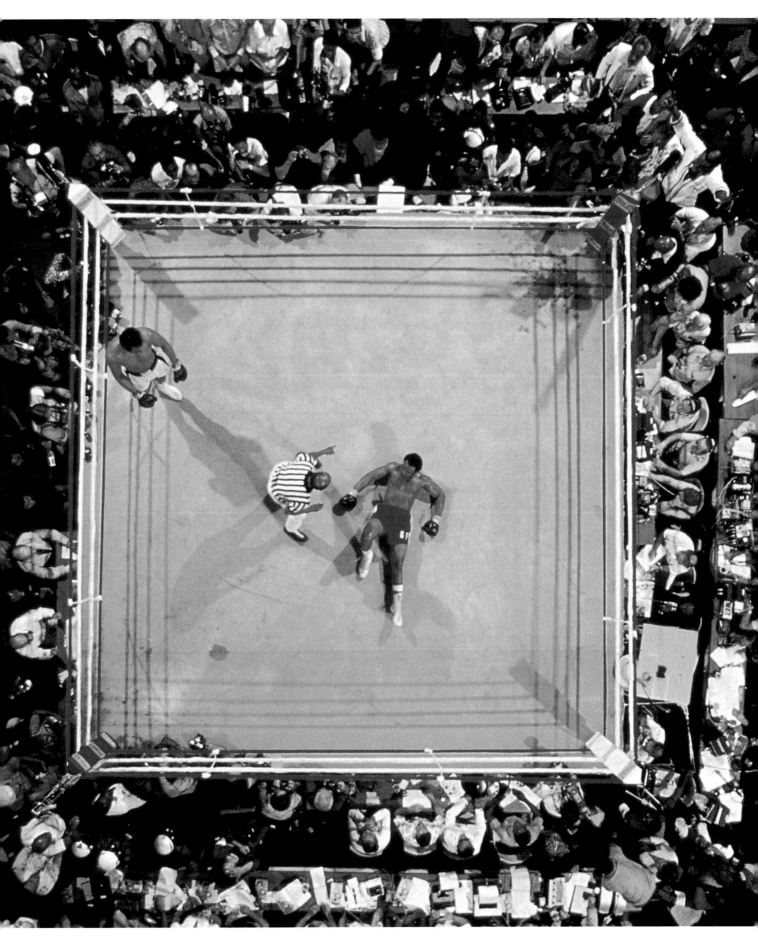

Ali landed a few days before Foreman did, to a tremendous turnout. There were people on the runways, on the tarmac; the airport was jam-packed, people were hanging off buildings – all because Ali was such a tremendous hero to Africans. It sounds preposterous, but there were people in Zaire who had no idea who George Foreman was. He was the heavyweight champion, and there were people who thought he was white! Ali was such a popular hero that the fight became clearly defined for the Zairians: It was good guy versus villain, and George had the role of the villain.

That first day there was a bunch of kids hollering, "Ali, *bomaye!*" and Ali asked one of them what that meant. "Ali, kill him!" He picked it up immediately, shouting "Ali, *bomaye!* Ali, *bomaye!*" Ali portrayed George as the invader: "He's in my country!" and he'd get the crowd to start hollering. When Foreman arrived, there was a very small turnout, nothing like Ali's reception.

Not just the Rumble in the Jungle, but Ali's entire career, was a symbol of strength and perseverance to a whole class of people that really had no voice at all. He had stood up to the American government by refusing to fight in an unjust and unpopular war. He had had an in-your-face personality from early on in his career.

Over the history of the boxing business, fighters typically had little to say and shied away from the spotlight, but Ali was probably the first boxer to realize that the camera was his friend, and to use it to his advantage. I could walk up and point the lens at him any time, and he'd always punch his fist in its direction, playing up to the camera in little ways as soon as he saw it. There would always be a moment when he would look away and wink at the press or flash a hint of a smile, and you'd realize it was all pretty much a performance.

As the fighters prepared for the fight in Zaire, Foreman looked so powerful and was destroying all his sparring partners – really punishing them. Usually, the sparring would last for three three-minute rounds. His partners would fight maybe two rounds, and then the trainer would have to stop them and bring in the next guy.

Standing outside Foreman's gym, you could actually hear his strength. When he was working on the big punching bag (which weighed between fifty and a hundred pounds and was attached to a chain), it would fly up in the air each time he hit it. There would be a punch, then silence, then this huge rattle, over and over. The sound of that chain, just the chain, could be heard all the way outside the training gym.

But eight days before the fight, Foreman was pummeling a sparring partner who defensively put his arm up. His elbow hit George underneath his headgear and cut him near the eye.

Suddenly, everything changed. The music festival went on, but there was a nearly six-week delay before the fight could happen to give Foreman's eye a chance to heal. During this time, the training continued, and I continued to shoot. Ali was always going out running in the bush, in Kinshasa and in the villages around there. But Foreman remained reclusive, spending very little time with anybody outside his inner circle. He finally moved from his camp into the Intercontinental Hotel, where everyone else was staying, but he was never accessible the way Ali was.

I believe it was during this delay that Ali began to turn things around. I think that, had the fight come off when it was supposed to, Foreman would have fought a much better fight. But the delay turned out to spur Ali's greatest psychological victory – by the time they got into the ring, he had totally psyched George out.

When the fight finally took place on October 30, Foreman entered the outdoor stadium to nine-tenths of the sixty thousand people there shouting, "Ali, *bomaye!* Ali, *bomaye!*" When the bell rang for round one, Ali didn't come out and dance away from George as everyone had expected. He ran right up to him and threw the first punch of the fight – a hard right that really set the tone for the rest of the bout. Ali was not going to run; he was going to be aggressive. He moved faster and punched harder than Foreman had imagined he would.

The story I heard about Ali's first strategy, which was later confirmed, was that he had had a talk with Cus D'Amato, the famous trainer who has worked with Mike Tyson and Floyd Patterson. Cus warned Ali that he would be fighting a bully, and that the only way to fight a bully is to stand up to him right at the beginning and let him know that you're not afraid of him. "My advice to you is, when the bell rings, just charge across the ring, haul off and hit him as hard as you can. Then you got to stay away from Foreman, he'll get tired and frustrated. You'll get him later on."

Ali obviously had listened to Cus. I've looked at that fight numerous times, a frame at a time, and in slow motion it's a big, looping right hand that hits George right on the head in those first few seconds and stops him in his tracks. He must have realized then that it would be a very difficult fight.

But Ali had such ring savvy, I'm sure that the other part of his fight plan – the "rope-a-dope" as he called it – was a strategy he came up with in the ring. Foreman was fast enough to keep cutting Ali off so he couldn't dance away. So with the ropes very slack (the three fights preceding theirs had loosened them, and the extreme heat and humidity had helped as well), Ali realized he could lean back against the ropes, cover himself with his arms and gloves and let Foreman wail away at him.

The punches seemed to be hurting Ali, and I could plainly hear the guys in his corner constantly yelling, "Get off the ropes, get off the ropes, oh, Champ, get off, you're getting killed!" They really believed that Foreman was going to knock him out! He hit Ali a number of times with the same punches that had knocked out previous fighters.

Throughout the fight, Ali continued his verbiage at Foreman: "That didn't hurt," "You've got to be able to punch harder than that," "You can't hurt me." I was eight rows back, but I could hear it all. In the end, Foreman just punched himself out.

The fifth round was when it really turned around – Ali's strategy was working, and Foreman's punches were becoming less controlled and less effective. All of a sudden, in the sixth round, Ali popped up off the ropes and started taking charge, landing some powerful combinations that had Foreman falling back.

In the eighth round Ali knocked George out, and the place went wild! There had been a strong threat of rain because the delay had moved the fight into the monsoon season, and just after the fight ended, the skies opened up. Rain poured down with hurricane force; it was so intense that the canopy over the boxing ring actually collapsed under the weight of all the water. The rain continued for about five or six hours. Had the storm happened during the fight, I'm sure the event would have been called off.

I personally feel that Ali could've beaten any fighter in the history of boxing because he was so much smarter than the others. He had Foreman beaten before they even got in the ring! In fact, I believe the Rumble should have been the final act of his boxing career – he really had nothing to prove afterwards. It was absolutely one of the greatest sports upsets of all time.

George Foreman had been the overwhelming favorite in Zaire. While there, I had called New York and spoken to a friend and said, "Ali is in great shape – if you're going to bet, see if you could bet a couple of hundred dollars for me on Ali." But everybody else was sure Foreman would win; the odds were between fifteen and ten to one in his favor. After the delay, the odds were around three or two-and-a-half to one, but still against Ali.

By the time of the fight, I wanted to bet a couple of guys from the press, but none of them would bet against Ali; the only guy who would bet on Foreman was Hunter Thompson. Hunter laid me three to one – a hundred and fifty to fifty dollars – and paid me after the fight. ⊕

george plimpton
on betting ali

WHENEVER A HEAVYWEIGHT TITLE changes hands, it's a seminal event. The Rumble in the Jungle certainly was that. Many of us had tried very hard, individually and collectively, to get Muhammad Ali reinstated to boxing. We believed that the various state commissions had illegally removed his right to fight – an opinion the Supreme Court eventually agreed with. But what gave the fight an added dimension was that Ali didn't rely on the courts to give him back his championship: He went over to Kinshasa and *won* it back.

Most of us in the press corps had thought Foreman was going to destroy him. George had KO'ed Joe Frazier in Jamaica in such a devastating way that it didn't seem as though anyone would be able to stand up to him in the ring. Still, though I'm not a gambling man, being an Ali fan, I made a gentleman's bet with someone that Ali was going to win.

I was a few rows back for the fight. During the first round, it was as if we were watching an execution in slow motion. It looked awful – Ali against the ropes, Foreman landing these big, slugging blows that could bruise anywhere they hit.

In the middle of this punishment, Ali flicked out a jab, and we saw the sweat fly off Foreman's face. Suddenly we realized that there was method to the madness! We could see that Foreman's blows – which had been like salvos from a battleship – were getting weaker, wilder and almost desperate. It was as though he knew that if he didn't land one of those shots he'd be in trouble – running out of ammunition, to continue the battleship analogy.

Then, in the sixth round, Ali came off the ropes. He seemed fresh, almost *titanic* in size, while Foreman before our eyes seemed to deflate, small in comparison.

What was most astonishing was that Ali's corner had been yelling at him to get off the ropes. His "rope-a-dope" tactic was not something he had told anybody he was going to do. But as I rode back on the bus that rainy night with Angelo Dundee, Ali's fight manager, he told me that he hadn't known anything about the strategy beforehand, that Ali had devised it in the ring during the course of the fight – a great tactical move that won him back his title. ⊕

lloyd price
on africa

MAN, IT WAS a motherfucker! The Rumble in the Jungle was more than the biggest boxing match, more than the best concert – it was a surge of commitment to black empow-
erment. The whole thing was being done by black people for black people in black
Africa, and Muhammad Ali was at the center of it all.

I still get questions from kids who've heard about the Rumble. Did it really happen? Were you really there? It did, and I was. Muhammad went down there – to a foreign country – after taking all the abuse and humiliation of a suspension and then a
defeat, and beat Foreman, a guy who looked tough and had never been beaten by
anybody. With a knockout punch, Ali snatched victory from the jaws of defeat, and
because he was the man who stood up and spoke out for black pride, his victory felt
like a triumph for the cause.

In 1974, I'd already known Ali a long time; we had met in Louisville when he was
still Cassius Clay. I played this place called the Rivers Club there. He loved to
look into the bar and see all the ladies inside, and he loved to hear me play, but
he was still too young to come in. I walked outside the club one day, and there he was
sitting on my car. I don't remember exactly what he said to make me pay attention to him,
but he was really aggressive, and I got to like him. He didn't let on that he was a boxer
at that point. I just thought he was another kid running around down there. After a while,
he started coming around every time I would play in Louisville, and we got to be good
friends.

I had met Don King in Cleveland when he was running a nightclub there called the Corner
Tavern, where I played. We got to be really close when he expanded his club so that my
big band could play there regularly. I can't remember
who came up with the idea for the Rumble first, Don
or myself. We were always talking.

Don and I had both been interested in boxing going
back to 1972, and it was clear that we would have to
do something big for Ali in his challenge against Foreman. What wasn't so clear was
who would put up the money. The 1971 Ali-Frazier fight had paid the largest purse
ever in the history of boxing up to that point: five million dollars between them. Rumble
was going to pay five million dollars for each. We knew nobody here thought the sport
was worth that kind of money, even for this fight, which was going to be a much bigger deal
than most. So we began to look for sponsorship outside the United States.

There was also a feeling that the heavyweight championship of the world shouldn't
just be in Chicago, Las Vegas or New York, but that it should be presented to other
parts of the world. I had a company called the West African Trade Counsel and had
met with a lot of Africans about doing concert events, and eventually it all just together. Before we knew it, there was going to be a Rumble in the Jungle. We were going to Zaire.

It had been the perfect time, the perfect thing to do. Everything was starting to feel
different. Black people were rising up and feeling proud. My idea was that the whole event
should be like a huge homecoming, with a concert even bigger and better than
Woodstock. I thought of it as a way to connect people to their roots, in a sense, a way
to take the slaves back to Africa as champions.

We were really dedicated to that idea, and we sold it to Muhammad and everyone
else. I knew I could get the entertainment side together, and that Don would rally the people for the fight. But, really, the success of it had everything to do with Ali. I knew it
would be that way.

Sure, he had boxing ability – his talent as a boxer was superb – but he was also a
guy who knew exactly who he was and stood his ground. He was not afraid to be a black
man, and that's why people admired him. He had embraced the Africans long before he ever

"Ali, *bomaye!*": Ali is cheered by a
Zairian crowd in Kinshasa prior to
his heavyweight-title bout with
George Foreman

went down there and had a real commitment to the spirit of being involved with the international community. He was like the self-appointed cultural ambassador. People everywhere loved him for that.

While the fight was the cause, my vision for the music event was about taking black rhythms back to Africa. So I hired the exact same crew that had put together Woodstock and asked everyone in R&B plus everyone in black and Latin music to come on down. I wanted to get as many entertainers and celebrities as I could to perform in Zaire. We had James Brown, Etta James, Tito Puente, B.B. King, the Fania All-Stars, Miriam Makeba, Sister Sledge, the Spinners, the Crusaders, Manu Dibango, Hugh Masekela, Fela and myself as performers. Plus, we had many local African entertainers.

The feeling of being down there with all that great music was pure magic. Everybody was buzzing on Africa, it was just amazing. The African music was so fresh, I thought they'd get the fish up out of the water. Even before it was over everybody started talking about putting together an alma mater so we could come back and do it again.

That's why the Rumble in the Jungle has become a part of black folklore today. It made our people feel proud, and it made them feel good about their origins. Everybody's got a base, a root, an origin. Everybody's got to be from somewhere. Irishmen come from Ireland, Englishmen come from England, Italians come from Italy and Africans come from Africa. But most of us who have been here in America for several generations have no experience of Africa.

When I got to Africa and was able to mingle and mungle with a lot of people who looked just like me, I began to see myself differently. I had been a world traveler already, but being there was something different, something wonderful. That's why I wish all the African-American people who are coming up now could visit Africa. Though not all Americans will be able to understand the cultural significance of everything that's going on down there, they certainly will realize that they do have roots on this earth. They'll connect to the place and the people, who look like them and who will recognize them as one of their own.

Nothing else I've experienced since has had the same kind of impact, and I don't know if anything in the future will. The Rumble in the Jungle was something that happened like magic – a magical moment in time. ⊕

goodbye, vietnam
by laura palmer

The target was Saigon. South Vietnam had been battered in a massive three-month offensive and, by April 1975, all that stood between Communist troops and a final victory in a war that had lasted for decades was the beautiful but beleaguered capital of Saigon.

For two years, from 1972 to 1974, Saigon had been my hometown. I arrived barely three months after graduating from Oberlin College and worked as a radio reporter and magazine writer; the first article I ever had published was in ROLLING STONE.

By 1975, I was working in Paris as a journalist, and as the northern provinces of South Vietnam collapsed in rapid succession under the Communist assault it became clear that the end of the war was inevitable – and it became impossible for me to stay away. So with the money I'd made reporting the death of Aristotle Onassis I bought my last youth-fare ticket: Paris-Saigon-Paris.

Shortly after returning I went to see a trusted fortune-teller with my closest Vietnamese friend. With a frightening matter-of-factness, the fortune-teller said she and her husband would poison their children and themselves if the Communists came to power.

I asked if it was her ability to see into the future that made her so afraid. She shook her head. "No. There are some events that overwhelm destiny."

This is absolutely how it felt to be swept up in one of the defining moments of the Seventies.

The images of the evacuation – helicopters lifting off from the rooftops of Saigon, then pitched like cheap toys into the South China Sea to make room on the overcrowded aircraft carriers – became some of the most indelible images of the decade, the chaotic last gasp of America's involvement in Vietnam.

At twenty-five, I was one of the youngest reporters there and the only woman to write a first-person account of the U.S. evacuation of Saigon. It is excerpted here.

I wrote the article on my small Olivetti typewriter as I sailed aboard a U.S. aircraft carrier to the Philippines.

At Clark Air Force Base, I watched as a telex operator typed out the six-thousand-word piece. It took an hour to transmit the telex to San Francisco, and as it clattered away it seemed as though my memories of Vietnam were becoming smoke.

Although I left Vietnam, it never left me. I returned for three weeks in 1989, and was reunited with my beloved friend Nguyen, who, as it turned out, had been a colonel with the Viet Cong. He welcomed me back with a bouquet of miniature roses wrapped in a lace doily.

April 29, 1975: As Saigon faces inevitable surrender to North Vietnamese forces, evacuees rush to the rooftops to meet waiting helicopters

"I wish I could have told you it would have been all right to stay," I remember him saying. "But I was worried that something would happen and I couldn't protect you. You were young, with your whole life ahead of you. I wanted you to marry and have a family." And I did.

"YOU FIFTEEN PEOPLE on that chopper! Run. Now. Go. Run!" We ran, through a cyclone of steaming air whipped up by the helicopter's spinning rotors. You don't think and you don't feel. With eyes gripped on that chopper, you run. Hundreds of marines in flak jackets and helmets, carrying M-16s, seemed to be bursting through space. The chopper had its tail ramp up; I threw in a bag, but couldn't make it. Someone grabbed my arm and I was dragged onboard and across the floor. Seconds later, in a roar, the chopper lifted off.

When I went to bed the night before, I put the two white vinyl armchairs on the twin bed next to mine. It looked so funny, like a miniature train compartment. But it would keep out a lot of shrapnel. The wide French windows were shuttered and latched. Saigon was slumbering and quiet – at least for the moment. I pulled the pillows around my head and slept in a stupor until the explosions started. It was loud, heavier than

military air evacuation of all remaining U.S. personnel and civilians in South Vietnam, begins, rescuing approximately 84,000 (by State Department estimates). Some 22,000 refugees are picked up by Navy ships waiting off the South Vietnamese coast.

30 The Vietnam War ends as North Vietnamese and Viet Cong forces enter Saigon and accept South Vietnam's surrender. The new government announces plans for a nationwide election, with reunification as the eventual goal. Within weeks, the rulers will expel Western journalists and ban the publication of all newspapers, books and other printed material by private citizens.

1975 MAY

1 Hank Aaron, now a Milwaukee Brewer, breaks another Babe Ruth record, knocking in his 2,209th career RBI.

The Rolling Stones announce their 1975 Tour of the Americas by rolling down Manhattan's Fifth Avenue, performing "Brown Sugar" at full volume.

5 After four years of resisting TV broadcasts, the South African government gives up, and the country's first TV program airs.

12 Khmer Rouge naval vessels seize the U.S. merchant ship *Mayaguez* 60 miles off the Cambodian coast. In a rescue operation that will embarrass and damage President Ford politically, 38 U.S. troops are killed (23 in a helicopter crash en route to the rescue), 50 are wounded and three are MIA.

Fans at a free Jefferson Starship concert cause $14,000 worth of damage to New York City's Central Park. The band and sponsor WNEW pick up the tab.

13 Fiddler and Western swing pioneer Bob Wills dies.

14 The White House, New York State and various banks refuse New York City mayor Abe Beame's requests for financial assistance. New York City will suffer a series of debilitating strikes by public service workers, then on July 31 begin austerity measures including wage freezes. On Dec. 9, Ford will sign legislation to save the city from default.

Three sitcoms depicting blue-collar life in urban America, *All in the Family*, *Sanford and Son* and *Chico and the Man*, are TV's most popular series.

on any of the previous nights, but still far away – about five miles. But nothing was crashing into downtown Saigon. Mired in the quicksand between sleep and reality, there was really no decision to make. People didn't seem to be in the halls of the hotel, and if it was serious, there would be a knock on the door.

Two hours later, there was.

"Pack your things. We're all getting out of here. The airport is burning. You've got about half an hour." I started doing things without thinking. The explosions were steady, but still not closer. What should stay? What should go? The blue jeans weren't back from the laundry, the birth control pills were on the bathroom table. Papers. Passport. Leave the bikini because you hate it and it's a good excuse to buy another. Would everything fit in? What about the other leather suitcase? The typewriter? Give it away.

It was about six in the morning. Dawn. If you've ever had a love affair with Saigon, you love her best in the early morning hours after curfew, when she's silent and her thin breezes blow. She stands alone in those hours with whatever pride is left.

I walked across the square through the lingering dawn, and past the National Assembly. It looked ghostly with its fresh paint. Policemen slouched out front on folding chairs, their rifles on the ground. I went to the rooftop of the Caravelle Hotel with a gaggle of other journalists to watch the war. The salmon-colored cathedral arched up by the main boulevard, one of the frayed remnants of elegance left in the capital. In the distance beyond, explosions and clouds of black smoke bolted through the dawn. There were burps of orange flames and the baritone thud of artillery. An airplane was shot out of the sky by an antiaircraft missile and spun slowly to the ground in a ballet of fire. Someone had died. Again.

A loudspeaker in the square blared out President Minh's acceptance speech from the day before. As he said when he picked up the gauntlet, "Accepting the responsibility of leading the country in such a moment is really not pleasurable." Little did he know. After the speech, the loudspeakers spewed out the South Vietnam national anthem. It was a gloomier, sloppier version than usual. There was no visible panic in the early hours. Many people were staying inside and few could anticipate the magnitude of what was about to happen.

It was the roughest with Nguyen. He's been the litmus paper for rumors over the last decade, and has one of the sharpest minds in town. Scores of correspondents have ebbed and flowed with his wisdom over the years. He chose to stay because he could not leave it all behind. He wanted to see how it all came out. Perhaps he knew he would never be happy again if he left. And there are the ten birds and German shepherds to care for. After a rocket attack, he said: "My skylarks sang so well last night, and the laughing thrush. But my dog barked and barked. He hated the B-52s and used to go wild." Nguyen was calm, because he is always calm. He calls himself the "General of Givral's" – the coffee shop across the street that is the Saigon rumor mill. "My troops have all deserted me. Now I must get new recruits." How do you say goodbye to one of the wisest, most compassionate men you know? A man who still dreams of strolling down Tu Do Street in a white suit with a tiger cub on a leash. You wish he would go away so you didn't have to face it.

He was there when I left. As I squeezed his arm and said I loved him, I told him I would never forget. Cheap sunglasses hid the tears as I walked away, and I did not look back. For the rest of the day there were seconds of fear and hours of sadness.

What do you notice as you walk away? Disney's *Lady and the Tramp* is playing at the downtown theater. The last rat that stops in his tracks and then darts back into hiding. The grotesque statue of a marine that lurches forward in Lam Son Square reeks of a stark stupidity in a city stinking of sadness.

The evacuation code name was originally "Talon Vise," but was changed to "Frequent Wind" after appearing in *Newsweek*. There were four evacuation options. The most preferable was a combination of the first two choices: fixed-wing aircraft and ships. The third option utilized only fixed-wing planes.

But the prerequisite for all three was an airport that was open and secure. By the time Frequent Wind started to blow, the airport was virtually closed, and plan four went into effect – a total helicopter evacuation staged from the Seventh Fleet.

We never heard the announcer say, "The temperature is 105 degrees and rising," followed by the first eight bars of "I'm Dreaming of a White Christmas," the secret signal that was supposed to be broadcast over the American radio station.

A signal came from somewhere, because suddenly everyone was saying, "This is it, let's go." Off we went, with shoulder-bag luggage, typewriter cases, Nikons and nervousness. I was in the first group of thirty or so journalists, and we felt like an obvious target as we headed purposefully down the street. But nothing happened. People were curious and stared as we went past, but there was no hostility. We were not Pied Pipers, luring Vietnamese into our wake. Still it was a short distance and a very long walk.

At the pickup point we all crammed into the lobby of a building, and in the sweaty confusion realized we were in the wrong spot. That "Oh, fuck, here we go again" feeling was rampant. This time the hike was long – another five blocks to another building. No one seemed to be in charge, but the word spread that we were in the right spot. Several carloads of Vietnamese families began arriving and hastily mingled into the crowd with their luggage. And then you realized, without any pride, that there is a little Da Nang inside us all. That, yes, you too could push and shove, kick and stomp. If panic broke out, the fittest and strongest would survive.

After an anxious forty-five minutes of waiting and drinking orange sodas, huge black passenger buses with grating across the windows pulled up. This had to be the ultimate target. Traveling in the bull's-eye. A blind man could lob a grenade over his shoulder as he heard the bus chug past and kill us all. Not to mention any of the soldiers swarming the streets with guns in their arms and ammo in their belts. Our bus was loaded first and we headed off.

The bus snaked through the streets of Saigon.

We were led by a patrol car with its red light spinning, and driven by a bus driver with a strange sense of humor.

"Okay, ladies and gentlemen. I just want you to know that I've never driven one of these things before. Last night they gave me an M-16; this morning, they gave me a bus." Ha ha ha. But it drew a response from the boys in the back.

"Hey, can we stop at the commissary on the way out? I want to pick up a few bottles of booze."

"Let's stop at the Cercle Sportif for a swim and a gin and tonic." The bus continued at a crawl, turning up one street, then down the next in the opposite direction. There was a delay and we had gone into a holding pattern. But the bus driver kept up the banter.

"Okay you all, this is the scenic tour. Now on your right, you'll see a statue of Trang Hung Dao." Up and down and back and down again. By now it was past noon. More people were on the streets with more luggage, driving aimlessly – but not wildly – about. Perhaps they were watching to see where the Americans went. Several hundred had gathered in front of the American Embassy, but they were not desperate. No one was strung out like a scarecrow on the barbed wire of the embassy fence. The bus came to a dead halt alongside Ambassador Martin's house. A fine, clandestine rendezvous point. We parked across the street from two other buses and waited for another to arrive. Like sitting ducks, we sat there for another thirty minutes. The sun was center stage.

The bus finally headed out onto Cach Mang Boulevard, the straight strip of road that runs to the airport. It crosses a river past an elaborate Buddhist temple and some of the seediest bars in town. The shops and bars were boarded up. The deserted American Legion, Post Number Thirty, was swallowed in hollow silence. A crowd of about fifty people had gathered in front of CARE – the American relief agency – with the hope that they might be carried off by Frequent Wind. Except for a speeding, swerving military convoy, the boulevard was calm. We passed the monument being constructed to the memory of Allied soldiers, but no one was working there. It's barely completed and consists of a platform of stairs trailing into space. Then, at the entrance to the air base, the sign: THE NOBLE SACRIFICE OF ALLIED SOLDIERS WILL NEVER BE FORGOTTEN. As if the Vietnamese did not have enough of their own dead to remember.

As we approached the main gate, the driver advised us to duck down. An earlier bus had been forced to turn back and they expected more problems. A crinkle of small-arms fire sputtered in the distance. At the entrance, the bus swerved to avoid barricades and plowed through a rut. As we stumbled off the bus, a rocket crashed nearby. It shattered more nerves than property. We were herded into the Defense Attaché Compound – a mammoth matrix of buildings once dubbed Pentagon East. As in any other government building, there was the dull hum of air conditioning, linoleum floors and bulletin boards. Some of the signs were mocking, like the one by the post office warning of letter bombs: TERRORISM IS PREVALENT WORLDWIDE. YOU COULD BE NEXT! CHECK YOUR MAIL. BE WARY!

They lined us up against the wall and it felt like fire drills in the fifth grade. There were several thousand people in the building, most of them Vietnamese. There was no system of priorities. Why should a Vietnamese or some British journalist go out ahead of an American? The issue became moot after we all got out, but it could have been volatile if the exodus were halted and Americans were left behind.

"All right, everybody, back there against the walls. Weapons, ammunitions, explosives and knives, into this box. Come on, everybody, no one's getting onto a chopper with any weapons." As the box passed me, there were at least a dozen small pistols inside – little Da Nangs. We still had no idea of how long the wait would be. After being counted off in groups of fifty, we were given little baggage tags as tickets and told to hang them from our clothes. The civilian leader for each group was responsible for seeing that his fifty made it on the chopper together. Like lemmings we had fled into a major military operation and there was no turning back. A marine told us that a battalion and a half – roughly nine hundred men – had landed and "secured" the area. The wait continued. Someone asked which groups would go first and the reply was, "There's no 'ahead' of anything."

The marines all had a certain physical similarity because of the flak jackets and helmets. There were tattoos and Omega watches and several very scared faces peering out from beneath those helmets. But the majority were pros. They looked and acted it. They risked tremendous personal danger on our behalf, which is not easy to forget. The outcome was uncertain, but they were ready for anything.

1975 JUNE

"Man, we've been sitting out there for sixty days, just waiting for this thing to start."

Putting your life completely into someone else's hands creates a prism through which the situation is filtered. You need to believe you're getting the best and it's one of the rare moments when you look for – and see – the best in others. I maintained a terrified composure, but deeper down there was a sense of calm. There is not much to do but wait and see how it all turns out. But then you think of the antiaircraft missiles that ring the airport. And the marches and moratoriums that no longer matter. It's guerrilla warfare with the self until the situation changes and one feeling dominates.

The garbled growl of helicopters was heard overhead. It was raining helicopters. We could not see them from inside the windowless corridors, but the lines began to move. Get up. Walk. Sit on your luggage. Light a cigarette. Wonder how much longer. Listen for incoming fire. Worry. You turn a corner and there's the door. Someone says: "About fifteen more minutes." The group leader counts *his* batch of fifty.

"All right, no baggage, just people. Leave your luggage." Unzip the bag and yank out the papers. "He doesn't mean us. That's for the people behind." Back the papers go. A rush of total terror, like after the steepest hill on a roller coaster. The bag digs into my shoulder. Thinking stops. The door opens.

"You fifteen people get on that chopper! Run. Now. Go. Run!" Seconds later, gone. The chopper tilted as we gained altitude and for an instant it seemed like we would pour back out. I clenched Bob Shaplen's hand in frozen fear. We turned to each other with tears in our eyes, then looked away. But he had started covering Indochina four years before I was born – in 1946. Odd that we should be squeezed together for the final farewell. I would never ask him what he thought about as we churned up into the

sky. The city was a tangle of buildings, unraveling into the distance. Overwhelmed by a sense of loss, drowning in a sea of sadness. Exploded apart from a past and battered by memories that, like flying shrapnel, rip you apart as they lodge inside. We were evacuated and left.

The chopper headed out toward the coast, through an air corridor that was protected by helicopter gunships and fighter bombers. The ground beneath us was a patchwork of rice paddies. Lazy clouds dangled in the sky and the flight seemed more noisy than dangerous. There were about fifty people in the chopper; most were Vietnamese. It was a painting, or one of Larry Burrows's photographs, which were paintings anyway. A Vietnamese woman with tears streaming down her face held two small children, fathered by a black man, in her lap. Dark eyes locked into luminous amber skin, and tufts of curly hair framed their foreheads. The seats and floor of the chopper were filled. An amoeba of people, a mass of up-and-down shapes. A mosaic of faces, confusion and fears. Two helmeted door gunners clutched machine guns with belts of long, pencil-like bullets.

The land dissolved into the sea and we were safe. The knot of tension and strangled feelings was released. A hazy sky and gray sea blended together as if we were nowhere.

Then the aircraft carrier. A huge steel mass that stood on the calm sea like a building on land. Just like war again. Circling, dropping and thump. The ramp was opened and we were led out. Again the whirlwind of air from the chopper's rotors. You stoop a bit and the powerful gusts push you forward. Every sailor on the boat who was not working was snapping pictures. I stopped, stood still and blocked everything out to feel the air, sun, sea and joy.

Our chopper landed on the U.S.S. *Okinawa.*

Operation Frequent Wind officially ended at eight thirty in the morning – nineteen hours after it began. I was lying awake and staring at the pictures of someone's wife that were tacked to the bunk above me. One of the ship's commanders announced the "termination" of the operation and proclaimed it the single largest helicopter operation in aviation history, adding that now we would have something to tell our grandchildren. At last.

"The government of South Vietnam surrendered unconditionally today . . ." North Vietnamese tanks had pulled up to the presidential palace. The turnover had been peaceful. The Battle for Saigon had been averted and the soldiers laid down their guns. We risked more by leaving than by staying and still had four more days of sailing ahead of us.   ⊕

notes from the underground
by lenny kaye

ONE NIGHT IN APRIL, Hilly's dog was hit on the Bowery.

A saluki. Ran out between two cars and got clipped at the junction where Bleecker runs smack into CBGB's front door.

He was named Johnny; and Johnny – the protagonist of "Land" – was always Johnny, long before the dog. Johnny would live, and during that spring, playing our version of "Land of 1000 Dances," the world gathered at our portal as the Johnnys moved their shadows across the walls of a Lower East Side bar.

Downtown. Manhattan: "Oh, look at this land where we am," declaimed Patti, and when we did, it became a time for retrospection and re-creation; a reminder of why we started listening in the first place. "There is not twilight on this island."

Call it what you will – and lumpen punk rock fits as well as anything – but you do it for yourself first, for the person in you that wants to pick up a sounding device and activate the sleeping self. To find through music life's beating heart and then wear it on your sleeve, genre sewn on like military patches, signifying your company, your rank, your serial number. Battle scars, campaign ribbons, war wounds. And every once in a while, you get to raise a flag. *Corregidor,* man. I was there.

It's only after you look around at the clearing smoke, counting the casualties and sweeping up the rubble, that you see how it fits into the fore and aft. Rather than note the differentials, or how something quasi-new is created out of the random weave of three rotating chords, I'll spin the similarities. The common thread.

For me, it all begins in the Sixties American garage. 'Tis a Nugget if you dug it, and I did, growing of age as rock & roll itself moved through the squalor of infantasy through protracted adolescence. Doo-wop on the corner might have been my first impulse, but too young to sing with the older guys, I had to wait until the Beatles and R. Stones first showed up on these shores to begin thinking about this new notion of picking up an electric guitar.

In the either/or mythos of teenagery, you either hang with the quasi-thugs or the bespectacled intellectuals, the jocks or the jokesters. But what if your developing personality doesn't fit such preconceived notions – or even, odder than odd, you move between both polarities, a mutation on a par with the paired opposites-attract matchmaking of rock & roll itself?

Why, then, you form a band. Find a bunch of other misfits and start playing the music that still other misfits pass along.

The primal impulse. A shared yearning. Mutual misconception. And sometimes you just want to make a racket.

This rock-as-alien-creature is part of the music's timeworn appeal, its otherness. It makes for a strange tension, a flux that takes two steps forward and three steps back, kind of like a dance in which the partners – in this case, the culture at large and its bizarro mirror image – beckon and reject.

Such is the mating call of alternate-culture mainstreaming, to be followed inevitably by recrimination, anger and a sense of betrayal as possibility becomes probability and then predictability. As a teen musician (dubbed "Crazy Like a Fox" by my doppelgänger Link Cromwell) and later a "rock writer," I followed the twisting tides of rock & roll, struggling to find its artistic voice and, by extension, my own.

Even then, I liked the indefinity, the song as it was becoming, and felt my own restlessness when destinations were reached. The rush of getting there. And for most of us roaming lower Manhattan as the Seventies made their presence felt, it was time to move on. Shake it up, baby.

The entrance fees had risen. The immediate gratification of rock & roll had been replaced by a workmanlike professionalism and studio sheen, a world away – or so it

rumors that his disappearance was a result of Mob ties will persist.

4 Led Zeppelin singer Robert Plant and his family suffer serious injuries in a car accident while vacationing on the Mediterranean isle of Rhodes; the band postpones a scheduled U.S. tour.

5 Stevie Wonder re-signs with Motown Records for $13 million – the largest sum in recording history to date – although the deal won't be finalized until the following April.

8 Jazz saxophonist Julian "Cannonball" Adderley dies.

9 *Don Kirshner's Rock Music Award Show* airs on CBS, featuring nonrockers like Olivia Newton-John and Mike Douglas presenting awards to Bad Company, the Eagles, Stevie Wonder, Joan Baez and Roger Daltrey.

13 Bruce Springsteen begins his legendary five-night stand at New York City's Bottom Line nightclub and lights the media fire that will engulf his breakthrough third LP, *Born to Run*.

15 A North Carolina jury finds black convict Joanne Little not guilty of the slaying of her white jailer, whom she claims forced her into a sexual act. Her case draws both support and derision, split along racial lines.

16 Vocalist Peter Gabriel officially parts company with art rockers Genesis. After many months of auditioning possible replacements, the band will hand the microphone to one of its own, drummer Phil Collins.

27 Former Ethiopian emperor Haile Selassie, a messianic figure to Rastafarians worldwide, dies.

More than five years after the Kent State shootings, a federal grand jury finds Governor James Rhodes of Ohio and National Guardsmen not personally responsible for the deaths of four students.

28 ROLLING STONE reports on the burgeoning disco craze: It's no longer primarily a gay or black scene; 12" singles and special "disco mixes" of popular dance songs arrive; and new and converted dance spots open, bringing the national total to 2,000 discos.

4 In Geneva, Egypt and Israel reach an agreement for troop

seemed – from the raw exuberance and spontaneous combustion of early rock. Slumbering singer/songwriters. Pyrite metal. Dinosaur bands lumbering under concept albums and pseudo-symphonies. The Sixties rock underground, now welcomed into the corridors of power, had made a collective bargain that, like most pacts with the devil, gave it three wishes and took its soul. Confronted with a music that was smoothed and sated, we looked for the angularity, the jagged edges that could draw blood, the atonal skid-mark screech of our own rite of passage.

The first thing we had to do was bring it back to ground zero; i.e., remember what drew us to the music in the first place. Along with this simplifying and slicing-away of dead weight (which we could hardly play anyway), we all desired – no matter what sounds would eventually be purloined or invented – a return to overdrive (or was it overdose?) energy, guitar feedback set on stun; as for content, our rockin' role models moved to the harder edge of the urban strut, no stranger to shock corridors and decayed tenement streets. Faster. Louder. Up the ante.

L.A. San Francisco. Detroit. You could feel the footfalls of the approaching momentum come ever nearer, yet if you looked around at the strange gaggle of scenesters – performance artists and avant-cinematographers and garage-rockers-in-a-city-that-didn't-even-have-parking-spaces-much-less-garages – you couldn't believe that this Boweryesque scene could ever be that kind of cataclysmic scenery. It was too far from the mid-American point. Too off the map, even if the Sixth Avenue edifices of the music business were only some fifty blocks north. It was the interregnum. Ever since the mid-Sixties Lovin' Spoonful–era Night Owl, New York had found it hard to support a local band scene. There was only one Velvet Underground. One Fugs.

One New York Dolls. They had begun in a small arts space on Mercer Street as the Seventies kicked off, creating their recipe of pick-it-up trash and vaudeville from the shards of the most romantic rocks: Brill Building teen pop and late-night hanging at Nobody's, the pseudo-English groupie bar. The glitter scene they led made a valiant stand at the cross-dressing Club 82, with such bandwagoneers as the Harlots of 42nd Street, the Miamis, and Another Pretty Face (from the wilds of Jersey); ultimately, it would be the antiheroes of the scene, Kiss, who would have the last laugh.

The clubs closed, including – for a time – Max's Kansas City, which had at least given the bands a milieu in which to live out their Rock Dreams cravings, and the resultant wander led to some mighty strange venues. Supper clubs like Ashley's, cabarets like Reno Sweeney or the occasional adventurous disco – Le Jardin in the Hotel Diplomat comes to mind – could only go so far. A dive was needed.

Television found CBGB. The owner, Hilly Kristal, had toyed with country and bluegrass and blues before, and even while he continued to live in the back room with his pack of dogs, he gave the bands a space to set up in on the left side of the room – as long as they didn't block the pool table.

Every Sunday night, Television would play. It was a good night to go for a hang because it was after the weekend flood tide, the bridge-and-tunnel waters receding and leaving mostly your fellow travelers on the shore, gasping for air and wriggling their tailfins. Everything was pretty cacophonous, erratic and jerky, teetering on the edge of grasp. Out of tune. On target.

The bands started to cluster. The fans, and most of them were the other bands, stayed to watch. Small world, isn't it?

Though it might have seemed insular to a wandering outsider, within the CBGB world everyone brought differing influenzas to the petri dish. Garbage-picking from the detritus of rock, the music leapfrogged a generation backward and forward, excavating scorned pop objects and hex-rated perversities. The bands were held together by philosophy alone – they were hardly alike in style, at least in these formative stages. The only time-share they cultivated was another way of looking at the world: good old Us versus Them.

Inbred and feeding on itself (though I'm sure it avoided Hilly's hamburgers from the kitchen, which is now the rear undressing room), CBGB became an exotic castle keep for this medieval morality play in the making. The bands that rooted there – stalwarts all, including Ye Talking Heads, the good Lady Blondie, those Knights of the Ramones Table, the aforementioned Sir Television and our humble selves – then rode off into the worldly night to seek fortune and frolic.

Self-propelled. Shot through the vortex of pop culture. Whooee!

But even at its most projectile, you have to realize it's not you that's the pebble in the sling. It's your moment. Your arc is the distance it takes to carry this blip of history-as-it's-lived to someone who picks up a piece of it, a large chunk or a sliver that drops off along the way, sometimes unrecognizable, and makes it their own.

National acts still performed at Madison Square Garden; radio playlists had little to do with local music. But word spread that a home for the disaffected had been founded on an avenue where many had traditionally come to lie in the gutter, to eat and sleep on the street and to see what life was like when they started from scratch.

It wasn't just New York at the time. Everywhere I traveled in that *Horses*-drawn year, every city and interstate, there were pockets of people with mutual affections. Did I say afflictions? Stylistically, this simpatico spit off a myriad of directional signals, a survival of the fittest for accouterments: slashed-and-burned clothes, motorcycle jackets, cranked guitars, overdriven rhythm. Wave that high sign and let the world know you gotta do it Your Way. But a few years later, when Sid Vicious sang the Frank Sinatra anthem as a flaming finale to punk-as-a-way-of-life (not that any of us wuz punk, see?), little did he know that it could never die, because it always reconfigures. New wave begets hardcore begets industrial begets grunge. For New York, CB's begat Hurrah begat the Mudd Club begat Danceteria, the concentric circles of an earth movement in seismic pulse.

Cut up. Imprismed. The lineage can be traced wherever you like, styles notwithstanding. The impulse to pick up a guitar, beat a drum, blow a horn, scream into a microphone, turn a table and ultimately stick your hand down your throat and pull out your heart for the universe to see, is ever replicating.

You never know where it's going to strike next. And that's what I remember most about those weeks in early '75: The possibilities endless, I'm standing outside the rock & roll club after we played, or Television played, two sets a night, Thursday through Sunday, sharing a smoke with "T" in the next-door hallway of the Palace Hotel, and looking up Bleecker Street as it starts its slow curve around the world. ⊕

hilly kristal
on cbgb

IT'S STILL fascinating when I consider which CBGB experiences I remember the most. I'll never forget the Talking Heads and the Shirts performing on the same audition night. I'll never forget the whole Patti Smith thing. I'll never forget John Cale when the crowd wouldn't let him off the stage and he played until 5:30 a.m. The Dead Boys opening for the Damned – they blew them off the stage! Das Fürlines – they were a great band. I still think of early Blondie – the Stilettoes – they were campy and fun. The B-52's had a different thing going.

I opened CBGB in December 1973. The name stood for Country, Bluegrass and Blues. That was the music I was into and wanted to present. One day around March 1974, when I was on a ladder outside, Tom Verlaine walked by and asked if I was interested in booking rock music. It was his band Television's manager who really started bugging me. He wanted to put Television on at CB's on Sunday nights. I agreed.

Television was horrible, just horrible. And nobody came, so I said, "No more." But their manager pleaded, saying he had another band, this one from Queens – and that's how the Ramones first started playing at CBGB. They were even worse. They were a mess.

Word got out and people started coming around, and the scene started growing. The summer of 1974, so many groups wanted to play CBGB. With the new bands, there was a movement back to basics. It was a self-expression thing for most of those kids. They certainly couldn't play their instruments as well as the musicians I listened to – Miles Davis, Thelonious Monk – so these CBGB bands were not thrilling to me at first. But soon I saw that many of them had their own vision. Sometimes limited technical facility can give a group its own distinct personality. And some of the groups became exceptionally original.

Patti Smith liked it here and ended up playing four nights a week, for quite a few weeks. Television, who had gotten really good, was the opener for those shows. As a poet, Patti was already well known. As a rock singer, she was surprisingly good – she had magnetism, and her voice sounded great. That was the beginning of a wider circle of people finding out about CBGB.

After the Patti Smith residency, I figured I had to do something to keep the crowds coming in, so I decided to have a festival. This was midsummer 1975. I called it the Festival of the Top 40 Unrecorded New York Rock Bands. I waited until there was nothing musical going on in New York City, after the Newport Festival, then I started taking out huge ads in the *Voice* and the *Soho Weekly News* – and at that time *nobody* took huge ads.

The ads did the trick. All the early CBGB bands played, except Patti's, because she was recording. The Ramones, Blondie, Mink DeVille – countless groups. And everybody played at least twice, seven days a week, for three weeks. People came from all over, from *NME* and *Melody Maker* and ROLLING STONE. The Japanese came, too. That's when CBGB and the bands playing here really got heard around the world. ⊕

disengagement from the Sinai, with the installation of U.S. observers. The accord is approved by Oct. 10, and Israeli troops begin leaving the peninsula for the first time since the 1973 war.

5 *Jaws* becomes the top-grossing film of all time.

Former Manson Family member Lynette Alice "Squeaky" Fromme tries to shoot President Ford and is immediately arrested in California. On Sept. 22, Sara Jane Moore also makes an unsuccessful assassination attempt on the president in San Francisco, and is likewise arrested.

6 Top of the charts: Glen Campbell's "Rhinestone Cowboy" (pop single); Jefferson Starship's *Red Octopus* (pop album).

8 The busing of Boston schoolchildren begins again amid protest demonstrations.

9 NASA's unmanned probe *Viking 2* takes off for Mars.

10 Bob Dylan joins swing bandleader Benny Goodman, bluesmen Sonny Terry and John Hammond Jr. and gospel singer Marion Williams in a TV tribute to legendary Columbia Records talent scout John Hammond. All of the event's performers had been Hammond's "discoveries"; he also signed and/or produced Billie Holiday, Bruce Springsteen and Stevie Ray Vaughan.

16 The delicate balance among Lebanon's religious groups begins to teeter out of control. Fighting erupts between Christian and Muslim factions, beginning a drawn-out civil war that will kill thousands and reduce Beirut to ruins.

18 Patty Hearst is arrested in her Bay Area hideout along with other surviving SLA members. Eighteen days later, ROLLING STONE makes headlines with its investigative account of the early days of Hearst's abduction and subsequent underground flight.

20 David Bowie's "Fame," hits #1 on the *Billboard* pop chart, his first to reach the top.

25 Soul singer Jackie Wilson collapses from a paralyzing heart attack while performing "Lonely Teardrops" in New Jersey. He will remain immobile and mute until his death in 1984.

1975 OCTOBER

1 Muhammad Ali defeats challenger and former heavyweight champion Joe Frazier at the

p.c. in the valley
by michael rogers

AS A NEW COLLEGE graduate in Palo Alto in the mid-Seventies, I had an interest in stringing words together to make prose and a knack for stringing wires together to make electronic gadgets. Growing up, I had always assumed I would support my quest for literary fame and fortune with an engineering job in some fluorescent cubicle at an obscure semiconductor company down Highway 101 in Sunnyvale. But then the opportunity beckoned to head north to San Francisco and become a ROLLING STONE writer. Now, twenty years after choosing Door Number Two, I'm writing this chapter for a fee only slightly higher than what my calculator-toting classmates who headed south to Intel pay to have the transmission fluid changed in their Ferraris.

Not that I mind: Rock & roll journalism was very good to me, and Ferraris are poor vehicles in heavy traffic. But I must admit that back then – even though I was a longtime subscriber to a little magazine called *Popular Electronics* – I entirely missed the historical significance of its January 1975 cover. That cover featured the MITS Altair 8800, the first personal-computer kit. The $397 Altair was a drab, boring box with blinking lights – a primitive fossil compared to today's personal computers. In fact, once you'd built the box, you still had to be exceedingly clever at programming in order to make the lights blink. Even so, a force had been set loose, and by the end of the decade much of today's computer landscape had already been shaped by a handful of powerful personalities, plus a hefty cultural hangover from the Sixties.

Regardless of my feckless career move, during the Seventies I continued to read *Popular Electronics* and remained drawn to the southward suburban sprawl then newly dubbed "Silicon Valley." I devoured the microcomputer enthusiast magazines (with whimsical titles like *Dr. Dobb's Journal of Tiny BASIC Calisthenics and Orthodontia*) and was a regular at the first hobbyist computer shows. The latter were ragtag high-tech bazaars of folding tables and hand-lettered signs advertising arcane electronic wares (BAUD RATE GENERATOR! TANTALUM CAPACITORS! IC EXTRACTORS!), gatherings sufficiently funky that business attire was defined as a clean T-shirt.

It didn't occur to me at first to write about my visits. Perhaps it was because there was absolutely nothing cool about electronics hobbyists in the mid-Seventies, unless you were one yourself, and even then you were probably plagued by wildly alternating moods of oblivious obsession and serious self-hatred. No fashion designer had yet glamorized nerdy eyeglasses or unkempt hair; there were no movies in which geeky yet oddly sexy young men and women

> At right: Steve Wozniak and Steve Jobs *(from left)* show off the Apple I; following page: The MITS Altair 8800

solved crimes via keyboard and modem; there were no gilded techno-mansions rising on Seattle lakefronts. Sure, some guys were already making buckets of money in the old-style computer industry, but they were flattop engineer types who never did anything really stylish with their loot. For outsiders, this whole personal-computer scene tended to appear either unpleasantly weird or exceedingly dull.

The closest thing to sexy that the electronics hobbyists offered the normal world in the early Seventies was the "blue box," a homemade device that generated telephone-company dialing tones and allowed free long-distance calling. There was an underground college market for blue boxes – in fact, building and selling the contraband gadgets was the initial business venture for the soon-to-be-legendary Steves – Wozniak and Jobs. (Supposedly, inveterate prankster Wozniak's first free long-distance call was to the pope, in order to confess that he'd built a blue box.) But blue boxes were illegal, hard to use and ultimately appealed mostly to adolescent males intent on deconstructing the global phone network. Wozniak long remained an idol to young "phone phreaks" just cutting their teeth on Ma Bell; years later, wealthy from his Apple stock, semi-retired in a mansion above Silicon Valley, he would pick up his home telephone to hear dozens of kids from around the world on the line simultaneously yelling "Hey, Woz!"

"Thrilla in Manila," in the Philippines.

Drummer Al Jackson Jr., the heartbeat of Booker T. & the MG's and a key part of the Stax Records sound behind soul legends Otis Redding, Sam & Dave, Wilson Pickett and countless others, is shot and killed by an intruder in his home.

7 At long last, John Lennon succeeds in his effort to become a legal American resident when a three-judge panel rules in his favor. Two days later, on his 35th birthday, John and Yoko celebrate the birth of their son, Sean Taro Ono Lennon.

11 NBC's *Saturday Night Live* premieres. George Carlin appears as the first guest host and the rookie cast includes John Belushi, Chevy Chase, Dan Aykroyd and Gilda Radner. A week later, the program begins its meteoric rise with a Simon & Garfunkel reunion.

12 Rod Stewart and the Faces perform their last show together at Long Island's Nassau Coliseum. Stewart will continue his successful solo career, while guitarist Ron Wood will sign on permanently with the Rolling Stones. The remaining members and Steve Marriott will re-form the Small Faces.

22 Due to financial pressures and low attendance, the World Football League falls apart 12 weeks into its second season.

The Cincinnati Reds down the Boston Red Sox in seven games to win the World Series.

27 Bruce Springsteen is featured on the cover of *Time* and *Newsweek* in the same week.

29 The Rolling Thunder Revue, Bob Dylan's ever-expanding folk-and-rock cavalcade concert, begins in Plymouth, MA. During the next few months, the loosely planned and roughly executed production will travel throughout the U.S., popping up guerrilla-style in various cities and featuring Joan Baez, Joni Mitchell, Ramblin' Jack Elliott, Bob Neuwirth, Allen Ginsberg, Roger McGuinn, Mick Ronson and many others.

31 Capricorn Records president Phil Walden produces the first of many Southern-rock benefits for Democratic presidential candidate, former Georgia governor Jimmy Carter. The Marshall Tucker

Like Jobs and Wozniak, many electronics hobbyists who started with blue boxes moved on to computers in the mid-Seventies. Intel had recently introduced a new item called a microprocessor, gathering thousands of transistors onto a single chip not much bigger than a Caribbean postage stamp. The microprocessor was initially intended for electronic calculators, when those were themselves still costly items. But hobbyists like Wozniak – who pored over the chip-company catalogs the way bookies read the *Racing Form* – quickly saw that it was now possible for an individual, rather than IBM or Sperry or Honeywell, to add some additional parts to these chips and create a computer. "Microcomputer" was the name first used to distinguish these new machines from the refrigerator-sized minicomputers (usually shared by many users) that at the start of the decade had represented the state of the art.

Ground zero of the microcomputer movement was the area around Stanford University, where the ambient culture shaped a deeper ethic that colors the industry to this day. By the mid-Seventies, of course, some trend-watchers saw the counterculture rapidly receding in the rearview mirror, but its influence remained strong. When, in 1977, one writer at ROLLING STONE proposed a satirical *Life* magazine–style photo-essay describing an isolated tribe of the last hippies left living in America, editor Jann Wenner rejected it: "You have to remember," he said, "some of our readers are still discovering that stuff." A case in point were the nerds of Silicon Valley, a few steps behind the Sixties beat but now bonding enthusiastically with everything from Power to the People to computer collectives.

The Homebrew Computer Club, for example, where the elite of the early computing days met regularly to swap plans and parts, was shepherded by an eloquent young hobbyist named Lee Felsenstein. His previous job had been with the *Berkeley Barb*, a newspaper noted equally for explicit sexual advertising and radical politics; Felsenstein cofounded Community Memory, a group devoted to making computer access available to every citizen for free, at least a full decade before most citizens had any idea they'd want such access in the first place. Added into that political mix was the influence of the Whole Earth Truck Store, a Palo Alto offshoot of Stewart Brand's *Whole Earth Catalog* of the Sixties, which rapidly moved into the new frontier of tiny computers. And nearby was the People's Computer Company, an organization that arose prior to the personal computer as a way for ordinary citizens to get access to time-sharing minicomputers, publishing books with titles like *My Computer Likes Me.*

Up in the hills above Silicon Valley, Jim Warren, a jolly, bearded fellow (whose penchant for nude hot-tub parties caused his departure from a teaching position at a Catholic college), turned his hand to small computers and launched the first West Coast Computer Faire (complete with precious Sixties spelling), at which the Apple II debuted. And a charismatic fellow named Ted Nelson (who likely inherited his stage presence from actress mom Celeste Holm) made regular public appearances to preach the virtues of Xanadu: a complex vision of a universal electronic world library in which all knowledge was linked to all other knowledge. Project Xanadu itself never happened – although more than a few believers pumped big dollars into the effort over the next couple of decades. Ironically, the Internet itself is now, rather on its own, taking the shape of Nelson's mid-Seventies vision.

As a result of these countercultural influences, many computerists of the Seventies shared both a profound mistrust of big business and a nearly religious belief that the computer was a tool of personal liberation. Even when the personal computerists went into business, their companies took names that mocked largeness or were simply silly. The Itty Bitty Machine Company lasted long enough for IBM's lawyers to draft a cease-and-desist letter; Kentucky Fried Computers had an only slightly longer life. Apple Computer, named for one of Steve Jobs's favorite fruits, is the last reminder of the days when whimsy was a more powerful force than one's marketing department.

Despite the excitement around the Homebrew Club, for most of the decade personal computers remained amazingly primitive. They initially stored their programs on cassette tapes, displayed text onscreen in big blocky capital letters and in general did very little of practical value. The buyers were almost entirely hobbyists – at that point, big businesses were perfectly happy with their mainframes and minicomputers ("Nobody ever got fired for buying IBM" was the corporate mantra, and IBM was years away from building a personal computer). Most small businesses still considered the Xerox machine the outer limit of technological risk-taking. Yet even so, the key personalities of the personal-computer industry were already well into the roles they would someday play on the global stage: models of the postindustrial capitalist for a new generation of entrepreneurs.

Consider Bill Gates. As a Harvard sophomore, Gates saw the MITS Altair 8800 on the cover of *Popular Electronics* and dropped out of school to develop, along with his buddy Paul Allen, the form of BASIC language needed to make its lights blink. Since no other language existed at the time, the first Micro-Soft (as it was then spelled) product was an instant hit. But Bill was soon unhappy, for he promptly collided with a prevailing notion spawned by Sixties idealism: "Information wants to be free." People were sharing Bill's software with one another, rather than purchasing new copies for themselves. He promptly challenged the personal-computer community with a testy "open letter" about how people should pay for his work rather than give copies to friends, and if they didn't, there wasn't going to be any more useful software coming from him, thank you very much.

The document was scathing, scornful and quite correct in asserting the importance of intellectual property rights. Computer hobbyists, however, immediately attacked Gates as a mercenary snake who wanted to own the Garden – in terms much like those used more than twenty years later by Microsoft's more contemporary critics.

About the time that Gates was standing up for intellectual property, Steve Jobs was cruising department-store aisles studying kitchen appliances in order to come up with a friendly look for the Apple II computer. (The 1976 Apple I computer had used the standard packaging of the era: a naked printed circuit board delivered in a plastic bag.) Thus, it was a watershed in personal-computer history when in 1977 he and Wozniak unveiled the sleek, beige-plastic Apple II, the first personal computer to look like something other than the interior of a telephone switchboard. The Apple II debut was at a five-thousand-dollar booth at the now-legendary first West Coast Computer Faire in the basement of San Francisco's grungy Civic Auditorium. The Apple II was astoundingly slick by the prevailing standard, but Jobs was only warming up. Ten years later and five blocks away, after a tempestuous departure from Apple, he would don black tie and rent the elegant Louise M. Davies Symphony Hall to unveil his brilliant but doomed Next computer – programming the stylish black cube's sound system to play a duet with a classical violinist.

The Seventies also shaped two key technologies for the

remainder of the century. Indeed, one can argue that the personal computer and the Internet were also basically finished by the end of the decade and that the next twenty years have involved working out the details. In the mid-Seventies at a laboratory called Xerox PARC in the hills above Silicon Valley, a small band of blue-sky thinkers had built a desktop computer uncannily like the mainstream personal computer of the Nineties, featuring a mouse, icons, windowing graphics, a laser printer. But Xerox hesitated, and then in 1979 Steve Jobs – again cruising the aisles for ideas, this time at PARC – saw the work. He instantly realized that he was looking at the future, ultimately giving rise to the Lisa and Macintosh, which in turn led to Windows, as Bill Gates stamped the concept with his brand.

And the Internet, whose formal birthday is often given as 1969 (when it was the ARPAnet, linking a handful of universities and governmental and industrial research labs), actually added its most crucial ingredient in the Seventies. In an obscure but landmark experiment in 1977, researchers in the United States and Europe routed a computer signal from a moving van on San Francisco's Bayshore Freeway, via radio, landlines and satellites, over to London and then back to Los Angeles – traversing 94,000 miles and, as one researcher later recalled, "We didn't lose a bit." That "bit heard round the world" proved the viability of the TCP/IP system – the ability to send data seamlessly between totally different kinds of computer networks – that is today the fundamental technical underpinning of the global Internet.

By the end of the decade, I'd written a novel about the incredible story unfolding forty miles south of San Francisco. The book's editor, Michael Korda, an astute observer of popular culture, liked the manuscript but not the title: *Silicon Valley.* "Do people really have any idea where that is?" he asked. It was an excellent point, but like a stubborn computerist, I refused to change the name: As I saw it, Silicon Valley in the Seventies was the story. And while my recalcitrance about the title did not do the book's commercial prospects any good, in retrospect I was right.

Although it would be another five years before the locale became legendary, the odd characters of Silicon Valley had already mapped out the technology for the rest of the century. And more importantly, the Seventies had also created a state of mind that informed the technology. It was a cantankerous, idealistic and occasionally messianic attitude that now influences everything from antitrust debates to arguments over Internet censorship – a spirit that also shapes young computerists not even born the day the MITS Altair 8800 made the cover of *Popular Electronics.* ⊕

tania got her gun
by howard kohn & david weir

THE INSIDE STORY? Who would have the chutzpah to put such a baldly unexplained headline on a magazine cover? And in blaring type! Yet by the time ROLLING STONE Number 198 hit the newsstands on a Tuesday in October 1975, no explanation was necessary. The whole country and half the world knew what it meant, to exaggerate not at all.

Until the moment of publication, ROLLING STONE went to great lengths to keep this one a secret. Even at the magazine's offices it was known only inside a small circle. On the previous Saturday the issue had rolled off the presses under the watchful eye of guards hired to make sure no one walked away with a copy. The precautions just helped to agitate rumors, of course, and the radio buzzed with them all day Sunday. Finally, after nineteen months, here was everything there was to know about heiress Patty Hearst's disappearance! The scoop of the decade, to be published by that underground music magazine in San Francisco! Everyone wanted to know what had happened to Patty Hearst, from the time when she was stolen away in her nightclothes by members of the Symbionese Liberation Army (SLA) to the shocking flash of her ten weeks later on a bank surveillance camera as the beret-wearing, machine-gun-wielding "Tania" and through the many months after she had dropped completely out of sight. On Monday morning the 'Today' show devoted twenty-two minutes to the scoop. On Monday evening, NBC and CBS led off their news broadcasts with "The Inside Story." The ROLLING STONE cover was flashed on the screen as big as life. By the following morning, the story had become a banner headline on newspapers throughout North America, Europe and Asia.

We remember ROLLING STONE's editor, Jann Wenner, toasting us with champagne in his office and then saying, "Okay, back to work, boys." For two weeks we hardly slept, and most of the sleep we did grab was in airport terminals or in parked cars or at our desks. Our notebooks show we conducted more than thirty interviews, ten on a confidential basis.

Getting the story was not the hardest part, though. Most other reporters seemed to be waiting for the FBI to break the case and then leak them the information, and it happened that the FBI, more than a year and a half after the kidnapping of Patty Hearst, still did not have a clue. The only people who were able to clear up the mysteries that had transfixed so much of the world (Was Patty an SLA stooge from the very beginning? Had she converted to the SLA? Or was she the consummate victim?) were former college radicals like ourselves who knew someone who knew someone.

Meanwhile, the New World Liberation Front (NWLF), a gang of armed leftists who believed it was their mission in life to carry out the vendettas of the SLA, issued a communiqué to say we'd been placed on their hit list alongside FBI bureau chief Charles Bates. Communiqués were then an accepted means by which underground groups made their wishes known to the larger community of the left or to any psychopaths who might be interested. The surviving members of the SLA, who were by this time under arrest, had expressed unhappiness over their portrayals in "The Inside Story."

For some time there had been a bitter debate over what the proper political perspective on the SLA and the NWLF should be. Were they a genuine expression of Sixties-era dissatisfaction with the status quo? Or were they acting out of a personal dementia? The answer wasn't really hard to come by, but the two groups had a certain genius for public relations. For instance, the ransom demand sent to the Hearst family for Patty's release was not for a bag of money to be dropped off in the dark but rather for truckloads of food to be handed out to Bay Area poor people in a spectacularly staged media event. Strange as such good Samaritanism might have seemed, there was considerable praise for it on the left. Our piece, on the other hand, had made it clear that, based on their overall conduct, these self-styled revolutionaries were nothing better than criminal thugs.

No one at ROLLING STONE doubted that the situation had become dicey. Recent history in the Bay Area favored violent political retaliations. Everyone on staff stayed away

from the windows of the makeshift offices in the old brick warehouse, and extra securi-ty was brought in.

In the late summer of 1975, Patty Hearst and her SLA companions, Bill and Emily Harris, were captured after being recognized by local residents who alerted authorities.

In the booking room, Patty was fingerprinted and asked the usual questions: name, age, date of birth, occupation.

"What do you do for a living?" the matron asked.

"Nothing."

"Are you a student?"

"No."

"Well, what are you?"

"Well, I don't do anything."

"Well, how do you make a living?"

"Well, I'm an urban guerrilla."

Publication of "The Inside Story" caused the Hearst family to hire high-powered attor-ney F. Lee Bailey and change legal strategies in Patty's trial for the Hibernia Bank case. Nonetheless, she was convicted by jurors who did not believe she had acted wholly under duress. The Harrises also were convicted. All three served time behind bars; Patty was pardoned in 1979 after serving nearly two years.

PATTY HEARST and Steven Weed were home in their Berkeley apartment watching *The Magician* on TV at nine o'clock on the foggy night of February 4, 1974. The young couple lived together in something that used to be called sin and smoked an occa-sional joint. But in Berkeley they were considered straight.

Outside, a stolen 1964 Chevrolet Impala convertible pulled up in front and dimmed its lights. Donald DeFreeze, Willie Wolfe and Nancy Ling Perry emerged and moved silent-ly to apartment number four. Perry rang the doorbell while DeFreeze and Wolfe waited in the shadows. Perry hunched over and held a hand to her face. "I just had a car accident out front. Could you . . . ?"

Weed cracked open the door and DeFreeze and Wolfe burst in, brandishing guns, knocking him to the floor and kicking him in the face with heavy boots. They grabbed Patty and carried her kicking and screaming to the waiting car. There they shoved her into the trunk with a brusque order: "Get in and keep quiet."

Patty was scared and half-naked but she stared hard-eyed at her kidnappers. "Don't give me any shit."

Even in those first terrible moments Patricia Campbell Hearst managed to summon up the daring and arrogance that had been her style through nineteen years of life as an heiress to the Hearst fortune. Her parents had provided every indul-gence, tolerated her dope smoking, her sneaking out to rock concerts at San Francisco's Fillmore and her faded blue jeans. When she couldn't accept the Catholic-school dis-cipline that required her to scrub toilets for breaking petty rules, her parents trans-ferred her to a more flexible, nonsectarian school.

It was there that she met Weed, a math teacher and the school's most eligible bach-elor. Two years later, when she was eighteen, she moved in with him. Her parents ini-tially disapproved, and Patty worked briefly at paying her own bills, holding a $2.25-per-hour job in a department store for four months. But when she gave that up to return to school, her father paid for her books, tuition and the out-of-wedlock apartment as well. Over the next year her father supplied enough money for her to buy expensive prints from her grandfather's collection, Persian rugs, a Tenth-Century Persian manuscript and dozens of plants.

Patty was not used to discomfort. Her life had been insulated from real-life drama and pain. She assumed her father would quickly ransom her.

The SLA, however, kept Patty blindfolded in an "isolation chamber" approximating a San Quentin "hole" – a stuffy, closet-sized room with a bare lightbulb and a portable cot. There were no windows, and it was hot. She lost track of time and didn't feel like eating. She was told her parents loved money more than her.

She was not raped or starved or otherwise brutalized. But Donald DeFreeze, the

SLA leader known as Cinque, kept up a constant intimidation. He berated her and her family for being part of a ruling class that was sucking blood from the common people.

"Your mommy and daddy are insects," he yelled. "They should be made to crawl on their hands and knees like insects if they want you back."

Patty tried to defend her parents. They had not hurt anyone. They were good people. Cinque was wrong. He had never met them.

But Patty feared Cinque. He told her she'd be killed if her parents did not meet the SLA's demands, and she believed him.

So Patty grew impatient as the ransom negotiations bogged down. "I felt my parents were debating how much I was worth," she said later. "Like they figured I was worth $2 million but I wasn't worth $10 million. It was a terrible feeling that my parents could think of me in terms of dollars and cents. I felt sick all over."

It angered her when her father visited San Quentin and reported that the living conditions there were fine. The SLA had informed him that her living quarters were identical to those in San Quentin. Her father seemed to be saying that tiny cells, stale air and gloomy walls were an acceptable environment for his daughter.

And she became alarmed when heavily armed FBI agents raided a house where they thought she was being held. She felt her parents were recklessly allowing the FBI to risk her life.

After a while it seemed that her parents had given her up for dead. "It's really depressing to hear people talk about me like I was dead," she said in her second taped statement. "I can't explain what it's like." Her mother had taken to wearing black and speaking of Patty in the past tense. Worse, her mother had ignored an SLA demand by accepting another appointment from then-governor Ronald Reagan, as a regent of the University of California.

"I felt like I could kill her when she did that," Patty said. "My own mother didn't care whether the SLA shot me or not."

By degrees her disillusionment with her parents turned into sympathy for the SLA. Cinque was the first to perceive the change. He rewarded her by allowing her to roam about the San Francisco apartment that served as the SLA headquarters. For a month she had been kept in the "isolation chamber." She'd become weak and could barely stand up. To be able to walk freely from one room to another seemed the world's greatest pleasure.

Cinque tempered his frequent berating of her. Patty was urged to attend the SLA's daily political study sessions. She was invited to listen to the SLA national anthem, an eerie jazz composition of wind and string instruments that Cinque had selected. And she was furnished with statistical evidence and quotations from George Jackson and Ruchell Magee that promoted her political development. Less than 10 percent of the U.S. population controls 90 percent of its wealth. Some people eat catered meals while others starve. Some can afford fancy lawyers while others rot in jail. Some live off inheritances while others live in squalor and despair.

Patty was shown a long list of the Hearst family holdings – nine newspapers, thirteen magazines, four TV and radio stations, a silver mine, a paper mill and prime real estate. Her parents clearly were part of the ruling elite. That's why they had quibbled over the ransom money. That's why they had handed out turkey giblets instead of steaks during the food giveaway that the SLA demanded. Money meant everything to the economic class of her parents. And the only power that could fight that money was the power that came out of the barrel of a gun.

It was a political philosophy that had bored her when Weed and his doctoral-student friends had discussed it in their Berkeley apartment. But Cinque's rough eloquence was more persuasive than the abstract talk of graduate students. The SLA's motives made more sense. They wanted to redistribute the Hearst wealth to more needy people. It was her parents – and the economic class they represented – who were to blame for her misery and that of countless others.

The SLA members encouraged her radicalization. They hugged her, called her "sister" and ended her loneliness. Patty's conversion was as much emotional as political.

Seven weeks after she was kidnapped, Patty asked to join the SLA. Despite their new respect for her, most of the SLA soldiers were opposed to the idea. Patty would deprive them of mobility because her face was so easily recognized. She could not be counted on for emergencies. She did not have the guerrilla training the others had.

But Cinque wanted her to become a comrade in arms, and Cinque was the undisputed leader of the SLA. His experiences were of broken families, hungry children, prison bars. He was an escaped convict, a black among eight whites, a man of violence and wild boasts. None of the others even had police records. They looked to him as a guru. Patty's conversion was proof of his power and strength.

Cinque – and Patty – prevailed. On April 3, she announced in a communiqué that hereafter she was an SLA soldier. "I have chosen to stay and fight," she said. Her parents had only pretended to save her. They were liars.

"The things which are precious to [them] are their money and power. It should be obvious that people who don't even care about their own children couldn't possibly care about anyone else."

But Patty's statement contained a final plea to Steven Weed. "I wish you could be a comrade," she said. For three years she had believed herself in love with Weed. She knew him to be weak-willed and unromantic. But she still secretly hoped he'd do something daring and loving. He styled himself a radical. Perhaps he'd find a way to join her.

Instead he spoke to her from Dick Cavett's talk show with words of condescension. Patty was brainwashed, Weed said. She would come to her senses if he had the chance to be alone with her.

"Frankly, Steven is the one who sounds brainwashed," Patty shot back in her next communiqué. "I can't believe those weird words he uttered were from his heart."

Weed was Patty's last tie to her former life.

live from new york…
by bill zehme

THEY SEIZED THE NIGHT – Saturday night – made it their own and took the National Broadcasting Company hostage in the coup. They were youthful improv guerrillas who tore into television and perpetrated acts of brio. Seven conspired on camera: Gilda (God rest her soul), Laraine, Jane, Garrett, John (God help his soul), Danny, Chevy and, a season later, Billy. They worked late. And *live . . . live from New York . . .* on a ninety-minute weekly insurrection then called *Saturday Night*. They trafficked in raw, disposable comedy for the post-Woodstock generation: sketch, drugs and rock & roll. They were unsafe for public consumption (the Not Ready for Prime Time Players, natch) and were therefore consumed voraciously: by us, by themselves and eventually by Hollywood.

Saturday Night Live, which was theirs at birth, became ours in life. Within weeks of its unveiling, on October 11, 1975, it was a comic institution, a platform for happy revolt, a reason to stay home and up and tuned. It even annoyed Johnny Carson, comedy's patriarch, who snippishly alleged that these upstarts couldn't "ad-lib a fart at a bean-eating contest." (Carson finally whiffed *something* in the air, though, because later, he slavishly indulged any *SNL* alums who deigned to crease couch on his *Tonight Show*.) "Before us," says Bill Murray, "people never watched television at night." (People with attitudes didn't, anyway.) Now viewers were looking for trouble – spoiling for it once a week. Suddenly, Saturday night was all right for fighting.

And everyone fought. *"I hate the fucking Bees!"* John Belushi would bellow, referring to the Killer Bees sketches that he felt so demeaned him. "I want to *burn* those fucking Bee costumes!" Backstage egos, as such, crackled and seethed. (Recurrent grousing themes included underutilization of the women and, most galling, the public's early perception of the program as *The Chevy Chase Show*.) The hostility bled into the material. Angst (theirs and ours) got giddily purged on camera: When Dan Aykroyd turned on the Bass-o-Matic and liquefied a real fish (*on live television!*), video violence never felt so palpable and refreshing. "Yes, it's just that simple!" said Aykroyd, glorious in his shill. "Fast and easy and ready to pour!"

Fast was not necessarily easy. The remorseless schedule was, and still is, first draft Wednesday, on air Saturday. "Which meant we stayed up all week," says Chevy Chase pridefully. "Night and day." Very near the beginning, Aykroyd said, "It's great. You write something down on a piece of yellow legal stationery, and three days later it becomes reality."

A s with love, long car trips and *Saturday Night Live*'s evolution, the first part is the best part. The bounty of seasons one through five now belongs to the ages: Nerds, Samurais, Coneheads, the brothers Blues and Festrunk (Czechs in slacks with big bulges). The original cast members would never live down their myth. (Future casts would never live up to it.) Nor would they forget the thrill of the risk, the fast turnaround on laughs. Murray likens his movie life now to bowel blockage. "I'm sorry, but it's like eating a meal and never getting the result out," he says mournfully. "I tell a joke in March, and I don't get a laugh until Christmas. You're left feeling awful weird, like the check hasn't cleared. Something's wrong."

We saw underwear a lot. Sometimes we saw less. We saw Jane Curtin rip open her blouse during "Weekend Update" ("Try these on for size, Connie Chung!" she cried). We saw the crack of Dan Aykroyd's ass on the set of Lisa Lupner's kitchen – he was playing a stooped-over Norge-refrigerator repairman who conveniently tucked his

Not Ready for Prime Time Players in their second-season glory: John Belushi, Dan Aykroyd, Bill Murray, Laraine Newman, Garrett Morris, Jane Curtin, Gilda Radner *(clockwise, from top left)*

marking pencil between his buttocks. And then there was Gilda Radner's Roseanne Roseannadanna, who waxed sticky over such pressing matters as nose hairs, phlegm balls and unchewed meat trapped between her teeth.

"I don't really think of *Saturday Night* as show business," Radner once said. "It's something different. You know what it is? It's telling secrets."

Lorne Michaels knows all of the secrets. He is the J. Edgar Hoover of *SNL*. As producer and chief, he founded the operation, crafted its golden era, left after five years to save his sanity and returned five years later to save his show. (Since 1985, *SNL* has been Lorne again.) "To me," says Chase, "Lorne *is* the show." Certainly, Michaels presides over its formulas. "I always felt," he has said, "that at its best the show was a record of what had gone on that week in the country, the world and the lives of the people doing the show."

Perhaps *SNL*'s best-kept secret has been Cow Dropping. "Cow Dropping" is in-house lingo for comic futility. It is said that whenever a sketch ends sloppily (an unfortunate *SNL* tradition), a cow is dropped. Chase explains: "Gilda and I were playing a typical WASP couple who go tag-team wrestling with Belushi and his Bees. We didn't have an ending, but we did have, for some unknown reason, a prop: a stuffed cow. I think it was Lorne who said, 'Maybe we ought to drop the cow.' So when the sketch could go no farther, we actually, actually did. And although we never physically dropped the cow again after that, it's happened in theory over and over."

Still, at its most uneven, the show was, and has continued to be, dependable. On any given weekend, it may be awful, but at least it's on. We know where to find it, and we know what we'll find. For instance, *SNL* has dependably provided sanctuary for truly *unique*-looking people. Consider the distinct contours of John Belushi, Bill Murray, Martin Short, Laraine Newman, Harry Shearer, Gilbert Gottfried, Eddie Murphy, Joe Piscopo, Mary Gross, Julia Louis-Dreyfus, Billy Crystal, Jim Belushi, Dana Carvey, Jon Lovitz, Dennis Miller, Victoria Jackson, Phil Hartman, Chris Farley, Julia Sweeney, Mike Myers, Chris Rock, David Spade, Al Franken, Molly Shannon, Janeane Garofalo, Nora Dunn, Norm MacDonald and Cheri Oteri – geeks who inherited the mirth.

The show has also dependably drubbed every presidency since its inception. Especially Gerald Ford's. "No problem," Chevy, as Ford, would assure us while inadvertently attaching staples to his forehead. As a gesture of goodwill, Ford press secretary Ron Nessen agreed to host, and thereafter, it became impossible to take Ford seriously. When Ford finally caught on, he gave up. He took to introducing himself with "I'm Gerald Ford, and you're not."

Which raises another critical point: No other television program has promulgated more pop catchphrases. Without *SNL*, scores of college students would have nothing to say to one another. From outer orbit, the Columbia astronauts announced, "We're here to pump you up!" (Hans and Frans defy gravity!) This sort of behavior is endemic. The vernacular is clogged with such residual expressions: It's always something. Jane, you ignorant slut! You look *mahvelous*. Noogie patrol! That's so funny I forgot to laugh. No fries – cheeps. No Coke – Pepsi. Look out, Mr. Bill . . . Oh, noooooooooooo! O-tay! But nooooooo! Never mind. We are two wild and crazy guys! I'm Gumby, dammit! Get to know me! I hate it when that happens. We invite you to consume mass quantities. Cheeseborger-cheeseborger-cheeseborger. Now, isn't that special? Yeah, yeah, that's the ticket! That's the news – guess what? I'm outta here. Goodnight and have a pleasant tomorrow. Now get outta here, you knucklehead, I mean it.

Anarchy wears. No rebellion lasts forever. *Saturday Night Live*, while not exactly warm and fuzzy, is comfortable with its tumultuous past. Which has passed. Writer Ann Beatts has often said, "It's only avant-garde for so long before it becomes garde." Today, Lorne Michaels is old guard, whether he likes it or not.

Perhaps comedy had to grow up. Perhaps we should let *SNL* off the hook, allow it to stop competing with its own legend. Then again, perhaps we should just be grateful for videotape and the fact that cable reruns old shows. Says Murray, "Everyone loves us because we were the old group. But if we were still on television, they'd hate us. It'd be like, 'Oh God, are they still doing *that*?'"

Yeah. Right. Just drop the cow and get outta here, you knucklehead. We mean it. ⊕

lorne michaels
on saturday night live

"*I* DON'T DO TELEVISION!"

That's what John Belushi said when we were casting *Saturday Night Live* in 1975. I didn't take offense; actually, it was kind of a compliment. He didn't like the idea of TV, but the implication was that he would do it with me.

It's hard to believe now, but back then it was a big deal. Musical acts and especially people in comedy would routinely say they "don't do television." They were afraid. I felt TV could be good – if people cared about it being good.

When I first worked in network television as a comedy writer in the United States in 1968, it was still dominated by people who'd come up in radio. So it had a Thirties/Forties sensibility. By the early Seventies, what was happening in movies, onstage and in music wasn't yet on TV. A couple of the shows that had tried something new had come and gone, the *Smothers Brothers Comedy Hour* being the most notable example. Then there was *Laugh-In*, where I had been a writer during the first season. Though my contribution was insignificant, it was an exhilarating place to be; it was the number one show, often tied with *The Lucy Show* even though they aired at the same time. So there was an audience in the tens of millions that wasn't watching traditional television.

In 1969 I moved back to Canada to do my own show, *The Hart and Lorne Terrific Hour*, at the CBC. It lasted three seasons. I learned a lot by writing, performing and producing. In 1972 I moved to Los Angeles. After I arrived, I started working for a bunch of different TV shows. Lily Tomlin, who'd seen and liked some of my work in Canada, had hired me as a writer on one of her TV specials. When she went to ABC to do a pilot special, she encouraged them to hire me as a producer.

By 1975, a few of the shows I had done had been well reviewed, particularly those starring Lily and Richard Pryor. Then I met Dick Ebersol, who had just become head of NBC's late-night programming and was assigned to replace the *Tonight Show* reruns that aired on Saturday nights. We got along. He was my age, and I agreed to do a pilot special for him. Late one night when I got back to the Chateau Marmont in Hollywood, where I was living at the time, there was a message from Ebersol. Would I meet with him and some other people the next morning at the Beverly Hills Hotel's Polo Lounge?

That meeting led to other meetings in New York. There we made the decision to do a live show, which meant that no executives, except Ebersol, would see it till it went on the air.

I had felt that the problem with classic variety shows was keeping them fresh – sooner or later, Sonny runs out of things to say to Cher. So I decided we would have a repertory cast, live music, politics, films and a different host every week. As my dad used to say, my eyes were bigger than my stomach. I wanted *SNL* to be *everything*.

I started working on April 1, 1975; the entire budget of the show was $134,600, and we had a cast of seven because that was the number in our original presentation. I began looking for writers and cast simultaneously. Michael O'Donoghue and Chevy Chase came from the *National Lampoon Radio Hour*. Howard Shore was responsible for selecting the kind of house band we had, giving it that sound. Eugene Lee and Davy Wilson put together the look of the show. Herb Sargent had produced *That Was the Week That Was*. Politics was very much a part of our coming of age – the Watergate trials had just ended – so I knew we were going to deal with serious ideas and we would have to have something like *Weekend Update*.

Ultimately, I knew the show would depend on finding and getting the best, most original people. It took me three months to find the right people to fill the cast.

By the time *SNL* premiered on October 11, a synthesis of all these elements had taken place. We had our problems, of course. George Carlin was the host of our first show, and NBC wanted him to wear a suit, but *he* wanted to wear a T-shirt. But *SNL* went on, George wore a T-shirt (under his suit), and somehow Western Civilization did not come to an end.

To a large extent the first show was overplanned – we had had six months to prepare for the first show, but only six *days* for the second. So we just shook it out and found the rhythm. I think *SNL* really gelled for the first time with the fourth show. The host, Candice Bergen, let the cast shine. Nobody had expected the show's key strength would be the cast. Candy was the first person who said, "These people are *really* funny."

We started to notice our impact by the end of the first season. The current show's musical guests would show up and already be doing bits from our sketches. We had won Emmys for best show and best writing. But then, I had never doubted for a moment that the show would work. Not that I wasn't worried it wouldn't be good – I *always* worried that it wouldn't be good – it was just that I also knew so many talented people were involved and what they were capable of.

Then, when Chevy decided to leave in the middle of the second season, the "Saturday Night Dead" thing began to happen, and we got to the point of asking ourselves, "Are we gonna flame out or are we gonna continue?"

Over the years I've worked with a generation of *SNL* members who had all been influenced by the first seasons, then with a generation that was influenced by *that* generation, and now with people who only know the Seventies show from cable. There are different ways of measuring it, but in my worldview the four longest years of a person's life are high school. That's when people discover the show, and make it theirs.

It's hard to talk about the very early years, because none of it exists anymore. In 1975 the country was ripe for a fresh approach. There had been an overthrow of the established order after Watergate, and people were looking for something different after the Sixties. The Seventies ushered in a kind of sobriety, a reassessment of the norms, which made it possible for *SNL* to come in and be honest.

Cable has now fractured it all. It was a big deal in the Seventies that rock & roll was finally on television. Now rock & roll has not only its own channel but several. Network news is on twenty-four hours a day, every day. *SNL* is a show they'll never make again because it just combines so many different elements. That's why it's important for us to keep doing it. ⊕

hot on the one
by harry weinger

IT'S THE SPRING of 1975. I'm a senior at Clarkstown South High School in suburban New York. After the last bell, I'm usually hanging in the lobby with some friends before play rehearsal or waiting for a ride to work. There's always a radio blasting the latest pop hits, like Olivia Newton-John asking, "Have You Never Been Mellow?" The answer for an eighteen-year-old with sex and *Soul Train* on the brain is immediate and obvious: No, not lately.

During that same time period, however, Top Forty radio was grooving with a funky delight the likes of which I've never heard since. I'm pinned to the wall by the stomping stutter beats and nasty machine-gun guitar-and-percussion breakdown in the Ohio Players' "Fire," seduced by the thunderous beats and the frank, sexual come-on of B.T. Express's "Do It ('Til You're Satisfied)," thrilled by the improvised sax break in Average White Band's "Pick Up the Pieces," riveted by the stabbing synthesized bass lines and thickly slurred lyrics of Stevie Wonder's "Boogie On Reggae Woman" and exhilarated by my favorite band, Earth, Wind and Fire, whose "Shining Star" counters its live-and-loose party feel with a tighter-than-tight horn arrangement.

Then, the Isley Brothers' "Fight the Power (Part I)" sings out loud the words I'm only thinking: "I try to play my music, they say my music's too loud/I try talkin' about it, I got the big runaround/And when I roll with the punches, I got knocked on the ground/By all this BULLSHIT goin' down."

This isn't your usual Top Forty groove. This is funk in the big time. I am ecstatic.

Some of my white classmates, though, are disgusted with my delight. "Although I liked knowing you this year," one of them would end up writing in my yearbook, "I really hate your taste in music."

I shouldn't have been surprised. Music cliques exist in every high school in America. We were teenagers; we defined ourselves by what we wore, what we watched, whom we hung out with and whom we listened to. Even in a liberal-minded suburban town there was a fine musical line a white guy was not expected to cross.

Ironically, Seventies funk was a leap forward from Sixties soul music, that earlier decade's great unifier and a profound soundtrack for the civil rights movement, which also had propelled a significant number of black faces into the Top Ten: Marvin Gaye and the Temptations – "The Sound of Young America" – on Motown; Sam and Dave, and Wilson Pickett on Stax; and Aretha Franklin. But in the Seventies, funk

Fueling the fires of funk: Earth, Wind and Fire deliver the goods onstage

revealed a more politically, spiritually and sexually charged countenance: the Parliament/Funkadelic mob in outlandish masks and Black Panther regalia; the Ohio Players courting pain and pleasure with S&M-tinged album jackets; Earth, Wind and Fire's religious mythology; Kool and the Gang's Afrocentric LP covers; James Brown, the Godfather of Soul and the inventor of funk, proclaiming "Get ready you mutha, for the big PAYBACK!"

That scared a lot of white folks. Funk was a whole new style with a whole new vocabulary. For much of white America, the sound and stance were just too, well, black. Too bad. For anyone who really listens, the basic message of funk is one of joyful connection, of embracing, of getting down just for the funk of it, as I had first learned in that same high school lobby two years earlier.

Making my way out the front door of the school, I overcame all shyness and fear to chant out loud the razor-sharp vocal line of "Funky Stuff": "Whoa-whoa-whoa-whoa-whoa-whoa-whoa-whoa-whoa-whoa – YEAH!" Anthony, a neighbor who happened to be black, whipped his head around to look at me, then nodded coolly. "My man knows Kool and the Gang," he said with a big smile. I was no longer a stranger in a strange land.

Funk offers an earthy connection that is difficult to explain, because funk is about feeling. Funk, if you allow it to flow, is its own reward. P-Funk founder George Clinton

has declared, "You can speak volumes about what funk isn't. You can't really pinpoint what funk is."

But I'll try.

Funk is a rhythm. It goes back to Africa. Current lexicons trace the word back to Ki-Kongo language: *"lu-fuki,"* literally meaning "strong body odor." More figuratively, the term connotes a powerful vibe. It also expands to mean a positive energy drawn from community: a lot of celebrating bodies throwing off an energizing scent, if you will. Many people, sweating, swaying, carrying on as one.

Funk involves many musicians – funk bands' payrolls have always been large – playing as one. As family. Motown's legendary house band thought so – they called themselves the Funk Brothers. One of funk's greatest anthems is Funkadelic's "One Nation Under a Groove" (a Number One R&B hit in 1978).

Oneness is funk's mantra. It is also the musical blueprint for funk: Funk deliberately leans on the first beat – the downbeat – the one of a measure of four. (This differs from the accent in traditional popular music, which equally emphasizes the two and the four, the backbeat.) With that heavy emphasis there is syncopation, a stutter – like a heartbeat. The first human heartbeat is on the one. Our first breath of life is on the one. In their song of the same name, Parliament sings, "Everything is on the one."

In funk philosophy, spring – the time of renewal, when everything comes around again – is the one.

Funk used to be a bad word. In the jazz world it's been used for close to a century. All-night jam sessions were not only loose and sweaty (two prerequisites for modern-day funk), but when taking part in one within close quarters, one couldn't exactly hide the farts. As Jelly Roll Morton sang in his classic blues: "I thought I heard Buddy Bolden shout/Open up that window and let that bad air out." Funk evolved from a complaint to a cry to play more down-home, more bluesy, more loose and unpolished – to "Get funky!"

From jazz to R&B to soul music, that sense of realness stuck. Playing funky meant homing in on a groove, adding soul with one's own fire and personality. In funk, such signatures abound. James Brown's *"Unh!"* is funky. So is Larry Graham's bass pop. Michael Jackson's nickname? "Smelly," says Quincy Jones. "'Cause he can be so damn funky."

More than any other style, funk owes its minimalist, dance-inducing form not to R&B or soul but to a few soulful jazzmen. Soul jazz – the more commercial, groove-oriented jazz bag pioneered in the late Fifties and early Sixties by Horace Silver, Jimmy Smith and Art Blakey (whose arresting punctuation on the bass drum exemplified the phrase "dropping bombs") – is the direct precedent to James Brown's instrumental experiments with syncopated grooves and extended, lyricless jams.

In 1967, J.B.'s funk lab produced what is largely credited as funkdom's declaration of independence. "Cold Sweat" stood out from all the other hits of the day with an apparent, yet hypnotic, simplicity: It was sparsely structured, with the band "vamping" (repeating catchy phrases for an extended period) while Brown sang the mere outline of a lyric and audibly called the solos on the fly. Recorded live in the studio, the funk-defining jam (for it was more a workout than a song) was rooted in every facet of black music: The slight melody was borrowed from an earlier Brown blues; the rhythm guitar part, intended by cowriter Pee Wee Ellis to be a traditional R&B "chank," went off beat to give it an up-in-the-air feel; the horn riff was borrowed from Miles Davis's "So What."

But it was those drop-to-the-bottom-of-the-stomach breaks grabbing and suspending the listener until the next downbeat that showed off the incredibly tight, successful operation Brown had created. With his own funk family at his fingertips, Brown could enter a studio with loose ideas and the knowledge that with one crack of the whip his men would be ready to turn on a dime. They had to. For missing the downbeat onstage, the fine was fifty dollars per flub.

A literal family of funk emerged soon after Brown's breakthrough: Sly and the Family Stone from the San Francisco–Oakland Bay Area. Sly – with his sister, brother, cousin and friends – burst forth in 1968 with "Dance to the Music," a song mind-blowing in its optimism, gospel energy and soulful street-corner harmonies all mixed over a funk-schooled rhythm section.

"When I heard Sly for the first time it pissed me off," George Clinton told me. "Because I had the same concept, weaving all that together. I had my doo-wop Parliaments, I trained as a songwriter at Motown and I was loving all that crazy rock & roll happening at the time. But it upset me in a good way. I got fired up when he hit."

Sly and James continued to pare back funk to its bare essentials, heralding the arrival of the Seventies with a pair of minimal funk classics. Sly delivered "Thank You (Falettinme Be Mice Elf Agin)," with its unadorned popping bass line, in 1970. But for my thirteen-year-old ears, the decade really kicked into gear a few months later with James Brown's "Sex Machine." Perched on the edge of adolescence, I was electrified by the song's primal energy and titillated by the title. A melodic horn line was conspicuously absent; a raw, irresistible guitar riff replaced it, front and center, over the same confident, syncopated beat. Though Sly had offered his own "Sex Machine" on 1969's *Stand!* – a slower, viscous vamp compared to its namesake – Brown now monopolized the funk torch with his stripped-down drive and an updated and youthful band.

He called his new Seventies model the J.B.'s and (for a short but important time) featured teenage bassist Bootsy Collins. Bandleader Fred Wesley further streamlined Brown's lean approach, helping him count off seventeen Top Ten R&B hits in less than three years, including "Hot Pants" (1971), "Make It Funky" (1971), "Get on the Good Foot (Part I)" (1972), "Doing It to Death" (1973) and "The Payback" (1974). My radio crackled with one monster J.B. hit after another, every hour on the hour.

There were many other ears tuned into the same frequency, checking out the man who had crowned himself the Godfather of Soul: the Meters out of New Orleans; Charles Wright and the Watts 103rd Street Band out of L.A.; Stevie Wonder, declaring his adulthood with his backup band Wonderlove. George Clinton dug deep into his J.B.–Sly–Motown tool chest to launch the Parliament/Funkadelic mob. Significantly, he developed his empire employing graduates of the J.B. School of Hard Fines: Bootsy Collins, his brother Catfish, Maceo Parker, Fred Wesley and Kush Griffith all helped spread the P-Funk message, with major hits like "Up for the Down Stroke," "Tear the Roof Off the Sucker (Give Up the Funk)" and "Bootzilla."

As the decade moved forward, black funk bands, including Slave, Brass Construction, Brick, Fatback, Rose Royce, Cameo, the Brothers Johnson, the Gap Band and Con Funk Shun, sprouted like the hairs on my chest. But, except for the occasional on-the-one dance jam inching into the Top Forty, funk went underground in the latter half of the decade.

Funk's free expression and party reputation had been eclipsed by a more homogenized form of dance music: disco. In a weird paradox, the music that had come out of a gay, black and Latino underground scene was soon adopted by mainstream America, hailed for its universal, unifying force: Everyone is beautiful on the dance floor.

There were a few danceable cuts with a funky core that made it through the funk-disco overlap, from acts like Rose Royce ("Car Wash"), the Brothers Johnson ("Stomp!") and Marvin Gaye ("Got to Give It Up"). But as Clinton pleaded on Parliament's "Flashlight," a huge disco-funk-pop smash in 1978, "Help me find the funk!"

Yes, they both inspired sweat-covered bodies to boogie. But funk's was always a looser groove. Count the beats – disco differs in a critical way: It's like martial music, dictating equal emphasis on all beats, as exciting as a metronome to my funk-schooled feet. It was difficult not to be judgmental, not to have felt jilted by the rise of disco. I didn't mind disco, I just didn't like it pounding in my head every two seconds.

Today, it's that musical clique thing all over again. I still define myself by what music drives me out onto the dance floor. Under different guises, the dichotomy that I discovered between funk and disco – freedom versus dictate – survives: hip-hop or house? New Soul or techno? Call it what you will. I don't want my beats on a per-minute basis.

Funk had its pop moment in 1975, but its true victory is in its undying influence. Through its imitation and replication, funk has had the last giggle. "Funk not only moves," George Clinton spoke on Parliament's classic *Mothership Connection* album, "it can *re*move," putting forth two meanings in one line: Funk makes your body dance and eliminates prejudice in one downstroke. It also has succeeded in moving and *re*inspiring all those who came after the Seventies, growing in influence with each successive generation.

Funk has been carried out of the Seventies and into the following decades through its use in contemporary dance tracks by Prince, Michael and Janet Jackson and countless hip DJs. Funk's syncopated drive and its paralleling of partying and politics are the foundation of hip-hop. Through sampling, funk became the literal and lyrical backbone of rap.

Classic Seventies funk tracks now sell everything from burgers to computer chips. P-Funk has an even wider subculture than back in the day, with a dedicated cult following akin to that of the Grateful Dead.

In street slang, too, the funk tradition still reaches back. Quoting George Clinton (paraphrasing Art Blakey), there's only one way to describe the best of the best nowadays: "It's the BOMB!"

These days – the age of hip-hop – Kool and the Gang's songs are back in the Top Ten again, as the foundations for hits by Madonna ("Erotica"), Mase ("Feel So Good"), Snoop Doggy Dogg ("We Just Wanna Party With You"), Lil' Kim ("Not Tonight"), Jade ("Don't Walk Away"), Janet Jackson ("New Agenda"), DJ Jazzy Jeff and the Fresh Prince ("Summertime"), Coolio ("Too Hot") and a myriad of others. Hearing the Gang on the radio again reminds me of a night at New York's Nassau Coliseum in 1974: "Hollywood Swinging" is in the Top Ten and the band is on an incredible bill with the O'Jays, Gladys Knight and the Pips and Donald Byrd and the Blackbyrds. I'm a marshmallow in a sea of hot chocolate. A Kool "parrrrrrty" whistle is secretly tucked under my shirt, and I'm just as nervous as the Blackbyrds – the newcomers on the funk block – about strutting my stuff.

Then I remember where my heart lies: on the one. When the lights go down, I blow my whistle loud and long. I'll never forget the smiles and the shouts from my fellow funk fans, and the sound of twenty thousand other party whistles a moment later.

"Can't get enough – I try! I try! – of that FUNKY STUFF!" ⊕

a time to live, a time to die
by deborah blum

MY GRANDFATHER started disappearing in late 1975, about two years before he died. He was replaced by a statue of himself – same silvery hair, same curved and jowly face (he used to laugh about the second chin) but some stranger's eyes. They were the frozen, impersonal blue of a Midwestern winter sky, unshadowed, empty of memory.

He turned to me once that last summer and, pointing across the room, whispered – stranger to stranger – "Who's that woman?" It was my mother. "That's your daughter," I whispered back, not saying the worst of it: your only daughter. For one still second we stared at each other in shared dismay. "Isn't this awful?" he said. And then his face went cold as he went away again.

It had been no time, maybe four years, since he'd humored me through a brief, desperate high-school desire to be an actress. I wanted that grandfather back.

I swore to myself that I'd never be him; wouldn't live – or die – that way. It was hardly an original thought in that day and time, when the questions of the way life ends, whether or not we should be able to choose the exit route, engaged so many people. The first of my grandfather's many strokes occurred the same year that right-to-die became a national issue; in the fall of 1975, the case of Karen Ann Quinlan went to court.

As a longtime science reporter – yes, I abandoned theater for the pursuit of "how and why": How does the brain work? Why does it fail? – I think we've forgotten what a serious, earnest-thinking decade the Seventies could be at times. "Ethical issues in the Seventies," muses a colleague, and starts laughing at the thought. "Did they have any?"

Yes, indeed. This wasn't a lighthearted time at all, coming out of the bitterness of the war in Vietnam. I remember the Nineteenth-Century chapel bell at the University of Georgia tolling in the dark for all the classmates who had died in Southeast Asia. It's not so surprising, after all, that questions of life and death and who has power over the answers ran like an undercurrent through the culture of the time. Against that background, our power to make such decisions was transformed in the 1970s.

At right: Joseph and Julia Quinlan, devout Catholics and parents of Karen Ann, with a scrapbook full of press clippings on their efforts to disconnect their daughter from an artificial breathing device; following page: Karen Ann Quinlan

It was a decade in which technology and medical research suddenly reached critical mass: We really could stir up life in a laboratory, analyze it and/or make it go away if we didn't like the results.

Who was to decide life or death? For every shining scientific advance – say, the ability to detect birth defects before birth – another moral question would arise. This debate was intensified in 1973 when the *New England Journal of Medicine* published a confession of sorts. Doctors at a big university teaching hospital had, with parental consent, let several dozen severely deformed babies die in their bassinets. As technology widened the window into the womb, the first response was worry. How perfect? how old? how rich or famous did one have to be to merit survival? When Harry Truman died in 1972 the newsmagazines responded with stories about the indignity of tubes in his nose and the battery of clicking machines around him and questioned whether he had "outlived his life."

Karen Ann Quinlan was only the poster child, really, for a backlash against medicine's power to prolong life and, I think, to cut it short as well. Her face was everywhere in the fall of 1975; her story inspired rock songs and morality plays. She was uncomfortably like my friends and me. We'd all had evenings like her last conscious one, too many drinks with friends having too many drinks. It was a nearly lethal mix of alcohol and tranquilizers, apparently, that caused her to slip into a coma. She remained beyond reach for half a year before her parents realized she would not be coming back. When they asked her doctors to turn off the respirator, claiming Karen Ann had once said she wouldn't have wanted to live like that, the doctors refused. So the Quinlans went to court.

What an unlikely family to fight for death! The Quinlans were wholly religious, devout Catholics. It was months before they would accept how permanent the coma was. In court, one neurologist described Karen Ann as "a child without a brain." The phrase "persistent vegetative state" became everyday language in America, as did the hateful details: Her eyes would open yet only flick back-forth, back-forth, pure nervous twitch, with no thought to focus them. She was fed by a tube, breathed by a respirator. Her body was beginning to curl inward as a fetus. "I want to put her back into a natural state," Joseph Quinlan told the New Jersey Superior Court. "This is the Lord's will." There was no one, no one I knew anyway, who disagreed with his claim.

The notion of a "natural state" seems to me a faint last breath, the soft ebbing away of the old world when we really knew – or thought we knew – what "natural" was, before science and medicine began to break the ancient rules of life. What's a natural birth? The success of in vitro fertilization came in 1978 with the birth of Louise Brown in England. It's everyday medicine today. We don't question, as people did then, whether a "test-tube baby" is natural. Sure, why not, when we can not only fertilize embryos outside the body but freeze them for future use even after the so-called donors have died.

Scientists can also do so much more to change nature: take apart the genetics of life itself, rearrange the code, build an entirely new species in that same glass tube. That power came about, too, in the Seventies, and while the rest of us were perhaps worrying about the ethical consequences, industry saw pure potential.

In 1972, General Electric filed for a patent on the work of a staff biologist, Ananda Chakrabarty, who had genetically altered a bacterium so that it would rapidly break down oil-based sludge. No one had considered it before: Can you patent and own a living thing? GE thought so. When Chakrabarty's case lost at the patent office, the company appealed it all the way to the Supreme Court, despite the angry protests and angrier predictions of environmentalists. Victor Frankenstein's dark castle and laboratory weren't so far from people's thoughts this time around. After all, biologists were playing with a lot more than just environmentally friendly bacteria. They were synthesizing the genes of mammals, gene-mapping, mixing the genes of unrelated animals, trying out variations on existing viruses. Who would keep their creations under lock?

Imaginations can run wild in biogenetics, and they did. I would always visualize this fear very specifically: some black-lagoonesque, multi-armed, frog-faced creature rising out of the petri dish while white-coated researchers fend it off with flaming Bunsen burners. There were other scenarios, of course. The guys in white coats might decide how to make a "perfect" human and engineer the imperfects (meaning the rest of us, I suppose) out of existence. They could let loose some plague of invincible viruses. The incidence of debate and voices of reason seemed few: "I decided not to do the experiment [on SV40, a monkey tumor virus] because I couldn't persuade myself there was zero risk," stated one lone researcher in 1974.

Indeed – and this seems outstanding black comedy to me – the Defense Department reported that it couldn't come up with anything worse than the viruses that were already around. Yet imagine combining the infectiousness of an influenza virus with the bloody destructiveness of an Ebola virus. That's why, in July 1974, a committee of topflight biologists published a letter in the journal *Science*, asking for a moratorium on mixing molecules into "elements whose biological properties cannot be completely predicted in advance." I have to confess that statement makes me laugh. As if we have the power, ever, to "completely predict" what will result.

In response to that letter, 140 scientists from sixteen countries assembled at the Asilomar Conference Center in Pacific Grove, California, on the Monterey Peninsula, in early 1975. It was an unprecedented event, the first time an international group had attempted to instill not only safety but ethics into what had been a purely research-driven process. Asilomar was a turning point: Scientists – on a global scale – were at least willing to acknowledge that pushing the frontiers of knowledge carries risks and unforeseen consequences (see: nuclear power).

The scientists brought their crystal balls. Then they put them away. No one could predict where this was going. Nor did they want to. The whole appeal of genetic engineering lies in its unexplored possibilities, uncharted realms and the sheer intellectual amazement of being able to hold the tiny, fragile links of life and turn them into a chain of one's own making. Thanks to GE, too, everyone at Asilomar knew that one's personal creation might hold the promise of not only scientific advancement, but financial gain. Was anyone going to spill the beans when brilliant genetic insights, kept to oneself, might be so valuable?

The Asilomar conference didn't set tough limits on redefining and altering life, but it did propose a cautious use of benign organisms and contained laboratories. The theme of the conference's last paper was "Conventional aspects of the law and how they may sneak up on you in the form, say, of a multimillion-dollar lawsuit." It was that threat, more than creatures of the petri dish, that carried the day.

Before the Seventies, we, as a society, tended to ask clergy, philosophers, our doctors, even our friends how to handle difficult questions about life and death. But the high-end science achieved in the Seventies blew those questions into such monumental shape that often the law ended up forming the answers.

Does anyone believe that lawyers and judges and government agencies understand better than anyone else the ethics of life and death? Yet that became the precedent. GE and Ananda Chakrabarty won the battle to patent life. Now such licenses exist on just about everything that isn't dirt or inert, and researchers continue to hide their work from colleagues for fear of patent infringement.

The Quinlans won their legal fight, too. In 1976, the New Jersey Supreme Court said yes, turn off the machine. There was nothing in that decision, though, about natural states or how much ethics should dictate the right and wrong in medicine. The court said the "individual right to privacy grows as the degree of bodily invasion increases and the prognosis dims."

Her parents took Karen Ann to a nursing home and had the ventilator removed. One wonders about the power of prediction. Karen Ann breathed on her own for another nine years. She never woke, though, and when she died her weight was below seventy pounds, her body so tightly curled into a fetal position that her bones had calcified. There was nothing "poster child" about her whatsoever.

Eventually my grandfather couldn't make his legs work and my grandmother carried him herself for as long she could. He went into a nursing home, although his diagnosis confirmed that he couldn't recognize the move. He died within months.

I thought of it as freedom for both of them. I was twenty-four, angry that it had taken so long and been so painful. I might have then dreamed up the Nineties approach to death-with-dignity: Dr. Jack Kevorkian does it with a nice, painless, little intravenous drip. But my grandmother would have kept him with her if she could have, and the Quinlans, of course, could have had their daughter's feeding tube removed.

Science may increase our power over such decisions, but it really doesn't make them any easier. We still don't know what to do about test-tube life and recombined genes. The questions are basically the same. These days scientists are tackling larger problems and organisms, like ourselves. We've achieved the new power to clone adult animals, starting with a Scottish sheep named Dolly and leading to flamboyant proposals to clone human beings. Bans and moratoriums are being discussed – sound familiar? – but there's no consensus whatsoever on the ethics of duplicating another person, person, person. So what should we do when, someday, we have to decide whether or not to turn off the life support system for our friend, or our own clone? ⊕

Twenty-year-old Swede Bjorn Borg overcomes Ilie Nastase to become the youngest tennis player in 45 years to win Wimbledon.

4 America celebrates its Bicentennial in grand style: 225 masted ships from 30 countries cruise through New York Harbor; Washington, DC, sets off 33½ tons of fireworks near the Lincoln Memorial as its new National Air and Space Museum opens; 1,776 new citizens pledge allegiance for the first time in Chicago; and President Ford rings the Liberty Bell in Philadelphia.

The Ramones perform a Bicentennial concert at London's Roundhouse. Two days later, the Damned will debut, opening for the Sex Pistols at London's 100 Club.

12 In New York City, Congresswoman Barbara Jordan (D-TX) becomes the first black person and the first woman to deliver the keynote address at the Democratic National Convention. Three days later, Carter will accept the nomination and select Senator Walter Mondale (D-MN) as his running mate.

17 The XXI Summer Olympics open in Montreal under a political cloud as Taiwan withdraws over the International Olympic Committee's insistence that they not use the name "China," and Tanzania leads a boycott in protest of New Zealand's continued rugby competitions with South Africa. Thirty-two nations decline to participate and six Eastern European athletes will defect before the games close two weeks later. New gold-winning stars include Romanian gymnast Nadia Comaneci, American decathlete Bruce Jenner and Finnish runner Lasse Viren (although Viren is suspected of taking illegal medication).

20 Viking 1 lands on Mars and begins transmitting the first photographs and weather reports from the planet. On Aug. 7, NASA scientists prematurely release a report suggesting the possibility of Martian life; a later review reveals the Viking tests were inconclusive.

21 An unidentified bacterial outbreak strikes a Legionnaires convention in Philadelphia, infecting 180 across the state and eventually killing 29. By Jan. 1977, the Centers for Disease Control identify a new bacterium responsible for the

leading country to rebellion
by chet flippo

REVOLUTION and counterrevolution may seem to be the most unlikely topics ever to be associated with country music, but the tendency to rebel is ingrained in humans, it seems, and it certainly is embedded in the persons most likely to be prominent in country music: white, Southern males of modest education, little or no formal music training, considerable ego and virtually no sense of an enduring musical tradition.

It's not often that one movement can coalesce around one event, but, conveniently, the whole "Outlaw" upheaval in country music came to define itself by the release of one record album.

The album – *Wanted! The Outlaws* – itself was not really anything spectacular, even by modest Nashville standards. RCA producer Jerry Bradley (the son of legendary C&W producer Owen Bradley) conceded that, but knew he had hit upon what could become the biggest marketing coup of his life. For once, Nashville was selling a concept rather than just peddling records. Bradley, in fact, said just that when he called me in 1975 to ask me to write liner notes for the *Outlaws* album. "I'll send you tapes on it," he told me, "but I'll bet you've heard most of it before. What I'm doing is putting Willie and Waylon and Tompall [with Waylon's wife, Jessi Colter] together as the Outlaws, because that's the way they are regarded here in town. This is a package, a total package that I'm looking to break outside the country market. That's why I'd like you to do the notes: You know the music and the musicians, but you're not a cheerleader like the writers here in town. You're definitely not considered part of the establishment."

Outlaws was released on January 12, 1976, amid great hoopla by RCA. It soon crossed over to the pop charts, was certified gold by the beginning of April and became country's first platinum-selling album by December. Country music was no longer just a singles market; it now was an album market and thus could rival the sales of rock releases. Willie and Waylon virtually became household names. Their albums began selling gold (500,000 copies) on their own strengths. They were invited to the White House by President Carter in 1978 (Willie and Jessi went; Waylon declined). Their names appeared more often in ROLLING STONE than in *Music City News*.

Leaders of the rebellion: Willie Nelson and Waylon Jennings at the height of their Nashville days *(from left)*

By the time it ran its course, the Outlaw movement had changed the face of country music forever. The producer as king – that feudal notion was shattered. Country artists gained control over their own record sessions, their own booking, their record production, everything else related to their careers, including the right to make their own mistakes. It was a major shift in country music. It also brought country artists into the million-dollar stratosphere of pop and rock artists and also, of course, into their cocaine-and-marijuana-laced decadence.

Without going into great detail, even a casual reading of country music's history shows a cyclical pattern of action and reaction, based on commercial factors – on what the Nashville movers and shakers thought would sell. As a conservative business, country music may safely be said to have always preferred to follow, rather than to anticipate, trends. Rockabilly is a classic example. It was imposed upon Nashville by outside influences – from just down the road, in Memphis, at Sun Records – and could not be ignored after Elvis Presley's success. The country-music industry initially tried to ignore it and keep selling honky-tonk music, deliberately disregarding the social forces behind the changes in musical tastes. But there was such a groundswell for the new music – particularly by artists – it became clear that it was a future that could not be swept away. RCA farsightedly signed Elvis and thereby guaranteed its commercial future.

As rockabilly waned and – not coincidentally – country moved closer to pop music, Owen Bradley and guitarist and producer Chet Atkins brought forth what came to be known as the Nashville Sound. In another age, it might have been called "Lite Country."

so-called Legionnaires' Disease.

27 Seeking to invalidate a contract that he finds creatively and financially stifling, Bruce Springsteen sues his manager, Mike Appel.

John Lennon receives green card #A17-597-321, making his U.S. residency official.

31 Top of the charts: the Manhattans' "Kiss and Say Goodbye" (pop single); George Benson's *Breezin'* (pop album).

1976 AUGUST

1 A Gallup Poll reveals that Carter leads both Ford and Reagan by substantial margins.

10 Elton John begins a seven-show stand at Madison Square Garden that will break a box-office record set the previous summer by the Rolling Stones.

13 British punk rockers the Clash give a private performance for the press and friends, unveiling their influential lineup: singer/guitarist Joe Strummer, guitarist Mick Jones, bassist Paul Simonon and drummer Terry "Tory" Crimes. Guitarist Keith Levene (later of Public Image Ltd.) also performs as part of the band, but departs soon after the show.

New wave/power pop songwriter and bassist Nick Lowe releases his first U.K. single on Stiff Records, the two-sided hit "So It Goes/Heart of the City."

16 The Republican National Convention opens in Kansas City with Ford and Reagan battling for delegates. Two days later, Ford will secure the nomination and select conservative senator Bob Dole (R-KS) as his running mate soon after.

19 Carter solidifies his music industry connections at Capricorn Records' annual picnic in Macon, GA.

23 In a *New York* magazine feature, journalist Tom Wolfe dubs the overly self-involved Seventies "the 'Me' Decade."

24 American Legion conventioneers boo Carter as he announces his plan to grant amnesty to Vietnam War draft resisters. The next day, he will lead a Gallup Poll with 49% of the vote, versus 39% for Ford and 12% undecided.

26 ROLLING STONE reports that 250,000 fans have caught Texas boogie band ZZ Top one month into an 18-month world tour that packs a 75-ton

The producer was truly king with the Nashville Sound in operation. He chose the songs, the pickers, the arrangements, the album cover, the strings and the vocal backing used to "sweeten" the whole package. The singer was almost an afterthought.

It was into this pop-country quagmire that a generation of young country singer/songwriters, such as Willie Nelson and Waylon Jennings, came in the Sixties. Nashville had tried to ignore the Beatles and all they represented – the whole youth culture, pop culture, counterculture. Country music seemed fixed in a death frieze, epitomized by the Grand Ole Opry and its aging, rural, loyal-to–Roy Acuff audience on the one hand, and the younger, moved-to-the-city blue-collar crowd on the other. Audiences were no longer isolated or segregated: Even in rural areas, younger people listened to the latest Top Forty pop and rock hits, and, as they did so, they began to ask more of country music.

By the early Seventies there came to be a broad-based revolution spawned by the non–power brokers – the writers and singers – that was as much influenced by the Beatles as by Bob Dylan, as much by the Vietnam War as by country star Johnny Cash (who had been a one-man phenomenon).

The term "Outlaw" had surfaced with Waylon's 1972 hit song and album of the same name, "Ladies Love Outlaws." The song, written by Lee Clayton, one of the junior Outlaws in Waylon's orbit, was intended to be, Clayton said, more or less tongue-in-cheek. But it quickly caught on as a sort of anthem.

As far as the Outlaw business being a genuine rebellion against Nashville, it was a true declaration of independence by those involved. Willie had never been served well by the Nashville system and simply wanted to be left alone to pursue his musical vision. If he had to go to Texas to do so, so be it. (Ironically, a year before *The Outlaws* was released, Willie went down to a little studio in Garland, Texas, with his band and recorded his true breakthrough album, *Red Headed Stranger*. When CBS Records' Billy Sherrill balked at releasing the sparsely arranged record, Willie won the test of wills.) Waylon had felt ill-served by the system for years, and rightly so. He mainly wanted a little freedom: to record with his road band and to record what songs he wanted to, when he wanted to – without a producer who had been assigned by Atkins – and especially where he wanted to.

It was this last wish that led to his alignment with Tompall Glaser and the formation of Outlaw Headquarters at Hillbilly Central, Tompall's studio on Nineteenth Avenue South in Nashville. And in 1972, after discovering that RCA had not automatically picked up Waylon's option to re-sign with the company, his manager soon had Columbia, Atlantic, Capitol and Mercury wooing Waylon. After tense negotiations, RCA eventually re-signed Waylon, but gave him the greatest artistic freedom of any of its country artists.

His music didn't change immediately, but his records did – especially the 1973 album that became the quintessential Outlaw work: *Honky Tonk Heroes*. It also set the formula for what became known as Outlaw music: sparsely accompanied and highly personal songs – a cowboy's diary set to a driving beat, as it were. This was Waylon Jennings working at full bore, finally able to do what he wanted to, capturing his lusty, gritty vision. Nine of the ten songs on *Honky Tonk Heroes* were written by another Texas Outlaw, Billy Joe Shaver, a gifted poet who was determined to try Nashville because of his idols, Willie and Waylon. Billy Joe hitchhiked to Nashville on the back of a truck loaded with cantaloupes, naive in his belief that such songs as "Black Rose" – about a black-white romance – could make it in Nashville. They did, although they could not have five years earlier or five years later. The Outlaw window was open, however briefly. Even though the credits say the album *Honky Tonk Heroes* was recorded at RCA, the bulk of it was cut at Hillbilly Central, with Waylon and Tompall producing.

The astonishing thing was that, until Waylon in particular began to receive exposure in the rock press and success with rock audiences and became aware of how things were done in rock, the Outlaws – as well as most artists in Nashville – didn't realize that having artistic freedom in the recording studio was a given outside Nashville. You could record what you wanted and record it with your road band, you could pick the cover of your album, you could try to find a booking agent capable of putting you into places better than the blood-and-guts honky-tonks. You could pick a manager from Los Angeles or New York or anywhere else, and it could be someone who wasn't part of the tiny Nashville old-boy network. And – the biggest heresy – you could control your own publishing, which of course was always where the real money was and had always been Nashville's darkest little secret.

In short, that was the crux of the Outlaw movement: It had nothing to do with long hair or wearing black leather or smoking dope or any other trivial sideshow issues. It was actually a fairly sober attempt at gaining self-determination and independence – not such a rare thing for creative people to seek. I can remember being touched by what I considered Waylon's naiveté when – after he started opening for such rock bands as the Grateful Dead – he was flabbergasted to learn that such groups could actually put riders into their contracts calling for specific food and drink to be served to them in their dressing room. It was almost like watching a barefoot kid discover shoes.

What they did not yet have to effectuate real change in the Nashville music hierarchy was big record sales. Sales, anywhere in the music business, equaled money, and money equaled power. Getting music writers from ROLLING STONE to rave about an Outlaw concert was one thing, but moving those albums out of the stores – that was the kicker, that would certify whether or not this little "movement" that Nashville seemed to have on its hands would amount to anything more than a temper tantrum being thrown by

from 1975 – Willie's *Red Headed Stranger* and Waylon's *Dreaming My Dreams* – primed the Outlaw audience. Had it been released six months earlier or six months later, its impact might have been negligible. As it was, its fallout was considerable.

Outlaw-clone music inundated Nashville, and Willie and Waylon clones flooded the South and Southwest. In Texas, particularly, the Outlaw look became an everyday uniform, and that led right into the "Texas Chic" trend, which itself directly spawned the whole *Urban Cowboy* business. Willie and Waylon soon declared themselves sick of the Outlaw moniker, but they were more or less stuck with it. In 1978, Waylon felt moved to write and record the song "Don't You Think This Outlaw Bit's Done Got Out of Hand," and he doesn't write all that much.

The excesses performed in the name of Outlaw, by musicians and fans alike, were legion. A backlash was inevitable, especially after other performers began to see the amount of success (and money) that accrued to Willie and Waylon. Their records and concerts were scrutinized and criticized to a degree neither had thought possible.

Oddly, what may have been the biggest legacy of the Outlaws was scarcely recognized. In effectively challenging

They talk about progressive country, but it's really progressive listeners – *Willie Nelson*

some talented, if immature, youngsters who had not yet learned the tribal ways. Jerry Bradley knew that. He knew, he thought, just how to fix all that with his big Concept Album.

Wanted! The Outlaws had only Waylon's name on the spine (because he was the only one of the four Outlaws under contract to RCA at the time). Jerry Bradley decreed that there be a burnt-at-the-edges wanted-poster look to the cover of the thing, with Waylon's picture front and center, to be flanked by Willie, Tompall and Jessi, with my liner notes on the back, in the form of a poster or broadside. The cuts on the record were unremarkable. Side one was made up of Waylon's "My Heroes Have Always Been Cowboys" and "Honky Tonk Heroes," Jessi's "I'm Looking for Blue Eyes" and "You Mean to Say," and "Suspicious Minds" by Waylon and Jessi. Side two opened with Willie and Waylon singing "Good Hearted Woman" and "Heaven or Hell" and Willie's rendition of "Me and Paul" and "Yesterday's Wine." It ended with Tompall's "T for Texas" and "Put Another Log on the Fire." Not exactly a song lineup to draw the angels' hosannas. Yet this *Outlaws* album was the first platinum album in country-music history. There have been many answers advanced to explain that and, I suspect, the most nearly correct one is that the timing of the album was perfect. Two spectacular albums

and then shattering Nashville's feudal system, the Outlaw movement opened the doors of artistic freedom wide – perhaps a shade too wide for some. Country music (and its new pop audience and attendant prosperity) not only had made room for a Joe Ely or a Rosanne Cash or a Ricky Skaggs, it also had made room (too much, some said) for crossover crooners like Kenny Rogers.

Nowadays, the Outlaw movement has proved itself a durable building block in the ongoing construction of the country-music edifice. Artistic freedom may well be its most lasting legacy – Garth Brooks could likely never have leveraged his degree of independence without the lasting lesson of Willie, Waylon, et al. to draw upon. Steve Earle perhaps would not have started his own record label – E-Squared – on Music Row in Nashville, in the very heart of the Country Establishment, without a maverick tradition as inspiration. The Mavericks themselves would probably still be outside the walls of Nashville, shouting to be let in, had it not been for these earlier rebels chipping away at those walls. Of course, it still all comes down to economics – an outlaw outfit selling a few records is ignored; an outlaw outfit selling platinum is not an outlaw gang, it's a successful, respected business entity. ⊕

hamilton jordan on walking to the white house

THE MOST THRILLING phase of the 1976 presidential campaign came in the early days, during the Iowa caucuses in January and the New Hampshire and Florida primaries in February and March. We were a band of guerrillas then, running a guerrilla war in the perfect situation: The political and press establishments had set lower expectations for us, while we had already been running longer and harder than most of the other Democratic candidates.

Because nobody outside of Georgia knew who the hell Jimmy Carter was, we figured out ways of using his fantastic base of support in his home state. We organized the "Peanut Brigade," teams of Georgian volunteers who fanned out to key primary states, distributing materials and information and even going from door to door to tell people about Jimmy Carter. It sounded hokey, but it flowed from a personal belief in Carter, and it worked. Soon Carter was on television each week claiming victory somewhere else, and the press had discovered Plains, Georgia, and was interviewing his brother, Billy, and Miss Lillian, his mother. But eight or ten weeks later, Carter was badly overexposed and people began to tire of all the coverage of his campaign. That's when Jerry Brown and the other "ABC" (Anyone But Carter) Democrats started winning a few primaries.

Carter's decision to run predated the 1972 election, when things were looking grim for George McGovern. I sent Carter a seventy-two-page memo in November of that year advising him on how to go about it. At that point Carter was a popular New South governor, and the 1972 candidates for

Presidential candidate Jimmy Carter with friends the Allman Brothers Band, Providence, Rhode Island, 1975

president had traipsed through Georgia and spent the night with him at the governor's mansion. Carter often said that he was never able to think of himself in a league with Washington, Jefferson and Roosevelt, but he had little problem comparing himself to George McGovern, George Wallace and Scoop Jackson. Based on that, Carter concluded he would at least have a chance at getting elected.

In that 1970–72 time period, a crop of progressive Southern governors had been elected. *Time* magazine did a story about these politicians, and Carter appeared on the cover, which began a process of separating him from the rest of those guys. Quite frankly, none of those others had the audacity to make the race for the White House, so while they were doing their jobs and maybe hoping to be vice president or in the cabinet someday, Carter was making methodical plans to run for president.

Then Watergate happened, and it made Carter's "outsider" candidacy more relevant and valid. It was, in a way, a confusing time. There was a feeling of great hope and expectation, particularly in the South, that we were moving into a new era, and had begun to put our race problems and Vietnam behind us. But Watergate dominated the news and the political landscape.

Out of that chaos came Jimmy Carter, a man not associated with Washington – a straight shooter. On one level, he was a very simple person – what you saw was what you got – but he was also a deep thinker and very sophisticated in his perceptions. Carter could stand up in somebody's living room in New Hampshire or in an auditorium in Iowa, speak about his family, his beliefs, his experiences and his love of this country and be very powerful. He never had a prepared speech and often spoke spontaneously. He'd write down only three or four phrases to outline a speech.

One of those powerful moments occurred during a Law Day speech in 1974 at the University of Georgia, where Governor Carter's appearance preceded Senator Ted Kennedy's major address. Politicians typically tell their audiences how important and wonderful they are; Carter's instinct, however, was to challenge his listeners to be better at what they do – and as human beings. In his Law Day speech, he talked about the failures and shortcomings of the justice system and about the roles the young lawyers should play in a just society. His performance was vintage Carter.

As it happened, Hunter Thompson was at that speech, following Kennedy around. He was so smitten that he played a tape of Carter's remarks all over the country to key press people and politicos. This ultimately led to a ROLLING STONE cover story and endorsement of Carter, which made the former Southern governor an acceptable choice for younger voters.

Later, when he was president, in formal addresses to Congress or televised speeches from the Oval Office, Carter was never quite as good as he had been in those more informal situations. He was small in stature, lacked a deep voice and simply was not comfortable in many of the contrived settings required of a modern president. Jimmy Carter was and is a complex man – and complexity is not well served in this modern age of communication. Reagan, on the other hand, is a simpler person, which served him well during his presidency.

I had never been involved in a presidential campaign before Carter's: Those of us who worked for him were not savvy enough to know that our goal was considered by most insiders to be impossible. We had a lot of challenges to overcome. The perception was that you couldn't get a candidate from the South elected; that to win, he had to be a sitting governor or senator from a big state and a product of the Democratic party machine – like Hubert Humphrey, LBJ or John F. Kennedy. There was also a feeling early on that since there were so many people running for president there would be no winner-take-all in the Democratic party, and we would have to have a brokered convention to choose a candidate in 1976. So the conventional wisdom was that several candidates would win 15 or 20 percent of the delegates

they needed for the nomination, and ultimately the nomination would be negotiated in the back room by party leaders – who were not likely to pick a former Georgia governor.

Our strategy defied that conventional wisdom and was built on the belief that we could win the nomination on the first ballot.

In reaction to Watergate and the election scandals, the Federal Election Commission had been recently created in order to regulate the influence of money on our political system. For the first time, there were limits imposed on how much a campaign could raise and spend and on how much an individual could contribute; and now, reports had to be filed by candidates in order for them to receive matching federal funds. Unfortunately, these changes turned our politicians into beggars by making fund-raising more difficult, but they did put a premium on small donors, which probably helped Carter's campaign, since he didn't have big contributors or corporate support.

To qualify for federal matching funds in 1976, we had to demonstrate a broad base of financial support all over the country. Phil Walden, the head of Capricorn Records, and Tom Beard, an Atlanta businessman and old college friend of mine, helped us do that by holding rock concerts to raise the necessary money. The Phil Walden relationship was crucial to Carter's candidacy both politically and financially. The Allman Brothers Band concerts that Walden organized sent an important cultural and ideological signal to voters *and* raised a lot of money.

Carter was a true music lover and even in the White House

kept up his connections with the music industry and his favorite performers, from Willie Nelson to Mstislav Rostropovich. And when Elvis called the first few times, Carter talked to him. But he soon realized Presley was pretty heavy into the sauce and wasn't making much sense. Then he would pass the phone to Tom Beard or myself, and we would pretend to be the president. Elvis never knew the difference – he called mainly to express his support and say he was real proud that a Southerner was our president.

When Carter was elected, he especially wanted to move away from the imperial presidency Nixon had maintained. So he chose to walk – not ride – the inaugural route to the White House on his first day in office and didn't allow the band to play "Hail to the Chief." But it turned out this was one change the American people didn't like. They *wanted* their president to be somewhat imperial, if not in his actions, at least in his stature or appearance. Some of Carter's changes weren't practical, either. He did away with many of the White House limousines, a policy that sounded good to us before we got there, but once he was in office we realized we had to be able to get from the White House to the Capitol in ten minutes, and how were we going to get there? Walk?

As an outsider, Carter went to Washington in hopes of changing the direction of both the Democratic party and the country and of strengthening the relationship between our government and the American people. I'm sad to say we were not successful in doing that. The gap between our elected officials and their constituency is wider today than ever before. Consider the trillions of dollars spent on the inner cities of this country during the last fifty years, and then go into any big city and talk to its citizens – they will tell you that life's no better there now than it was a quarter of a century ago. And underlying their dissatisfaction is a greater and greater distrust of Washington and the officials these folks chose to represent them.

It seemed that Carter was a marked man as soon as he got to the White House. He had triumphed over the political establishment and the pundits, but once he got to Washington those same people were determined to show him who was boss. The very qualities that had made him attractive to the American people were perceived as liabilities inside the Beltway. His Southernness and his religious beliefs were poked fun at and said to be contrived. By 1980, he was being portrayed as manipulative and political, a man who would do anything to win reelection.

Ironically, Carter tackled the country's toughest and most politically difficult issues, ones that other presidents had sidestepped or ignored: the Panama Canal treaties, the Middle East peace process, the SALT agreements – none of them political winners. Nevertheless, for me, during the White House years, the magical moments with Carter occurred at Camp David at the time of the Middle East peace accords. His attention to detail, his knowledge of the issues and his tenacity and willingness to take enormous risks all came into play. And when logic or persuasion failed, Carter took Israeli prime minister Menachem Begin and Egyptian president Anwar Sadat and simply banged their heads together to get the desired result. Most of the progress made in the Middle East in the past couple of decades has been based on those Camp David Accords.

During our White House stay, we also had some terrible luck: When we went into office, the price of a barrel of oil was twelve dollars; it reached thirty-five dollars shortly before we left. The shah was ousted and the Iranian situation blew up. These crises might have happened five years earlier or five years after we left but, as luck would have it, they happened on our watch, and we had to deal with them.

Jimmy Carter was and is a Renaissance man, interested in every problem and every issue. This sometimes caused him to appear to be a bundle of contradictions; one day he was an environmentalist passing new programs, the next a belt-tightening moderate trying to balance the budget. It became impossible to sustain a consistent support group in Congress for our agenda.

Carter always saw government as a means of magnifying the impact of his own life and work. When we left the White House, he immediately used his ex-presidency to help others – and he's *still* trying to solve all of the world's problems. The Carters have established two health programs in Africa that have nearly eliminated two diseases – Guinea worm and river blindness. Jimmy Carter typically spreads himself too thin. He takes on more than he should, but he also consistently accomplishes more than you think he will. He's made a difference with his life. ⊕

phil walden
on rockin' for jimmy

WHEN JIMMY CARTER was still governor of Georgia he came by a couple of recording sessions for my label, Capricorn Records, in Macon. I remember that one of those times we were recording Dickey Betts's solo album *Highway Call*, and Jimmy sat there with Dickey and recited every line of the Allman Brothers Band's "Ramblin' Man," which Dickey had written, and asked him about each lyric – about Highway 41, which runs through the center of Georgia, and all the other words. Dickey was just blown away, and the two became an unlikely pair of friends! That's how Carter established himself with the bands.

Ninety percent of the time I was not present when he met the artists; I just arranged the meetings and he would close the deal himself. The Charlie Daniels Band, the Marshall Tucker Band, the Outlaws, the Atlanta Rhythm Section, Lynyrd Skynyrd – all of them got behind Carter when he was running for president. But the Allman Brothers Band started it.

The first Allman Brothers benefit for Carter was in Providence in 1975. I had been telling myself for days, over and over, that I was going to ask him not to make a speech. So right before the show I said, "Governor, Geraldo Rivera is going to introduce you, and let me just tell you how this rock concert thing works. The audience has bought tickets not to help you get elected president of the United States, but to see the Allman Brothers Band. A lot of times, if someone is out there talking for any lengthy time period they may start booing."

"Phil, don't worry," he said. Then he walked out onstage and said, "Hi, my name is Jimmy Carter. I'm running for president. I hope I can count on your support, and I hope you'll join me in welcoming our friends the Allman Brothers Band." The audience started clapping, and he walked offstage.

I first met Carter when he was governor; he was doing a series of "listening" tours in Georgia, in which he would visit various businesses and speak with employees and their employers. He came into Capricorn, and we had a great initial meeting.

After that I started hearing from him on a pretty regular basis, and later, he invited my wife and me to the Governor's Mansion. We spent the night there with Rosalynn and Jimmy. During the course of our visit, I asked the governor about his plans after his term expired. He answered, "I've decided what I'm going to do. I'm going to run for president."

I actually said, "President of what?"

"Will you support me?" he asked, and, of course, I said yes.

I became one of the first members of his financial planning staff, and I still remember our first meeting in Atlanta. The budget for the first year's campaign was in the area of $600,000! I raised my hand and asked, "Are you sure this is enough? I wouldn't think that this would be sufficient funds to run for mayor of Macon."

Carter's response was: "I'm gonna fly tourist and I'll wash my own socks and we'll stay at people's houses and we'll keep our costs way down."

I forget how many months later it was, but Carter called me early one morning and said, "You were right, we don't have any money anymore, we're broke. Unless I can come up with a quick remedy, I've got to drop out."

Bear in mind that this was happening during the post-Watergate era, when there were many new, and very strict, fund-raising limitations. So I said, "You know, we're looking into the possibility of doing a concert." We had discovered that under the new election laws we could do concerts to raise money and, if we followed the regulations, we would be eligible for matching funds. Up to this point, we had viewed the concert more as a means of publicity than as a fund-raiser.

Carter said to me, "If you could give me two or three concert dates, then we could go to the bank and borrow against that." So that solved the cash flow problem right away because the Allman dates were all but guaranteed to be sellouts.

The moment I actually began to believe we might go all the way to the White House occurred later, at a special event at the Hyatt Regency Atlanta, after Carter had won a series of Southern primaries. I was standing next to Hamilton Jordan, and he just looked at me and said, "Do you believe it? We're going to win this damn thing!"

I said, "I think you're right."

ON INAUGURATION DAY there was an open house at the White House. Thousands of people were there, and by the time we got up to the line to shake President Carter's hand, he looked exhausted. My wife started crying, and we all just looked at each other, overpowered by this feeling of happiness and relief.

I visited the White House the following February, Carter showed me around, and then we walked outside and looked back at the White House. I said, "You're the thirty-ninth president of the United States. Are you in awe of that at all?"

He looked down, smiled and said, "You know, I hadn't really thought about that, but I guess I am a little bit." Then we turned around and walked back inside. It had been a nice first visit and he had been a nice person to have had walk me around.

I HAD DINNER with Jimmy Carter recently, after which we went to see a Bob Dylan concert. Carter was so amazing: Everyone knows how difficult it is to decipher what Bob Dylan is singing or even to know which song he's playing, now that he rearranges his songs. But as we sat there listening to him, Carter would punch me and say, "Hey Phil, this is from the new album." ⊕

reggae inna u.s.a.
by roger steffens

IT'S THE HEIGHT of a clammy summer in Tennessee in 1976. My wife, Mary, and I are driving cross-country to our home in L.A., fresh from a frustrating, three-week search for reggae music in Jamaica. Disembarking in Montego Bay a month earlier, we had encountered José Feliciano singing "California Dreamin'" on the airport PA system, and in the minibus to our destination, we were serenaded by a succession of C&W artists ranging from Hank Williams and Patsy Cline to Gale Garnett and Nancy Sinatra. Jamaican radio proved to be bereft of any local music at all. Where was the reggae?

We decide to stop for lunch in Nashville. Cruising through Middle America's C&W capital, we spot an old brick building ahead with a fading sign: ERNEST TUBB RECORD SHOP. As we draw abreast, we see a huge display window filled from top to bottom with burlap sacks. Printed on each one is the unmistakable image of a fierce-looking man with dreadlocks poised beneath a blood-red Bob Marley and the Wailers logo. It's the distinctive cover of what will be Marley's – and reggae's – highest-charting album ever (Number Eight pop), *Rastaman Vibration.*

Perhaps there's hope after all, we think. Maybe the heartbeat strains of reggae are finally beginning to penetrate the American heartland. A few days later in San Francisco, we fall by Kingston Records, a Rasta shop run by our old friend Ruel Mills. As we recount our trip, Ruel smiles slyly and laughs, "You have fe leave Jamaica fe find Jamaica."

Reggae was the natural inheritor of the progressive, socially conscious vibes of the Sixties. No other music of the Seventies so successfully preached and pranced simultaneously, enrapturing the listener with its uplifting millenarian outlook, its unwavering belief in the unity of God in man and nature and, of course, its abiding worship of the sacrament. Call it joint or spliff, bong or chalice, the herbal connection bonded the cultural handshake: Reggae revived flower power and rolled in the buds, stems and seeds.

But Marley saw a distinction, too, as he surveyed the growing, mostly white tide of reggae converts in 1976. "Rastamon him not like hippie . . . Him hold-a on long time an' hippie no hold-a on, him fail. De hippie should-a hold on five more year until we come. Den dem hippies be de Rastamon, too!"

Yet American blacks, Marley's most coveted audience, remained impervious to him and his message throughout the Seventies. They were under the sway of elaborately costumed funk and disco and seemed determined to avoid any reminder of their own African roots, fearful of the stigma of primitivism.

Unlike the recipients of the earlier infusion of ska and rock steady into Great Britain, when a wave of Jamaican laborers immigrated with families and various infectious mento and ska 45s in tow, American ears had to wait until 1969 to hear Jah music. That year witnessed Desmond Dekker and the Aces cracking the U.S. Top Ten with the unlikely, Old Testament–inspired "Israelites" – a summertime novelty tune in the context of the Beatles' "Get Back," Zager and Evans's "In the Year 2525" and other hits of the day. But it marked the first ripple of the one-drop wave to crash onto American shores a few years later. Bobby Bloom's sunny lament "Montego Bay" (1970) and Johnny Nash's one-million-seller "I Can See Clearly Now" and Paul Simon's Kingston-recorded "Mother and Child Reunion" (both 1972) provided other signposts along reggae's early-Seventies inroads to the U.S., culminating with Eric Clapton's chart-topping – if rock-blunted – cover of Marley's "I Shot the Sheriff" in September 1974.

My personal conversion to reggae began one particular Northern California week in the summer of 1973 when a triple-punch knockout hit me in the form of an article, a movie and an album. ROLLING STONE had published an essay by journalist Michael Thomas on his Jamaican journey – speaking of a deeply philosophical music-maker named Marley, an equally profound and life-loving bush dweller called Cunchyman and an exotic, naturalistic but serious religion called Rastafarianism. Perry Henzell's rude-boy epic *The Harder They Come,* starring Jimmy Cliff, with its high-powered

baits the band into cursing on the air. The resulting uproar will cause the band to be banned from performing in all but five cities on their upcoming British tour; by January, no concert hall or club in the U.K. will book the band.

2 ROLLING STONE reports on the controversy surrounding a song by the rock band Starz titled "Pull the Plug," the lyrics of which evoke a scenario suspiciously reminiscent of the Karen Ann Quinlan right-to-die case.

3 Seven gunmen shoot up Bob Marley's Kingston, Jamaica, residence in what appears to be a politically motivated attack. Miraculously, no one is killed, even though the house is filled with family, friends, band members and Marley himself.

A 40-foot inflatable pink pig floating over London – part of a photo shoot that Pink Floyd commissioned for its *Animals* album cover – breaks loose, causes major aircraft warnings and eventually reaches an altitude of 18,000 feet before it is last sighted over Kent.

4 Former Deep Purple and James Gang lead guitarist Tommy Bolin dies in Miami of a heroin overdose.

13 Rick Dees and His Cast of Idiots' novelty record "Disco Duck (Part 1)" becomes the fourth platinum single in pop history.

19 Rev. Al Green holds the first Sunday service at his Full Gospel Tabernacle Church in Memphis; more than 1,000 people attend.

21 Rubin "Hurricane" Carter and John Artis, whose 1974 murder convictions had spawned public outcry and protest, are again found guilty of a triple homicide.

23 Isaac Hayes, Stax artist, songwriter and the genius behind "The Theme from *Shaft*," files for bankruptcy with debts of $6 million and 14 lawsuits pending against him.

28 Texas bluesman Freddie King, creator of the perennial instrumental "Hideaway," dies.

30 ROLLING STONE reports on the release of *All This and World War II*, a 20th Century–Fox movie coupling war footage and Beatles songs (sample pairings: Pearl Harbor being bombed to "Sun King," Hitler seen in his Alpine retreat *Berchtesgaden* to "Fool on the Hill"). The film is

soundtrack, opened in a little theater on the north side of the UC-Berkeley campus. I sat with a full house of scruffy post-hippies in an atmosphere that became cloudy and cloudier as the story unfolded and the music raved on. The following day, down on Shattuck Avenue, I picked up a used copy of Bob Marley and the Wailers' *Catch a Fire* for a couple of bucks, cheap enough to take the chance.

That was it. From its eerie fade-in, sneaking like a thief in the night, until its final midnight-raving denouement, I sat speechless as I heard music at once odd yet strangely familiar. The rhythm was backwards, the offbeat emphasized, the blunt bass licks coiled thickly into the lead guitar, echoing the melody one or two beats behind. And those voices! Bunny Wailer, Peter Tosh and of course Marley – half-singing, half-chanting the ethereal, plaintive vocal triad that is the foundation of Jamaican harmony. "Iron sharpen iron," as they say in Jamaican patois to describe the finely honed effect of the reggae vocal technique of word, sound and power.

As the months passed, I realized I was not alone in my newfound discovery. Marley was becoming the darling of American rock critics, though reggae was struggling to be heard outside a cult audience. Marley toured the U.S. in 1975 for the first time without Peter Tosh and Bunny Wailer, who had separated to pursue their own muses. His appearance at L.A.'s Roxy was the hottest ticket of the next year, with music-biz heavies and Hollywood stars vying for entry: John Lennon, Yoko Ono, Ringo Starr, Warren Beatty and Jack Nicholson ended up on tabletops, cheering what tour emcee Tony G called "The Trench Town Experience."

To understand the full effect of reggae's bottom-rich riddims, to put a face on the music, it had to be experienced live. In 1975, a hastily arranged concert at Oakland's Paramount Theater offered Mary and me our first chance to see Marley in action. It was staged by Bill Graham, and the place was virtually sold out by word of mouth. We sat in the front row of the balcony, leaning expectantly over the rail as Marley took the stage. Although his locks barely grazed his shoulders at the time, his appearance seemed so bizarre, so unearthly, that many folks around us gasped at the sight of him. He wore street clothes and sang with his eyes closed, trancelike, and never said a word between tunes. Marley was mesmerizing. During instrumental solos, he would snap his head back as if he were about to fall over, then flail his body forward as dreadlocks whipped around his face, making him appear like some Upper Niger fetish or mask come to life. Every time he did this the audience would rise to its feet with a leonine roar. Frenzied cheers rent the air when he delivered the street-fighter lines of "Talkin' Blues": "I feel like bombin' a church/Now that you know that the preacher is lying/So who's gonna stay at home/When the freedom fighters are fighting." This was something other than "boogie till your coke spoon falls off your neck" music – it was as soulful and meaningful and un-Seventies-glam as one could get in that boisterous decade.

None of our growing number of reggae-listening brethren could have known it at the time, but 1976 was to prove a banner year for Jah music. It was a high-water mark – not just

most effective ambassador. Bob Marley was wounded in a politically motivated assassination attempt, ironically echoing the Biblical words he had quoted on the cover of his then-current hit album: "The archers have sorely grieved him, and shot at him, and hated him." (Even more eerie was the title of Marley's only ROLLING STONE cover article during his life the preceding August: "Rastaman With a Bullet.")

The next year, Marley was in exile in England, teaming up with Perry to produce the raucous twelve-inch single "Punky Reggae Party." "The Wailers will be there," he sang. "The Damned, the Jam, the Clash, Dr. Feelgood, too." The solidarity and influence among dreads and mohawks was blessed, and reggae began to overtake other musical styles. The Clash's "White Man in Hammersmith Palais" and Elvis Costello's "Watching the Detectives" adapted skank rhythms to a fiercer, punk-based attack, foretelling the full-force ska revival to come in 1979–80 with two-tone bands like the Selecter, the English Beat, Madness and later the Police, UB40, Men at Work and on. And on. And on.

Now, almost a quarter-century later, the sound of 1976, of "roots" reggae, has become so familiar as to be old hat. It has been successfully diffused through other musical styles (rap, untold ska permutations, Dread Zeppelin), while reg-

Me hafta laugh sometime when dem scribes seh me like Mick Jagger or some superstar t'ing like dat. Dem hafta listen closeh to de music, 'cause de message not de same. Noooo, mon, de reggae not de twist, mon! –Bob Marley

because Marley had a hit and was on the cover of music magazines, but because now everybody was paying attention. The major labels went scurrying to find the next dread-locked shaman. In that short twelve-month span these now-timeless record titles came out alongside *Rastaman Vibration*: Peter Tosh's anthem to the herb, *Legalize It;* Bunny Wailer's immortal debut, *Blackheart Man;* Toots and the Maytals' R&B-infused *Reggae Got Soul;* Burning Spear's *Marcus Garvey* (and its dub companion, the sepulchral *Garvey's Ghost*); Max Romeo's Lee "Scratch" Perry–produced call-to-arms "War ina Babylon." For sheer creativity and clear-eyed vision, the leading voices of reggae have never packed it so forcefully, same time, same place.

As 1976 ran out, the harsh and bitter realities brewing under Jamaica's idyllic island unity almost robbed us of its

gae itself has mutated and updated itself (dub, dancehall, hip-hop). On a level more widespread than almost any music since jazz, reggae's riddims and message of uprising have journeyed from a small Caribbean island to become a global, musical esperanto uniting peoples, countries and struggles. One can find roots-type bands singing "One Love" lyrics in Portuguese in Brazil, in Polish in the shipyards of Gdansk, in Zulu in South Africa and in Fijian in the South Pacific. Among black and brown cultures, Bob Marley has been elevated to a Che Guevara–like stature, as revered for his political stance as for his creative vision. Stranger transformations have occurred. As *New York Times* music critic Jon Pareles predicts: "In 2096, when the former third world has overrun and colonized the former superpowers, Marley will be commemorated as a saint." ⊕

a commercial and critical flop.

1977 JANUARY

destination: mars
by timothy ferris

WHEN 'VIKING ONE' landed on Mars on July 20, 1976, none of us at the Jet Propulsion Laboratory in Pasadena – guests, press, scientists, the flight teams – had the slightest idea whether the thing had worked. JPL was in "control" of the flight, but at a distance of 220 million miles, there was no such thing as direct control. Radio signals from *Viking*, traveling at the speed of light, took nineteen minutes to reach Earth. So the JPL people – longhairs, dry old men in drip-dry shirts, a few women in miniskirts, a backwater fop in bright Dacron, one thin black man in shades – rocked back and forth in their desk chairs, smoked cigarettes and waited. It was 5:00 a.m. "It's on Mars," someone said, "one way or another."

When the good news arrived, *Viking* project director Jim Martin, who had been hunched over a set of computer terminals in a Plexiglas-walled office he'd had built so he could keep an eye on everyone, stood and accepted congratulations from a half-dozen colleagues who rushed in and surrounded him. He wrested himself away long enough to take another look at the screens, just to make sure, then walked out into the lander-team area wearing a dazed smile. He pulled on a T-shirt given to him hours before by a local mescalito. It portrayed a frightened Martian shouting, THE AMERICANS HAVE LANDED! Martin posed for photos.

The arrival of the first photographs suspended the celebration. Technically they were superb (in fact, they made it from Mars to Pasadena in better shape than they did from Pasadena into the newspapers and TV shows). I think what made them so startling was that they so obviously came from another world. Many of us had been accustomed to talking and writing about "Mars," throwing the word around as if it served to capture Mars the planet, just as I can write "whale" on the page, without having touched a finger to even one genuine whale gliding beneath the waves of some specific sea. Now the whale was at the door. The photos on the screen came not from a dot in the sky, but from a piece of a sovereign world.

Clustered around the TV screens in JPL's Von Karman Auditorium were a few old Mars dreamers who had made the interplanetary trip years ago in their imaginations – Poul Anderson, Robert Heinlein, Theodore Sturgeon and Ray Bradbury. "We're in a dangerous situation," Bradbury was saying. "We can't stay here on Earth. We have to move out. We should go to Mars for the reason that we do everything we do – for survival. Space travel is a responsible way of reacting to the gift of life."

That night Carl Sagan and I sat scrunched down in a sofa in his Pasadena apartment with a two-foot-long lander panorama photo wrapped around our heads. Sagan, a planetary astronomer with a Ph.D. in astrophysics and a particular interest in Mars, had spent much of the eighteen hours since the photo arrived on network television explaining what it showed, but he had not had a chance to sit back and study it in detail. Sagan and I stared silently for twenty minutes.

"Bring full concentration to it," he advised. "Try to imagine yourself there."

Look hard enough and you'll find something: Soon the jumbled rocks and dunes had arranged themselves into elegant swirls, and I imagined freshets roaring down from the giant Marineris Valley, cutting those swirls in the days when water flowed on Mars. But then the swirls slowly turned into a network of straight lines, and the lines into a honeycomb. I had to admit I'd been looking too hard, had entered that zone where the geometries of nature become indistinguishable from those of the mind.

Maybe this was Mars Fever and we were catching it.

"Look at this," Sagan said, indicating an outcropping of rock about a quarter-mile from the lander. "What do you see?"

I looked closely and was startled to find a shimmering lake. Tangled mangrove trees rose from its banks. A lone palm stood to one side. The oasis was miniature, no more than five feet across.

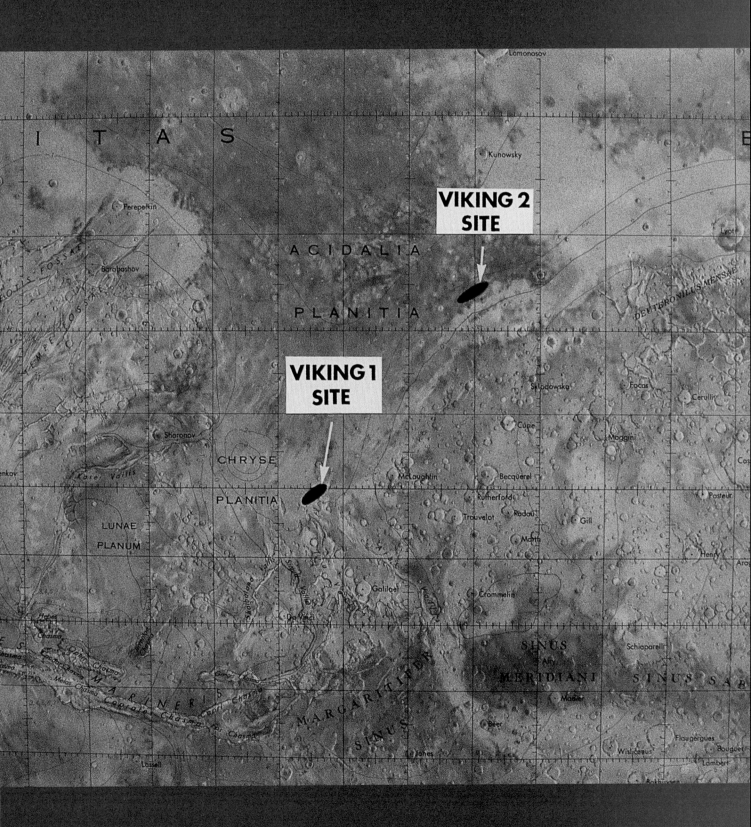

Cher, Linda Ronstadt, Aretha Franklin, Loretta Lynn and Paul Simon. The next day, Carter pardons most Vietnam War draft-dodgers, and the celebration continues at the White House, where the Marshall Tucker Band and the Charlie Daniels Band perform such songs as the CDB's obligatory "The South's Gonna Do It."

23 Carole King's *Tapestry* breaks the record for chart longevity, marking 302 weeks on *Billboard*'s Top 100 Album Chart and holding the record until 1980, when it is broken by Pink Floyd's *Dark Side of the Moon.*

26 Patti Smith, opening for Bob Seger in Tampa, falls offstage midset, sustaining severe head lacerations (requiring 22 stitches), a badly bruised shoulder and two fractured vertebrae. "I look like an asshole. I got a big plaster cast on my neck and a Sex Pistols haircut," she reports.

Memphis soul label Stax Records is auctioned for $1.3 million to an L.A. liquidating company. Assets include master tapes, unreleased recordings and stacks of old records. San Francisco–based Fantasy Records will later obtain distribution rights to the catalogue and begin reissuing the label's R&B gems.

Fleetwood Mac founder and blues-rock guitarist Peter Green is institutionalized after attacking a messenger who was attempting to deliver a £30,000 royalty check from his accountant's office.

28 Latino comedian and *Chico and the Man* star Freddie Prinze, 22, fatally shoots himself in L.A.

30 The final episode of the eight-part television adaptation of Alex Haley's African-American saga *Roots* draws 80 million viewers, the largest TV audience to date.

1977 FEBRUARY

6 Best-selling books in the country are Leon Uris's *Trinity* (fiction), Alex Haley's *Roots* (nonfiction) and Woodward and Bernstein's *The Final Days* (paperback).

7 Publisher Little, Brown & Co. pays Henry Kissinger an estimated $2 million for his memoirs.

8 *Hustler* publisher Larry Flynt is found guilty of pandering obscenity in Cincinnati.

ERA approval is rescinded by Idaho.

9 Rubin "Hurricane" Carter and

I described all this to Sagan.

"I had," he said, "exactly the same hallucination."

The next day Jim Mitchell, a graduate student studying with Seymour Hess, the chief *Viking* meteorologist, told Hess that his study of climate data from the lander indicated the Chryse site on Mars might be "a good place for mirages." Two days after that, Alan Binder, a young project geologist, had the misfortune to notice what looked like a letter *B* on the side of one rock. A television reporter bulletined a story of MARTIAN GRAFFITI, and Binder, remarking ruefully that his own name began with a *B*, had to devote the better part of an hour explaining to the press that your vision can play tricks on you in a desert, even if the desert is Martian.

High-resolution photos, and photos taken at other times of day when the sun illuminated the Martian scene from a different angle, determined that there was no *B* and that the oasis Sagan and I saw was nothing more than patterns of sunlight on stone. All were illusions, as expected, though I like to think of them as shared illusions, in which we play a part but the landscape plays its part, too. We have our dreams, and Mars, lifeless or not, may perhaps be permitted its strange dreams as well.

Life beyond Earth formed the axis of Carl Sagan's career. He listened at giant radio telescopes for signals from alien creatures, affixed plaques to spacecraft leaving the solar system to demonstrate the possibility of sending them greetings, and argued that primitive organisms might be found not only on Mars but on Jupiter or even the moon. Influential in *Viking* from its genesis, he was sometimes called the "guiding spirit" of the project, with the emphasis on spirit. His official role was small – he served as a member of the lander imaging team – but his unofficial role was major: He had become one of the best-known scientists in the world, and it was he who turned up on *The Tonight Show, Issues and Answers, Meet the Press* and the network news shows, explaining *Viking* when it landed.

When Sagan took up the pursuit of extraterrestrial life as a student in the Thirties, most serious scientists regarded the subject with no great enthusiasm. "The general sense was that it was the province of weak-minded sci-fi enthusiasts, and that anybody with an ounce of sense knew the whole subject was ridiculous," Sagan recalled.

Ranged against Sagan were less optimistic scientists, chiefly geologists. Sagan dealt characteristically with their opposition. First he kept calling attention to the excitement and merit of sending life-detection equipment to Mars. "The discovery of even an extremely simple organism on Mars would have profound biological significance," he wrote. "On the other hand, if Mars proves to be lifeless, a natural experiment has been performed for us: two planets, in many respects similar; but on one life has evolved, on the other it has not. By comparing the experimental with the control planet, much may be discovered about the origin of life."

Congress, confronted with the enormous costs of the manned moon landings and the Vietnam War, canceled the original $2.4-billion plan for a lander that could have roamed the surface of Mars, and replaced it with a scaled-down, $1-billion project named *Viking*. In subsequent cost cutting, *Viking* was postponed an additional two years. As project director since 1968, Martin wasn't happy about the delays, but he used the time to improve *Viking*'s design, and the project scientists were able to boost the lander instrument package from 80 to 160 pounds. What had begun as a simple exploratory vehicle became a sophisticated bundle of gear intended to see, feel, taste and smell Mars in dozens of ways. *Viking* was to search for life. Finally, on August 20, 1975, the *Viking One* was launched from Cape Canaveral.

In 1976, the *Viking One* lander, a gray spider with the bulk of a big motorcycle, detached from its orbiter and dropped down between the outstretched crescent arms of Mars. It cut into the upper atmosphere, a metal surfer holding its own poise and counsel. As the air grew thicker, the lander cast off a protective shell, spread a parachute, descended toward the red landscape. At four thousand feet three engines ignited. The parachute fell away; the winds of Mars will tear that parachute into a girdle of bright threads, ornaments from Goodyear. The lander slowed, steadied itself and touched down on Chryse Planitia, the broad delta of a dead Martian river, late on a summer afternoon.

The bleak vistas of two sites where *Viking* landers touched down did little to discourage

Sagan about the prospects for finding life on Mars. Life flourished on Earth for billions of years, he pointed out, before any of it evolved into something the *Viking* landers could have seen; until four hundred million years ago the only signs of life on Earth's surface were a few algae colonies by the seashore. Because Mars is bathed in ultraviolet light – its atmosphere lacks a layer such as Earth's to shield it from ultraviolet rays – few biologists expected life would be found on the surface. More likely it would be underground. That was the reason for equipping the landers with digging hoes. Soil samples were dug and dropped into the hoppers of the biology instruments, and the scientists waited.

The design of three biology experiments reflected differing guesses at what Martian microbes might be like. Since early fall, chemists in laboratories across the country had been trying to explain how nonliving chemistry could have triggered the *Viking* life detectors, while biologists tried to

tions on either side of the matter. The pessimists knew that even a clear negative finding would not entirely rule out the possibility of life, since organisms might exist in oases beyond the landing sites, deep beneath the soil, or in forms not detectable by *Viking*'s relatively simple experiments. And among even the most fervent optimists, none wanted to be remembered in history as the one who declared there was life on Mars and then was proved wrong.

By the end of the year the *Viking* mission had loosened up like an old car. Many of the scientists packed to go home. The orbiter and lander photos played to a shrinking audience.

Carl Sagan returned to his research and writing, his film scripts, television shows and teaching. "Quite apart from the ambiguities of biology, the scientific knowledge obtained from *Viking* has revolutionized our knowledge of Mars," he said. "At the very least, we are seeing inorganic chemistry which to some degree duplicates organic chemistry. This is a dis-

By the time I'm forty, interplanetary travel will be common. Nobody will want to talk to me at that age anyway. I'm gonna be on Mars. It doesn't matter, this planet won't be here in fifty years –Kiss guitarist Ace Frehley

explain how there could be life in the absence of organic molecules. Neither group was able to account for the data.

We still don't know if there is life on Mars.

Under pressure from the press, the public and colleagues to come up with an answer, some of the *Viking* scientists went through what one described as "marvelous oscillations of opinion." One revised his estimate of the chances for life from a-million-to-one to fifty-fifty. Another started out neutral, then said privately that life was the only possible explanation, then did an about-face and said only nonbiological chemistry would do.

The man in the spotlight was Harold Klein, head of the biology team. He resorted to the measured language of a diplomat. "These are the facts we have," he said. "They do not rigorously prove the existence of life on Mars. They do not rigorously exclude the presence of life on Mars."

The project scientists avoided making public declara-

covery of great significance for our understanding of Mars. When you think about it, we find ourselves at a crucial moment in history: We have four working stations on or in orbit around Mars, making the first long-term observations of another planet. It's a harbinger of future exploration of the solar system, and it's of the greatest importance that we did it."

Carl Sagan died in 1996, but his vision continues to inspire popular imagination and scientific study. At the time of his death, he was at work on 1997's 'Contact,' a film based on his book about a scientist who detects a radio signal from an extraterrestrial civilization. NASA's 'Pathfinder' landed on Mars in 1996 – the first successful expedition to the planet since 'Viking' – and the 'Pathfinder' lander was subsequently named "Sagan Station" in honor of the scientist who did more than any other modern thinker to inspire research into the question of whether there is life beyond Earth. ⊕

feverish
by nik cohn

IN THE WINTER of 1975, when I made my first trip to Bay Ridge, Brooklyn, I had been in America for just a few months. I was a contributing editor at *New York*, where I wrote a rock-music column. But the music business, by this time, no longer excited me. I'd been in London during the Sixties; by comparison, these seemed withered days. Rock, which had once been an explosion, had become just another industry, a matter of churning out product.

What I sought, primarily, was an energy fix – the kind of rage and obsession that had drawn me to write about rock in the first place. Clearly, it wasn't to be found at record-company parties, or in the New Establishment music press. So I hit the streets.

Up in Rockland County, I stumbled across a disco dancer named Tu Sweet. He was entered in the Great American Dance Contest, and he was dazzling. He was also black, which meant that he was forced to share first prize, an injustice so rank that even his rivals jeered. But he took the setback in stride. "That's why they named me Tu Sweet," he told me, when I cornered him. "It means 'right on' in French, and that's the way I am."

Later on, when we got back to Manhattan, he took me to a dance club called Othello, near Madison Square Garden. There, fueled by a nonstop supply of Grand Marnier–and–Cokes, he proceeded to give me a grounding in Disco 101.

Some of it I already knew. Van McCoy's *The Hustle* had recently been a hit, and I was aware that new dance clubs were opening 'round town. But I had no idea where disco came from, or how far it had spread. According to Tu Sweet, the craze had started in black gay clubs, then progressed to straight blacks and gay whites, and from there to mass consumption – Latinos in the Bronx, West Indians on Staten Island and, yes, Italians in Brooklyn.

Of these, he knew the Italians best. Some of them went in for the same dance contests as himself, and though he found their style in general too crude, a little too blatant, he liked their passion.

"Some of those guys, they have no lives," he said, staring into his Grand Marnier–and–Coke. "Dancing's all they got."

For me, that was an automatic hook. Growing up in Northern Ireland, and later living in England, I'd always thought of teen style in terms of class. Rock, at least the kind that mattered to me, attained its greatest power when have-nots went on the rampage, taking no prisoners. *Dancing's all they got.* It sounded to me like a rallying cry.

The spirit of Tony Manero lives on at Brooklyn's 2001 Odyssey, the disco that sparked the story that ignited the movie that spread Fevermania

When I proposed the story to Clay Felker, then editor of *New York*, his response was lukewarm at best. At night, over dinner at Elaine's, he conducted a flash poll, with discouraging results. No one present knew anything of disco, Felker reported back, and no one gave a damn, either.

Still, he let me go ahead. On an icy, storm-wracked Saturday night in early December, Tu Sweet commandeered a gypsy cab, and we sallied forth for Brooklyn. There was this little club out in Bay Ridge, 2001 Odyssey, where he'd been a few times. Most blacks were not welcome there, but Tu Sweet wasn't most blacks. Once he'd got out on the dance floor and showed off his moves, even the racial hard core had given him grudging credit. "They still don't like me," he admitted. "But they're not about to demise me."

Leaving Manhattan, he knew exactly where he was headed. Many hours later, he still did. By that time, we had trawled all of Bay Ridge, Borough Park and Bensonhurst, and most of Sheepshead Bay to boot. The gypsy cab was unheated, ice layered the windshield and the engine had started to grumble as loudly as me. I would have given serious money to be back in Othello, warm and stoned, but Tu Sweet refused to admit defeat. "It's right around this corner," he announced, for perhaps the twentieth time. This

time, by some fluke, he proved correct.

We were in a dead land. There were auto shops, locked and barred; transmission specialists; alignment centers. There was the Crazy Country Club, which advertised "warm beer and lousy food." And then there was, at the far end of a deserted block, a small patch of red neon light.

When we pulled up outside the club, a drunken brawl was in progress. Just as I opened my side door, one of the brawlers emerged from the pack, reeled over toward the gutter and threw up, with fine precision, all over the side of the cab and my trouser legs.

I took it as a sign. Quickly slamming the door, I ordered us back to Manhattan. Tu Sweet, sniffing the blood-rage in the air, for once didn't argue. So ended the first chapter.

One image stayed with me, though: a figure in flared crimson pants and a black body shirt standing in the club doorway, directly under the neon light, and calmly watching the action. There was a certain style about him – an inner force, a hunger and a sense of his own specialness. He looked, in short, like a star.

I knew that look well. I'd seen one version as a child, in my hometown of Derry, when I came across a teen gang outside a coffee bar and watched one of them, their leader, perform magic tricks with a rubber snake. And again, in London, around 1965, when I turned up one night to see the Who, and met a Mod named Chris, just turned seventeen, who claimed to buy three new suits each week and change his shirt five times a day.

They didn't do much, these faces. Didn't sing or play guitars, and their daytime job, if they had one, was irrelevant. Their whole power – their *stardom* – was inbuilt.

The following weekend, I went back to 2001 Odyssey with Tu Sweet, and this time we got past the door. I didn't learn much, though. The noise level was deafening, the crush of sweaty bodies suffocating, and none of my attempts at striking up conversations got beyond the first few sentences. I didn't see the figure in the doorway again, and the others I tried talking to were unresponsive. Plus, I made a lousy interviewer. I knew nothing about this world, and it showed. Quite literally, I didn't speak the language.

So I faked it.

I conjured up the story of the figure in the doorway, and named him Vincent. Taking all I knew or guessed about the rubber-snake charmer in Derry and, more especially, about Chris the Mod in London, I translated them as best I could to Brooklyn. Then I went back to Bay Ridge in daylight and noted the major landmarks. I walked some streets, went into a couple of stores. Studied the clothes, the gestures, the walks. I imagined how it would feel to burn up, all caged energy, with no outlet but the dance floor and the rituals of Saturday night. Finally, I wrote it all up. And presented it as fact.

There was no excuse for it. At the time, if cornered, I would doubtless have produced some high-flown waffle about Alternative Realities, tried to argue that writing didn't have to be true to be, at some level, real. But, of course, I would have been full of it. I knew the rules of magazine reporting, and I knew that I was breaking them. Bluntly put, I cheated.

Oddly, no one seemed to notice. Or, if they did, they failed to confront me. Clay Felker still showed small enthusiasm for the project, it's true, and if not for James McMullan's illustrations, the piece might never have seen daylight. In the end, though, it struggled into print.

By then it was June, and certain compromises had been reached. My own title, "Another Saturday Night," had become "Tribal Rites of the New Saturday Night," and an introductory note was appended, in my name, insisting that every word in the story was the gospel truth.

On the Monday morning that the article hit the stands, I left my apartment early and didn't return till after lunch. When I got home, the lady I was living with told me that I'd had a mysterious phone call. "Some guy called Rabbi Stigfeld," she said. Suspecting that he was calling to hustle a contribution to Jewish causes, she had stonewalled by telling him that I was asleep in a pool of my own vomit at the foot of the bed and couldn't come to the phone. "I got you off the hook," she told me proudly.

It took a little thought to work out that Rabbi Stigfeld was, in fact, Robert Stigwood, the producer, whom I knew quite well. At that juncture, he was probably best known in rock and theater – he managed the Bee Gees, and had produced *Jesus Christ Super-*

star – but had recently branched out into films. When he called me back, he told me that he'd read my Bay Ridge story, and would I care to pop 'round for tea?

This was unexpected, to put it mildly. Magazine writers, in those gauche days, hadn't yet learned to think of their stories as potential films. When I ambled over to Stigwood's place, however, I found him fat with deals. It turned out that he had recently signed a three-picture deal with John Travolta, who was then best known as Vinnie Barbarino, the dim-witted Sweathog on TV's *Welcome Back, Kotter*. The first of these was to be *Grease*; and my Saturday-night story, Stigwood felt, was tailor-made for the second.

I didn't argue with the man. I didn't even complain when

Manero, *Tribal Rites of the New Saturday Night* turned into *Saturday Night Fever*. Bizarrely, I had the nerve to feel wronged.

From then on, I lost control of my creation. Or rather, the creation ceased to be mine. When filming began, I kept away from the set, partly not to intrude, and partly to avoid John Travolta.

From his persona in *Welcome Back, Kotter*, I assumed he was genuine Brooklyn, born and bred, and therefore would see right through me. By the time I realized that he actually came from a genteel suburb in Jersey and was no more *echt* disco than I was, it was too late: I'd dealt myself out.

Saturday Night Fever had its premiere on Pearl Harbor

It would be an hour before anyone saw me [at Odyssey], and during that time I concentrated on every detail of their behavior I could. Their whole way of dancing, moving, conversing, relating to their girls, was ritualistic. It had its set rules. –John Travolta

he served me stale chocolate-chip cookies with my tea. As best I can recall, all I said was, "That sounds feasible."

Shortly afterward, I traveled down to Texas, where I rented a hunter's cabin, way back in the woods near Llano. For the next six weeks, I sat under a spreading shade tree, surrounded by cow chips and flies, pounding out a screenplay about mean streets and discos. I hadn't a clue how to write for films, but dumb ignorance had been my sleeve card all through this enterprise, and there seemed no good reason to change tacks now.

This time, though, I'd overpushed my luck. According to the late Don Simpson, then a Hollywood fledgling, my draft script was quite likely the worst in movie history: "The alpha and omega of turkeys." So I was quietly removed from the firing line, and Norman Wexler, who'd won Oscar nominations for *Serpico* and *Joe*, took over. Vincent became Tony

Day, 1977, at Grauman's Chinese Theater. A fleet of limousines was laid on to convoy the main protagonists down Hollywood Boulevard and dump them at the feet of their adoring fans. Since my only adoring fan had just tossed a microwave at my head, I went as the date of Yvonne Elliman, who sang "If I Can't Have You" on the film's soundtrack. Exactly as I'd seen it on countless newsreels, we stepped out into a barrage of flashbulbs, while a man with the vowel-chewing delivery of a boxing announcer bellowed out our names. "MISS EEEVONNNA ELLLEEEMAAAN," he intoned, then glanced at me and hastily checked his name card.

"Who are you?" he demanded.

"I wrote the story."

"Oh." For a moment the emcee looked blank. Then he regathered his forces. "MISS EEEVONNNA ELLEEEMAAN," he announced again. "And acquaintance."

The film itself made only a small impression on me. I could see that it was competently made, and John Travolta was superb, but it all seemed oddly hackneyed – a rehashed "problem teenagers" flick from the Fifties, updated with four-letter words and gang bangs.

Afterward, as I clawed my way through the crush outside the theater, I felt more panic than elation. "Fevermania," as it would soon be labeled, was something I'd never bargained for. Watching the hysteria around me, it seemed like a rogue chemical reaction I had triggered by chance that was now running off with me.

Dimly, I already sensed that this would change everything. From here on, I was going to be stuck with another self – a virtual stranger, defined by *Fever*, who'd hog the limelight and try to take me over. I didn't think we would get along.

Returning to New York, I went back to work – specifically, to another story for *New York*. This time around, again with Tu Sweet's assistance, I was going to spend twenty-four hours on Forty-second Street. I planned to dive in blind, without preconceptions. If a story came up, I'd grab it. And if it didn't, no matter, I'd make one up.

That was the idea, anyway. But something odd happened. When I reached the Deuce, people talked to me. Perhaps, having nothing to lose, they couldn't be bothered to put up defenses; or perhaps I had learned something about listening. Either way, I was able to make the kind of connections that had eluded me in Bay Ridge.

First, there was a dealer selling lactose as cocaine, then a drugstore cowboy selling sex, then a street preacher called Sister Pearl. Almost without my prompting, they poured out their stories. And what they told me was so vastly more interesting, so much wilder and weirder and more heartbreaking than anything I might have invented that I could do nothing but shut up and marvel, then slouch off to the nearest gift shop, where I bought myself one notebook and one refillable pen.

True stories proved highly addictive. Once I'd consumed this first batch, I had to have another, and another. The habit grew so compulsive that it quickly blocked out all other concerns. As a result, I missed the full force of Fevermania.

I did notice that a surprising number of people had taken to hugging me and calling me Nickie, and that I was now referred to in the tabloids as Fever Man Cohn. I also noticed that large checks had started rolling in. This was gratifying, but also troubling. I was painfully aware that everything *Fever* brought me was shabbily come by. That knowledge, more and more, came to eat me up. But I failed to return the checks even so.

Not that *I* mattered now, in any case. *Fever* had taken on a life of its own. 2001 Odyssey, and "Staying Alive," and Travolta's white suit, above all, with the tight vest and billowing flared trousers, and his right hand pointing to the stars – these had entered pop mythology, embedding themselves in the collective memory, until they came, for many, to define a whole decade.

Even ten or fifteen years afterwards, whenever the Seventies were evoked, it was a safe bet that someone would strike a disco pose and morph, Bee Gees–style, into a singing mouse. And now, of course, the whole Seventies machinery has cranked up again. The Seventies are sexy, in fashion, in rock and in films like *Boogie Nights*.

Mostly this phenomenon strikes me as being nothing more profound than fashionable hype. Each decade goes through a similar process of regurgitation, and it always boils down to the same core: a shiny, new phrase for making money.

What is genuine, however, is the staying power of *Saturday Night Fever* itself – or rather the power of its mystique. This doesn't stem, Lord knows, from my story. Nor, to judge from the brief snatches that sometimes flash past me on TV, has the film worn well. But the central figure, whether he's called Vincent or Tony Manero, still resonates. Much of that is because of Travolta, of course. Nonetheless, I keep returning to that first night outside 2001 Odyssey, and the figure in the doorway, standing under the neon light. The grace in him, and the hunger. All that passion, and no place to let it loose but here, in this nowhere club, on this nothing dance floor, where no one would ever know. Or would they?

That figure never fades. He was in Derry, and in London, and again in Bay Ridge. And he's still out there, somewhere or other, in his own neighborhood, caught in his own set of traps. Just staying alive.

punk primitive
by billy altman

I CAN STILL SEE the headline on the London tabloid that greeted me as I arrived at Heathrow Airport from New York City on December 2, 1976. THE FILTH AND THE FURY, screamed the banner on the *Daily Mirror*. As I passed the newsstand, I stopped dead in my tracks. What the hell was this basically unknown punk band, the Sex Pistols, doing on the front page of a big city's newspaper?

Picking it up, I learned that the snotty foursome had apparently ruffled just about every prim-and-proper feather in the whole bloody United Kingdom by using (to quote young Master Rotten himself) a compendium of "rude" words – "shit," "fuck" and "bastard," to be precise – during the final seconds of a (horrors!) live, uncensored interview with British TV talk-show host Bill Grundy the previous day.

The Pistols had been there to plug their just-released debut single, "Anarchy in the U.K.," and as I read of the chain reaction of outrage detonating all over the country – from the cab driver who kicked in the screen of his TV to prevent his son from hearing any more of "this sort of muck" to the refusal by a group of elderly women who worked as record packers at an EMI pressing plant to take part in any further manufacturing of the Sex Pistols record (stuff *this* in your pic sleeve!) – I couldn't help but marvel at just how quickly and effectively the Sex Pistols had executed their mission.

That their appearance was reportedly a last-minute replacement for Queen only made it that much more bizarre, and somehow perfectly fitting. After all, hadn't Queen originally been hyped as "British rock in the royal tradition"? And weren't the Pistols – the budding (perhaps oozing was more like it) symbols of this entire nihilistic punk-rock "movement" – the best practical joke imaginable to play on that same bloated, decrepit tradition? It certainly seemed so to me, but then I suppose I *was* prejudiced.

Back in 1973, while attending the State University of New York at Buffalo, I'd edited and published my own fanzine – called, appropriately enough, *Punk*. To be honest, the working title had been *The Shakin' Street Gazette* – in honor of the 1970 MC5 song written and sung by guitarist Fred "Sonic" Smith, a song that a bunch of us rock & roll lunatics in Western New York had adopted as an unofficial theme song and rallying cry. ("Shakin' Street, it's got that beat/Shakin' Street, where all the kids meet/Shakin' Street, it's got that sound/Shakin' Street, you gotta get down.")

The 'zine was subsidized, I might add, by the university itself; I'd been working as the school newspaper's music editor for several years and had finally talked our unsuspecting editor in chief into letting me put together a rock & roll supplement. Just as we were finishing up the debut issue, my co-conspirator in this journalistic caper, Joe Fernbacher, decided to call my bluff. "Look," he said, "we've got articles on Iggy and the Stooges, the Sonics, the Bubble Puppy, professional wrestling, Don Ho and Brian Wilson being separated at birth, a cover story on the Seeds. *Shakin' Street Gazette*'s okay, but if we had any guts we'd just call it what it really is, a magazine for punks like us: *Punk Magazine*."

Joe had a point, and it wasn't just the fact that he outweighed me, 300 pounds to 150 (they didn't call him "El Mono" for nothing), that helped drive it home. The term "punk" had been wafting through rock criticism for some time, mostly in the pages of Detroit's gleefully irreverent *Creem*, where writers like Lester Bangs, Dave Marsh and R. Meltzer were helping articulate an aesthetic based on the preference for ranking attitude far ahead of what pioneer Meltzer called "mere music." If ever there was a time when rock & roll needed more attitude and less "mere," it was the early Seventies.

Yeah, sure, the Sixties counterculture had flopped, Woodstock had turned into Altamont, the dream was over, blah blah blah. But, having determined at some point during the tumult and the shouting that rock & roll wasn't going to change the world but could indeed save your life (thank you, Lou Reed), there were those of us looking around and asking, "Is

Original Pistols bassist Glen Matlock keeps his mind on the music while Johnny Rotten takes center stage *(from left)*

that all there is?" (Thank you, Peggy Lee.) As we watched our brothers and sisters basically packing in whatever they thought "it" had been in the first place and readying themselves to become "happy idiots and struggle for the legal tender" (thank you, Jackson Browne), there were those of us who came to the conclusion that if we didn't want a world soundtracked by, in one ear, the bland sounds of country rock, and in the other, the soulless strains of prog rock, we'd better quit griping and do something about it.

Ergo, the punk attitude, which in 1973 meant championing current music that was considered either beyond the fringe (the Stooges, Captain Beefheart, the New York Dolls) or below our supposed generational line (Black Sabbath, Alice Cooper, Blue Öyster Cult). There was also nostalgia for years like 1966, when a British Invasion–inspired, triumph-of-the-will spirit enabled garage groups who could barely play three chords (? and the Mysterians) – if that many (yea, Seeds) – to somehow triumph, if only for the duration of one side of a single. (The Seeds, bless their chaotic souls, though they knew only two chords, had somehow made five – count 'em – whole albums!)

Collectively, this was the music that had stuck to our viscera. Music that, especially considered within the dead zone that was the early Seventies, embodied the essence of what it was that made us love rock & roll in the first place: the unruly, incorrigible sound of freedom flashing.

So it was that Buffalo's *Punk Magazine* ("The Curse of the Metaverse") reared its ugly little head in May of 1973. In my editor's note I wrote the following Charles Foster Kane–styled "statement of principles": "Wimps take heed! You will find this tabloid boring, offensive, possibly insulting. And that's just the way we want it. The legions are now forming, and soon all us rockers will bury you beneath your pile of James Taylor, Cat Stevens, Grateful Dead and Moody Blues records. 'Cause the time is now and we're seizing it while most of you nod out." And we meant it, man.

To make a long story short, *Punk*'s notoriety led to my being invited to the first- (and last-) ever rock critic convention, held in Memphis, Tennessee, that summer (one of many highlights: They take us over to Graceland – Elvis isn't home – but Bangs and Meltzer nonetheless commemorate the occasion by pissing through the front gate). Before I knew it I was a nationally published rock critic, even though all that writing about rock & roll "professionally" in those days meant was that you were getting printed but hardly getting paid. (Did I say "those days"? Sorry.)

By the next fall, I finally amassed enough credits to graduate (last class I took: golf), with (believe it or not) an actual six-years-in-the-making Bachelor of Arts degree in pop music and no job prospects. I decided to move back to my hometown, New York City, to seek my fame (ha) and fortune (double ha) as a rock writer. While we managed to put out only one more issue of *Punk* – featuring such literary opuses as "Blue Cheer – An American Tragedy," "Hoyt Wilhelm – Man or Myth" and "A Dream Date With Wild Man Fischer," plus contributions from both Bangs and Meltzer, who became lifelong friends (not long enough, either, Lester) – I was damned proud to have been one of the first ones to make it to the front lines. (One of my fondest memories from 1974: handing a copy to Meltzer's pal Patti Smith, who was performing her readings/concerts around town, and running into her a week later. "Thanks for the magazine," she said. "I read *every word*.")

I felt prouder still over the next few years. At dark-lit recruiting stations like Max's Kansas City and CBGB, folks like Ms. Smith, the Dolls and the Dictators (the first group, by the way, to use the word "punk" on a record – 1975's *Go Girl Crazy*) and their younger cousins, Blondie, Television, Talking Heads and (last but eternally not least) the Ramones, started filling the trenches and drawing more and more volunteers from the ranks of rock & roll's disenfranchised for the guerrilla war at hand. Along the way, a couple of local brats named John Holmstrom and Legs McNeil had started up another rag called *Punk*, which, as I told them (at a meeting at the White Horse Tavern in the West Village that Meltzer had arranged), was okay by me – even if they expressed a distressing fondness for the Fonz from *Happy Days* (hey, any black leather jacket in a storm).

By then – 1976 – I'd become an almost legit, working rock-writing stiff. On the strength of recommendations from ex-editors Bangs and Marsh, I'd joined the staff of *Creem* as Record Review Editor and New York Editor (New York office: my living room). It was in that capacity that I found myself on that aforementioned plane headed to Merrie Olde, etc.

Of course, timing is everything, and as for what I was doing in England when all the Pistols stuff broke . . . well, it just so happened that the Pistols' label, EMI, had flown over a trio of American rock journalists – *Hit Parader*'s Lisa Robinson, *Circus*'s Steve Demorest and myself – to do stories on another one of their acts, Steve Harley, leader of Cockney Rebel. Like numerous other early-to-mid-Seventies English performers (Slade, T. Rex, Roxy Music), Harley had a sizable following at home – his 1975 single, "Make Me Smile (Come Up and See Me)," had been a Number One U.K. hit – but hadn't been able to crack the U.S. market. EMI was determined to make that happen, and to that end was bribing our respective magazines with a press junket to London to meet Stevie and watch him perform a sold-out show at the Hammersmith Odeon.

Of course, our pooled agenda changed significantly once the Pistols "problem" developed. We first fulfilled obligations: sit-down interviews with Harley and attending his concert (the guy wasn't bad, kind of a workingman's Bowie, with a little Dylan thrown in). Then we managed to talk the cheery EMI publicity bloke (Roger something) into motoring us up to Manchester for what was, it was fast turning out, one of the few Sex Pistols shows on their Anarchy in the U.K. tour that hadn't been canceled due to "public outcry" (read: nervous-Nellie promoters and club owners fearful of a white riot breaking out in their yard).

Speaking of white riots, it was the then-unsigned Clash who opened the show that Thursday night at a club called the Electric Circus, presumably named after the old New York hippie haven on St. Mark's Place, and indeed looked like a place that had lain dormant since the Day-Glo–hazed days of Boone's Farm and downs – right down to a bona fide, fully functional light show projected on the back wall. Add to that image a gangly batch of spike-haired, safety-pinned, torn-T-shirted, bondage-paraphernalia-accessoried kids pogoing on the dance floor, and the entire scene became so surreal I was tempted to stick myself with one of those safety pins just to see if this was actually happening or whether it was only that some long-ago-ingested drugs were finally kicking in.

Once the Clash started playing, though, I knew something was happening, and, yes, Mr. Jones, I certainly *did* know what it was. Sheer, unadulterated rock & roll energy, dispensed with such freneticism that I could almost see the sparks flying off Joe Strummer as he sang "I'm So Bored With the U.S.A." (the only words I could make out during the entire set; not that it mattered). Indeed, the Clash as an entity looked and sounded like electroshock therapy in progress – all jerks, jumps and leaps, as if every guitar chord and microphone were in live-wire stun mode. Which, in a word, described their set: stunning.

The Clash was followed by ex-Dolls Johnny Thunders's and Jerry Nolan's Heartbreakers, and it was during their ragged-but-right performance that the natives started getting restless. Soon up-and-down pogoing had devolved into side-to-side slamming ("moshing" to you younger folk). There were numerous exhibitions of the emerging British punk tradition of "gobbing" – taking a healthy swig of beer, wine, phlegm or bile and expectorating in the direction of the stage. As things got wetter and wilder, the journalist (as well as the survivalist) in me decided to trek upstairs to the club's deserted balcony, and it was from there that I witnessed the Sex Pistols in all their *retch-ed* glory.

Being above the fray afforded me the opportunity to see something I'd never seen before (or since, for that matter) at a music show. Almost the instant the Pistols began performing, the audience began moving *away* from the stage rather than toward it. Hanging from the mike stand in his ripped clothes, glaring bug-eyed at everyone, spewing out the invective-filled lyrics of songs like "Liar" and "Pretty Vacant," Johnny Rotten looked and sounded like the blitzkrieg-bopped orphan of rock & roll – an irradiated musical mutant lurching out, daring all to feel his disease. Guitarist Steve Jones was a swirling dynamo of leaps, splits and raunchy power chords, while Paul Cook, wearing a Dickensian street-urchin smirk, nonchalantly bashed away at his drum kit. From the left side of the stage came the only real hint of melody in the band's music, courtesy of bass player Glen Matlock, who was clearly the point person in the group's instrumental sound and who, between that musicality and his Bay City Rollers–ish neat looks, gave the band an ironic pop sheen.

That irony hit home about midway through the Pistols' set when the gobbing and between-song heckling ("Piss off!" "You jerks are just loud!") suddenly gave way to a barrage of solid rather than liquid floor-to-stage projectiles – until Matlock got hit square in the chest with an empty Grolsch bottle (thickest one on the market at the time). The Pistols finished the song, then all marched to the lip of the stage. "You fuckin' cunts," yelled Rotten, "throwin' things in the dark." "You guys suck, the Who are great," replied someone, and with that, Jones cocked his guitar and zoomed into the intro from the old Who song, "Substitute," which the band proceeded to then demolish faster than you can say Baba O'Riley. Before this forty-odd minute exercise in two-way-street abuse was over, the Pistols careened their way through a few more songs, including "God Save the Queen," which, with Matlock's bouncy bass line leading the way, had me humming the "no future" line all the way back to the U.S. a few days later.

Of course, by the time the Pistols finally made it over here for their one fateful U.S. tour, Matlock was long gone, replaced by (as the *New York Times* called him) Mr. Vicious – a symbol, it seemed, of the smart-ass Pistols committing the dumbest showbiz mistake of all: believing their own hype. And when, you might ask, did this old soldier know the punk wars were really over? The first time I heard the Police, or the Knack?

No, it was actually in January 1978, right after the Pistols had announced their breakup following the infamous "Ever had the feeling you've been cheated?" show in San Francisco. But it wasn't the Pistols' official demise that clinched it for me. A few days later, I walked into CBGB and who should I see but *NME* photographer Joe Stevens, back from the Pistols tour, sitting quietly at a table downing a beer with none other than Johnny Rotten himself. Rotten had flown to New York and was holing up at Joe's place.

Here he was, the most famous celebrity in punk, going completely unrecognized. I looked around the half-empty club and realized precisely why that was. You see, there were at least two dozen people in the place who looked exactly like him. ⊕

a death in the family
by mikal gilmore

In the autumn of 1976, I learned that ROLLING STONE accepted an article of mine for publication. I was elated. Then, about a week later, I learned something horrible, something that killed the elation: My older brother Gary Gilmore was going to be put to death by a firing squad in Utah. It didn't look like there was much that could stop it, and I didn't know if I could live with what that meant.

In early November of 1976 my mother told me that Gary had withdrawn his rights of appeal from Utah's legal system and was requesting that the courts and prison enforce his death sentence as soon as possible. I remember feeling stunned and angry, and I remember thinking that nothing would ever be the same. Not for myself, not for my family, maybe even not for the nation around me.

Shortly after I heard about Gary's wish to be executed, I told my editor at ROLLING STONE, Ben Fong-Torres, that Gary was my brother. By this time, Gary Gilmore was a daily name in nationwide headlines, and I felt that the magazine had a right to know that I was his brother. Fong-Torres, who had lost a brother of his own through violence, was extremely sympathetic and supportive during the period that followed, and he gave me the opportunity to write about my experience of Gary's execution for the magazine. To be honest, not everybody who worked at ROLLING STONE back in 1977 thought it was such a great idea to run this story, and I could understand their misgivings: After all, what would be the point of publishing one man's apology for his murderous and suicidal brother?

JULY 30, 1976, wasn't any different, just another Friday night that left me drained. *The Wild Bunch,* Sam Peckinpah's genuflection to violence and honor, was on TV, and as I settled back on the couch to half-watch it, I picked up the late edition of the *Oregonian.* I almost passed over a page-two item headlined OREGON MAN HELD IN UTAH SLAYINGS, but instinctively I began to read it. "Gary Mark Gilmore, thirty-five, was charged with the murders of two young clerks shot during the holdup of a service station and a motel. . . ." I read on – in a daze – about how Gary had been arrested for killing Max Jensen and Ben Bushnell on two consecutive nights in July. Both men were Mormons, about the same age as I, and both left wives and infant children behind.

The Gilmore family, before Mikal was born, circa 1950: father Frank Sr., mother Bessie, younger brother Gaylen, middle brother Gary and oldest brother Frank Jr. *(clockwise from top left)*

I let the paper fall to the floor, caught my face in my hands and tried to brace the nausea that built inside. One of my greatest fears had come to pass: My brother Gary had murdered.

I sat on my couch the rest of the night, alternately staring at *The Wild Bunch* and rereading the sketchy account. I felt shame, remorse, guilt . . . and rage. It could've been *me,* I thought, the victim of some senseless robbery.

The next day, I went to visit my mother in Milwaukie, six miles away from my house in Portland. I had no way of knowing whether she had read the news except to call and ask, which seemed too distant and cold. It turned out that she had known of the killings for more than a week, but couldn't bring herself to tell me. In tears, she asked: "Can you imagine what it feels like to mother a son whom you love that deprives two other mothers of *their* sons?"

Nine weeks later, she called me on the night of Gary's sentencing, October 7, to tell me that he had received the death penalty. I was stunned, but I found myself echoing my friends' consolations: "Mother," I said, "they haven't executed anybody in this country for ten years and they aren't about to start with Gary." Still, nausea rushed through me as I hung up the phone. All I could see that night was Gary's face, those bloodshot eyes rushing toward me like some red avalanche.

The first I heard of Gary's desire to be executed was on November 8, a week after his request. I was furious. "The fool!" I screamed. "Doesn't he know he's throwing loaded dice? In Utah they *will* kill him if he pushes it." My mother tried to calm me, explaining that just that day – the 8th – Gary's original attorneys had filed for a stay – against his protests – and the Utah Supreme Court had granted one.

The next day I decided it was time to confront Gary. I put a call through to Draper Prison. To my amazement, Gary was on the phone within two minutes.

Our first few exchanges were polite but tentative. Gary grew impatient quickly. "Something on your mind?"

"Gary, are you serious about this?"

"What do you think?"

"I don't know."

"That's right. You don't. You never knew me." Gary had thrown a hurdle I couldn't leap, one he was entitled to. I was at a loss for a reply. "Look," he continued, a softer tone to his voice, "I'm not trying to be mean to you, but this thing's going to happen one way or the other; there's nothing you can do to stop it and I don't particularly want you to like me. It'll be easier for me if you don't. It seems like the only time we ever talk to each other is around the time of somebody's death. And now it's mine."

I hadn't counted on Gary taking the offensive. I felt helpless against it. "What about Mother?" was all I could reach for.

"Well, I want to see Mother before this goes down. I want to see all of you. Maybe that will make it easier. But I *am* serious about this, and I don't want you or anybody else to interfere. It's totally my affair. I killed two men, the court sentenced me to die and now I'm accepting that sentence. I don't want to spend the rest of my life on trial or in a prison. I've lost my freedom. I lost it a long time ago. Now I'm just going to make them finish the job they started twenty years ago."

I tried to stifle a cry. "What's wrong?" asked Gary.

"It's hard to hear this stuff from somebody you love –"

"Hey, I don't need to hear that," Gary broke in. "I won't let anything hurt me anymore and I don't want you to think I'm some 'sensitive' artist because I drew pictures or wrote poems. I killed – in cold blood." A guard told Gary his time was up.

I SAT DOWN and wrote Gary a long letter. I wrote him that whatever choice I made, it was a matter of love, an issue between him and me, and not the courts or newspapers. I outlined my belief that redemption was more possible in the choice of life over death, and confessed that for years he'd frightened and confused me because of his violent whims. If time enough existed, I wanted to lift that barrier.

That afternoon, when I visited Gary at the prison, he read my letter quietly, pensively, and when he was finished, he cried. Then he managed a smile. "Well put," he said. "Are you familiar with Nietzsche? He once wrote that a time comes when a man should rise to meet the occasion. That's what I'm trying to do, Mikal. . . . Look," he said, suddenly changing the subject, "I was thinking about what I said, about 'where were you.' I realized that was unfair. I wasn't around much when you were a kid. I don't hate you, although I've tried to act that way lately. You're my brother. I know what that means. I've been angry with you, but I've never hated you."

I forced myself to ask the one question I'd been trying to ask all along: "What would you do if I tried to stop this?"

He winced. "I don't want you to do that," he said evenly.

"That doesn't answer my question."

"Please don't."

"Gary, what would you do? All you've said is that you wanted the sentence of the court carried out. What if that sentence were commuted?"

"I'd kill myself. Look, I'm not watched that closely in this place, no matter what you hear. I could've killed myself any time in the last two weeks, but I don't want to do that. You see, I want some good to come from all of this. If I commit suicide, then I can't be a donor – to people who have more right to life than I do – and my whole will could become suspect. . . . Besides, if a person's dumb enough to murder and get caught, then he shouldn't snivel about what he gets. I don't think death will be anything new or frightening for me. I think I've been there before."

We talked for hours, or rather Gary talked. I'd already missed a flight back home and had forgotten about the person waiting out in the parking lot for me. But this was the first real communication we'd shared in years; neither of us wanted to let go.

A friend told me that week that if we are confronted with a choice between life and death and choose anything short of life, then we choose short of humanity. That made it all seem so clear-cut. I wrestled with the decision and finally realized that I couldn't choose life for Gary, and he wouldn't. He had worked out what he reasoned to be some means of atonement. Eventually the Utah death penalty statute will be judged either constitutional or unconstitutional. Perhaps Gary was to be executed under an illegal law. I raised all those arguments with him. They didn't faze him. He wanted death, his final scenario of redemption, his final release from the law. To Gary, the greatest irony was that the law – which in his eyes had always sought to break him – finally wanted to save him when he no longer wanted salvation. In order to beat the law, he had to lose everything – everything but his own unswerving definition of dignity.

I couldn't reason with that, I couldn't change that. And in the end, I couldn't take it away from him.

ON SATURDAY, January 15, 1977, I visited Gary for the last time. By that time, camera crews were camped all over the grounds of Draper, preparing for the finale. During our previous meetings that week, Gary had always opened with some friendly remarks, a joke or even a handstand. Today, however, he seemed slightly nervous, although he denied it. "Naw, the noise in this place gets to me sometimes, but I'm as cool as a cucumber," he said, holding up a steady hand. But the muscles in his wrists and arms were discernibly tense. He started to show me letters and pictures he'd received, mostly from children and teenage girls. He said he always tried to answer the ones from kids first, and then he read one from a boy who claimed to be eight years old: "I hope they put you someplace and make you live forever for what you did. You have no right to die. With all the malice in my heart, (name)."

"Man, that one shook me up for a long time," he said.

I asked him if he'd replied to it. "Yeah, I wrote, 'You're too young to have malice in your heart. I had it in mine at a young age and look what it did for me.' "

He had a guard bring a book Johnny Cash had sent. It was his autobiography, *The Man in Black,* which Gary wanted left with Mother.

"I'd really like to give you something or leave something for you. Why don't you let me leave you some money? Everybody needs money." I tried to decline and suggested that he give it to the Bushnell and Jensen families. "There's no way money can buy back what I did to those people," he said, shaking his head.

Gary's eyes nervously scanned the letters and pictures in front of him, finally falling on one that made him smile. He held it up. A picture of his girlfriend, Nicole. "She's pretty, isn't she?" I agreed. "I look at this picture every day. I took it myself; it's the one that I made that drawing from. Would you like to have it?"

I was touched, and said I would be pleased to have it. We talked about his drawings and I asked if he wanted them turned over to anybody in particular. "No. You can keep those, sell them, give them away, whatever you want. You can even publish them. I'd like to have that one of the old shoe printed someplace. I always considered that my self-portrait – an old empty prison shoe."

At that point, Warden Samuel Smith entered Gary's room. They discussed whether Gary would have to wear a hood. I put the phone down. Minutes passed.

I rapped on the glass and told Gary I would have to leave soon and asked if the warden would allow us a final handshake. Gary grasped my hand, squeezed tight and said, "Well, I guess this is it." He leaned over and kissed me on the cheek. "See you in the darkness beyond."

I pulled my eyes away from his. I knew I couldn't stop crying at that point, and I didn't want him to see it. "Are you okay?" he asked. I bit my lip and nodded. A guard handed me the book and picture of Nicole and started to walk with me to the rolling bar doors. Gary watched me pass through them. "Give my love to Mom," he called. "And put on some weight. You're still too skinny."

The guard walked with me through the two fence gates and patted me on the back as I left. "Take it easy, fella," he said.

On Monday morning, January 17, Gary met his firing squad. I was with my mother and brother and girlfriend when it happened. Just moments before, we had seen the morning newspaper with the headline EXECUTION STAYED, and turned on *Good Morning America* for more information. They announced that Gary was dead. No words could adequately express our feelings that morning, the seesawing of our emotions. We were braced for anything but that final twist. When I left later, photographers were gathered around the trailer-court gate, aiming at my mother's tiny trailer.

For millions, Gary provided a focus for revenge, while for others he fulfilled the American dream of hero and madman, saint and outlaw. Gary was a network of contradictions. He was a man who loved his mother with a childlike fervor and who protected children and dogs. But he was also a man who discarded opportunities and, in rage, could be violent and could kill.

If Gary was one of society's losers, then he was also one of its losses; a fine line separates the role of the breaker from the broken and Gary crossed that line many times. It's tempting to seek a lesson from this episode. The only one I can find in the aftermath is what seems to be the most obvious of all: that life is all we have, and we should never deprive others of its certainty. And murder and execution are not the only ways in which we kill. ⊕

cancerous cells will later settle in his brain, bringing about his death in 1981.

10 Elijah Blue Allman is born to Gregg Allman and Cher.

12 Protesting the construction of a gymnasium on the site where four students were killed in 1970, 194 Kent State demonstrators are arrested without incident.

13 Even in a New York City blackout, the shows must go on: Boz Scaggs, cut short in the middle of "Full Lock Power Slide" at Avery Fisher Hall, sits down on the edge of the stage in the beams of ushers' flashlights and promises to reschedule. At the Bottom Line, NRBQ continues acoustically, and the Happy Trails Dance Band does the same at the Lone Star nightclub where, ironically, an annual party held by Con Edison, the city's power company, had just ended.

14 The Sex Pistols perform "Pretty Vacant" on *Top of the Pops,* marking their return to British television for the first time since appearing on *Today* with host Bill Grundy in Dec. 1976.

23 Led Zeppelin drummer John Bonham, manager Peter Grant and two Led Zeppelin employees are implicated in the savage backstage beating of one of Bill Graham's production employees in Oakland. They are later charged and heavily fined.

26 Four days after the release of his album *My Aim Is True* on the small U.K. upstart label Stiff, Elvis Costello is fined for performing on the street outside London's Hilton Hotel, where an international conference is being held by CBS Records. The misdemeanor proves worthwhile, as he soon signs with the larger label.

29 Punk is the fall's most distinctive fashion arrival, says *Women's Wear Daily.*

1977 AUGUST

3 Revelations of a 25-year program of secret CIA-sponsored mind-control research involving drugs, hypnosis and other behavior-controlling devices are made public. CIA director Stansfield Turner admits the agency's role in such studies, which he reveals took place in over 80 institutions, 44 of which were universities. The next day Turner is granted expanded powers, including control over his own budget, over two new intelligence

before out was in
by patrick pacheco

ON A JANUARY day in 1977, the phone rang in my cubicle at *After Dark* magazine. Arnold Schwarzenegger was calling – and he was very upset.

"Patrick, this is terrible," he said, in heavily accented English. "One of the pictures in the magazine shows my penis. I did not approve this picture."

When Schwarzenegger had come into the offices of *After Dark* on Manhattan's Columbus Circle to approve the layout, he was an Austrian bodybuilder who was just then breaking into film, starring in George Butler's documentary *Pumping Iron* and Bob Rafelson's movie *Stay Hungry.* He was charming and ambitious, then in the midst of a press blitz calculated to whisk him out of the rather freakish world of bodybuilding and into the New York social spin. The campaign featured stories about him in all the New York fashion and arts magazines, including *After Dark,* which, by virtue of its early championing of Bette Midler, had earned the cachet of being something of a star-launcher.

I picked up a copy of the February 1977 issue of *After Dark* and looked at the beautiful cover photo of a superbuffed Arnold clad only in a pair of black briefs, his head pensively cradled in his hand. There on page forty-one, among a collage of photos of preening, pumping bodybuilders, was a small picture of the future superstar and Kennedy in-law drying off in a locker room. And there, just peeking out from beneath the white towel, was the tip of the offending wienerwurst.

I calmly explained to Arnold that he had indeed approved the spread. "I didn't really notice it," I said, assuring him that the candid, unstudied pose robbed the picture of any salaciousness. Besides, male frontal nudity wasn't all that shocking in those days, certainly not in *After Dark.* "I don't think you have anything to be worried about."

Arnold sounded assuaged. "Oh, well, if you didn't notice it, and I didn't notice it, maybe no one else will either," he said.

Not likely, I thought. Not with our readers.

In fact, with that issue, *After Dark* magazine would hit the peak of its twelve-year run as a national magazine of entertainment, as it then billed itself, reaching a paid circulation of about 73,000 national subscribers with a readership five times that. The vast majority of those readers, as the advertising demographics read, were urban single men in their thirties and forties, with a high median income, who spent a lot of money on grooming aids, clothes, going to theater and movies and traveling to exotic places. In other words, gay. But the particular strength of the publication, one that would doom it later, was its reputation for defining a certain urban gay aesthetic without actually coming out and saying it – successfully walking that thin line throughout much of the Seventies when "don't ask, don't tell" was the motto of a sizable segment of homosexual men.

Led by editor William Como, a rather melodramatic queen given to wearing outsized jewelry, strong cologne and shirts unbuttoned to the navel, the staff – young, gay and underpaid – was used to handsome, buff young men like Schwarzenegger coming through the door looking for exposure. And exposure of both talent and flesh was something we specialized in. Profiles of emerging stars Bette Midler, Peter Allen and others like them, and tributes to legends such as Joan Crawford and Ava Gardner, were mixed among pages largely devoted to covering contemporary New York culture (*The Rocky Horror Picture Show*) and the gay-lifestyle scene ("The Disco Craze!"). Readers could also count on beautiful, tasteful pictures of naked or nearly naked men – but always with shots of women strategically placed to allay any anxiety such overt displays of homoeroticism might arouse in readers or advertisers.

Gay liberation, which had begun with the Stonewall riots in June of 1969, had brought the homosexual revolution out of the closet and into the streets, but only among a flying wedge of activists and freethinkers. There was, at the same time, a large contingent of more conservative gay men who had made their way from farms and small

THE NATIONAL MAGAZINE OF ENTERTAINMENT
FEBRUARY 1977

$1.50

AFTER DARK

**LEONARD COHEN
GINGER ROGERS
DINA MERRILL
GEORGE GRIZZARD**

**BODYBUILDING:
THE NEW
PERFORMING ART**

**ARNOLD
SCHWARZENEGGER**

towns across America to urban centers like San Francisco, Los Angeles and New York. Many within this group were open about their sexuality with close friends, usually other gays, but for both professional and personal reasons they kept it hidden from others – straight friends, family and business associates. They frequented gay bars, discos and cabarets; lit candles before such gay icons as Liza Minnelli, Barbra Streisand and Diana Ross; loved theater, ballet and opera; made a priority of seeing films by Luchino Visconti, John Schlesinger and Ken Russell; and traveled to gay tourist meccas such as Fire Island, Key West and Provincetown.

After Dark, reflecting the sexual zeitgeist of the decade as it progressed from the political upheavals of the Sixties into a hedonistic era when beauty, sexual pleasure and hip awareness were valued, quickly caught on with this group. New York back then resembled nothing less than a gigantic masked ball of fluid identity, recreational drugs and casual sex, which would reach its apogee at the end of the decade at Studio 54. *After Dark* captured the ongoing party with irreverence and eroticism coyly packaged so that you could leave the magazine on the coffee table of your studio apartment, telegraphing urban chic to your straight neighbors and friends while dropping an additional hint about yourself to other gays, who understood the code of the magazine.

It certainly got my attention. In fact, *After Dark* was what propelled me to New York from Los Angeles after I'd graduated from UCLA in 1972. Coming from a conservative Latino family, I was out to only a small group of friends, one of whom showed me a copy of *After Dark* with a cover photo by Kenn Duncan of a handsome, shirtless man, his head thrown back in laughter. The back pages were filled with ads of attractive men in brief underwear – a visual concept Calvin Klein would parlay into a national marketing obsession during the next decade.

Captivated by the erotic, fun sophistication captured within *AD*'s pages, I sent a résumé and picture to Bill Como, and in the fall of 1972 I was hired as an editor and gofer, joining a skeletal staff that, belying the magazine's sophisticated image, was a ragtag band of starstruck, unpolished kids. Once referred to as "Como-sexuals" by the drag comedienne Charles Pierce, we were thrilled to be working at *After Dark*, even if only for subsistence wages and all the press freebies we could hustle. The first of many comp tickets I wangled provided memorable insight into the magazine's culture and the New York of the early Seventies. On my first day, Louis Miele, *AD*'s caustically funny advertising director, said, "It's Bette Midler's last night at the Continental Baths on Saturday, so you better call and get yourself on the press list."

I had never heard of Bette Midler before, but she was, by then, something of a fixture around the *After Dark* offices, having been on the cover twice. More than anyone, the "Divine Miss M" (a Midler persona that was crafted to a large extent by *AD* writer Bruce Vilanch) epitomized the evolving "urban gay aesthetic" of *After Dark* – campy, glamorous, torchy, sensitive, a bit slutty and raunchily funny. (Her Sophie Tucker jokes were a good example: "So my boyfriend Ernie was screwing me the other day and he says, 'Soph, you got small tits and a tight box,' and I said, 'Ernie, get off my back!' ") Now, borne aloft on her new Atlantic recording contract, Bette was going mainstream, leaving the small cabarets – through which she had developed a fanatic gay following – for the Broadway theater and concert arenas around the country.

The Continental Baths was a gay bathhouse in the basement of the Ansonia, an architectural wedding cake of a residential building on the Upper West Side. When I arrived that night with my roommate, Mary, who was then working as a Playboy bunny, there was a line of people snaking around the block, waiting to get in – a party in itself. Young men in jeans and bomber jackets dragged on joints, drag queens checked their mesh stockings, hustlers smiled at potential johns and straight record execs alighted from limousines with their trophy wives.

Inside, patrons sat on folding chairs and stood three abreast around the perimeter of a room, at the end of which was a jerry-built stage. Half the audience, patrons of the baths as well as the cabaret, wore only towels and would occasionally drift upstairs to cubicles to satisfy their sexual appetites. Back then, relief from the dangers that promiscuity posed was just a prescription of penicillin away, or so we believed.

Bette Midler and the Harlettes, accompanied by Barry Manilow, her pianist and arranger, whipped the audience into a megavolt state of sheer exhilaration in the cramped, steamy quarters. "How do you like these maracas, boys?" she said, shaking her tits in a halter top and dancing around the stage in stiletto heels. When she launched into her hits "Friends" and "Do You Want to Dance?," the audience, at least the half in towels, sang along. By the early morning hours, the place looked like a scene from Fellini's *Satyricon.*

For most of the decade, Bette was *After Dark*'s lodestar – the glamorous Queen of the Carnival who energized and blessed our revels. Most of that revelry was centered around the nightclubs and discos, out of which came the pulsating, driving lifestyle and music that would make stars of Barry White, Donna Summer and the Village People, to name a few. Years before *Saturday Night Fever,* we staffers published reports of the burgeoning gay disco scene we were sampling. We started at the Sanctuary, a deconsecrated church in Hell's Kitchen, then proceeded to the Anvil, a raunchy backroom bar (where Felipe, the Indian character among the Village People, had been discovered dancing on the bar by record producer Jacques Morali) and finally ended up at Le Jardin, a disco in the Hotel Diplomat. My own personal favorite during those years, however, was G.G. Barnum's, a wild, Mafia-owned dance palace with a two-story-high dance floor over which "disco bats" – transsexuals and humpy Puerto Rican boys on trapezes – would fly.

If Bette Midler was our queen of the revels, Arnold Schwarzenegger set the gold standard for the male celebrities we presented. *After Dark* touted women entertainers as retainers of an enviable glamour, talent and beauty, while men were presented as objects of sexual fantasy – an innovative concept, at least for a "mainstream" publication. Arnold was perfect because he was not only beautiful but he was also muscle-bound – the embodiment of the physical culture that our magazine celebrated long before the gym craze would sweep America.

While most women were thrilled to be in a publication that had such high-gloss values, men were a little more circumspect, fearing that it would compromise their careers. Not surprisingly, heterosexual males, like Schwarzenegger, Paul Newman and Robert Redford, had fewer reservations than gay actors, most of whom were, and remained, in the closet. *After Dark,* for example, never got an interview with Rock Hudson or Liberace, who sent his regrets. Even so, we were always very discreet. "Outing" was a concept that was simply unheard of then.

After Dark was typically uncritical, almost fawning, in its coverage of the arts. This approach was partly a reflection of the personality of its insecure, eager-to-please editor, but also had origins in what I used to refer to as the "yowzah" streak in gay culture – its hat-in-hand attitude toward the mainstream, heterosexual power brokers. Nor did we want to offend advertisers, particularly the big national accounts, who were often on the fence about *After Dark.*

To show dick or not to show dick was the constant debate at editorial meetings. The magazine, of course, had ridden to its peak on its combination of sex and sass. When it began in 1968, theater stages and movie screens reflecting the sexual revolution that was then at full throttle lost few opportunities to show bare ass and tits. The Broadway

musical *Hair,* in particular, mined box-office gold with its celebrated – albeit dimly lit – nude scene, and *After Dark* "let it all hang out," focusing particularly on films that had erotic and campy overtones. Directors who could always be counted on to deliver the goods were John Waters (*Pink Flamingos*), Ken Russell (*Women in Love*), John Schlesinger (*Midnight Cowboy*), most European directors, including Pier Paolo Pasolini, and Andy Warhol, whose ripe, fleshy discovery Joe Dallesandro was an *After Dark* icon.

But as nudity became less and less fashionable, the magazine became more and more hard-pressed to provide the titillation that, along with coverage of the arts, was key to its success.

By 1980, sales of the magazine had flattened out, publishing costs were rising and *After Dark* sank into the red. Gay men could now get all the flesh shots and entertainment news they wanted in more hard-core publications like *Blueboy* or so-called women's magazines like *Playgirl* and Bob Guccione's *Viva.* A halfhearted attempt to turn the magazine "more mainstream" – more straight entertainment reporting and less nudity – failed, and the magazine slowly ground to a halt in 1981.

I don't suppose the magazine's demise was much mourned at first. A lot of what it had chronicled as bold and daring was now mainstream. The Village People were playing college campuses; our favorite drag queens, like Craig Russell and Divine, were in hit films (*Outrageous, Polyester*) and Tom Cruise was dancing around in his underwear in *Risky Business.* The great masquerade ball that *After Dark* had documented was coming to an end. Politically active gays had always been slightly contemptuous of the magazine's coy and closeted hedonism, their stance reflecting a rather brittle and bitchy side of the community. There hadn't been much communal feeling among gays during the *After Dark* era.

All that changed when the first signs of the "gay cancer" appeared in 1981: The ensuing AIDS pandemic revolutionized the gay community. The urgency of the crisis and its traumatic emotional toll made the frivolities of the preceding decade seem ridiculous and even dangerous. The obsequiousness and tentativeness of many closeted gay men was replaced with the in-your-face radicalism of ACT-UP; Rock Hudson and thousands of other gays were effectively "outed" by the failure of their immune systems, and promotion of casual drug use and easy sex now seemed irresponsible. Besieged by an implacable enemy and ignored by an uncaring public, gays rallied together in their grief and rage. A true warmth and caring replaced the petty backbiting of the gay community.

In Washington, D.C., in 1994, the AIDS Quilt was being unveiled for the last time on the Mall, and I drove down with a couple of friends "to mourn and party," the informal mantra of the AIDS era. The individual squares of the quilt commemorating the dead often incorporated favorite memorabilia of the honored deceased, and on more than one square, I saw an issue of *After Dark* magazine. In the brilliant sunshine of that beautiful spring day, I joined countless others in mourning – and celebrating – our lost youth, which now seemed like some joyful, silly, fevered dream. ⊕

significant fund-raising activities in support of Brown's unsuccessful 1976 presidential bid.

26ERA supporters march on Washington, DC, as President Carter declares Women's Equality Day.

29St. Louis Cardinals infielder Lou Brock breaks Ty Cobb's long-standing record as he steals his 893rd base.

Four are arrested in a plot to steal Elvis Presley's remains from a Memphis cemetery. Plans are immediately made to move his and mother Gladys's bodies to a garden at Graceland.

31An advertiser boycott of the new ABC daytime-drama parody *Soap*, in which Billy Crystal plays a gay man, gathers steam as religious leaders express outrage over the show's outspokenness on sex and gay issues.

1977 SEPTEMBER

1Pioneering black vocalist Ethel Waters dies.

4Reflecting growing fascination with Top 10 and other similar hit inventories, *The Book of Lists* is the week's best-selling nonfiction book.

5Voyager 1 follows *Voyager 2* on a multiyear journey toward Saturn, Jupiter and beyond.

Bandleader and well-known New Year's Eve host Guy Lombardo dies at age 72.

7Convicted Watergate conspirator G. Gordon Liddy is released from federal custody after serving a term of 52$\frac{1}{2}$ months.

An American Medical Association study of TV violence cites programs on ABC as the most violent, and those on CBS as the least. A week later CBS is ranked last in the Nielsen ratings.

8ROLLING STONE reports on the brewing legal battle between VCR manufacturers and the movie industry as home taping of broadcast TV begins to "threaten the rerun and replay market of films on TV," according to a lawyer for Universal Studios.

9Soviet authorities confiscate various titles, including copies of George Orwell's *Animal Farm* and *1984*, which had been brought into the U.S.S.R. for the first-ever international book fair in Moscow.

10Top of the charts: the Emotions' "Best of My Love"

hotel california
by anthony decurtis

"I don't know why fortune smiles on some/And lets the rest go free," sings Don Henley in "The Sad Café," the concluding song on the Eagles' last studio album, 1979's 'The Long Run.' Those lines capture eloquently the degree to which the Eagles had come to see the superstardom they enjoyed in the Seventies as a kind of curse that generated dissension among the band's members, critical controversy, creative paralysis and a nearly metaphysical discomfort with the hedonistic delights – however fully indulged – that were the reward and price of their success.

In 1977 the Eagles were at their absolute height. Toward the end of the previous year, the year of the bicentennial, they had released 'Hotel California,' the album that would stand as their greatest achievement and solidify their place as one of the decade's definitive bands. 'Hotel California' is a clear-eyed, wistful examination of California as the last stop on the American journey westward, the country's destiny made manifest and then foreclosed. Novelist Joseph Conrad used the phrase "fascination of the abomination" to describe the hypnotic power that self-destruction can exert on the soul, and that phrase sums up the album's depiction of a gorgeous paradise – the geographical end point of American aspiration – transformed into a sunny hell of unsatisfying pleasure.

The singles "New Kid in Town," "Hotel California" and "Life in the Fast Lane" all dominated the charts in 1977, as did 'Hotel California' itself. The Eagles then began working on 'The Long Run,' but battles over the direction of the group, anxiety over crafting a worthy followup to 'Hotel California,' legal struggles with the band's management and a growing perception by critics of California rockers as spoiled, narcissistic sybarites stalled the band's productivity. Two years and a million dollars later, 'The Long Run' appeared. But by then, the Eagles were exhausted and disaffected, and when Glenn Frey announced in 1980 that he had begun work on a solo album, their breakup became official.

The Eagles sang in the perfect voice of the Seventies, in soaring harmonies aching with a Sixties hangover. It was a voice of desperate joys sought in the wake of a failed dream, a messenger of damaged ideals and disappointed longing. The Eagles' voice still carries those meanings. The band has been inducted into the Rock and Roll Hall of Fame, and 'The Eagles: Their Greatest Hits 1971–1975'

The Eagles in full *Hotel California* flight: Don Henley, Joe Walsh, Don Felder, Glenn Frey, Randy Meisner *(from left)*

has become one of the best-selling albums of all time, second only to Michael Jackson's 'Thriller' – convincing proof that while the Eagles' music is an essential expression of the Seventies, it far transcends nostalgia.

On a bright day in August of 1989, Henley and Frey met at Henley's home in Beverly Hills to do their first interview together since the Eagles' split. (At the time, rumors were flying about a possible reunion, though that would not happen for another five years.) They looked back on having provided the soundtrack to a time, a movement from youthful exuberance to depleted cynicism – the transition from the Sixties to the Eighties.

DO YOU THINK *of the Seventies as a distinct era, or does it blur around the edges?*

FREY: Well, it can sort of be defined by the life of our band, because the band started in the fall of '71 and broke up probably sometime in 1980, so we were working together for the whole decade.

HENLEY: The decade has some definite parameters for me because I came to L.A. in the summer of 1970 from Texas. And then the band. I think of the *Desperado* period, which was '73. And then '75, which was *One of These Nights*. I think '75 was around the point when the Seventies changed – '74, '75, '76. And then late '76 started another period – the *Hotel California* period. That's when disco and punk were starting to come in, and I guess that was the beginning of the Eighties.

FREY: We changed, too. I think we got a little more serious; maybe we were a little more politically active. You know, something happened around the time of the bicentennial.

We got *Hotel California* out by Thanksgiving 1976 – we wanted badly to have an album out in that year.

Let's go back a bit. What brought you to California?

HENLEY: I came here for the first time from Texas with my little band Shiloh. I believe it was February of 1970. We came out to cut a single, not really to move here. I remember driving into town, we came up on the Hollywood Freeway. It was a nice, clear February night, one of those nights when the town looks really pretty. I had never seen the Capitol Records Tower – I was freaking out. It was like there was this big metal and concrete symbol of the record industry. I had so many Capitol records when I was a kid – 45s, you know, when they had that purple label with the Capitol dome. I believe the writing was in silver. It was a manifestation of all my childhood dreams. I was awestruck. I had never seen any terrain like this. Where I come from, there are rolling, gentle hills but no vistas like this. And, of course, I had never seen a grid of lights like that in my life. It just went on forever.

What about when you got the Eagles together? What were your ambitions?

FREY: I think we had a lot of optimism. You don't know any better than to think that you can do really well. I mean, every time you put together a band, you think, "This is going to be the one."

HENLEY: The best band in the world – until you really get to know everybody. We were young, and the times were exciting, and the world lay stretched out before us. The beginning is when it's great. Money and girls were the two big motivations – that's what it was for everybody. Then you become a serious artist and set out to change the world.

FREY: There was a time during 1976, 1977, where the record business went crazy. That was when *Hotel California* came out, and *Saturday Night Fever* and also *Rumours* by Fleetwood Mac, and . . .

HENLEY: *Frampton Comes Alive!* – for a minute.

FREY: That was the music business at its decadent zenith. I remember Don had a birthday in Cincinnati, and they flew in cases of Chateau Lafite Rothschild. I seem to remember that the wine was the best and the drugs were good and the women were beautiful and, man, we seemed to have an endless amount of energy. *Endless* stores of energy. Hangovers were conquered with Bloody Marys and aspirin, you know what I mean? There were no two-day purges or hiding in your bed. It seemed that you bounced back, you were resilient.

HENLEY: There was much merrymaking. Those kind of record sales were unprecedented. I guess everybody thought it was going to continue like that. Lots of money was spent on parties and champagne and limos and drugs. And then, of course, the bottom fell out.

FREY: Led Zeppelin might argue with us, but I think we might have thrown the greatest traveling party of the Seventies. It was called the Third Encore. Almost every night when we were on the road, we would throw this fabulous mixer. We'd hand out 3E buttons, and we'd invite all the key radio people and as many beautiful girls as we'd meet from the airport to the hotel and whatever. We had our own sound system and we played Motown and blues records and had this terrific party every night.

HENLEY: Shit, yeah! I mean we were living . . . this was the dream that we all had. This is why we came to California. It just got bigger than we ever expected it to. It kind of scared us, I guess.

FREY: We tried to maintain that underdog frame of mind.

HENLEY: But it was hard to be an underdog when you're selling twelve million records! [*Laughs.*]

FREY: The band just got bigger and bigger, and it became unmanageable. I think the underbelly of success is the burden of having to follow things up. We started to run out of gas. Don sort of blew his literary nut on *Hotel California*. I mean, we covered it, from love to sex to drugs to the future of the planet to . . .

HENLEY: Religion.

FREY: We weren't thinking about selling fifteen million records at the time. It's one thing if you have a couple of hit singles and get a gold record. That's different from selling fifteen million albums. There's only a few artists who have had the education of having to continue working on stuff after some sort of blockbuster success. So it wore on us. We spent a lot more time in the studio toward the end of the decade, and we got a lot more critical of our own work, because we wanted it to be better than the last thing we did. We probably should have just given up and written a couple more love songs and put out *The Long Run* a couple of years earlier. Now I realize that.

HENLEY: I think we knew intuitively that it would pass. I think we could sense the future. I think intuitively we were aware of the end of the boom. Not exclusively for ourselves, but the nation.

I remember interviews in which you'd say that 'Hotel California' was about more than California. It was really about America.

HENLEY: America in general, California being the microcosm. That didn't seem to take. I mean, it just went in one ear and out the other.

FREY: There was a time, somewhere in 1976, when I thought things were going to get better. We had gotten rid of Nixon. We had a Democrat in the White House. Jimmy Carter and the boys were going to have barbecue on the Hill.

HENLEY: It seemed like the Sixties were back for a second.

FREY: And then Khomeini . . .

HENLEY: And the helicopter mechanics. Events conspired against ol' Jimmy.

Do you feel that politically the Seventies suffered a hangover from the failed idealism of the Sixties?

HENLEY: Yeah, I'm still writing about it. The dream was unfulfilled. In the late Seventies, greed reared its ugly head. We turned from a society that was concerned with our brother and our fellow man into a society that was very self-centered, self-concerned, about money and power. That took us into the Eighties, but it really got started at the end of the Seventies. I guess it was a result of a disillusionment that the Sixties didn't quite pan out. For all the publicity about the babyboom generation and how we were going to change the world, we weren't in control. The same people who had *always* been in control were *still* in control. While we were out taking drugs and preaching flower power and having rock concerts and loveins, people were running the country.

FREY: I think when the Seventies started, music wasn't giving much hope. There was almost no way that musically the Seventies were going to be on a par with the Sixties. The only people that even got remotely close were Crosby, Stills, Nash and Young, but all their problems – they sort of blew it. But they had that myth going for a while. Looking back on things, the music of the Seventies doesn't sound that fucking bad to me at all. You can name the great albums of the Seventies. I don't think you can name the great albums of the Eighties, but if you do, how great are they compared to *Layla*?

HENLEY: It was a very natural time. And it all made sense with the music. Then, in the late Seventies, there was a backlash against that. Music started to become very urban-oriented, a reflection of the concrete and steel and the pace. So we didn't, to paraphrase Joni Mitchell, get back to the garden. If we did, we didn't stay there. The country, the natural sound that is connected with nature, has gone out of music pretty much. I lament that loss, that contact we had with nature.

What other records do you think really stand out?

FREY: I might forget some things, but I'm thinking of a string of Elton John hits. We had the Spinners, we had the Philadelphia Sound – I liked those records. It's kind of funny even to have resented disco compared with where that kind of music has gone. Some of the older disco songs, shit, if it's Harold Melvin and the Blue Notes, those are pretty good fucking records. Some of the Donna Summer records I like a lot better than things I've heard recently. There's a lot more craft and a lot less programming involved, that's for sure.

Who did you see as your competition in those days?

HENLEY: Fleetwood Mac was the competition, but it was a friendly competition.

FREY: I thought about competition more in the earlier days. You know, once you become successful, you realize that you're competing with yourself. Somebody else making a good record can't keep you off the charts. We used to have those T-shirts that said SONG POWER, because we felt that was what we had going for us. There was, even in the early Seventies, too much emphasis on packaging. There was already dry ice and smoke bombs. I looked at Jethro Tull and some of those bands as the people we were competing against.

Bands that were about spectacle?

HENLEY: Yeah, we were deliberately minimalist, to a fault probably. We were accused by one critic of loitering onstage – which pissed us off then. Now we can laugh about it.

It sometimes seems that the Eagles are on the radio now as much as in the Seventies. How does it feel to be driving in your car and hear your songs?

FREY: It seems like all of our best songs have risen to the top – they're the ones that get played over and over again. You know, you get these printouts of your publishing, all the songs you've written, and of the Eagles songs, there are about eight or ten that just consistently do big numbers – and they also happen to be the ones I like. It just reminds you that maybe you are good at what you do and that what you did when you were young is still good now. That makes me feel good.

HENLEY: I feel good about it, too. It depends on the mood I'm in. Some days "Hotel California" will come on the radio and I'll turn it up and listen to it. Some days I'll just turn it off or punch another station.

You are in the position of having lent an expression to the language: "Life in the fast lane."

HENLEY: Yeah, I wish I had a nickel for every fucking time somebody's used that.

FREY: We do! [*Laughs.*]

What do you feel is the Eagles' legacy?

FREY: It's hard for me to say. We've left this collection of records, this body of work. In the end, I think our work mirrored the times and that's what remains. That's what people will probably enjoy. For some people it will be nostalgia, and for other people it's like archaeology, like me listening to records from the Forties. That's not nostalgic for me, because I was never there. We are fortunate enough to be one of the bricks in the building. ⊕

couldn't keep a liquor license) – opens on New York's Upper West Side, in the same location as what had been the gay Continental Baths.

jenny boyd
on fleetwood mac

IN 1977, *Rumours* had become the Number One album in America, and Fleetwood Mac was riding high.

I remember that during their shows, when the lights were dimmed between each song, the road manager would walk onstage like a butler, holding a tray of bottle caps filled with cocaine for each member of the band. We wives and girlfriends were allotted ours backstage. After the gig, the party would really get going when someone would start showering wine over someone else's head, or pick a food fight in the restaurant.

What astonishes me now about those years is that, at the time, our lifestyle really didn't seem so outrageous. The first time it dawned on me that life with the band had distorted my perception of reality was when we were in London during the Rumours European tour, and my husband, Mick Fleetwood, and I went to see our old friends Peter Green and Danny Kirwan, who'd been Mick's band mates in the early days. Both Peter and Danny were down and out. Peter had turned into an overweight paranoid schizophrenic and Danny was compulsively scratching himself as if he had fleas. I remember turning to look at Mick in his elegant, Chinese-silk waistcoat, and thinking how out of touch we both had become in the three short years since we'd left the U.K.

After making the mass exodus from England to Los Angeles in the spring of 1974, Mick and I and his band mates quickly embraced the sunny, laid-back California lifestyle. In the beginning, we mostly hung out around the pool of the house where John and Chris McVie were staying in Laurel Canyon, which was dubbed "The Brain Damage Club." There, the release from our rather prim, stiff-upper-lip upbringing took full rein. Spirits were up, and lots of wine encouraged us to shrug off our British propriety – and (with the exception of Mick) our bathing costumes – and indulge in underwater acrobatics.

Fleetwood Mac: Lindsey Buckingham, Stevie Nicks, Mick Fleetwood, Christine McVie, John McVie *(from left)*

The music scene in L.A. captivated us. A distinct sound, particular to Los Angeles, had emerged. It was more like country rock than the hard-rock sounds of the English bands Fleetwood Mac had toured with, such as Deep Purple and Savoy Brown. The radio stations blared out one great song after another: Linda Ronstadt, the Eagles, Jackson Browne, James Taylor and Joni Mitchell. Their sounds fell through the air like leaves from the same tree; little did I know at the time that Fleetwood Mac's music would soon become a major branch of that tree.

The Eagles played at the Santa Monica Civic Center not long after we had arrived. John had been a great fan of theirs for a long time and loved everything they represented. So we all went to their gig and stood at the back of the hall. Their hip California sound was very cool: outlaw themes and laid-back voices made sweeter by wonderful harmonies. We were enraptured. They looked like a hybrid of Native Americans and modern-day cowboys, and this made our English hearts soar.

Mick came across Stevie Nicks and Lindsey Buckingham one day at a recording studio he was checking out for Fleetwood Mac's next album. He was so impressed with them that, a week later, when guitarist Bob Welch quit the band, he invited them to join Fleetwood Mac. Nicks and Buckingham completely revitalized the band's energy. Listening to the new lineup practicing, I noticed that the players really clicked. A magic emanated from them as they played. Their energy was palpable, their sound magical.

As the band began getting attention, we got caught up in the social whirl of people who suddenly wanted to be around Fleetwood Mac's vibrancy. After a successful tour, life became an increasingly decadent, ongoing party. Whether we were in the studio, in a restaurant or at someone's home, we were always celebrating and getting high. I liked the merriment, yet felt like an outsider.

I had always felt a bit awkward about my role in the scheme of things because, as

Mick's wife, I was constantly with the band yet not actually a member of it. Inside I felt a conflict between what I wanted to do and what I was doing. But the band was the center of everything, it was like the sun in my solar system – my life revolved around it.

Rather than trying to understand why I felt ill at ease, I went along with the excessive revelry of the crowd. I'd start drinking right away to mask my shyness. At parties, after having been given the nod by whoever was holding the cocaine, I'd proceed to pick at yet another expensive meal. It got to the point where, often, I couldn't remember the end of the evening.

Life had changed dramatically since the Sixties. Back then, we were smoking pot and experimenting with LSD in order to expand our consciousnesses. In the Seventies, we were drinking alcohol and snorting cocaine, caught up in the fast, high-flying world we now inhabited. With youth, fame and money running rampant therein, our world had turned into a false paradise.

At the time *Rumours* was being recorded, Stevie had split up with Lindsey, Christine and John were getting divorced and Mick and I – after divorcing and then remarrying six months later – were again on the rocks. The terrific songs on that album came out of tremendous personal turmoil. During the sessions, the Record Plant was thick with every possible emotion. We were all continually walking into rooms and then having to apologize to couples interrupted in the middle of earnest talks or floods of tears.

Mick spent all his time in the recording studio, coming home in the early hours of the morning, if at all, and leaving again first thing the next day, usually without more than a grunt. Our communication became nonexistent. The more larger-than-life Mick got, the smaller I felt. As my life became less and less comprehensible, my search for some meaning in it became stronger. Astrology classes, spiritual books, gurus, meditation and psychics became my despairing attempt to feel whole in a world that was fast becoming a roller-coaster ride. Eventually, I met a doctor of Oriental medicine and, with the help of his acupuncture, stopped drinking alcohol and using cocaine. I was the only one I knew who was straight. So, for the sake of my own sanity and the well-being of our young daughters, I returned to England to start a new life.

It took a couple of months before my departure had any impact on Mick, at which point he pleaded with me to return. He waited until I arrived in L.A. and he'd had enough vodka before telling me about his affair with Stevie. I was shattered. Then he dug the knife in further, saying, "I can't make up my mind if I want you or her." Disheartened, I realized I was back in the midst of the insanity, which, after a few months, I left for good.

Since resettling in England, my life has been completely different. I'm still sober, and now I organize workshops for people recovering from drug and alcohol abuse. I've faced up to the fact that the band life was never enough for me and that it was everything for Mick. And while I still love Fleetwood Mac's sound and all the other music I listened to in Los Angeles, I try to maintain a safe distance from that time and its powerful rumors. ⊕

segment of his performance in Los Angeles.

A chartered plane carrying Lynyrd Skynyrd and its crew crashes near McComb, MS, killing lead singer Ronnie Van Zant, guitarist Steve Gaines and his sister, backup singer Cassie. MCA Records immediately recalls their new release, *Street Survivors,* the cover of which shows the band surrounded by flames, and substitutes new artwork.

25 A $576-million-plus deal is signed between the NFL and all three major TV networks in the most lucrative broadcast agreement to date.

28 After much ballyhoo and trepidation, *Never Mind the Bollocks Here's the Sex Pistols* is released.

29 The Consumer Products Safety Board predicts at least 375,000 skateboard-related injuries for 1977, doubling the previous year's total.

1977 NOVEMBER

1 Animal tranquilizer phencyclidine (PCP) is seen as a new major health hazard as its use as a recreational drug increases.

3 In a landmark ruling on "battered wife syndrome," Francine Hughes is exonerated for reasons of insanity after setting fire to her abusive former husband as he slept.

Elton John announces his retirement from live performances midconcert at the Empire Pool in London. John will remain true to his word for 15 months, but will return to the stage on Feb. 3, 1979, in Sweden.

4 Martin Scorsese's "rockumentary" of the Band's last public performance, *The Last Waltz,* opens.

Former CIA director Richard Helms is fined $2,000 and given a two-year suspended prison sentence for failing to fully disclose past U.S. covert activities in Latin America.

5 Ozzy Osbourne departs Black Sabbath, only to ask for his job back after a few weeks. Within months, he will leave the band for good, pursuing a lucrative solo career.

8 Proto-punkette Suzi Quatro appears on the TV show *Happy Days* playing Leather Tuscadero, the leader of a rock band called the Suedes.

14 Hare Krishna founder A.C. Bhaktivedanta Swami Prabhupada, whose followers include George Harrison, dies.

beyond the velvet rope
by glenn o'brien

IT'S HARD TO REMEMBER specific nights at Studio 54. 1977? '78? '79? They all seem to have blended into one endless night, but I remember many details. I remember waiting for hours for Grace Jones to show up and perform. I remember Studio 54 co-owner Steve Rubell giving me drink tickets and asking if I had any blow (a question that always astounded me, like the pope asking for my blessing). I remember almost killing myself on a beer bottle rolling across the dance floor. I remember Quaaludes and people accidentally going home with the wrong people.

I remember *Interview* editor Bob Colacello dancing with Truman Capote and Nureyev dancing with Mick Jagger, and I remember Farrah Fawcett dancing with her blouse open enough so that I could catch a flash of breast if I maneuvered into the right position. I remember Liz Taylor with her husband, the senator, who looked like he was going to have a heart attack any second (fortunately there was amyl nitrate within easy reach). I remember Andy Warhol's brief flirtation with vodka and thinking, Hey, Andy's stoned! I remember thinking, How can I pick up Patti D'Arbanville? but never coming up with the right answer. I remember finding a bottle of cocaine under the cushions of a sofa. I remember finding a couple having sex in the far reaches of the balcony. I remember when you could just pull a joint out and smoke it. I remember saying, "Hey, anybody want to go to the Mudd Club?"

I remember sitting with Nile Rodgers of Chic watching the TV news reports the day after a great party. The anchorperson said that the disco had been fined five thousand dollars by the fire department for "blocking an egress."

"Five-thousand-dollar fine for blocking a negress?!" Nile roared. "It must have been Diana Ross!"

D ante Alighieri would have found Studio 54 harder than hell to get into – a paradise, purgatory and disco inferno all in one. The nightclub offered corporeal ecstasies and cardinal sins, descending levels of decadence and ascending circles of celebritydom. Like other visitors to this netherworld, where the nights lasted forever and the sun never rose (and a smiling, crescent-shaped, cocaine-toking moon illuminated the interior), Dante would have required fame, fortune or a friend to guide him through the portal.

Mobs clamored at the velvet ropes, petitioning for admittance. Petitioners shrieked "Steve!" (for Rubell) or "Marc!" (for doorman Marc Benecke, perhaps the first celebrity doorman), hoping a glance at them would jog their memory and the ropes would part. Men stood behind attractive girls (or boys) hoping the other's glamour would do the trick. Some hired limos, hoping that a limo exit would help them make a Studio entrance.

Despite its exclusionary image, Studio 54 probably admitted more people than any nightclub had up to that time. Housed in a former opera house and television studio (with a legacy – it was the home of the infamously rigged *$64,000 Question*), Studio was almost

At right: Bianca Jagger is feted on her birthday at Studio 54, December 1977; following pages: a galaxy of stars celebrates *Interview*'s newest cover, 1979: Lorna Luft, Jerry Hall, Andy Warhol, cover gal Deborah Harry, Truman Capote and Paloma Picasso *(from left)*

guaranteed an eclectic crowd due to its scale alone. It took hundreds of patrons to make the place look happening. The dance floor by itself was three thousand square feet.

From its opening night, April 26, 1977, Studio 54 was a perpetual publicity machine, preordained to be the most famous nightclub in existence. A film-company employee was hired specifically to wrangle celebrities, receiving $250 for A-list stars, $125 for minor celebs. Overnight, the buzz was out and the limos started arriving. Studio 54 filled a void that no one knew had existed; the world needed a metadisco, a new firmament for pop superstars to shine in, a social nexus where café society, Seventies hedonism and the process of celebrity-making could mix.

It was disco society, stimulated by chemicals far stronger than caffeine. Studio 54 blasted off at the height of the disco era, riding the waves of that basic, primal, frenetic dance music designed to maximize the display of sexuality. "Push, push, in the bush."

During the early Seventies, trendy heterosexuals had discovered gay discos and all they offered: hipper music, better dancers and a sexually charged atmosphere that attracted models and other beautiful people who could carry on wildly without being constantly hit on. This mix of gays and high-end heteros, pioneered at New York clubs like Tamburlaine, the Sanctuary and Le Jardin, set the tone for the full integration of Studio 54.

Anybody could dance with anybody. Studio 54's attraction crossed more than just sexual boundaries: Celebrities, Eurotrash and new-wave rockers mixed freely. The radical eclecticism of the joint was a big part of the electricity of the atmosphere. One expected to see anyone and anything, and sometimes did.

Studio 54 brought together celebrities and the hoi polloi in a new way, making celebs and civilians comfortable together – and apart. The stage door on West Fifty-third Street served as a VIP entrance, obviating indignities at the ropes on Fifty-fourth. Inside, Studio placed its first-tier VIP area behind a scrim that sharply divided the dance floor. With entrance attained, the rich and famous and those otherwise lucky enough to be let in consorted with one another, let their hair down, flirted fearlessly and consumed controlled substances freely.

After working up a glistening sweat in their exclusive area, VIPs had access to the rest of the club to dance amid, and be admired by, their public, scout for young talent and flirt with the always scantily clad waiters. Or – if their wealth or fabulousness truly merited access to the inner sanctum – celebrities could descend a staircase, behind the bar, that led to the club's basement where, amid cheesy decorative touches and an AstroTurf floor, they could find greater privacy for more elaborate self-medication or a good cry.

Studio 54 not only mingled gays with straights, celebs with regulars, it also was probably the first club that had integrated bathrooms. The toilets were still nominally "men's" and "women's," but few paid any attention to that distinction. Mixed couples disappeared into stalls to share pharmaceuticals and/or intimacies. And some people entering the facilities were not readily identifiable as any particular gender.

Celebrities have always had places to meet one another, but no nightspot has ever been as consistently eclectic, fertile and lively as Studio. Movie stars, rock stars, artists, writers, ballet dancers and politicians mixed and mingled. Nureyev could meet Wilt Chamberlain, and Jerry Rubin did meet Diana Vreeland. Even Hamilton Jordan, President Jimmy Carter's chief of staff, was known to frequent the club. Its denizens forgot their troubles and partied under that neon man in the moon with the coke spoon dangling under his nose. At the center of it all was Studio's core constituency, consisting of those who knew everyone: Liza Minnelli, Truman Capote, Bianca Jagger, Halston, Calvin Klein, Georgio Sant'Angelo.

And occupying an almost papal position in this religion of fame – bestowing it, proselytizing for it and bringing it to the masses – was Andy Warhol. From the beginning, Studio 54 drew members of the Warhol Factory, and soon the boss himself was there every night. Warhol had made cultural idolatry a fine art. Studio, with its heady mixture of New York, Hollywood and European climbers, provided him the means to take his concept to the next level. He could recruit famous covergirls and coverboys for his magazine *Interview*, he could scout out ingenue beauties to put in his movies or fix up with his friends. Studio also proved a place to meet patrons with a spare twenty-five thousand dollars to plunk down for a portrait.

For Andy and *Interview* and Steve and Studio 54, it was the perfect symbiotic relationship at the perfect time. Studio provided *Interview* editor Bob Colacello a gold mine of celebrity shenanigans to report on in his column OUT. A diary of the social life of Warhol and his entourage, OUT was remarkable in its unabashed enthusiasm for social climbing, shamelessly dropping names and dispensing flattery. But the sheer chutzpah and exhibitionist ambition of his "Mondo Boswell" diary gave it a fresh and genuine, if bizarre, charm. It's hard not to like someone who's enjoying himself that much.

Interview eschewed any pretense of objective reporting in favor of unmediated celebrity-to-celebrity dialogues. Interviews were brilliantly unedited. The reader was a fly on a fabulous wall, in with the "in" crowd, eavesdropping on the rich and famous, enjoying a written cinema verité on how they talk and what they talk about. *Interview* was, in fact, at the vanguard of a new kind of journalism.

There had always been "celebrity journalism" – supermarket tabloids have graced check-out lines for decades – but in the Seventies, a new era of stargazing reportage came into being. *Time* spun off their "People" column into its own weekly magazine of the same name – Mia Farrow graced the cover of its first issue in March 1974. The same year, Liz Smith was engaged by New York's *Daily News* to produce a gossip column of similar focus. Walter Winchell – arguably the granddaddy of all rich-and-famous tattletelling (and Liz Smith's teenage inspiration) – died on February 20, 1972, but his spirit immediately rose again and, being on the guest list, walked right into the Studio decade.

As gossip rocketed from tabloids to mainstream publications, a glossy new world awoke, where Warhol's line, "In the future everyone will be famous for fifteen minutes," was accepted as prophecy. The future was now, at Studio 54. Consider the arithmetic: A world with 162 cable channels suddenly needed many more stars than a world with only three networks.

Studio 54 may have represented a tribal democracy in socializing, but it proved to be more about celebrities' need for an audience and fans' need to admire and aspire. Studio 54 itself came to bestow momentary immortality: There were famous waiters and DJs, and one of the first patrons to achieve notoriety was Disco Sally, a dumpy senior citizen who boogied her nights away there (she became known for being a dumpy senior citizen who boogied her nights away there). And the owners – Steve Rubell and Ian Schrager – became celebrities in their own rights. When both were arrested for tax evasion, their legends remained intact: superhosts, the Runyonesque Robin Hoods of discodom.

Studio was democratic in sharing with all its patrons the same feeling, the feeling of having arrived: Past the ropes, you were in. It was a universe of infinite possibilities, where you might meet anyone, where you might do things you hadn't imagined. That's why the legend lives on in a dreamscape of wild images.

Margaret Trudeau with no underwear on. Michael Jackson lurking in the DJ booth. People having sex in the balcony. Bianca Jagger riding a horse across the dance floor. Steve Rubell giving Andy Warhol a garbage can full of money for his birthday. Roy Cohn dancing. Forty-eight Rockettes kicking up their heels for Liz Taylor. President Carter's mom, Lillian, wondering why the boys were dancing together.

The last time I went to Studio 54, it was no longer a disco. Bob Weir of the Dead was playing to a house full of tie-dyed teens who probably had never heard of Steve Rubell. Later, before it was shuttered, Studio 54 breathed its last gasp as a topless bar.

Today, there's nothing quite like it was, when it was. Most people don't stay up so late anymore, they work much too hard, and if they go out to see celebrities, they book reservations months in advance to get into that new, famous restaurant that everyone's been talking about. And those people who never made it past the velvet rope – I guess they now go to Planet Hollywood to see something that was once worn by, or belonged to, a celebrity. There are even velvet ropes in front. Maybe they're there to keep the customers in. ⊕

deborah harry
on studio 54

INITIALLY I had heard only bits and pieces about Studio 54 – in 1977, I had been on the road with Blondie in Europe and Australia. But when I got back to town, I heard it was the place to go.

The first time I went, they let me in because Blondie was happening. The place was complete chaos – packed with people! You'd sort of push your way upstairs, roam around and then you'd roam around downstairs and you'd see people: Andy Warhol, Truman Capote, Diana Vreeland.

I met Diana through Bob Colacello, who was running Andy's Factory. I met Lauren Hutton. I met everyone; that was part of going out: You'd go and you'd meet a tableful of people. Diana, I remember, was brilliant: totally eccentric and elegant, semi-European, with an exaggerated personality. She was into fascinating, clunky jewelry and wore things that flattered her kind of figure.

I was a scruffy downtown kid and I liked it like that. I wasn't part of the showbiz crowd. Liza, Bianca – it was *their* clubhouse. I never made it to the "secret chambers." Not that I was terrifically interested in the secret chambers, since I'm not a gay man, well . . . there you have it.

There were always guys walking around with no clothes on, gay men without shirts, wearing leather chaps. Up until that point the gay scene had for the most part been a quiet, private one. Studio 54 made a difference: It was a downtown atmosphere in an uptown place. Nightlife has developed over the years to the point where, today, it's a part of normal behavior, but then it was fresh.

Studio 54 became a Blondie scene because it was truly mixed, a general-admission crowd, not just a rock crowd (though my leanings were more toward rock). There was more of a division in people's minds about social groupings then. There was the "Death to Disco" movement. Now, people aren't so concerned about crossing over.

In 1979, "Heart of Glass" managed to do that "crossover" thing. It was one of the few pieces of music of the time that was popular with the rock-pop scene and also took off in the area of urban music. It was just one of those things that worked.

Later on, I got friendlier with Andy. When I was on the cover of *Interview* in 1979, they threw a big party for me at Studio 54. It was pretty exciting, quite a big deal, a lot of fun and packed with celebs. My picture on the cover was the backdrop for the stage. That was cool: my shining moment at 54. ⊕

galactic gold on the silver screen by peter travers

I HATE 'STAR WARS.' Scratch that: I don't hate *Star Wars*, I hate what it begat. After George Lucas's seminal space fantasy struck box-office gold in 1977, movies never recovered. Big wasn't good enough – you had to supersize it. The *Star Wars* bonanza helped transform the last great decade of film into a harbinger of the digitized, depersonalized, megabudgeted and megahyped event flicks that clutter our multiplexes today. Hollywood became the evil Empire, the true Death Star, as the studio bean counters used movies to engender sequels, toys, T-shirts, lunch boxes, bedsheets and video games.

But I'm rushing ahead. A long time ago, in a galaxy far, far away – namely Seventies Hollywood – cinema was, as the slang of the time had it, a happening thing. Movies were pop-culture artifacts. People had fun at them, friends argued about them, some even took them seriously. Comparing box-office figures hadn't yet become a national pastime. Trade publications reported a movie's grosses, but audiences were blissfully ignorant, staying open to a wide variety of choices. As a fledgling film critic, I was eager to weigh in on a medium that, in a decade bookended by two extraordinary visions of war – *M*A*S*H* and *Apocalypse Now* – had already produced *Mean Streets*, *Gimme Shelter*, *A Clockwork Orange*, *The Last Picture Show*, *Badlands*, *Husbands*, *Dirty Harry*, *Cries and Whispers*, *Chinatown*, *Nashville*, *The Conformist*, *One Flew Over the Cuckoo's Nest* and the first two chapters of Francis Ford Coppola's epic *Godfather* trilogy.

Star Wars was one of the first movies I had been assigned to review. This was before my days as a critic for such large-circulation publications as *People* and ROLLING STONE. In fact, I was living in a suburb of New York and writing for a local newspaper, the same rag I had delivered to neighbors years before as a paperboy. I mention this for two reasons: One, like most critics new to the job and working for peanuts, my attitude was irritatingly smart-ass; two, since nobody had ever heard of me or my newspaper, there were no invitations to the advance screenings the studios customarily provide for bona fide critics. On the opening day of *Star Wars*, I waited in line like everyone else.

Obi-Wan Kenobi (Alec Guinness) confronts his nemesis Darth Vader (voice of James Earl Jones) in the original *Star Wars*

And what a line it was, made up mostly of teens and twentysomethings, who talked excitedly to each other about the "cool movie" they were about to see. Amazing, when you consider that 20th Century–Fox, the studio behind *Star Wars*, had hardly broken the bank on a prerelease publicity campaign. Lucas's entire budget for the film didn't run more than a paltry ten million dollars, and sci-fi was not considered a hot genre in a year that saw audiences and Oscars gravitating to Woody Allen's *Annie Hall* and such weepies as *Julia* and *The Turning Point*. These were the days before the Internet, before the *Drudge Report* and *Ain't It Cool News*, and yet a buzz was in the air. *This* audience was hungry to see *this* kind of movie.

Not me. Here I was, accredited to criticize movies at last, and what do I get as an assignment? A space opera. I wanted stronger material. The first half of the Seventies had percolated with hot stuff. Screen violence, from *Dirty Harry* to *Taxi Driver*, provoked debate and political analysis. Blaxploitation had been on the rise with *Shaft*, *Superfly* and *Foxy Brown*. Censors were outraged by alleged cinematic violations of the moral code: Linda Lovelace went down on cast members in *Deep Throat*, Divine nibbled on dog doo-doo in *Pink Flamingos* and Marlon Brando buttered Maria Schneider's butt in *Last Tango in Paris*. Even the mainstream offered the sight of a prepubescent Linda Blair masturbating with a crucifix in *The Exorcist*, raising outcries of pornography and sacrilege.

No subject was sacrosanct. You could satirize war (*M*A*S*H*) or presidential politics (*All the President's Men*). You could even take on censorship (*Lenny*) and the hypocrites of TV (*Network*), music (*Nashville*) and religion (*Monty Python's Life of Brian*).

New directing mavericks, such as Coppola, Martin Scorsese, Terrence Malick, Brian De Palma and John Waters, joined the masters – Robert Altman, Stanley Kubrick, Sam Peckinpah, Roman Polanski and Sidney Lumet – in raising hell with convention. Actors tore into career-defining roles: Al Pacino making NYPD waves as the crusading cop in *Serpico* and making offers you can't refuse as the don in the *Godfather* films; Jane Fonda getting inside the skin of an unhappy hooker in *Klute*; Robert De Niro confronting himself in a mirror ("You talkin' to me?") as the tortured Vietnam vet in *Taxi Driver*; Gena Rowlands unraveling as the ultimate mad housewife in *A Woman Under the Influence*; Jack Nicholson telling a snarky waitress to take some chicken and "put it between your knees" as the drifter in *Five Easy Pieces*; Sissy Spacek wreaking supernatural havoc as the teen misfit in *Carrie* (the first Stephen King story to hit the screen); Sly Stallone taking his best shot at being boxing's champ as the Italian Stallion in *Rocky*; Diane Keaton la-de-dahing as Woody Allen's unattainable shiksa in *Annie Hall*; John Travolta making all the right moves as the disco king in *Saturday Night Fever*; and Pam Grier as the real embodiment of girl power in *Foxy Brown*.

What kind of actors did we get in *Star Wars*? Unknowns. No one standing in line seemed to know or care who Mark Hamill was, and Hamill was playing Luke Skywalker, the hero. Harrison Ford, cast as the daring adventurer Han Solo, was also a nonentity at the time, better known for his carpentry work around L.A. than for his bit parts in films *(The Conversation, American Graffiti)*. Carrie Fisher, the nineteen-year-old daughter of Debbie Reynolds and Eddie Fisher, had made a brief but telling impression onscreen in 1975 as jailbait for Warren Beatty's hairstylist in *Shampoo*. Now, as Princess Leia, Fisher was on her way to becoming a screen icon. But who knew? Aside from Alec Guinness, who played Obi-Wan Kenobi, the Jedi counselor wise in the ways of the Force, James Earl Jones was the most distinguished member of the cast, and Jones's contribution was limited to his voice as he boomed words forth from the mask of the evil Darth Vader.

Make no mistake, crowds did not line up for *Star Wars* to see the acting. They wanted special effects, robots, furry creatures, holograms, laser swords and space battles. They wanted what Lucas had promised when he first devised the film that would spawn two sequels – *The Empire Strikes Back* (1980) and *Return of the Jedi* (1983) – and possibly two more trilogies. They wanted *Flash Gordon*, or at least the kind of cliff-hanging adventure that Hollywood had forgotten how to craft with feeling. Lucas made good on his promise.

Good for them. Bad for me. Or so I thought. Hadn't I put in countless hours haunting movie theaters, tracking down key films in museums and revival houses (this was the pre-VCR age) and studying the craft of celluloid deconstruction at New York University? Hadn't my formative years been spent – misspent in the view of my parents, who pleaded that I pursue "a real job" – to prepare me to review real movies with real people instead of robots and Wookies? I pushed into the theater with a chip firmly in place on my shoulder to have a go at *Star Wars*. The way I figured it, George Lucas, who had done a fine job directing *American Graffiti* – the 1973 film about high school graduates in 1962 – had reverted to grade-school juvenilia.

Star Wars ultimately wore down my resistance. Somewhat. The dialogue, with all the navigational jargon, was stilted. Ford had famously chided Lucas about it: "You can type this shit, George, but you sure can't say it." Ford was right. The fussy C3PO and the mischievous R2D2 are the funniest and most human characters in the movie, and they're robots. Chewbacca, a huge and hugely neurotic Wookie, runs a close second to the 'droids. Sometimes, Lucas just shows off. He references other movies, from *The Wizard of Oz* to *2001: A Space Odyssey* to *The Hidden Fortress*, and seasons the script with corny folklore. Lucas had read Joseph Campbell's writings on the persistence of myth, and what he gleaned is meant to give resonance to Luke's paternal conflict with the dastardly Darth Vader that culminates in *Return of the Jedi*.

The audience responded according to plan. They clapped at the battles, laughed at the jokes and hushed when Lucas laid on the heavy stuff. In my newly professional opinion, the Freudian mumbo-jumbo didn't work. What got to me about *Star Wars* was the sheer exhilaration so obvious in the filmmaking. Lucas was trying to bring his fantasies to life onscreen. This wasn't cynical filmmaking, the work of a hack on the make. In the image of a double sunset, Lucas fuses wit and wonder. At its best, so does the rest of the film. The cantina scene, in which creatures from various planets gather to party, leaps off the screen. Can you blame audiences for wanting to leap with it? David Fincher, the director of *Seven* and *The Game*, remembers being fourteen when he saw *Star Wars* for the first time and wanting to escape with Han Solo in that big, rusty spaceship: "All of a sudden this whole world of possibilities opened up. At fourteen, you're thinking about cars and getting out of your parents' house. You go, 'Wow, that's what it would be like to blast out.' "

Blast out, indeed. *Star Wars* quickly built itself a youth cult. The time was right for a seismic shift in audience tastes from introspection to escapism. Corruption in high places, epitomized by the Watergate break-in in 1972, inspired Hollywood to produce darkly brilliant works on political paranoia, such as *The Parallax View* (1974) with Warren Beatty, *Three Days of the Condor* (1975) with Robert Redford and *All the President's Men* (1976) with Redford as Bob Woodward and Dustin Hoffman as Carl Bernstein, the *Washington Post* reporters who helped expose the Nixon cover-up. It's ironic that the best movie about the Watergate era is still *Chinatown* (1974), a detective story set in 1937. In telling the story of Jake Gittes (Jack Nicholson), a private eye who uncovers an L.A. land scam that extends to the highest levels of government, *Chinatown,* with a career-peak script by Robert Towne, signaled an end to Sixties idealism. "Forget it, Jake, it's Chinatown," says a Gittes operative when the detective attempts to dig further into the chaos of corruption for answers. The line became emblematic of the pessimism at the heart of the first part of the decade.

By 1976, the mood of the country and its movies had changed. *Rocky,* Stallone's underdog triumph about the triumph of a boxing underdog, won the Oscar for Best Picture over the harder-edged *Taxi Driver, Network* and *All the President's Men.* Nixon had resigned, Jimmy Carter was soon to win the presidency and America wanted to forget its troubles. You could see the signs in 1975, when Steven Spielberg's *Jaws* brought out audiences in record numbers to watch a great white shark nibble at the swimming population of a New England town. But it took Spielberg's pal George Lucas to relieve public malaise in a record-breaking way with *Star Wars.* As a team, Spielberg and Lucas were onto something. They were building movies like theme parks. The *Star Wars* trilogy would morph into an Indiana Jones trilogy in the Eighties with Harrison Ford, Han Solo himself, as the whip-cracking Indy. In the Nineties, Spielberg would mint money by cloning dinosaurs in a *Jurassic Park* series while Lucas prepared trilogy number two in the *Star Wars* series.

For the record, the reissue of *Star Wars* in 1997 – with zapped-up visual effects that Lucas couldn't afford and technology didn't allow in 1977 – fattened the gross by $138 million to make it the biggest box-office winner of all time, followed by Spielberg's *E.T.* and *Jurassic Park.* Not even a year later, James Cameron's *Titanic* – the most expensive movie ever made, at $200 million – knocked *Star Wars* off the box-office throne in a matter of weeks (thirteen to be exact) after its opening in December 1997. It's only fitting, since Cameron, whose pre-*Titanic* output included *Aliens, The Abyss* and two *Terminator* films, is the principal disciple of Lucas and Spielberg in the Nineties. The public obsession with the budget-busting *Titanic* and its grosses is a direct outgrowth of what Lucas and Spielberg started in the Seventies. When these golden boys started breaking records that had been set in 1939 with *Gone With the Wind,* audience expectations rose to a level that began turning studios into gladiators and moviegoing into a blood sport. Even the country's leading film critics reduced their verdicts to a simple thumbs up or thumbs down. Audiences demanded that each new film epic top the one that came before.

> **Right after *American Graffiti*, I was getting this fan mail from kids that said the film changed their lives, and something inside me said, do a children's film. And everybody said, "Do a *children's film?* What are you talking about? You're crazy." –George Lucas**

In response, Hollywood changed radically. Gone were the days when a movie would open in a few key cities and spread by word of mouth. Now studios fling their costly epics into wide release, buoyed by lavish marketing campaigns that amount to as much as a third of the film's budget. Teaser trailers precede a movie by months to prepare the way. No longer can a studio hide its failures. Everyone from Internet nerds to your crazy cousin Mo monitors a movie's weekend grosses. If the product doesn't measure up, it hits the discard pile, damn the budget. The result? Sequels, retreads and rip-offs built to exploit formula rather than foster originality. Lucas and Spielberg have much to answer for.

Depressed yet? The Seventies proved a nurturing audience once existed for maverick movies that thrived on content, character and rule-busting defiance. But that was before the dark times when computer-generated imagery replaced humanity as the leading box-office draw. Thinking back on *Stars Wars* and all the sleek, soulless movies it spawned, most egregiously *Starship Troopers,* I wonder if Lucas will ever again find that creative spark that marked his work before marketing took it over. *Forget it, Jake, it's Chinatown.*

Or maybe not. Something else sticks with me about *Star Wars*: At the end, the kick-ass rebels take on the evil Empire and win. ⊕

record plant refuse to press the Buzzcocks' "Oh Shit," the flip side of their single "What Do I Get?" It will eventually make it to record stores and the U.K. charts.

21 The *Saturday Night Fever* soundtrack, featuring the Bee Gees, the Trammps, Tavares, K.C. & the Sunshine Band, Kool & the Gang, MFSB and others, reaches #1, dislodging Linda Ronstadt's *Simple Dreams* and beginning 24 weeks as the country's top seller.

24 *Cosmos 954*, a nuclear-equipped Soviet satellite, falls out of orbit and into the dense Canadian wilderness. Investigators will find debris a week later and determine that it poses no threat to humans.

27 The Illinois Supreme Court upholds the American Nazi Party's right to march through the predominantly Jewish town of Skokie. On June 12, the U.S. Supreme Court will refuse to hear an appeal of the case, allowing the June 25 parade to occur.

28 Terry Kath, guitarist and singer for Chicago, accidentally shoots and kills himself.

30 Baseball commissioner Bowie Kuhn blocks the sale of Oakland A's pitcher Vida Blue to the Cincinnati Reds, judging the move to be against the best interests of the game. Twice miffed (Kuhn had prevented the sale of three A's in 1976), A's owner Charles Finley will call on fellow owners to oust Kuhn from office. On Mar. 3, 20 of the 26 owners will announce their support for Kuhn, and on Oct. 2, the Supreme Court will do the same. Blue will finally be traded to the San Francisco Giants.

31 Blood, Sweat & Tears saxophonist Greg Herbert dies of an accidental drug overdose in Amsterdam, during a European tour.

1978 FEBRUARY

1 Polish filmmaker Roman Polanski, facing statutory rape charges in California, flees the U.S.

Bob Dylan's foray into film, *Renaldo and Clara*, premieres in Los Angeles. A quasi-documentary of the Rolling Thunder tour, featuring appearances by Roger McGuinn, David Blue, Joan Baez, Allen Ginsberg, Ramblin' Jack Elliott, Dylan's wife Sara and many others, the film clocks in at 232 minutes (later cut to

saint elvis
by chet flippo

In the Seventies, Elvis Presley's hip-swiveling vigor had become a heavy plod. His early, historic records still inspired generations of rock & rollers, but the charge and thrill – the irreverent danger – of his music and stance were muted and weary.

On August 17, 1977, the young man from Tupelo, the white man who could "sing with the soul and feel of a Negro" (as producer Sam Phillips reportedly said), the poor man with a "million dollars worth of talent" (as his manager Colonel Tom Parker stated), was found dead behind the gates of Graceland. But as a life ended, a career was reborn. In the years that have followed, the tragic elements of Presley's story – his political innocence, his abuse of prescription drugs, his Garbo-like retreat in the end – have only added to his ascension. To this day, his throne remains empty.

THE FIRST WHISPERINGS of a clandestine Elvis church service came out of Fort Wayne, Indiana. A group of paunchy, heavily sideburned, middle-aged men, as the rumors went, started holding Elvis services once a week. With an altar and all, but not too formal. Low Elvis, as it were. Then, for more than a year, I started hearing serious rumors about an Elvis church in Manhattan. I heard of sightings from too many otherwise sobersided people to dismiss it totally as garbage: They had all heard of an Elvis church ceremony floating among various vacant storefronts on Manhattan's Lower East Side.

In both cases, the rumors remain tantalizing but impossible to confirm. And the more I explore the phenomenon of Elvis Alive the more I understand the Mystery: Nobody wants to be labeled an Elvis nut. No matter how innocent the connection. Many hard-core Elvis cases remain "in the closet" because their devotion to El might cause problems with the boss, wife, in-laws, school, job. Even so, it is obvious two decades after his death that Elvis touched a great many people more than they realized at first.

Like many a grand Southern funeral, Elvis's was conducted on a larger-than-death scale: every flower in Memphis heaped up in memorial, every limousine within hundreds of miles pressed into service, tens of thousands of weeping, prostrate mourners, the eyes of the world glued to this great spectacle taking place on August 18, 1977. Elvis Presley's passing evoked memories of illustrious funerals past: Huey Long crossing to glory over in Louisiana, Hank Williams taking his last ride down in Alabama, General Robert E. Lee giving up his last command in Virginia.

As a casual Elvis fan, I pretty much quit paying attention to him after he went into the army. As a journalist, I kept up with him but had no idea what was really going on with his career until I went to his funeral. As a reporter, I've covered only two such occasions: JFK's and Elvis's funerals. Needless to say, there were many similarities. What most amazed me, however, was the emotional intensity present at each. In many ways, Elvis's laying-to-rest was the more intense, especially because there was no protocol for the fans attending. At a president's funeral you know what you're supposed to do and not supposed to do. At Elvis's, on the other hand, there was an undercurrent of such untapped . . . spirituality, if you will, that it was always unsettling and at times frightening. The potential was there for anything to happen. I had had no idea there were so many people, so fiercely devoted, who now felt such a devastating loss and emptiness.

In many ways, Elvis's death is best compared to that of Robert E. Lee, both because of the cultural similarities and the extraordinary degree of public grief. Both Lee and Presley were identified by Southerners as ideal Southerners who were sullied or brought down by outside forces beyond their control. Both were deified as a result of their grand failures – which were caused by someone else. In Lee's case, the blame for Gettysburg was assigned to Longstreet. In Elvis's, it was the dope-doctor, Dr. Nick; it was the Judaslike bodyguards who exposed his pill-popping final years; it was the pointy-headed music muckraker Albert Goldman wallowing in Elvis's filth; it was anybody who brought down the noble Elvis. Elvis was martyred overnight. I can tell you, the

112) and leaves most critics and fans baffled and impatient with its cryptic dialogue and loose narrative structure.

4 *Saturday Night Fever* is #2 at the nation's cinemas, while the soundtrack and its current single, the Bee Gees' "Stayin' Alive," are both #1 on the pop charts.

15 Muhammad Ali loses his title to Leon Spinks in a split decision in Las Vegas.

23 The Southern California scene dominates the Grammys as the Eagles claim Record of the Year for "Hotel California" and Best Arrangement for Voices for "New Kid in Town," and Fleetwood Mac grabs Album of the Year for *Rumours*. Disco artists Thelma Houston ("Don't Leave Me This Way") and Leo Sayer ("You Make Me Feel Like Dancing") each land one award, and film-score master John Williams wins for the hit soundtrack to *Star Wars*.

ROLLING STONE reports that several radio stations have banned Randy Newman's "Short People" because of listener complaints. Sales skyrocket in cities such as Boston and Chicago, where the record was removed.

British punk band the Stranglers delay their L.A. debut as police continue the search for the "Hillside Strangler," whose murders of L.A.-area women remain unsolved.

28 British punk rockers the Damned call it quits for the first of several times.

1978 MARCH

2 Charlie Chaplin's coffin is stolen from a cemetery in Switzerland. His body will turn up May 17, in a field ten miles east of the cemetery.

6 *Hustler* publisher Larry Flynt is shot and paralyzed from the waist down outside a Georgia courthouse where he had been facing trial for the distribution of obscene material.

15 *American Hot Wax*, a cinematic portrayal of pioneering rock & roll DJ Alan Freed, opens in New York City. Chuck Berry, Jerry Lee Lewis and Screamin' Jay Hawkins perform, while *SNL*'s Laraine Newman plays a songwriting sidekick, loosely based on Carole King, to Tim McIntire's portrayal of Freed.

16 After a long public battle, the Senate passes President Carter's Panama Canal Treaty, guaranteeing that the Canal

silent intensity of feeling for the lost Elvis that day was so overwhelming among the crowds thronging Graceland that it could have levitated an unbeliever.

If you had to pick a day when Elvis started becoming a religion, the day of his funeral would be as good a choice as any. But it had begun even before. As longtime Elvis watcher and biographer Dave Marsh once told me, "It all depends on in whose mind Elvis became a religion. Remember, in the early days, Sam Phillips was running around comparing himself to John the Baptist and Elvis to Christ. And that was in '54 or so."

Patsy Guy Hammontree, an English professor at the University of Tennessee, Knoxville, wrote the seminal Elvis reference book, *Elvis Presley: A Bio-Bibliography*, and has monitored Elvis happenings for many years. She went to her first Elvis concert in 1972. "It was a religion back then," she says. "Forget saying that Elvis is becoming a religion now. It was one from the beginning. The first thing that struck me was that it was very much like a Baptist revival – without any of the sadness. People were weeping but they were weeping for joy. They were joyous, I learned, because each one felt that Elvis was singing personally to them and only to them, directly to them. He was looking directly into their souls, they thought."

Yes, Elvis's passing brought back memories. But the one thing no one imagined at the time was that, unlike other famous dead Southerners, Elvis could not be counted on to remain dead. Either in the flesh or in the spirit. Amazingly, decades after his "alleged" death, the hue and cry and glory and worship are not only persisting, but they are increasing to an almost sacrilegious recognition of sainthood. For Elvis! There are literally thousands of otherwise partly sane citizens walking around thinking out loud that Elvis never croaked at all and is still walking among us, perhaps rearing back and performing an occasional miracle in between trips to Dunkin' Donuts and Wal-Mart. Others – many others – are elevating Elvis to a hallowed spot somewhere just a tad below the Holy Trinity, making him the focal point of a religion. As Hammontree points out, less and less is known about Elvis himself as the years pass: The myth has quickly swallowed the man. Just how and why did such things come to pass?

There were a number of reasons for Elvis's phenomenal popularity while he was alive, most of them self-evident. What took over with a fierce vengeance after he died, though, is a matter less easy to capture or chart. Still, it is impossible to deny that something far beyond the ordinary now informs the Elvis Mystique, something that has a genuine hold on millions of people. These are normal, workaday people you pass on the street every day without realizing they have a secret: They are Elvis worshipers. For most, it doesn't go beyond a very strong attachment to the man and his music: a collection of as many Elvis records as possible and the really important stuff beyond that, the personal Elvis icons, like the ticket stubs from the Hilton show in Vegas, the Elvis scarf snatched out of the air almost from the master's hand, the ashtrays and place mats and other junk from the souvenir shops on Elvis Presley Boulevard across from Graceland.

Still others are more possessive, more obsessive. They're the ones with the Elvis rooms in their houses, those eerie shrines to the King, displaying jars of pure Elvis dirt from the grounds of Graceland; rare photos (it's been estimated that at least a billion photos were taken of Elvis in concert during the last seven years of his life alone); snippets of his clothing; pieces of carpet from Graceland; a dried and pressed flower from his funeral; a scrap of aluminum foil that once blacked out his windows at the Hilton; "Always Elvis" wine. They vacation every year at Graceland. They listen to little but Elvis. They may have personalized Elvis plates on their vans. Some of them channel Elvis.

Then there are the really way-out cases, those lives that are virtually turned over to Elvis. They wear Elvis, think Elvis, eat and sleep Elvis, and maybe see him or hear from him occasionally. There's an unsettling documentary called *Mondo Elvis* that you should rent if you ever get the chance. It's a series of interviews with some extreme Elvis cases: twin teenage girls who are convinced Elvis is their father; a woman who abandoned her family to move to Memphis and be near El's spirit; and a truly dedicated Elvis impersonator who is acting as an ordained priest, but to carry on this King's spirit. There are straight-faced Elvis fans in this film who predict that he will one day (in the not-so-distant future) be the first Protestant saint. Or should be. (From all accounts, his interest in the spiritual began early in life and greatly intensified in his last years.)

Well, that's in accordance with his spiritual history. Especially since there are now frequent sightings of the King, along with the occasional miracle (shakily documented though they may be). For example, this comes from a supermarket tabloid: "After she lost her sight saving her Elvis LPs from a fire in her home, Rosa D'Angelo was visited by the late idol's spirit and healed." There's even a whole book dedicated to "unusual psychic experiences surrounding the death of a superstar." It's titled *Elvis After Life,* and contains several case studies of Elvis's "activities" since his alleged death. Why did Ruth Ann Bennett's Elvis records mysteriously melt just after Elvis died? Why did Arthur and Marian Parker's Elvis statue fall to the floor and crash? What exactly happened when Beverly Wilkins was temporarily "dead" and met Elvis?

Much of the supernatural and spiritual phenomena surrounding Elvis Presley in both death and life can be explained away in simple psychological terms: wishful thinking, psychosomatic effects of grief, anniversary reactions, photism, mass hysteria and so on. There was also, though not everyone realizes it, a strong spiritual attachment to Elvis on the part of others that was built up throughout his life. Elvis was certainly never comfortable with it, but the fact remains that there was an intense spiritual reaction to him from the first, and not just on the part of teenage girls. Those who saw his first appearance on *Louisiana Hayride* remarked on his phenomenal effect on women of all ages in the audience, an effect that went beyond any kind of reaction to the music or his raw sex appeal. Increasingly, members of his audience came to describe their initial reactions to Elvis in religious terms. And what they were talking about, more often than not, was the ecstasy of conversion, a fairly standard religious experience. It was obviously something that went beyond the usual appeal of a charismatic leader. Critics and observers of the early Elvis phenomenon went so far as to compare his effect on audiences to that of Gandhi or Hitler. Or Jesus Christ.

Elvis's own image did not deviate from the holy: He loved his mother, he loved gospel music, he did not seem to sin and he loved his fans. And he never forgot his roots. No more could be asked of a matinee idol. Indeed, he himself seemed to become more spiritual, if not mystical, as the years went by. His hairdresser, Larry Geller, became his spiritual advisor and was apparently responsible for what books actually made it into Elvis's limited library over the years: Linda Goodman's *Sun Signs,* Kahlil Gibran's *The Prophet,* Cheiro's *Book of Numbers, The Secret Doctrine* by Helena Blavatsky, books by Edgar Cayce and so on. Elvis also carried and read the Bible, and said that his favorite passage was I Corinthians 10:13.

Televangelist Rex Humbard, who straightaway called up Vernon Presley and volunteered to deliver a eulogy the minute he heard that Elvis had passed, affirmed Elvis's spirituality. After he had seen Elvis perform in Las Vegas, he went back to his dressing room after the show and later said, "While Elvis and I talked, something supernatural happened – a light filled the room. We wept together. Elvis said to me, 'Mr. Humbard, this is the greatest Christmas gift I could have.' "

Humbard did not preach at the funeral, although he did deliver a short, emotional eulogy. Reverend C.W. Bradley of the Wooddale Church of Christ officiated. Bradley was Vernon's pastor, and while he said he liked Elvis, he attributed no divine qualities to him.

Soon thereafter, however, the world at large began to get some inkling of the fanaticism with which enormous numbers of people worshiped Elvis. What struck me most at first was the stolid passivity of these people, who wanted nothing more than to stand at the gates of Graceland and weep. I watched in amazement as they literally stripped the grounds of Graceland Christian Church, next door to Graceland proper. They clawed at the very earth and denuded the shrubs and greenery, seeking something to carry away. Fans just assumed – incorrectly – that it was Elvis's parish church, and they treated it accordingly. That poor church finally knuckled under and sold out to Graceland.

Many Memphians themselves were sick of the whole crazy business and wished it would just go away. Even today, Elvis plays better outside Tennessee than within. The high holy days of Elvismania are officially known in Memphis as "Elvis International Tribute Week" but are derisively referred to by locals as "Dead Elvis Week." The third week of August encompasses Elvis's and his mother, Gladys's, death days, and the week is the high point of life for a true El-fan. Elvismania itself is too far-flung and too extensive to be catalogued comprehensively, but in this one week most of what goes on around Elvis can be glimpsed or experienced in Memphis. And what goes on is a splendiferous subculture at work. The motels up and down Elvis Presley Boulevard are booked solid for months in advance by the fan clubs and impersonators. Motel room windows are decorated competitively. There are candlelight vigils galore, an Elvis 5K run, a Fan Appreciation Social and more craziness than can be easily explained. The people who participate in these activities are otherwise normal people who just happen to feel that Elvis had a major impact on their lives, one that cannot be ignored. The rest of the year they may be in the closet, but come August's holy week they're flaunting it in the streets of Memphis.

Thanks to them, Graceland itself, and the Elvis estate in general, is doing much better than Elvis did when he was alive. It has a captive audience, after all.

I once had the good fortune to visit Graceland in the company of Jerry Lee Lewis. He was Elvis's biggest rival until his marriage to his thirteen-year-old cousin effectively caused him to be blacklisted by the music industry. He is no great Elvis fan – the last time he had been to Graceland, while Elvis was still alive, he had been arrested at the gate with a gun in his car. Even so, he had mellowed enough in the intervening years to consent to be the honored guest on a nationwide radio show broadcast live from Graceland. Jerry Lee was gracious enough on the show – surprisingly so, given his volatile nature. Later, though, he told me, "Yeah, they makin' all this damn money off damn Elvis Presley. I don't even know whether he's dead or not. I thought he was, anyway. If that sumbitch comes back alive, I'm gonna kill myself." ⊕

platinum rising
by stan cornyn

IN 1978, I was executive vice president of Warner Bros. Records. I'd been moved into the company's Number Two office, sharing a private bath with Number One – Mo Ostin. My new office was, no kidding, big enough to host an indoor volleyball match.

By then, I'd put in almost two decades at Warner, having been hired in its beginning, fumbling years to help Joel Friedman, the label's early marketing head. Then, because I spelled excellently, my job was to write whatever the company needed written – liner notes, sales slide films, even order forms. At the time, Warner was, like its future stablemates Elektra and Atlantic, an independent label beneath notice – as important to retailers as Yugoslavian cars have become to the American auto market.

It was the Fifties. If you went on the road, you slept two guys to a room (and hoped not to draw Joel Friedman, who snored like all Detroit after every poker-and-whiskey game). In 1959 the major labels (RCA, Columbia, Capitol) ruled. The big guys got 90 percent of their entire catalogues stocked in stores, while indie labels like Warner got 5 percent stocked, which meant if you had a list of 150 albums, 7.5 of your albums would show up in a store, and 142.5 of them would be dusty somewhere. Indier labels (like Atlantic and Elektra) showed up in stores, on average, with zero percent.

In the twenty-odd years since joining Warner, I'd been fired and rehired, seen Joel Friedman move on to head up the Warner music group's distribution company (called WEA, for Warner-Elektra-Atlantic). I'd been in the right place at the right time (the Sixties and Seventies) with the right attitude. We got big, flourishing under the corporate umbrella of Warner Communications Inc. (WCI). Now it was we who got 90 percent of our albums stocked in stores. I, personally, had risen as well. My new, Seventies job in my new sports arena–sized office was to administer a company of executives who did not wish to be administered.

This impasse came home to me one day when, in reviewing an expense account, I saw that one of our valuable executives had bought himself a Montblanc pen on the company tab, and had dispatched a limousine to the jewelry store to fetch it. When I brought up this excess to Mo Ostin, he waved his hand in dismissal, as though I were acting like some kid at a big-time restaurant, counting out nickels and pennies to pay a three-hundred-dollar bill. In the Warner family, you didn't screw with the executives or the artists. *Buying pens via limo – haven't we anything better to think about, Stan?*

Growth wasn't limited to our music group. The entire record business was exploding. Wall Street took note and started calling it the "Record Industry." In 1978, WEA grossed $394.5 million – a big contrast to 1963, when a one-million-dollar, finally-in-the-black year for Warner Bros. had called for champagne (albeit in Styrofoam cups). By 1978, WCI's record companies had, in the United States, a 24.7 percent market share. That means we were selling one of every four albums sold. *Hey, no sweat! Styrofoam in '78? Unthinkable.*

In this new, good-to-be-the-kings age of the latter Seventies, there was no two-to-a-rooming going on; it was one-to-a-suite. Our corporate daddies sugared our travel with the WCI jet, especially when it came time for Mo Ostin, myself and a couple of others to fly almost every October from Burbank to New York and delight the WCI bosses with astonishing profit reports.

Later in 1978, the plane ride began to feel rockier. For the first time in my experience, our company's gross gush of cash did not cover its grosser excesses of expenses. We execs were caught between (a) dealing with Corporate, who loved us for earning increasingly bigger profits for the company, and (b) dealing with our own execs and artists, who loved us because we tolerated damn near anything.

Which brings us to New Orleans.

Elektra Records had scheduled a "Coming Out" party for its next major album release. The party would be thrown in New Orleans's French Quarter. When Elektra asked its

English camp-rock stars Queen to attend this party for the group's new album, well, the only possible, the only conceiv- able way for Queen to get to that party was to fly there via private jet. With a bedroom. And a shower. With a glass door.

The theme for this bash was obvious: Really Fun Women. Queen had come up with an album called *Jazz*. From it, there was a single called "Fat Bottomed Girls," with a picture sleeve that featured an ass-focused rear view of a pink-bikini-clad woman on a bicycle. There was also a promotional photo of about sixty similarly attired female cyclists, the result of a bike "race" that Queen had staged in London. Nudes-on-bikes rapidly became a Queen motif. At a later Madison Square Garden concert, the audience cheered half-naked women cycling across the stage during the band's performance.

To draw even more attention to "Fat Bottomed Girls," Elektra, climbing way out on some limb, threw what may well have been the most ribald rock party ever held in pub- lic view. Elektra rented the entire city of New Orleans, or so it seemed. The party became a two-hundred-thousand-dollar exercise in debauchery, even by French Quarter standards. Queen disembarked from the rented plane, leaving behind the fur bedspread and satin sheets.

After sundown, Queen met New Orleans. Both boogied through the humid night. Sweat melted shirts and blouses until most anything above the belt became free to rub.

Through this all-night romp roamed hired, hermaphroditic strippers. Topless waitresses bore trays of condoms and Vaseline. Rock blared, reverberating through cobblestone streets better suited for Dixieland parades and the strains of "St. James Infirmary." Amped-up rock deafened streets with names like Bourbon. The Quarter's old-timers bent over iron balconies, agog at behaviors no Lenten Carnival had ever put on parade. Stoned secretaries, whirling their arms, spun themselves dizzy, opening themselves freely to any- thing. Hired escape artists did their Houdini tricks. Freelance dwarfs, some hired, some not, tugged on people's pants, yelling up obscenities. Crowds flocked to see the woman who was smoking cigarettes from an orifice that precluded any possible concerns about lung cancer.

Flying in the corporate jet wasn't just for singers – it was also for signers of singers. But the people who actually dis- tributed the albums – the straphangers who manned WEA's pick-pack-and-ship distribution centers – did not fly in private.

Behind the flash and glamour of rock stardom lay the day-to-day routine of distribution pipelines. In charge of WEA's pipeline – in charge of the cardboard boxes and the tak- ing back of returns and collecting of cash – was that five- feet-six-inch *bubeleh* from Brooklyn named Joel Friedman.

In that heady sell-'em-by-the-ton age, when even albums by exercise guru Richard Simmons could ship platinum (a million copies out), Friedman was caught between his own conservative sense that the market was oversold and his responsibility to the "ship out more" euphoria emanating from the sales departments at his three labels supplying the albums. However, when it came to making how-many- to-ship policy with the labels, Joel Friedman had been taught to speak his piece, then to shut his mouth.

He had been one of the founding fathers of Warner Bros.

Records back in 1958. As that label grew, three of its exec- utives bonded. These three – Ostin, Friedman and Joe Smith – shared East Coast ancestry. They now lived in the same town: Encino. They synagogued together. Saturday morn- ings at Dupar's Deli, they eggs-and-pastramied together.

When, in the Sixties, Steve Ross gave Warner Bros. Records new management, he elevated Ostin and Smith to the Number One and Number Two spots. Joel Friedman felt passed by.

Friedman had to take it. He knew how. He'd grown up in low-rent New York, where he'd learned the Hustle before it became a dance step. Friedman had found his way into the business from behind a manual typewriter, working as a reporter for both *Cash Box* and *Billboard* magazines. Then he signed up to head marketing at the just-forming Warner Bros. Records. Joel Friedman looked people in their eyes and bear-hugged colleagues more often than Smokey. He remembered the first names of shipping clerks' kids.

Like most independent labels in the postwar era, the three WCI labels – Warner Bros., Atlantic and Elektra – grew to success using somebody else's selling machine. To open their own nationwide distribution systems would have cost more than indie labels could afford. So the young labels suffered through the years with "independent distributors." Indies had no clout. They got paid when their indie distribs needed their new hit. If they were cold, they likely didn't get paid. To have, as the Warner label heads envisioned it, "control over our own destinies," had taken these labels decades to achieve.

The moment came in 1971 when the three labels gath- ered under the ownership of, effectively, one guy: Steve Ross, the head of what came to be known as WCI. Joel Friedman had been voted into his chance to become one of those privileged jet riders by creating one common distributorship for the three feisty labels. For the next six years, from 1971 to 1977, with Joe Pesci–like drive, Friedman and a small WEA team built the first new branch records system in America since the Forties, and the last one ever since. Getting your own branches meant, at first, tough divorces from your collection of old, slow-paying indie distributors like New York's Harry Apostoleris, who kept a lead pipe in his desk drawer for just such situations. It meant setting up warehouses in eight different cities in less than a year; making hires, getting loading docks fig- ured out and dealing with all the street realities. Friedman, day after day, constructed a machine. And it worked.

The labels made it easier: They put out hit albums. WEA shot up to a Number One market share ($144 million) with- in its first year, outselling its big rival, Columbia. That made WEA the goldenest goose in the whole record business. It pissed off Columbia. WCI, the guys in Manhattan with the private jets, steadied the basket under the goose, lovingly counting WEA's 1971 golden eggs: Roberta Flack. Jimi Hendrix. Aretha Franklin. Crosby, Stills, Nash and Young.

After six years of working out of sight, back in the record group's kitchen, Friedman still only rated flying first-class commercial. He knew not to ask. And to wait his turn.

He trudged on. Like others in this business, he worked a lot of nights and weekends, ate every meal with extra marinara and halfway through the meeting had to empty the ashtrays. Even in this up-all-night crowd, Friedman became legendary

Night," a song cowritten with Bruce Springsteen. The song will reach #13.

More than 40 rock & roll performers petition President Carter to end America's commitment to nuclear power. Many of the participants, including James Taylor, Bruce Springsteen, Jackson Browne, Carly Simon, the Doobie Brothers, Gil Scott-Heron and Tom Petty & the Heartbreakers, will later play at antinuke benefits and record the *No Nukes* album.

Dead Boys drummer Johnny Blitz is stabbed in a street fight near CBGB; a four-night benefit to defray his medical costs follows.

In a Washington, DC, news conference, a former Cambodian information minister reveals that as a result of the tyrannical rule of the Khmer Rouge, more than two million of his countrymen have been murdered or have died from starvation or disease and that the deaths are continuing.

21 Former Fairport Convention singer Sandy Denny dies after falling down a flight of stairs in a friend's London home.

22 Bob Marley & the Wailers headline the One Love Peace concert in Kingston. Performers include Culture, Dennis Brown, Big Youth, Jacob Miller and a spliff-smoking Peter Tosh. The climax comes when Marley brings out rival politicians Prime Minister Michael Manley and Edward Seaga, who grasp hands in a gesture of unity.

23 Ex–Sex Pistol Sid Vicious films his rendition of Paul Anka's "My Way" for the band's movie *The Great Rock 'n' Roll Swindle,* pulling out a revolver and shooting at his audience to end the performance.

28 *FM,* a film about the battle between progressives and regressives at a rock radio station, featuring Linda Ronstadt, Jimmy Buffet, REO Speedwagon and Tom Petty, premieres. Three weeks later, Casablanca Records chief Neil Bogart will unveil *Thank God It's Friday,* his answer to *Saturday Night Fever,* with music by Donna Summer, the Commodores, Diana Ross and the Village People. A day after that, *The Buddy Holly Story,* a tribute to the bespectacled rock & roll pioneer, starring Gary Busey, will open in Dallas.

1978 MAY

9 Tubes lead singer Fee Waybill

for his drive. At La Costa sales meetings, if it was tennis break, Friedman would be out on the court, four-eyed, bandy-legged, big-bellied, gold neck chains bouncing off his chest, yelling across the net at younger, fitter opponents, "That all you got?" His staff knew just what to get Friedman for the holidays: They chipped in for an Exercycle.

In 1977, just six years after its birth, WEA felt flush. Rather than its usual save-a-buck regional meetings, WEA decided to convene all its infantry, over seven hundred of them, in one major convention. There, in a darkened auditorium in the Diplomat Hotel near Miami, for the first time, the seven hundred looked up onstage where a banner proclaimed (who knows what this thing meant?) THE FUTURE IS NOW.

Joel Friedman's distribution company had been elevated to glamour status. Can't you see? Right there, in the auditorium's front row, sat the Very Big Guys: WCI chairman Steve Ross, record group exec VP David Horowitz and WEA International's head, Nesuhi Ertegun. Validation: They'd actually flown in for their Golden Goose!

Friedman finally got his turn in the spotlight. At the mike, he announced his opening hurrahs:

• Each year for the past six years, WEA's sales had risen more rapidly than anyone else's in the industry.

• WEA labels had earned more Recording Industry Association of America–certified gold and platinum awards than any other company in the business.

• Fleetwood Mac's *Rumours* and the Eagles' *Hotel California* had gone quintuple platinum. Once, quintuple-platinum sales (such as Carole King's *Tapestry* and records by the original Tijuana Brass) had been considered freaks. Now they'd become a commonplace fact of life.

• The previous year, more than seventy Warner artists had sold in excess of one million units in the U.S. alone.

• The previous year, WEA had sold one of every four albums sold in America, a 24 percent share. (Nearest rival Columbia felt gall at 17 percent.)

• "We haven't even scratched the surface," exulted Friedman. "We hereby predict a new level of award: the Titanium Album, for ten million unit sales!"

Flamboyant and campy rock stars in the style of Queen got shipped in to perform for the convention. Onstage, these men flailed, their guitars swinging aloft, their shirts unbuttoned in deep Vs, directing your eye to the bulging Wonder Jocks. Meat on stage, performing for Row A, where sat Money.

Previous spread: November 16, 1978: Queen's Freddie Mercury receives onstage support from free-wheeling cyclists; at right: Warner Bros. execs Mo Ostin and Joel Friedman *(from left)*

During one such courting of the sales force, down in the darkened auditorium, puffs-after-climbing-three-steps Friedman seized the arm of his Number Two exec, Henry Droz, whispering, "Hold me. I can't see." Droz steadied Friedman. Within a minute, Friedman recovered. In the dark, Friedman pooh-poohed, "I'm okay now." Hey Joel, maybe too much celebrating last night?

The following week up in Manhattan, Joel shook hands with WCI's David Horowitz on his new contract, one that gave Friedman that "equal status feeling." Now, at long last, he was doing as well as his former colleagues Mo and Joe. On American Air, returning to his home in California, Friedman munched his Rolaids and leaned over to his seatmate, a promo guy from Atlantic. "Well, kid, I can't believe it. They gave me everything I wanted. I got so much money coming in, I don't know what's going to happen next."

He paged through that week's *Billboard* with glee. Of the top five albums in the country, WEA distributed four: Number One, Fleetwood Mac's *Rumours*; Number Two, Linda Ronstadt's *Simple Dreams*; Number Four, Foreigner's *Foreigner*; Number Five, the Rolling Stones' *Love You Live.*

And eight in the Top Twenty! He turned to the promotion man. "That's a 40 percent share!" And then, with a couple of Jack Daniel's down, Joel Friedman drifted off to sleep.

At home that evening, Joel told his wife about his new deal at WCI. Finally, he felt like one of the Big Four. The next morning – right into another ferocious workday: tie loosened, impatient, looking for more. Later that night, as he left the office, he stubbed out the workday's last Parliament, shook his head and told Droz, "I gotta stop with these."

The next morning, November 8, Joel Melvin Friedman woke at 4:00 a.m., complain-

ing of chest pains. Paramedics rushed over, but Friedman's aorta had ruptured. He was fifty-two.

The next day, work colleagues gathered at the Friedman home just to be there. They stood in groups in the backyard, not wanting to let Friedman's lingering presence escape. They told stories of late-night poker games with Jack Daniel's on the table. They spoke of Joel, their up-from-Brooklyn kinsman. They revisited stories of the endless nights of restaurant-made pasta-with-meatballs and cornball jokes. In that backyard, it was a day when, instead of laughing at those good old jokes, we could only nod, Yes, I was there; Yes, I know.

On the back porch, the assembled noticed Friedman's Exercycle. WEA executive Vic Faraci walked over to the machine. To the others, he read off the odometer: "Six."

The Warner records group's Age of Innocence just happened to die around the time of Friedman's death. Market realities came in through death's door, and market realities moved in to stay. LPs that had exuberantly "shipped platinum" – who told Richard Simmons he should sing? – got returned platinum. For the whole record industry, and for the WEA labels, 1978 turned sour. Optimism was stifled. Bonus bonanzas looked like a thing of the past.

Following the collapse, the labels-and-corporate-budget meetings were chilly. Mo Ostin, on the jet headed to Warner's meeting, polled his executives for a list of "1977's Accomplishments at WBR," hoping it would cover up way-too-short profits for the year. Ostin wrote a list on his yellow tablet: the number of Warner's Grammy awards, the number of Warner's Number Ones on the chart . . .

At the budget meeting, as Ostin was presenting this Accomplishments list, he was gently interrupted by his boss, WCI's Steve Ross, with the chide, "Mo, thanks, but the name of the game . . . is performance." With that sentence, that final word, "performance," a new reality became clear. Parties in New Orleans were fine, so long as they paid off in profits. In that sentence, that one word by Ross, our record business had changed from a vast fling featuring nude bicyclists to a new focus on a different bottom line.

I'd written down one other sentence that Steve Ross said in that meeting: "This business is like a car going up a hill. The first time you go into neutral, you're going backward."

Those six-hour, private-jet flights back to the West Coast seemed, at decade's end, to move through cold fronts. A whole year – 1978 – at zero profit. Could it be over? label heads wondered. What if our numbers keep shrinking? Is this back to the Sixties level, back to Trini Lopez and Pet Clark?   ⊕

finding hope in the middle east
by joe klein

I. WELCOME TO FATAHLAND, 1978

My first day in Beirut, I approached two young men standing like hunters in front of the PLO press office with rifles hitched up under their armpits, the snouts rest-ing on their forearms. They smiled, shook my hand and directed me up to the third floor, where there was a small waiting room for foreign press papered with PLO posters, all of which had one thing in common: guns. The most jarring were pictures of young children carrying rifles and trying to look defiant; also a drawing of a chorus line of Kalashnikovs parading into the Promised Land. Beneath a poster of Fidel Castro cuddling some children – one of the few that didn't include a gun – sat a Palestinian college student who handed me a form to fill out. With a minimum of fuss, I was assigned a PLO guide to take me down to the front lines in South Lebanon. The guide was a calm, soft-spoken young man named Naji, who had curly black hair and gold-rimmed eyeglasses. He was twenty-one years old; his family had fled the West Bank after the Israelis took the area in 1967, and now it was dispersed through Europe and the Middle East. Most of his brothers and sisters were well educated and holding down good jobs – a pretty typical story, since Palestinians have the highest rate of college graduates in the Arab world. When I asked him why, with his family doing so well, he was still intent on regaining Palestine, he said impatiently, "Because it is ours."

We were driven down the Lebanese coast in an old green Plymouth by a hired mad-man named Fouad, who felt no reluctance about using anything concrete – sidewalks, oncoming lanes – to get us where we were going.

It was a day of fast-moving, intense rainsqualls and pale sunshine. Syrian check-points slowed the traffic through the sad, ruined towns that had been classy Mediterranean resorts before the civil war. Just south of Sidon, at an oil refinery, we moved into territory controlled, de facto, by the Palestinians. *Fatahland,* the journal-ists called it. Now it was guerrillas – usually members of Fatah, the dominant PLO faction – who guarded the checkpoints. Most wore standard green fatigues, but oth-ers sported T-shirts, longish hair and all sorts of wild paraphernalia. I saw one fedayee wearing a cowboy hat, Texas Tech T-shirt and platform shoes. The guerrillas managed to affect a tough, street-smart pose and yet seem very friendly (later, I'd come across checkpoints where the Palestinians would stick their rifles into the car, then insist on shaking hands with everyone). Some were very, very young: The Qasmieh bridge, *the* crucial north-south link over the Litani River and target of numerous Israeli bombs, was "held" that day, rather nonchalantly, by two apple-cheeked boys just pushing puberty.

"See those hills over there?" Naji asked, pointing to a line of gentle, green slopes running parallel to the road as we crossed the bridge. "The Israelis hold those."

South of the bridge, the Palestinians controlled little more than the coast road and the city of Tyre, a picturesque port with famed Roman ruins. Before the Israeli offen-sive, Tyre had been run by the PLO and left-wing Lebanese and called itself "The People's Republic of Tyre." Now it was mostly deserted. The Israelis, obviously want-ing to clear the place out, had randomly bombed civilian neighborhoods. Naji showed us piles of rubble that once had been houses. Bits of domesticity were trapped in the concrete: children's notebooks, men's shoes, splintered chairs.

We drove several miles south of Tyre, through banana groves, to the Rashidieh refugee camp: a thicket of narrow dirt alleys and cinder-block shacks tucked in behind a citrus orchard. It was deserted now, except for guerrillas who were older and more men-acing than the ones we had seen on the road. These were on the order of tough, griz-zled Mexican bandits. One of the guards, a vicious-looking man with randomly scattered teeth and a ratty old sweatshirt, briefly disputed Naji's credentials but then allowed

us to pass into the camp with a motorcycle escort. At the top of a rise, a man with a telescope was sitting on a bridge chair looking out across a plowed field (studded with cluster bombs, I later learned, a minefield imposed from the sky) at the Israeli positions not more than a mile away. When the car stopped, he came over and offered his telescope. "Want to look at some Jews?" he asked.

"Zionists," Naji quickly corrected him. The man shrugged and smiled. I felt nervous.

Back in Beirut several hours later, Naji took us into the Arab University, down several stairways that grew progressively smokier, past groups of Palestinian boy and girl scouts, through a thick crowd of people and into a jammed meeting hall. I looked around. It wasn't a huge hall – long and narrow, with maybe a thousand seats. But all the seats were filled, and the aisles were packed as well. Every last person – they were mostly young men – seemed to be smoking a cigarette. The room was lit by strings of bare lightbulbs that transformed the cloud of smoke into a yellowish smog. PLO posters were all over the place. And in front, where I stood, were gathered about a hundred men with guns of all different descriptions.

The weaponry seemed a bit much, even by Palestinian standards, until I glanced to my left and saw the entire leadership of the PLO, including Yasir Arafat, sitting in the front row. Arafat, with his usual three-day stubble, was small, mouselike, a politician. He laughed at the jokes, applauded the rhetoric. A large semiautomatic pistol dangled from his hip.

Arafat turned out to be a great speaker, spellbinding even in Arabic. The last two words of his speech were "until victory . . ." and he repeated them until the crowd picked up the chant: "until victory . . . until victory . . . until victory . . ."

It was hard to believe that in the late 1950s, Yasir Arafat had been just another refugee, running a construction company in Kuwait. Palestinian nationalism seemed a wild idea back then, the plaything of a handful of Arab intellectuals. But as the refugee camps grew more crowded and conditions worsened, the idea began to take hold. Just as suffering in the Jewish Diaspora created the dream of Israel, suffering in the Arab diaspora had created Palestine. And now, in the dense, squalid anger of the camps, Palestine was the only dream around.

It had been nurtured in places like Sabra and Shattila, which form a vast running sore on the south side of Beirut, home to 210,000 people. In a winding alley between two of the jumbles of cinder block that pass for housing, I found several families that already had begun to seep into the camp from the south. We were beginning to talk via a PLO interpreter when a massive woman wearing men's pajamas under a housecoat approached and gently began to wring my neck. "Why don't you ask him about the F-15s and the cluster bombs?" She slapped me on the head, playfully, and then rested her arm on my shoulder as she reached down to pick up a pebble. "With this rock, I will liberate Palestine," she said, and the gathering crowd laughed.

I asked her name, and she said, "You can call me . . . Mrs. Sadat."

She began to tell her story: Her family had been forced out of Galilee when she was a little girl. They had been tenant farmers, and the rich Arabs had sold the land to the Jews. When her father protested, he was killed by the Israelis. "They killed many of our young men. The rest of us came to this camp in 1948. I have lived here ever since."

"Do you have any children?" I asked.

"Twelve sons, and they are all fighting the Israelis."

"Aren't you afraid they'll be hurt?"

She shrugged. "It would be all right if eleven of them died in war if the twelfth could die in peace in Palestine."

II. SECURITY IS A PHANTOM

Pa Za'el is a speck of green in the desert, surrounded by a Cyclone fence topped with barbed wire: a metaphor for Israel. It is one of the West Bank settlements, considered by the diplomats to be more a political statement – an Israeli attempt to hold conquered territories – than a community, and, in truth, it does seem rather precarious. It is home to forty families who live along tiny avenues of squat, cement "security" houses with adjoining bomb shelters. The avenues are arrayed like spokes off a dusty, crescent-shaped community center. There is an empty swimming pool and a neglected basketball court – one gets the impression that recreation is an afterthought.

The women of Pa Za'el were relentless homemakers and somewhat the worse for wear; invariably, their husbands looked younger than they. But then, the women were faced with the more difficult task of trying to impose permanence on a decidedly makeshift operation. They had created an atmosphere that resembled, when one forgot about the barbed wire, a garden apartment complex for young marrieds in the suburbs. There were no political posters or flags, but pathetic little flower beds and toys strewn about. Despite their best efforts, though, even the simplest ceremonies of domesticity seemed like acts of defiance.

Galia Kaspi is an American, a graduate of UCLA who wanted to see what Israel was like and decided to stay. She has short, severely cut black hair and her pallor seems a shock, compared to the ruddiness of the men – her husband is lanky and brown, the picture of health. "I believed in the necessity of settling these territories for security reasons," she said, but there were deeper reasons too. There was the sense – an almost mystical sense that Menachem Begin conveyed when he called the West Bank by its Biblical names, Samaria and Judea – that no matter what any politician said, this land was *Israel*. "We get our water from an ancient well that we found here," Galia said, proudly. "It's likely that the well was built by Jews and two thousand years ago Jewish people were drawing water from it, just as we are."

"What happens to you if this becomes a Palestinian state?"

It was as though the idea had never entered her mind. She seemed shocked: "It won't happen. It couldn't happen. A West Bank state would put them forty miles from the Mediterranean. It would be too easy for them to cut Israel in half."

"But what if it did happen? What would you do?"

"I wouldn't stay here," she said. "I wouldn't want to have someone stick a gun to my head when I was sleeping."

"But do you feel safe now?" I asked, as we went outside to the backyard. "There are all those militant Arabs who won't be happy until they have a Palestinian state."

"Let them have a state on the *other* side of the Jordan. It is the Arabs' problem – let them solve it."

"But you know that's no answer," I said, looking at the flimsy barbed-wire fence. "That fence doesn't seem like much security against all the anger."

A Phantom jet streaked across the horizon, then made a sharp, banking turn straight for Pa Za'el. "Oh, you're lucky," she said. "You're going to see a show."

We went around to the front yard. The plane dived down and buzzed the housetops and then pulled up. "He comes by every so often," Galia said. "His sister lives across the street and he comes by to say hello. Last week he was out in the fields with our men; this week he's up there."

The Phantom had turned again and was making another pass over the houses. A crowd had gathered in the street. People were laughing and applauding. Galia's husband, holding their young daughter, started to laugh. "Look, he has his landing wheels down." And he came in again, this time straight down the avenue of cement houses as though he

were going to land. Several of the children grew frightened and started to cry. The jet seemed to approach faster and lower now; the ground trembled and the air buzzed with the shriek of the engines. The plane whipped through, up, off into the distant mountains, and the settlement grew quiet and drowsy again under a white-hot sky.

Galia smiled. "You were asking about security . . ."

Hillel Schenker is thirty-six, a small man with dark, curly hair turning gray, and large, soft brown eyes. He is an intellectual, a writer, a folksinger, an editor of the socialist magazine *New Outlook*. He is unfailingly rational and so gentle in his ways that he never curses. Obviously, he is not a martial sort, but in Israel everyone has a war story, even Hillel Schenker.

Hillel served in the Yom Kippur War in 1973, mining the Golan Heights. One day his unit was at work in a field – they eventually learned that it was safer to put down mines at night – when the Syrians opened fire and he jumped down into a ditch. There were five corpses in the ditch. "It was disgusting, and one of my friends began to vomit. My thoughts were strange: My first thought was, 'Thank God, they're theirs.' But when we looked closer, it turned out that two of them were ours. They had all looked the same."

The strangest thing about Hillel, given the circumstances, was how hard he fought to remain rational, how devoted he was to solving problems that most likely had no solution. There was no doubt that a special series of events – the centuries of persecution, the Holocaust – had made a Jewish state absolutely necessary; there could also be no doubt that Zionism – the formation of a new country on the basis of race (or religion or whatever it is to be Jewish) – seemed a form of racism to the Arabs, who had the misfortune of being born on the lands the Jews had staked out. It was one of those untidy situations where both sides had a case, and where decisions were made emotionally. Hillel refused to deal with the past altogether: "It's not important now what happened thirty years ago. The important thing is that Israel exists, the Palestinians exist and how are we going to find a way to live together peacefully?"

"But how do you convince Israelis to trust the Arabs," I asked, "when there's no earthly reason why they *should* trust the Arabs?"

"You do it slowly," Hillel said, calmly optimistic. There was a growing peace movement in Israel. It wasn't very radical: The leaders made vague statements about peace being more important than occupied territories, but no definite proposals . . . and not a word about Palestinians. Still, it was good to see PEACE NOW bumper stickers on cars, and the crowds gathered around the petition tables in downtown Tel Aviv. It was, in fact, the first really positive trend Hillel had seen in years.

III. AN ARAB'S STORY

In 1940, a road gang worked near the town of Nazareth under the direction of a young Arab. Yusuf Khamish was eighteen and very frustrated. He had wanted to go to the university, but his father didn't have the money. So he was stuck with a boring job, supervising Arabs from town and Jews from a nearby kibbutz. He didn't like the Jews; they scared him. In school, the British taught him that kibbutz Jews didn't believe in God and didn't have families.

One day the kibbutz sent, as part of its crew, an old man. "You can't work," Yusuf told him. "It's too hot for an old man."

"Nonsense," said the man. "Of course I can work."

Yusuf hesitated, intrigued. "Well . . . come with me," he said. "You'll work inside today."

It turned out that the man was a professor of economics, a Marxist. They had long discussions together, and the professor began bringing Yusuf pamphlets about the Russian Revolution, then books. He taught Yusuf not to hate his father for being too poor to send him to college: The capitalist system was to blame. He gave Yusuf a beautiful vision of the future, when all people would live and work together in peace. One day the old man came to work and said, "You must come to the kibbutz with me. The leaders want to talk to you about building an access road."

"No," Yusuf blurted, a reflex reaction.

"Don't be silly," the professor said. "We won't hurt you."

Yusuf stayed at the kibbutz for three weeks, saw socialism in practice and became a true believer. He was arrested twice in the next several years. First by the mufti of Jerusalem, for being a radical. Then by the Israelis, for being an Arab radical. He quickly was sprung by his friends in the Mapam party and decided to stay in Israel even though many other Arabs were leaving. The growing forces of Jewish and Arab nationalism seemed, well . . . irrelevant to the class struggle. And hadn't the Russians aided the Israelis in those first days of independence?

Unfortunately, though, most Jews weren't like the old professor. Yusuf saw there were cases where Arabs were brutalized, their lands confiscated, their civil rights abused. But he was safely in the Mapam cocoon by that time, rising through the party ranks, becoming a public figure, eventually getting elected to the Israeli parliament, the Knesset.

Now, as he sat with me in the cafeteria at Mapam headquarters, a middle-aged man with thinning white hair and cocoa skin, Yusuf Khamish seemed a rather lonely figure, an oddity of history. He was not tremendously popular in Israel because he supported a Palestinian state, "not in place of Israel, but next to it." At the same time, when he went to international meetings, the Arabs would make fun of him, call him a "so-called Arab" bought by the Jews. "How can they do that to me? How can they do that?" he said.

The Israelis, who'd seemed so wonderfully rational at first, had become extremists. The Palestinians, a political movement that barely existed when Yusuf was making his life decisions, also were extremists. Even the Russians had turned out to be a major disappointment. All that had survived was the dream the professor had given him – and that still burned brightly, against all odds.

"You ask about the future," he said. "Okay. I would like to see a Palestinian state and a Jewish state next to each other. Gradually, I think they would see how much they had in common – both people look so much alike, both so hard-working, so intelligent. Gradually, I think they would come to depend on each other economically. Gradually, I think they would begin to mix and become one. I know, I know – it's ridiculous," he chuckled. "People tell me that all the time. They say that it's just an old man dreaming. Well of course! Of course it's a dream! But what's so bad about dreaming? When you live in this part of the world, dreaming is usually a lot more pleasant than real life."

The dreams of Yusuf, Hillel and a few others have slowly – agonizingly slowly – become those of many. Three months after this piece appeared in 1978, President Carter brought together Israeli prime minister Menachem Begin and Egyptian president Anwar Sadat at Camp David, Maryland, and hammered out an accord that, among other achievements, returned the Sinai to Egypt and laid the foundation for a lasting peace between Israel and at least one of its neighbors. Thus the Seventies ended with a glimmer of hope in the apparently hopeless cycle of violence.

Since then, Middle East peace efforts have seemed to flow in waves, in a frustrating two-steps-forward-one-step-back manner. After each handshake, after a new agreement has been effected, the brief romance seems to recede into a rash of terrorist attacks and retaliations: The assassinations of peacemakers like Sadat (in 1981) and Yitzhak Rabin (in 1995) are the most visible signs of the unending attempts to deny the rational peace process.

But with each wave of hope, more has been achieved, and most importantly, more begin to believe. What was unthink-able in the Seventies – Israel speaking directly with the PLO, the Palestinians actually policing themselves in their own, albeit poverty-stricken, homeland – has occurred. Peace will never suddenly and dramatically break through the Middle East war clouds, but one can finally discern an outbreak of rationality on both sides of Israel's heavily guarded borders.

Today, an increasing number of people – Arabs, Israelis and Palestinians – not only desire peace, but speak of it as a lasting and inevitable proposition.

marks his biggest hit to date as Funkadelic's anthemic "One Nation Under a Groove" enters the R&B charts; it will claim the top position for six weeks beginning Sept. 30.

24 New Orleans bandleader and wild man Louis Prima dies after a nearly three-year coma.

7 Who drummer Keith Moon dies at the age of 31, after overdosing on Heminevrin, a drug prescribed to stem his heavy drinking. Former Faces drummer Kenney Jones will replace him.

Sid Vicious performs at Max's Kansas City in New York City with New York Dolls drummer Jerry Nolan and Clash guitarist Mick Jones. An intoxicated Vicious mostly sticks to sloppy covers of rockabilly classics.

ROLLING STONE reports that Mick Jagger has thrown RS correspondent Chet Flippo off the Rolling Stones tour in a fit of pique after reading Flippo's less-than-complimentary review of the Stones' new album, *Some Girls.*

15 At age 36, Muhammad Ali becomes the first fighter to have claimed the heavyweight title three times, defeating Leon Spinks in 15 rounds in New Orleans.

16 At a cost of $500,000, the Grateful Dead realize a ten-year dream, performing the last of three concerts under a lunar eclipse in front of the Egyptian pyramids, before an audience of 2,000 Deadheads, travelers and Cairo-based Westerners.

17 After 12 days of intense negotiations, Israeli premier Menachem Begin and Egyptian president Anwar Sadat conclude the Camp David Accords, agreeing on a general framework to a Middle Eastern peace plan, including an Israeli withdrawal from Arab territories and a Palestinian role in the five-year transition phase. A week later, four hard-line Arab states, Libya, Algeria, Syria and South Yemen, will denounce the agreement and sever ties with Egypt, as will the PLO.

9 Belgian singer/songwriter Jacques Brel dies.

12 Sid Vicious is charged with the murder of his girlfriend, Nancy Spungen, after he finds her body in their room at New York City's Chelsea Hotel.

bongs, trips, 'ludes & lines
by bill van parys

SPRING 1978: *Three high school seniors are driving along country roads in a metallic-blue Mazda with a pistonless Wankel engine. Hummmmmmmm! They are listening to 'Exile on Main Street' – on cassette because they live in Leavenworth, Kansas, and the radio only plays crap by Player and the Bee Gees. They've just blown off a current-events class. The topic: Stephen Biko and apartheid; the instructor: John Etheridge, Melissa's father. They have opted instead to discuss the impending valve job on one guy's Celica and smoke Thai stick, drink Miller Ponys and do reds. They will soon return to their sixth-period physics class, where one of them will pass out in his front-row seat. I am that person. I am also student council president.*

If you've ever seen John Waters's *Polyester,* you've seen my hometown: dull, desensitized, stuck in the middle of nowhere. My friends and I were bored out of our skulls and wanting to be whatever we were not. The media was our lifeline to civilization; the people we read about in magazines, heard on the radio and saw on television were our gurus.

And, in the Seventies, the people we were devoted to were doing drugs. In fact, the entire decade seemed defined by the damn stuff: Rock and Hollywood stars were blowing, snorting and shooting; presidential son Jack Ford was toking up while Dad was in office. His mom, Betty Ford, would end up in detox by 1978. And a year into his term, Jimmy Carter was asking Congress to abolish all federal criminal penalties for minor pot possession. Pittsburgh Pirates pitcher Dock Ellis hurled a no-hitter on acid, tooted-up *One Day at a Time* star Mackenzie Phillips was out of her mind on Robertson Boulevard and a downed-out Buffy from *Family Affair* bought the farm. America's funny girl, Barbra Streisand, was firing up joints onstage in Vegas and even Mary Hartman – well, Louise Lasser – was popped for coke.

What had started with the mantra of "Feed Your Head" ten years earlier progressed into a mainstream mandate and recreational drug use became (gasp!) almost Establishment. In 1970, a well-funded, politically connected initiative to change pot legislation – the National Organization for the Reform of Marijuana Laws (a.k.a. NORML, har-har) was founded and rapidly eclipsed Vietnam as the cultural cause célèbre. *High Times,* a full-color magazine featuring scintillating centerfolds of the highest-grade cannabis buds, hit the stands four years later to sell-out demand, reaching a peak circulation of five hundred thousand in 1978. In that same year, the National Institute on Drug Abuse reported that 54.2 percent of high school seniors deemed themselves "heads." It proved to be the golden age of availability, with the romantic Sixties notion of drug use as introspective voyage tossed aside in favor of a somewhat blunter objective – destination: blotto.

You only had to turn on the radio to see how the aesthetic of indulgence had sunk into the collective psyche. Eric Clapton's song, featuring a frenzied audience chanting the hook lyric, got a lot of FM radio airplay. It was the decade's battle cry. Might that have been "Layla"? I don't think so. More like: "CO-CAINE!" This would play right after Toni Tennille had begged you to do that to her one more time. Hey, what can I say? It was a kooky time. No one dreamt that "zero tolerance" lurked just around the decade's bend. (By 1990, only an abysmal 32.5 percent would cop to getting stoned.)

Since I'm the "head" of the Class of '78, my physics teacher doesn't rat on me for passing out that day, but unfortunately my photography teacher does. She calls my mom, who comes down to my room the next morning to have "a little talk" about my chances of growing breasts, freaking out and spawning flipper babies. "And besides, Bill," she pleads, "you're just giving your money to drug dealers." To which I reply, "But mom, they're not drug dealers. They're my friends."

Poor woman. They *were* my friends, each with personalities as distinctive as the drugs they introduced me to. And each an unwitting Svengali-like influence on my development.

NOVEMBER 1975: *The son of a visiting college professor, Coleman was booted from a snooty prep school for doing bong hits in his closet. He is teaching us how to make bongs out of PVC tubing – purchased at a plumbing supply store – and how to turn electrical clamps into roach clips and fashion aluminum cans into emergency pipes.*

By the mid-Seventies, Colombia had eclipsed Mexico as "the source," the fifteen-dollar lid was giving way to the thirty-five-dollar "zee" (ounce) and the Drug Enforcement Administration estimated that Americans were buying sixteen billion dollars worth of marijuana a year. Freakdom was the fashion; we idolized Gilbert Shelton's Fabulous Furry Freak Brothers (whose only daily goal was to get high) and safely consumed a quarter-pound or more of pot a week in a friend's used hearse. And fuck sports: After school, we strove to become reefer connoisseurs, and we also fancied ourselves daring pot entrepreneurs, sometimes pooling four hundred dollars to "invest" in a pound. Alas, this was never wise on my part, as my silly socialist notions led me to sell my bags for cost to a group of people with names like Mongo at Haven's Park, a pothead hangout overlooking our town.

Head shops were mushrooming into a million-dollar business, offering underground comics, sex aids and secret stash kits (a hollow Coca-Cola can was a favorite) along with a wide array of pipes, roach clips, rolling papers and bongs. Seventies consumerism fueled paraphernalia fetishism; our choice of gear was crucial, a barometer of freak status. Double-wide strawberry E-Z Widers or papers with a built-in roach clip were considered a touch . . . well, *déclassé* when compared to the minimalist Bambu or the hemp-based Cannabis Indica. Conversely, two-foot-tall Graphics or the angular Apogee bongs were the Cadillacs of water pipes compared to squat, commodelike ceramic ones. Especially when they were cleaned with a high-tech bong cleanser like Grunge Off. Kiss that bong-breath ta-ta! And hey kids, don't forget the Ozium spray!

AUGUST 1976: *Chris is a little older than the rest of us, an intellectual and way into transcendental meditation. He claims he can levitate. He's studying chemical engineering at an East Coast institute and is home on a break with several vials of liquid LSD. He puts the acid on our tongues with an eyedropper, giggling quite often, making me wonder how much he is dispensing.*

It took a few years for the cultural imagery of the Sixties acid scene to reach the Midwest – okay, so we were a little slow – but by the end of the Ford era we embraced anything depicting or referencing consciousness expansion and drug-induced mysticism as part of our national heritage. "Steal Your Face" and "Umma Gumma" were tripster code words; jokes about Diane Linkletter (Art's daughter who jumped off her balcony while tripping) and Barbara Hoyt's hamburger (which had been laced with LSD by a Manson-family sorority sister) were a constant source of humor. When the home-brewed LSD dried up, we constructed our own incubation box for psilocybin mushrooms. My mom discovered it in my closet and wondered why I had cow turds in there. I told her it was for a science project.

OCTOBER 1977: *I'm 'luded out at Scooter's, the local disco, shaking my resistant booty to "Flash Light." The top part of my body is doing a prescient precursor to the Cabbage Patch, flopping around like a rag doll; too bad I can't move my feet. My best friend, Whitney, has parlayed his diagnosis of scoliosis from a school nurse into a prescription for Quaaludes, Seconal and Valium. Whitney reaches over the doctor's desk, adding zeros to the amounts prescribed while the doctor's back is turned. He takes his prescription with him on his senior exchange program in Europe, where he fills and refills his prescriptions enough to market the drugs and finance his trip.*

Disco is never the same.

By 1977, my world seemed to become sex-obsessed and more synthetic at the same time, even in "Heavy Leavy." Maybe it was all hormones and Donna Summer's fault: I shifted from tie-dye to Ultra-suede, from *High Times* to *Playboy*, from acid rock to Funkadelic. Psychopharmacology had become the sophisticated and synthetic way of the future. Downers ruled: The eminently abusable 'barbs and sedatives Tuinol, Seconal and Quaalude were garrulously absorbed into the mainstream. Raiding the parents' bathroom cabinet became a national pastime.

As early as 1972, reports showed that "'luding out" – downing Quaaludes with a wine chaser – was emerging as a popular college activity.

So, hello pills, and specifically, hello Quaaludes. They got you downed out without destroying your sex drive. Perfect. The entire country seemed crazy for this onetime antimalarial drug now known as the "disco biscuit." Even President Carter's drug-policy chief got busted for writing a Quaalude 'scrip for his assistant. By the end of the decade, I'd disguised myself as a giant 'lude for Halloween and stumbled into people as part of my "act." My costume might have won a prize that year. Funny, I can't really remember.

MARCH 1978: *Benjamin, the son of a South American diplomat, is living with his aunt in our town. We view him as a godsend. Especially when the mailman delivers him letters from home weighing several grams.*

By the late Seventies, cocaine was heralded as the champagne of the drug-culture set. In fact, it practically received official sanction from all levels of society. *Newsweek* celebrated cocaine as a swank status symbol, asserting it "was not addictive and causes no withdrawal symptoms." A Harvard Medical School psychiatrist publicly pooh-poohed Victorian-era warnings that the drug was "the most powerful and devilish drug which has ever been the misfortune of man to abuse," proclaiming it "relatively innocuous." The Domestic Council Drug Abuse Task Force contended cocaine use "does not result in serious social consequences" and encouraged law enforcement to focus instead on smack, the Mack-daddy of demonized drugs. This came just as Customs seizures of cocaine were increasing sevenfold in Miami alone, exposing an unheard-of increase in the inflow of the powder.

Too bad the drug totally changed our behavior toward one another. The dark suspicion that your drug partner might

Ten days later, he will attempt suicide after being released on bail from Riker's Island Detention Center.

16 The Roman Catholic Church elects Pope John Paul II, born Karol Wojtyla in Poland, the first non-Italian Supreme Pontiff in 455 years.

18 *Rockers*, a reggae film starring Leroy "Horsemouth" Wallace, with appearances by Burning Spear, Gregory Isaacs, the Mighty Diamonds, Big Youth, Jacob "Killer" Miller and others, opens in Kingston; it will reach the U.S. in 1980.

26 President Carter signs the Government Ethics Law, requiring financial disclosures by all executive-branch staff, and adding restrictions for all federal employees moving to private businesses.

30 The heavy-metal movie *Kiss Meets the Phantom of the Park*, in which the band battles evil robot doppelgängers, airs on NBC.

1978 NOVEMBER

4 Top of the charts: Anne Murray's "You Needed Me" (pop single); Linda Ronstadt's *Living in the U.S.A.* (pop album).

Platinum studio rockers Boston, whose first album in 1976 was the fastest-selling debut in U.S. rock history, play their namesake city for the first time and sell out two shows at the Boston Garden.

8 William Jefferson Clinton is elected governor of Arkansas, becoming the youngest governor in the nation at the age of 32.

10 CBS Records releases the Clash's second album, *Give 'Em Enough Rope*, in England. Columbia Records will release it in the U.S.

15 Disco innovators Chic, led by guitarist/vocalist Nile Rodgers (who will become one of the Eighties' hottest producers), receive their second gold disc in 1978 for "Le Freak."

18 Followers of Jim Jones's Peoples Temple of the Disciples of Christ shoot and kill California Congressman Leo J. Ryan and members of his staff after his inspection of Jones's 27,000-acre ranch in Guyana. Fearing reprisals, a paranoid Jones orders a mass suicide by lethal injection and consumption of poison-laced Kool-Aid, and then shoots himself. The death toll is more than 900.

23 British new waver Ian Dury releases his biggest hit, "Hit

be a narc was replaced by the fear that he was holding and wasn't going to share. It hit home with me the night Whitney came by my house to ask me to steal syringes from my mom, a diabetic, so that he could shoot some cocaine before we went to Scooter's. He didn't offer me any.

Drugs were now a game of exclusivity, not democracy. I've got mine, you go get your own. I think this is about the time I decided to become a stockbroker.

THE CLASS OF '78: *I decide to leave Kansas, opting for college in Wisconsin with its legal drinking age of eighteen and pot-friendly enclaves (old habits die hard). Values change and friends scatter. Coleman's mom, convinced his pot-smoking indicates a deep psychological disorder, drags him off to a Primal Scream clinic in Texas, never to be heard from again. One day the FBI arrives ten minutes after an eight-gram letter comes in the mail for Benjamin. Uh-oh. He moves to Montreal – quickly. I don't know what becomes of Chris – the last I hear he has quit his engineering job to bake bread at a commune. Whitney never leaves Kansas. He gets hooked on Valium and ultimately Demerol. He dies in his sleep shortly after trying to kick.*

Over the next few years, I land that stock-exchange job, but quit to indulge my arty-farty sensibilities. I find new friends and new drugs in new places and we watch in collective horror as cocaine and its demon-spawn, crack, turn the tide on drugs and make them totally uncool. By the mid-Eighties, Leavenworth shuts down Haven's Park.

Look at these kids. At first glance, they could be me and my hell-raisin' friends back in Leavenworth, rebelliously skipping class on a devil-may-care spring day sometime in the Seventies, cranking tunes and killing time until Janice the security guard drags everyone's ass off to detention. Except these kids are too clean. We would've been shitfaced (and I ain't talkin' Boone's Farm) – too far gone to notice if any nosy photographers were lurking about. –B.V.P.

TODAY: I still have no flipper babies. Drugs for me now are more about maintenance than recreation. I had to take a piss test the last time I changed jobs, and I admit that I passed. Age has refocused my adventuresome soul; drugs and the consciousness expansion just aren't part of the plan anymore. Now it's more about red wine and a trip to Bora-Bora.

I recently shared some of these teen-freak tidbits with a coworker, a hip twenty-seven-year-old. "Wow," she said, shocking me, "you were a really big druggie." I honestly pleaded that I wasn't, that I was completely normal for a time when John Belushi and Linda Blair were the heroes and doing drugs was the rebel's rite of passage.

We were young, resilient, curious and testing the limits – physical, social, legal and otherwise. And we had lots of company. The lessons my friends and I learned (some a little too late) were the same that society was reacting to by the end of the decade in its "Just Say No" sloganeering manner: moderation, balance, common sense. It just took us a while to realize that this was one case where more was not necessarily more. There are some things in life you gotta learn for yourself. ⊕

Me With Your Rhythm Stick," a huge seller in the U.K. but a noncharter in the U.S.

25 Talking Heads become the highest-charting new-wave act to date, as their second album, *More Songs About Buildings and Food,* hits #29, spurred on by a jagged reworking of Al Green's "Take Me to the River."

R&B veterans Jerry Butler, Gene Chandler, Gladys Knight, Joe Simon and the Temptations all appear on the R&B charts with disco songs.

27 San Francisco mayor George Moscone and openly gay city supervisor Harvey Milk are shot dead by disgruntled former supervisor and homophobe Dan White.

1978 DECEMBER

3 *Mommie Dearest,* Christina Crawford's tell-all book about her mother, Joan Crawford, is the current bestseller.

6 Retired General William Westmoreland states that medical progress made during the Vietnam War saved more lives than were lost, emphasizing advances in blood transfusions and treatment of malaria and trench foot.

8 Johnny Rotten's new band, Public Image Ltd., releases its debut album, *First Issue*; "Public Image" will become an underground hit.

14 Studio 54 co-owner Ian Schrager is busted for possession of cocaine with intent to distribute. IRS agents also found Hefty bags containing nearly a $1 million in cash.

The Vietnam War saga *The Deer Hunter,* starring Christopher Walken, Robert De Niro and Meryl Streep, premieres.

17 Stiff Records' Be Stiff Route 78 tour opens its American run at the Bottom Line with performances by Lene Lovich, Rachel Sweet, Jona Lewie, Wreckless Eric and Mickey Jupp.

20 The "Treasures of Tutankhamen" exhibit, featuring gold and other valuable relics from the burial chamber of the Egyptian prince, opens at New York City's Metropolitan Museum of Art. Over 1.2 million people will see the exhibit, which also inspires Steve Martin's Top 20 musical tribute (debuted on *Saturday Night Live*), "King Tut."

25 Public Image Ltd. plays its first concert, at London's Rainbow Theatre.

on the inside looking in
by daisann mclane

TWO CLUNKY men's Harris tweed jackets hang in mothballs in the back of my closet, woolly reminders of my first job out of college, my dream job: two years as a ROLLING STONE rock & roll reporter. I don't wear the jackets anymore – nowadays, my work wardrobe leans more in the direction of black taffeta party dresses – but at the time, they were as indispensable to my professional life as a Kevlar vest is to a New York City cop. The dozens of rock & roll profiles I wrote for the magazine between 1978 and 1980 wouldn't have happened without the tweed.

Wearing the straight, sexless uniform of the Ivy League to represent the most celebrated anything-goes journal of the counterculture may seem a bizarre fashion statement, but remember, this was 1978. Back then, the main roles available to women interested in rock & roll careers were: pensive singer/songwriter, lead chick singer (Patty Smyth), boho androgyne (Patti Smith) and grossly underpaid publicist. Back then, the etiquette, worldview and vocabulary of your average record-biz mogul was not so far removed from that of a boxing promoter or mobster (sometimes, in fact, these particular individuals *were* boxing promoters or mobsters). Back then, all the power and almost all the money in the music business belonged to men, the sort of men to whom it might never occur that the single young woman in possession of an All Access Pass and a seat on the tour bus was the ROLLING STONE reporter on assignment.

The jacket was there to take care of that. It also, as it turned out, accomplished something much more crucial in terms of the work I was doing: It lowered my profile. In a testosterone jungle of egos, the Girl in the Tweed Jacket projected the gangly gee-whiz of a kid sister. Neither sexy nor hip, she all but disappeared. Managers, agents and rock icons usually forgot she was around, forgot why she was there and – most importantly – who she was there for. In time (and there was always plenty of time, back then) many of them would loosen up and do and say things they would never have thought to do or say in front of "ROLLING STONE." Like show up, as Aerosmith's Steven Tyler did for his interview, holding a needle and thread and a ripped Spandex bodysuit, shrugging sheepishly: "Uh, hey, like, can you do me a favor? Can you sew?"

In 1978 I was twenty-four, the only female staff writer at ROLLING STONE and, except for Cameron Crowe, the youngest. For about ten minutes every morning, this fact was an occasion for intense head swelling on my part. Then I'd get to the office, a place guaranteed to turn one's vanities to dust balls. For this was no renovated hippie warehouse in San Francisco, but 745 Fifth Avenue, New York, New York – an expensive, serious-business address with an expensive, serious-business view of Central Park rolled out twenty-eight stories below like Jann's own carpet. To stroll (or, more like it, pace) these corridors was an exercise in humility not unlike that practiced by the *castigates* of rural Mexico during Holy Week. Summoned by my – usually tweed-jacketed – editor, Peter Herbst, to receive my next assignment, I ran a gauntlet of legendary bylines: Cameron, Chet Flippo, Ben Fong-Torres, Chuck Young, David Felton. Even my office cubicle was no refuge from the Giants of Rock Journalism; I shared it with (and he was not happy about this) Dave Marsh. Over in the next cubicle loomed the most looming *presence* of all, Paul Nelson, an *éminence* aswirl in wisdom and Dunhill smoke.

All of them were writers who were stars . . . *personas.* ROLLING STONE in 1978 was one of the last places that encouraged its writers to develop strong, offbeat, personalized voices. Most other national magazines, anticipating the celeb-sucking reportage of the yuppie Eighties, had begun to red-pencil the no-holds-barred idiosyncratic first-person writing of the New Journalism. But at ROLLING STONE, we maintained our stake in the territory that had been opened by Tom Wolfe, Norman Mailer and, especially, Hunter S. Thompson. At ROLLING STONE, it wasn't enough to go out and merely report a story; a writer was supposed to bag it, tie it up securely, then march it back home at spearpoint, still alive and twitching. (Chuck Young showed up at the office, after

his London escapades with the Sex Pistols in '77, with his T-shirt ripped and bloodied, a trophy of a job well done. Now *that* was the way to go.)

Not surprisingly, these strong, offbeat, personal ROLLING STONE voices tended to bleed off the printed page and into the offices of 745 Fifth Avenue. The office, at times, resembled a boisterous, competitive basketball court where Michael Jordan–sized personas lobbed and passed and dunked shoptalk and, sometimes, each other. At 745 Fifth, it was risky to neglect one's writerly image. Image-building, however, had its own perils. I remember one warm, sticky summer evening when a handful of us had gathered on the outdoor terrace of the twenty-eighth floor for one of those impromptu, raucous end-of-day sessions that usually revolved around genial verbal games of one-upmanship and the consumption of plastic tumblers of white jug wine. I'd had a few, and was leaning against the retaining-wall ledge, exhilarated by the view from the top and the fresh, cool, twenty-eighth-story breeze, when suddenly I noticed that all talking had stopped. I turned around then, and saw staff writer Fred Schruers tipsily walking along the six-inch-wide roof ledge, on his hands.

In this highly competitive league, I cast around for my edge, my angle, and discovered that, despite a total lack of gymnastic skills, I had certain advantages over the boys. For starters, I could sew. I could also, if need be, sit for an hour with Stevie Nicks on the lace coverlet of her antique Victorian four-poster bed in Bel Air and tut-tut over her recently hysterectomized puppy. Being female made me less threatening, encouraged a certain intimacy; sometimes a familiarity that became surreal, as when Steven Tyler said to me, absolutely straight-faced, "Do you remember what it was like, when you used to go finger-fuck girls under the aqueduct?" Of course, I said yes. At moments like these, I'd excuse myself, and run into the bathroom, scribble notes on my palm with a Flair. Then I'd come back to the office and furiously type these chronicles of the rock & roll road, every last bizarre, ridiculous, telling detail.

"But *what was it like?*" is the question people still ask me, years later, when they find out I used to earn my living stalking lead guitarists in the airport baggage claim areas of Tulsa, nodding asleep backstage at arenas in Salt Lake City, playing poker in Lear jets over Dallas and balanced on bar stools in Holiday Inn cocktail lounges in Shreveport, tape recorder ready to grab the least significant utterings of Aerosmith, Peter Frampton, Heart, Fleetwood Mac, ZZ Top or Cheap Trick. And this is how I always answer: To understand what things were really like for me, you must first remember that the music business in 1978 was a world in which new records by Peter Frampton shipped platinum, and where it was not unusual for a concert contract rider to include specifications concerning the number and dressing-room placement of chilled buckets of Dom Pérignon.

In short, it was a fat time, a moment in which rock had moved from the hip margins to the profitable mainstream and was sailing on a (seemingly) endless high tide of promotion, tour support, recording budgets, recreational intoxicants and loose cash (it was no coincidence that ROLLING STONE, which then depended on record-ad revenues for solvency, made its move from the funky San Francisco warehouse to the Fifth Avenue suite in 1977). Of course, we know now that much of the music that came out then was as cellulite-ridden as its production and tour budgets (this was, remember, the era of the three-record set, *Saturday Night Fever* and Kiss solo albums). But it all sounded great when you were listening from a seat in first class, which is where most of the musicians, moguls, functionaries – and sometimes tweed-jacketed journalists – got to sit. To be on the rock & roll road back then (when nearly every band with a new album could afford to tour) was to glide through the universe on cruise control. For weeks, often months, decisions were made, and problems resolved by managers, lawyers, publicists and accountants. Wake-up calls came at noon, road managers collected luggage from outside one's hotel-room door. I recall that most musicians I interviewed didn't wear watches. The myth of the rock & roll road was freedom; the reality was that one emerged from this pampered bubble as dependent and querulous as a spoiled adolescent.

This was a seductive world, indeed, but the tweed jacket always served to remind me who I was, a stranger at this party. I didn't – as did some of my colleagues – befriend rock stars. Nor did I pay too much attention to what they actually said to me in a formal interview situation, since what they actually said was usually so predictable that Cameron Crowe and I used to begin our phone conversations with a parody of it:

Me: Hello, Cameron . . .

C.C.: Fuck NO! We are *not* breaking up. The solo LP is just so I can, y'know, express some of my identity . . .

Me: But you canceled the tour, and your manager doesn't return calls . . .

C.C.: Bullshit. [*Voice lower, cracking with emotion*] Hey, listen. We're a *band.* This new album's gonna be a band album. We've got a new producer, we're goin' back to our roots. You'll see. We love the road . . .

Words were cheap in the high-rolling rock & roll subculture of 1978; they were as plentiful as white powder, and about as long-lasting. The stories of these years in the music business – the ones that interested me – lurked between the lines, in what was *not* said, in the nuances. And so, when I was sent out to write about a band, I began my work by listening to what they wanted to tell ROLLING STONE. Then I'd hang around afterward as long as possible, weeks if I could, accumulating details.

Little did I realize that this method of working was a method

around the corner and that the footloose possibilities of the (literary) New Journalism would be supplanted by the orchestrated, tight-security (televised) media event. Vietnam would make way for the Grenada and Panama invasions, for the Gulf War, but who knew? And who imagined that the champagne-bright, platinum-selling empire of rock would collapse, in a heap of returns, budget-slashing and layoffs? But it would, by 1980, the same year that Ronald Reagan was elected president, and my profession began to acquire a new, Eighties-style look: Celebrity Journalism.

The music journalism world I knew has been transformed. It's a visually dominated landscape now – photo layouts and video appearances are what sets a music publicist's heart racing. "Oh, you're the writer?" yawn the P.R. gatekeepers as you jockey for access to the star across a roomful of stylists and photo assistants. "I promise, you'll get your half hour, as soon as we wrap this. Of course we understand that [name of star here] needs to speak with you and we are *trying our best* to make it happen."

Rock journalism is people who can't write, interviewing people who can't talk, for people who can't read. –Frank Zappa

that would shortly become impossible, because its success depended on unlimited time with the subject. Here is my itinerary for a story I did on Fleetwood Mac in 1979, pegged to the release of *Tusk*: October – one week in Los Angeles to hang out at band rehearsals and visit members individually. November – three days in L.A. to interview Nicks. Late November – opening tour dates in Idaho, Denver, Salt Lake City – one week. December – press party in New York, three nights backstage at Garden. ALL ACCESS, said my plastic backstage tags, and all access I got; in this pre-MTV era, bands bent over backward for press coverage, and for ROLLING STONE they did cartwheels. I could not have imagined that, one day, doing a piece on a rock band would involve weeks of negotiating with publicists, resulting in a two-hour hotel-room session, then – zip. This was not how we worked in 1978. Back then when my editor suggested that I could write a 3,500-word feature about Peter Frampton after spending only three days with him at his home in the Bahamas – with no tour time, no follow-up visits – I did what any of my colleagues would have done at the time: I complained.

I don't think anybody realized that the all-access days were sputtering to an end, that spin control was lurking just

The rules have changed – but even if they hadn't, it would still be harder to write about rock stars today than it was then. Because with the passage of time, the stylistic tricks of Seventies journalism, once so fresh and liberating, have devolved into clichés. Magazines, such as *Esquire,* that once showcased the latest innovations in feature writing, now fumble and strain to resuscitate the hoary skeleton of New Journalism. But the corpse refuses to sit up, and I don't think it will again, because it can't. Audiences today are sophisticated readers of the signs and surfaces of the modern media world; they don't need a writer to go behind the scenes to tell them what is "really" happening. And so what if a celebrity is "really" different from his/her carefully constructed image (the basic trope of most Seventies profiles)? Hello! Tommy Lee . . . Madonna . . . Bill Clinton? As we say now: Been there, done that.

But back at ROLLING STONE, in the fat years, it was a different story. The limousines were waiting, the champagne was chilled and Jagger was on the phone, on *hold.* And twenty-eight stories above Central Park, we did handstands on the edge. In 1978 it never occurred to us, to me, that this world would tumble, or that we might fall. ⊕

paranoia, panic & poison
by tim cahill

FROM THE HELICOPTER it looked as if there were a lot of brightly colored specks around the main building. At three hundred feet the smell hit. The chopper landed on a rise, out of sight of the bodies. Other reporters tied handkerchiefs over their faces. Tim Chapman, a husky twenty-eight-year-old photographer for the *Miami Herald*, didn't have one, so he used a chamois rag. It turned out to be a good idea.

In Georgetown, the capital of Guyana, he had talked his way onto a flight to Jonestown, where the bodies still lay, three days after the massacre that culminated in the death of more than nine hundred members of the Reverend Jim Jones's Peoples Temple.

"The first body I saw," Chapman said, "was off to the side, alone. Five more steps and I saw another and another and another and another – hundreds of bodies. The *Newsweek* reporter was walking around saying, 'I don't believe it, I don't believe it.' Another guy said, 'It's unreal.' Then nobody even attempted to speak anymore. There were colors everywhere – raincoats and shirts and pants in reds and greens and blues; bright, happy colors." Chapman saw two parrots on a fence, a red-and-yellow macaw and a blue-and-yellow macaw. He moved around to get that angle: the contrast of life and death.

The bodies, Chapman said, were in grotesque disfigurement. One woman's false teeth had been pushed out. He saw a child, maybe five years old, between a man and woman who were swollen in death. He remembered that the child wore brown pants and a blue shirt. He wasn't as swollen as the man and woman. The children didn't seem to swell as much. Just for a moment Chapman stood there, hating the parents. They had a choice and the children didn't.

"I moved to my left. There was a vat, and then I saw Jones. As I moved toward him, I got a real bad whiff. I stepped away, almost tripped on a body and stumbled to get my balance, and as soon as I bent down, I was suddenly too close to one. There was a tremendous adrenaline shot, a fear."

Chapman chose not to shoot any photos of Jones. It had been done, and besides, he felt that somehow any more photos would glorify the man.

"His head was all blown out of proportion. There was a wound under his right ear and it was oozing. One arm was up over his head, stiff in rigor mortis. The skin was stretched tight over the hand, and it looked desperate, like a claw."

There was something else, something about the arrangement of the bodies that struck Chapman. Jones was on his back. Most of the others were face down, their heads pointing to Jones. "I could tell," Chapman said, "that it wasn't their final statement. It was Jones's."

Somehow that single thought was the most terrifying thing Chapman said that morning.

I t was a massive job, loading up all the corpses at Jonestown, and it took eight full days. On the ninth day, the government allowed about fifty news ghouls into the jungle enclave. We flew up to Matthews Ridge and were ferried the twenty or so miles to the ghost town in a helicopter that accommodated twelve. We landed on the rise Chapman had mentioned and made our way to the pavilion, where bodies had lain.

To get to the pavilion proper, we had to step across muddy rills, and the thought of that ocher-colored mud clinging to our shoes was unpleasant. The pavilion had a corrugated metal roof set on wooden columns and a hard-packed mud floor. In front of the stage, along with a collection of musical instruments, were several bits of gore: blackened flesh, shriveled bits of scalp, all crawling with flies. On the walls were signs that said LOVE ONE ANOTHER, and the like.

The path outside led down a shallow slope to Jones's house, a brown, wood affair, slightly larger than the rest, surrounded by tangerine and almond trees. The place was locked up, but scattered on the porch were Jim Jones's mail, a collection of books

Murray (for "You Needed Me") and Barry Manilow (for "Copacabana"). *Saturday Night Fever* is the big winner with three, including Album of the Year and Best Pop Vocal Performance by a Group.

The Temple City Kazoo Orchestra appears on *The Mike Douglas Show* with guest soloists David Brenner, Cheryl Tiegs, Lee Grant and Lou "The Hulk" Ferrigno.

16 During an acoustic performance at the Palomino, a North Hollywood club, Elvis Costello first reveals his country roots, playing songs by George Jones and his own "Stranger in the House," which Jones will later record.

17 The Clash kicks off its first U.S. tour at New York City's Palladium, with Bo Diddley supporting; "I'm So Bored With the U.S.A." is their opening song.

As an outgrowth of Vietnam's continued involvement in the Cambodian civil war, Communist China attacks Vietnamese troops along the length of Vietnam's border. Three weeks later, Chinese forces will begin to withdraw, but hostilities will persist.

22 ROLLING STONE reports that in an music industry first, Journey has developed an advertising relationship with Anheuser-Busch, leading to Budweiser posters in the group's programs and Journey-produced beer jingles. Similar deals appear imminent between Pabst beer and the Marshall Tucker Band, Panasonic and Hall & Oates, and JVC and Sea Level.

1979MARCH

1 According to a *Washington Post* poll, 99% of Americans own TVs, although 41% like the programming less than they did in 1974.

2 Havana Jam, the first cosponsored U.S.–Cuban music event in 20 years, offers Cubans three days of rock music, boasting a lineup of Stephen Stills, Billy Joel, Kris Kristofferson, Rita Coolidge and Tom Scott & the L.A. Express.

15 At a Columbus, OH, Holiday Inn, Elvis Costello, Bonnie Bramlett and members of Stephen Stills's entourage get into a fracas following disparaging remarks made by Costello about American R&B legends Ray Charles and James Brown. By way of explanation, Costello admits

and magazines and his medicine cabinet: three things that reveal much about a man.

The books and magazines were about conspiracies, spies, political imprisonment, people who manipulate the news and Marxism. A large red book contained dozens of Russian posters; one showed Lenin speaking before a crowd of workers.

Near a footlocker full of health foods and vitamins, I found hundreds of Valium tablets, some barbiturate-type pills and several disposable syringes, along with ampoules of synthetic morphine. Near the drugs, by a pile of blank Guyanese power-of-attorney forms, was a great stack of letters addressed "to Dad." Most were labeled "self-analysis" and began with "I feel guilty because . . ." The self-analysis letters were confessions. No one admitted to being happy and well-adjusted.

I read one from a young male: "I am sexually attracted to a lot of brothers and would rather fuck one in the ass than get fucked." After the original confession, the letters churned with hate. "I have feelings about going to the States for revenge against people." From an eighty-nine-year-old woman: "Dear Dad, I would rather die than go back to the States as there is plenty of hell there. I would give my body to be burned for the cause than be over there . . . If I had to go back, I would like to have a gun and use it [she names several temple defectors who worked with the anti-temple Human Freedom Movement] and have them all in a room together and take a gun and spray the row of them. I am glad to have a Dad and Father like you . . ."

The letters were chilling, suggesting lives filled with guilt and hate, and fear. More frightening was the tone of absolute submission to "Dad," a man who, by all evidence, seemed to be a hypochondriac, a drug addict and paranoid.

In the past, Jim Jones had real enemies. They were, for the most part, louts, bigots and segregationists: the kind of people who referred to him as a "nigger lover" and who spat on his wife when she appeared on the street with one of their adopted black children. Sickened by racist attacks, Jones moved his ministry from the Midwest to Brazil, then to Northern California, where the hostilities began anew. Vandals shot out the windows of the Redwood Valley temple, and dead animals were tossed on the lawn. In August 1973, a mysterious blaze devastated the San Francisco temple. Legitimately harassed, Jones began making connections between events, part real, part delusion.

Finally, a blistering exposé of the temple was published in the August 1, 1977, issue of *New West* magazine. Various defectors told stories of false healings, humiliations, beatings and financial improprieties. Jones used all the political clout at his disposal in a vain effort to kill the story. He fled to Guyana shortly before it was published.

In the isolation of the jungle, in the intimacy of the pavilion, Jim Jones raged against the defectors. They were organized now, and the traitors called themselves the Concerned Relatives. They were plotting against him, smearing him in the media and were in league with the shadow forces arrayed against him.

He was Father to all of them. He had taken the junkies and prostitutes off the street. He took in lonely old folks and fed the hungry. The young idealists had been floundering, unsure of how to make a better world. And he showed them. Without him there was nothing. Without him they would be back on the street or lying on a slab in the morgue. The community was totally dependent on him. Without him they were nothing and he told them so. It frightened them to realize he was ill.

His hate and fear were contagious. Elderly women united to kill the defectors. He held his hands up for the people to see, and they were running with blood. "I'm bleeding for the people," he said. ("Ground glass," a surviving Jonestown nurse told me later.)

Sometimes during Peoples Forum, when members spoke of being homesick or wanting to leave, Jones would have a "heart attack." The community could see what it was doing to Father, and they'd turn on the speaker in a fury. It wasn't just people leaving. That might be acceptable. But no one ever left and remained neutral. They sold out. They told lies. They joined the traitors. Perhaps those who spoke of leaving were infiltrators. Everyone could see what their words did to Father. He had to protect himself. "No one leaves Jonestown unless they're dead," Jones said.

The conspiracy came to a head on Saturday, November 18, 1978, during California congressman Leo J. Ryan's visit. Some temple members had deserted in the morning, when security was concentrating on the Ryan party. Now others were saying they wanted to leave with Ryan. Whole families – the Parkses, the Bogues – had turned

Rev. Jim Jones

traitor. They were more concerned with blood relations than with the cause and Father. Jones looked beaten, defeated. A man named Don Sly flew into a rage and menaced Ryan with a knife, but he was subdued. Newsmen were present. There'd be more smears. Ryan would report to Congress, and the full weight of the United States government would fall on Jonestown.

When Ryan and his collection of traitors left for the airstrip in Port Kaituma, gunmen followed. The shadow forces had won.

An alert was called and the community rushed to the pavilion. Jones told them the congressman's plane would "fall from the sky." He could do things like that. At Port Kaituma, Ryan's party was going to take two planes but a Jones loyalist named Larry Layton, who had left with Ryan, pulled a gun. Although Layton later denied it – saying it was his idea to go after the congressman's plane – Jones may have instructed him to shoot the pilot when the plane was airborne. But the party was too large and they were going to take two planes. Layton wounded two. He leveled the gun at Dale

Parks's chest and fired. Dale fell back, thinking he had been shot, but the gun had jammed. He jumped Layton and, with the help of another man, wrestled the gun away.

Meanwhile, gunmen arrived from Jonestown and began firing at the other plane. Ryan, Patty Parks and newsmen Bob Brown, Don Harris and Greg Robinson were killed. Others were wounded. The gunmen retreated to Jonestown.

"Those people won't reach the States," Jones told the community. Then he said it was time for all of them to die. He asked if there was any dissent. An older woman rose and said she didn't think it was the only alternative. Couldn't the temple members escape to Russia or Cuba? She had the right to choose how she wanted to live, she said, and how she wanted to die. The community shouted her down. She was a traitor. But she held her ground, an elderly woman, all alone.

"Too late," Jones said. He instructed Larry Schact, the town doctor, to prepare the poison. Medical personnel brought the equipment into a tent that had been used as a school and a library. There were large syringes, without the needles, and small plastic containers full of a milky white liquid.

Jones told the community that the Guyanese Defense Force would be there in forty-five minutes. They'd shoot first and ask questions later. Those captured alive, he said, would be castrated. It was time to die with dignity. The children would be first.

A woman in her late twenties stepped out of the crowd. She was carrying her baby. The doctor estimated the child's weight and measured an amount of the milky liquid into a syringe. A nurse pumped the solution into the baby's mouth. Then the mother drank her potion. Death came in less than five minutes. The baby went into convulsions, and Jones – very calm, very deliberate – kept repeating, "We must take care of the babies first." Some mothers brought their own children up to the killing trough. Others took children from reluctant mothers. Some of the parents and grandparents became hysterical, and they screamed and sobbed as their children died.

"We must die with dignity," Jones said. "Hurry, hurry, hurry." One thirteen-year-old girl refused her poison. She spit it out time after time and they finally held her and forced her to take it. Many people in the pavilion, especially the older ones, just watched, waiting. Others walked around, hugging old friends. Others screamed and sobbed.

Jones stepped off his throne and walked into the audience. "We must hurry," he said. He grabbed people by the arm and pulled them to the poison. Some struggled, weakly.

After an individual took the poison, two others would escort him, one on each arm, to a clearing and lay him on the ground, face down. It wouldn't do to have the bodies piled up around the poison, slowing things down.

The survivors, some of them children, stared at the reporters with vacant, ancient eyes. There were literally hundreds of journalists, from at least five continents, in Georgetown. It was madness. Virulent lunacy. And when you tried to assemble bits and pieces of the story, none of it fit together. There was no perspective, no center.

There were three distinct groups of survivors. First came the voices of dissent: those who had gone with Congressman Ryan and survived the shoot-out at Port Kaituma. This group included the Bogue family, the Parks family and Harold Cordell. They hated Jones and Jonestown. The press counted them as the most reliable sources.

The second group consisted of those who had escaped the carnage at Jonestown. Odell Rhodes and Stanley Clayton made up half of the total number. Both were articulate, both had witnessed the final moments.

Of the third group, Tim Carter, thirty, and Mike Prokes, thirty-one, had held leadership positions in Jones's organization, and they looked terribly frightened.

They sat at one of the tables and the press pounced. Lights, cameras, microphones, tape recorders, half a dozen people shouting out questions. Tim Carter, in particular, fascinated me. It was his eyes. He looked like a beaten fighter in the fifteenth round, one who just caught a stiff right cross he never saw coming. Tim Carter was a beaten man, and his eyes had the watery, glazed and unfocused look of a boxer who can no longer defend himself and who is simply going to absorb punches until he falls.

"I heard a lot of screaming," Carter said, his voice breaking, "and I went up to the pavilion and the first thing I saw was that my wife and child were dead. I had a choice of staying there," he continued, close to tears, "and I left."

"You saw your wife and child take poison?" someone asked Tim Carter. His eyes swam. "I didn't see them take poison. My baby was dead. My wife was dying. I'm trying to forget about it. Everything you thought you believed in, everything you were working for was a lie, it was, it was . . . a lie."

We had heard a remarkably similar story from the dissenting survivors. Jim Jones had promised that anyone who left Jonestown would be tracked down and killed. And yet, leaders of the organization had left in the midst of the suicides. They had with them a suitcase containing five-hundred thousand dollars in American currency.

"The money was given to us by one of the secretaries," Prokes said. He identified Maria Katsaris, a top aide and mistress to Jones. "She said, 'Things are out of control. Take this.' We left. The money was in a suitcase."

We all crowded at their table to suckle more information. The letter to the embassy, for instance. The one in the suitcase with the money. It was addressed to the *Soviet* embassy. Mike Carter explained, "Jones told us the Soviet Union supported liberation movements."

The bits and pieces wouldn't fit. It was like trying to hold too many ball bearings in one hand. Every time you got something, everything else threatened to clatter to the floor and roll out of reach.

Odell Rhodes was a soft-spoken, articulate thirty-six-year-old, an eyewitness to the first twenty minutes of the massacre at Jonestown. The first time we met, we sipped bourbon, strong and sweet and straight. Odell had been a junkie for ten years. He'd been through two drug-treatment programs, and both times he had gone back to drugs and some sleazy hustle on the street. "They tell you an addict shoots junk because he likes it," Odell said. "I never liked it. I had to shoot it."

When the Peoples Temple buses came through Detroit, an alcoholic friend decided to join. The next time they came through, the friend looked up Odell. The friend was dry, sharp, well dressed. "He looked like a successful businessman," Odell said. And Odell, who had failed twice trying to kick his habit, decided to check out the temple.

Jim Jones, he said, gave him a new self-image. He was intelligent. He was useful. Odell was given a job in the San Francisco temple. "The area it was in," he said, "was like where I had come from in Detroit. But I could walk down the street with money in my pocket and pass it all up."

When Odell first arrived in Guyana, things seemed fine. His job was teaching crafts to children, and he was good at it. He'd spend hours poring over books, looking for projects children could complete in a couple of hours. The kids teased him – "Hey, that'll never work, man" – and he'd bet them cookies that it would. They laughed a lot. "I really loved those kids."

But then things started going sour in Jonestown. The food deteriorated. The workdays increased. It seemed, to Odell's experienced eye, that Jim Jones was developing a serious drug problem. Crazy things began to happen, and he made plans to escape.

But then the news of Congressman Ryan's visit hit Jonestown. Security was increased. Then came the incident at Port Kaituma, followed by the terrible night of screams in which more than nine hundred died.

"I watched them die," he said. "And I haven't cried yet. It's like I'm dead inside. Water comes to my eyes, but I can't cry."

Odell sipped at the bourbon and blinked several times.

Jonestown was the last cult-oriented story I ever wrote. What else was there to say?

When I began writing about cults in the early Seventies, I was attracted, immediately, by the inherent comedic possibilities. Some groups flatly predicted the end of the world and they set actual dates for the firestorm. I always liked to be on hand to watch the sun rise and set without substantial incident. Then I got to ask the question: "Uh, wasn't something a bit more dramatic supposed to happen here today?" The intellectual flailing about in the wake of a failed Apocalypse was always both hilarious and pitiful.

Not that I thought cults should be banned or outlawed. Quite the contrary. If personal freedom meant anything at all, it had to encompass the process of belief, and that meant belief in the sublime as well as the ridiculous. For this reason, I was on record as opposing forcible "deprogramming," in which parents hired thugs to snatch adult children out of cult situations in order to turn them against their leaders. My exact words – a peculiarly Seventies formulation – were: "Kidnapping in the name of freedom is like fucking for chastity."

So the new religious organizations began contacting me, a writer they saw as an obvious sympathizer. Some were harmless, and a few actually did good work: I recall one group that formed a lifesaving volunteer ambulance service in the Bronx. Few groups, to my disappointment, advocated sexual license – there was enough secular sex to go around in the Seventies, I suppose – but one cult, the Children of God, did make a pretty good pile of cash out of old-fashioned prostitution. Jesus said, "Be a fisher of men." They were "flirty fishers."

The Seventies' spiritual smorgasbord also included Moonies, Hare Krishnas, Christian fundamentalists like the Tony and Susan Alamo Christian Foundation as well as a thirteen-year-old Perfect Master, lots of older ones, along with gurus, maharishis and American avatars. There were leaders who talked to God, and others who were God. I spoke to them all, sometimes writing stories, sometimes just collecting research.

Looking back over a span of twenty years, I suspect I had hoped that, in doing this work, I'd find the Truth: the belief system that would fill my soul with Utter Certainty. But, as the decade progressed, the stories that presented themselves to my attention became darker and more frightening. In various new religious sects, there were rumors of beatings, of unexplained deaths. Guns, in some cases, were being stockpiled, and members disappeared without a trace.

The one sentence I heard most often from cult members was: "If the press just told the truth about us, they'd have the greatest story ever told." But the press seldom wrote about the structure of the religion or its belief system. They wrote about cult leaders taking sexual or financial advantage of followers; about secret paramilitary drills; about actual physical torture. This, some cult leaders felt, was evidence of a vast conspiracy directed against them.

Hatred and fear of the outside world was the cement that held the most appalling groups together. Comedy had given way to a vague, unfocused fear that sometimes blossomed into outright terror. I was not surprised when I heard the first reports of the danse macabre of suicide and murder orchestrated by mad Jim Jones. It was almost to be expected.

The article I wrote about those deaths failed to change the world, and certainly hasn't stopped people from joining destructive or deadly cults. I suspect it is human nature to seek the solace of Utter Certainty. In San Diego, members of Heaven's Gate knew the Truth, as did the followers of David Koresh in Waco. Call it the Jonestown Syndrome: If the damn Apocalypse is going to keep dragging its feet, why not simply engineer one of your own? That way you never have to answer any of the hard questions. And if they laugh at you, or find you pitiful, you won't ever even have to know about it.

Because death is the only Utter Certainty. ⊕

a soldier's tale
by john milius

I DIDN'T GET THE FULL impact of *Apocalypse Now* when I saw it at the Hollywood screenings in 1979. I had been angry at Francis Ford Coppola because I thought he was trying to hog all the press. Then I took a bunch of people to see it at the Cinerama Dome here in L.A. The place was full. There was a trailer for *1941* with John Belushi – another movie I had been involved with – and it was a very raucous audience, yelling at Belushi and generally being loud. All of a sudden *Apocalypse Now* came on, with the helicopters and the Doors' "The End" playing. The theater went silent. There was never a comment, not a fucking noise in the audience, until the movie was over.

When the lights came up, I looked around and saw that people were sitting transfixed. Vietnam vets were there, too, weeping. I was stunned by how good the film was and what Francis had done. I was proud. I knew that we had accomplished *something*; whether it was good or bad, we had somehow kept the faith with those people.

Apocalypse Now achieved its highest aspiration: Not only was it immersed in the historical period and place – Vietnam – but it was an allegory of people facing reality and truth. The truth of life and the nature of war, of man, of civilization and of savagery. That is why the novel *Heart of Darkness* worked as a model. It's a timeless story.

Apocalypse Now has now attained *Citizen Kane* status and is revered as one of the great films of all time. It wasn't always that way. Critics excoriated Francis and me when it was first released. It is certainly, though, my most famous, and one of my best, efforts as a writer. When I die, they won't say anything but, "John Milius, who wrote *Apocalypse Now*, died this week."

The screenplay started when I was in USC's film school – the West Point of Hollywood – with George Lucas. We hadn't met Francis yet. George and I were the two ringleaders at school, making student films and winning awards. George was sort of the good boy and I was the bad boy. I lived in my car, I was an anarchist surfer, a complete, consummate rebel and an anti-intellectual of the worst kind. I was threatened with dismissal every other day. I've always had a problem with authority.

The specter of the Vietnam War was hanging over all our heads. I was the only one who wanted to enlist – everybody else wanted to go to Canada or get married. I figured sooner or later I was going to go, so I signed up for the Marine Air Program, but I had asthma, so I washed out. Then I had to reconfigure my life because I hadn't planned on living past twenty-six – nobody in the Sixties planned on living very long – and I had assumed my legacy would be a smoking hole in the ground over there.

Today in filmmaking there are mainly people who want to be famous, who aren't driven by the need to tell a story. They just want the fame. Back then, I never thought about the potential rewards of anything I did. I didn't think about whether I was going to be paid, whether I was going to get a new BMW or a house in Bel Air or any of that kind of shit. I had what I needed. I had my surfboard. I was fit. I had girls. I was trained. I was a weapon. I just needed a mission. I was STRAC: Strategic, Tough, Ready Around the Clock.

At USC I had a writing teacher, Mr. Irwin Blacker, who gave that mission to me. He'd tell us exotic Hollywood stories, including one about how many filmmakers had tried to do *Heart of Darkness* – most notably Orson Welles – but that nobody had been able to lick it. I had read the book when I was seventeen and had loved it.

So that did it. I said, Not only am I going to do my Vietnam movie, I'm going to use *Heart of Darkness* as an allegory because if you're going to be passing under the skeleton of an elephant, it will be much better if that skeleton is the tail of a downed B-52. I had the ambitious idea of going to Vietnam and shooting the film there.

When George tells this story, exaggerating everything, he'll say Milius was really insane. The truth is, they all wanted to go. Cinema verité had become a popular idea then with the emergence of films like *Medium Cool,* which had been shot during the riots at the '68 Chicago Democratic convention.

We were going to do it dirt cheap: shoot a feature film in 16 millimeter in Vietnam while the war was going on. Who knows, maybe we would have been killed. It certainly wouldn't have been the same movie – nor would it have been as good without Francis.

After USC I was a young, cheap screenwriter, hanging out at American Zöetrope, Francis's company. Then I cowrote *Jeremiah Johnson,* which became a hit for Robert Redford. I was hot. I got offers to fix up other screenplays. So I was now at the crossroads where I could become a rewriter or I could go off and write my own stuff, do my *Apocalypse Now.*

After *The Green Berets* it was unhip to do anything about Vietnam, because no studio wanted to touch the controversy. Yet in 1969 Warner Bros. struck a deal with American Zöetrope, and the screenplay for *Apocalypse Now* was part of that. I received fifteen thousand dollars for the script, and later, when the movie was finally made, another ten. That's it. But you know, fifteen was enough. I was getting my surfboards at a discount anyway.

The title came from the buttons hippies wore that said NIRVANA NOW with a peace symbol. I made one with a tail and engine nasals, so that the symbol became a B-52, and read APOCALYPSE NOW. As a matter of fact, I put it on one of my boards.

Surfing was inevitably going to be featured in *Apocalypse Now.* One of the movie's themes is that Vietnam was really a California War. By the Seventies, California culture had become the leading edge of the world, of hip youth. Not only the hippies, the guys in the Valley with their cars, the Beach Boys, the whole surfing culture, but also rock & roll. The British – the Beatles and the Rolling Stones – had faded; the real hip people were listening to the Byrds and the Doors.

I was obsessed with the Doors. It was my idea to use their music in the film. I remember hearing "Light My Fire" while the Six Day War was going on, when Israel was trouncing the Arab armies and retaking the Wall. I always thought of the Doors in terms of war, though the bandmembers were horrified by that connection. It just worked for me, though. Friends of mine who were in Vietnam said, "God, I was always plugged in to the Doors when there was a lot of stuff to be done." One friend who was in a Special Forces camp said his group had put on "Light My Fire" and played it all night while being attacked.

Adults didn't handle the Vietnam War very well. Remember, it was a war that was fought by teenagers, who hopped up their helicopters and put flame jobs on the gun pods. It became this sort of East-meets-West thing, an ancient Asian culture being assaulted by this teenage California culture.

In *Apocalypse Now* you're given a view of transplanted America in that scene in the compound of expandable trailers where Playboy bunnies are putting on a show for the soldiers. The depiction conveys the enormity of importing all this incredible American culture and power. You get that even with the film's image of cows being brought in by helicopter.

A friend of mine, who requests anonymity, was an important influence on *Apocalypse Now.* He did three tours of Vietnam in the Special Forces, and he told me the greatest power we had over there was that we could call from the sky either fire or a cow. We could burn a village down from the sky, or we could make a cow appear out of the air.

This friend was the model for Willard (played by Martin Sheen) in *Apocalypse.* Remember the story that Marlon Brando tells about the Communists chopping off the inoculated arms of children? It's a true story.

My friend was a Special Forces adviser to a South Vietnamese unit when the Forces were doing civic-action programs, inoculating people from a village not too far from Saigon. Afterwards, the Viet Cong came in and chopped off all the villagers' inoculated arms. To retaliate, the Green Beret team and the Special Forces civic-action team rounded up a bunch of known Viet Cong leaders and killed them all. My friend and the others got in trouble for it, though, because the dead had been the sources the Americans were buying intelligence from.

It's a harrowing true story that he will have to live with for the rest of his life. Every movie that I write contains a scene like it: Somebody tells a story of an event that is more harrowing than anything that can be depicted.

I love the smell of napalm in the morning." I had been sure that that would be the first line taken out of the *Apocalypse* script. As leader of the First Battalion of the Ninth Cavalry Regiment, Colonel Kilgore was a wildly drawn character – straight out of *Dr. Strangelove* – who, I must admit, I didn't think would ultimately work.

But Francis left the role as it had been written, and Robert Duvall is such a good actor he made it work. He made Colonel Kilgore a professional military guy who has acquired this California surfer cool and never deviates. He's still a warrior. He's just a warrior who surfs. He isn't just some fucking guy who says, "Yeah man, I like to surf. I wish I could find a good point here or something." Duvall's approach was: "That's Charlie's point? Yeah, well Charlie don't surf!" You know, "Fuck Charlie! I'm going to take this point and I'm going to surf it. I'm going to surf Charlie's waves. I'm going to fuck his women *and* surf his waves."

Of all the versions there have been of the movie, there's one that is my favorite. Francis made a tape of it for me. It's three hours and five minutes long and includes some of the famous cut-out French scene, more footage on the beach and more of a resolution in the end with Brando.

The version of *Apocalypse* most people have seen is what Francis calls the Modified Milius Ending, which hadn't been his preferred ending. Francis's ending shows Willard throwing down the sword, walking through everybody, getting on the boat and going down the river – that's the end of it. No air strike. But I said, "This is *Apocalypse Now.*

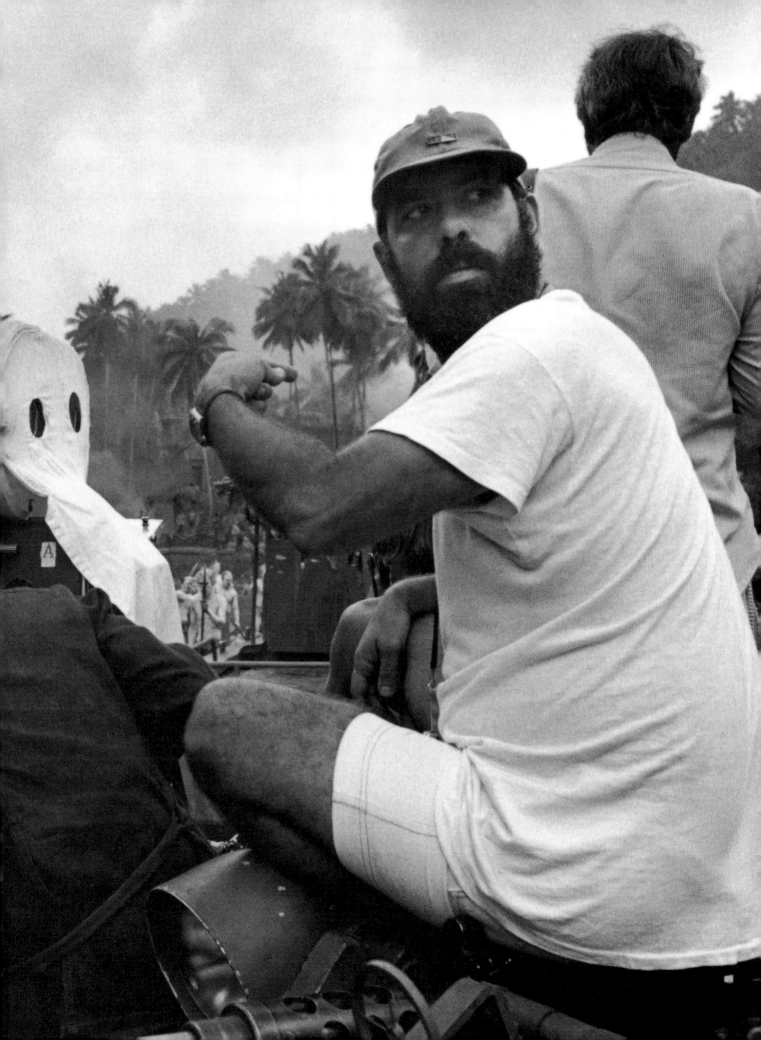

2 The Who film *Quadrophenia* premieres. Starring Phil Daniels and Police lead singer Sting, it chronicles the rise and fall of England's Mods in the '60s. The same day, the band, with Kenney Jones on drums, performs its first concert since the death of Keith Moon. Three weeks later, Jeff Stein's documentary of the band, *The Kids Are Alright,* will open in New York City.

3 Reports of an exodus of thousands of Vietnamese "boat people" fleeing their impoverished, war-ravaged homeland for any port that will accept them – including Hong Kong, Malaysia and even unpopulated islands along the Indonesian archipelago – fill the news. Reports state that thousands reach a port, but a significant number are incarcerated or turned away to perish at sea.

18 A jury awards $10.5 million to the family of Karen Silkwood, the nuclear-power-plant employee killed in a mysterious car crash in 1974 en route to meet with union representatives and a reporter.

19 Top of the charts: Peaches & Herb's "Reunited" (pop single); Supertramp's *Breakfast in America* (pop album).

At Eric Clapton and Patti Boyd Harrison's wedding reception, an obligatory jam includes Clapton, Paul McCartney, George Harrison, Ringo Starr, Mick Jagger, Denny Laine, Lonnie Donegan and Ginger Baker.

21 Fans mob Elton John in Leningrad during his first U.S.S.R. tour.

A presidential council report shows rising marijuana use in the U.S.

22 Cheap Trick's *Live at Budokan,* one of the best-selling live albums of the Seventies, goes platinum.

23 *Alien,* the science-fiction horror film starring Sigourney Weaver and John Hurt, is released.

1 The Seattle Supersonics defeat the Washington Bullets to clinch the NBA title in five games.

3 Two diet books, *The Complete Scarsdale Medical Diet* and *The Pritikin Program,* are among the five best-selling nonfiction books.

11 Hollywood legend John "the

JOHN MILIUS   GEORGE LUCAS   ROBERT DALVA

BARRY BECKERMAN   AL LOCATELLI   FRANCIS COPPOLA

This place is evil, it has to be cauterized by fire." Finally he came around to that idea and decided to have the air strike under the closing titles – his way of saving face but, in fact, it really worked.

F rancis had the arrogance, the hubris, the ambition to make *Apocalypse Now.* Whenever I direct a movie, I say, "If I get sick, I'm willing to die here," and that's the same kind of drive Francis had. There'd be a terrible typhoon, and Francis would say, "Let's shoot! Let's do something! Get a camera! Let's shoot! That's what we came here for." He became Kurtz.

Francis's personality is also the one most similar to Hitler's that I know: Hitler could convince anybody of anything, and so can Francis. Francis is my Führer. I'd follow him to hell.

Apocalypse took so much out of so many people that everyone who worked on it feels like a veteran. When they all came back from the Philippines, the same things that happened to Vietnam Vets started happening to them. They didn't work for a long time and suffered intense depressions, they drank and had nightmares. Everybody who worked on that movie got post-traumatic stress disorder. They had messed with *the war* and it had stained them.

I think filmmakers don't have that kind of push anymore. James Cameron with his *Titanic* is the only example I can think of from the last twenty years. I can just hear Cameron saying something like, "I don't care how much this movie costs, they're going to have to kill me to get me off this movie." That's the only way great movies get made. I'm not saying you have to spend $200 million. You can make one

Previous pages: Francis Ford Coppola *(right)* directs *Apocalypse Now* in the Philippines; above: American Zöetrope celebrates its founding in 1970 – those wearing hats are: John Milius, George Lucas and Coppola *(from left)*

for $2 million, but you have to be willing to push. You have to take the samurai attitude, be willing to die in the attempt.

Today in moviemaking, there's a pervasive fear of not being hip enough, not making the right corporate move, not having enough money. Corporate nazis have replaced individualism, dignity and ethics.

Take the Heidi Fleiss scandal. It came out that executives at a major studio were hiring Fleiss's call girls, and the corporation was paying for them. Can you believe that, having your corporation pay for your sex? The corporation telling you when and with whom and how long you could take your human pleasure? That's fucking science fiction. Can you imagine Sam Peckinpah being given a whore and the studio saying, "We'll pick up the tab"? He'd say: "Fuck you! I'll pay for my own whores!"

In a way, *Apocalypse Now* is about a guy who decides to make his *own* decisions. The further he gets in his career the more he's convinced he's not going to listen to the crap. He says to himself, "I'm not going to fight the war they want. I'm going to win. I'm going to go out there and do what it takes to win." And he's willing to pay.

In the Seventies our country still retained a tinge of idealism. It was a much freer society, where the individual was important. The Vietnam War made people evaluate their lives. If you were going to be drafted, either you went and fought for your country, or you had to make the decision to fight against that. But *you* had to decide.

I knew one guy back then who went to every fucking riot there was and got the shit beaten out of him. I told him he could have gone to combat and done that and probably would have had less chance of being killed. But he fought the cops and loved doing it – throwing himself into the middle of riot cops. He was a fucking warrior, just displaced.

One of my purposes in doing *Apocalypse Now* was to tell the story of the Vietnam War soldiers who had been treated with such incredible injustice and disrespect when they returned to America. I wanted to give them a sense of dignity and a place in history.

In order to be great, a movie has to be true. It must stay loyal to certain ideals and challenge them at the same time. *Apocalypse Now* challenged the inanity, the total unreasonableness of war. Everybody in the movie has gone insane, and they're all pointing to this madman at the end of the river, who's the one that finally tells you the truth.

Francis and I, we still talk like old veterans. "This was a great thing we did, shouldn't we go to war again? I mean this is what we were made for. We should go make *Napoleon* or do something outrageous and great and challenge Hollywood and ourselves."

As for the Vietnam War, my opinion hasn't changed too much since then. My feeling is that, if we were going to fight the war, we should have won. The original mistake was made by Allen Dulles and the CIA. They got us into Vietnam because they fucked up the Bay of Pigs. It was also Kennedy-family machismo – Kennedy had the ability to get us out and didn't do it. But I believe that once we were in and saying, "Okay, this is where we draw the line," we should have fought the war quickly and decisively. You don't send young men to die in a war you don't intend to win.

Besides *Apocalypse Now* and *Platoon*, I don't think any of the Vietnam War films capture just how clearly ill-fated the conflict was, much as the Peloponnesian War was. It was a war that should never have happened, that became hideously immoral, and so there couldn't be any correct political opinions about it. And yet, in a way, every opinion was right – it was simply the war that was wrong.

Francis is a real artist. I don't believe he's made up his mind about the Vietnam War, so he didn't let Kurtz have any answers. I think he wanted *Apocalypse Now* to be a work in progress, and every year he'd rerelease it.

Is *Apocalypse Now* anti–Vietnam War? Nearly all the people involved in making it, from Francis on down, were against the war and held what were considered politically correct views at the time. Except for me: I wasn't for the war, but I *was* for the American soldier and I wanted the film to reflect that. I wanted the grunts to be the heroes, to make a movie that they would look at and say, "This is ours."

I believe that one of the only noble attributes of our society is its concept of the American Citizen soldier. I'm a militarist and an anarchist. But don't expect that to make sense. As David Bowie once said when accused of contradicting himself, "Well – I'm a rock star." What do you expect? I'm a movie director.

Meanwhile, the mystique of *Apocalypse Now* lives on. The Marine Corps invited me to Camp Pendleton to watch a demonstration of an aerial assault combined with an amphibious landing. As the helicopters came in, "Ride of the Valkyries" was playing over the loudspeakers. It's become an anthem! I don't think the United States can go to war without it.

I went to Desert Storm to photograph the war for the Marine Corps, and just after the war ended, I went out to the oil fields in Iraq. The oil was burning where the manifold had been bombed and Saddam had released the oil into the gulf, so the sky was black. They put a perimeter up and these kids were out there in the minefields in their Desert Storm outfits. Every four hundred yards there was another American solider wearing a gauze mask because of the black smoke. It was nine o'clock in the morning. It was dark. Except for the fires of hell.

A journalist friend and I walked out to the furthest guy, who was all alone in the far reaches of that hell. I said to this kid, "What unit are you with, son?"

"FIRST OF THE NINTH AIR CAV, SIR. YOU KNOW THE FIRST OF THE NINTH? HAVE YOU SEEN *APOCALYPSE NOW*?"

"Yeah – 'I love the smell of napalm in the morning'!"

"YOU GOT IT, SIR!"

The soldier gave me a high five. When we were walking back, my friend asked me, "Why didn't you tell him?"

"I think he would have shot us." ⊕

18 The SALT II talks end with long-range nuclear missile limits set at 2,250 launchers per superpower. President Carter and Soviet premier Leonid Brezhnev sign the arms accord in Vienna; Carter will return home to seek congressional approval.

29 Little Feat lead singer and guitarist Lowell George dies of an apparent heart attack.

30 Gary Numan's band Tubeway Army tops the U.K. charts with the synthesizer-heavy "electropop" single "Are 'Friends' Electric?" Numan's single "Cars" will later become a Top 10 hit in the U.S.

1979 JULY

11 *Skylab*, the 77-ton orbiting lab that three separate NASA missions used and that has been slowly dropping to Earth, enters the atmosphere and breaks apart; large pieces fall into the Indian Ocean and the Australian wilderness.

12 Soul singer Minnie Riperton dies of cancer.

The second game of a White Sox doubleheader is canceled and 34 are arrested when a "disco demolition" rally in Chicago's Comiskey Park goes out of control. A crowd of 50,000 chants "disco sucks" and blows up an estimated 10,000 disco records, then rushes the field, refusing to get off.

16 President Ahmed Hassan al-Bakr of Iraq resigns, naming vice president Saddam Hussein as his successor.

17 In a surprise move, President Carter reshuffles his entire Cabinet due to its less-than-satisfactory performance, names Hamilton Jordan chief of staff and spends the next month appointing replacements. Predictably, public confidence in Carter ebbs.

19 After a seven-week civil war, Nicaragua's Sandinista rebels take control of the capital, Managua, two days after the resignation of President Anastasio Debayle Somoza. His departure ends 46 years of his family's rule.

26 Two years after the British release of the Clash's eponymous debut album, Epic Records releases it in the U.S.

ROLLING STONE reports that promotional music videos are becoming "the newest selling tool in rock," and cites David Bowie's "Boys Keep

death of the cincinnati eleven
by chet flippo

AT ABOUT 7:15 on the evening of December 3, 1979, Larry Magid sat down to dinner with Frank Wood in the luxurious Beehive Club, a private club in the upper reaches of Cincinnati's Riverfront Coliseum. Wood, who was general manager of the city's premier rock station, WEBN-FM, remarked to Magid, who was head of Electric Factory of Philadelphia (one of the country's leading rock promoters) that the crowd streaming onto the coliseum floor far below them for that evening's Electric Factory–promoted Who concert seemed to be quite orderly. A "happy crowd," he said, not at all like the rabble that had disrupted previous "chain-saw concerts" there, like the Outlaws' fighting crowd and Led Zeppelin's mob.

The crowd below them was sprinting to get as close as possible to the stage, in the grand tradition of "festival" or unreserved seating. By agreement of the coliseum management (the coliseum is privately owned), Electric Factory and the Who, mostly general-admission tickets had been sold: supposedly 3,578 reserved seats in the loges at eleven dollars each and 14,770 general-admission tickets at ten dollars each.

A few of those thousands of young people – the youngest known was four years old – had blood on their shoes as they ran happily down the concrete steps into the "pit," the seatless area in front of the stage where the true fanatics stand throughout the show. But no one noticed.

Magid and Wood continued their leisurely dinner. They still had plenty of time before the Who would come on, which would actually be about twenty minutes after the scheduled starting time of 8:00 p.m., because the band would be preceded by clips from the film *Quadrophenia*. Cal Levy, who ran Electric Factory's Cincinnati office, cruised the aisles. Things looked okay to him. At about 1:30 that afternoon he had noticed a large crowd congregating around the main entrance – two banks of eight glass doors each, arranged in a large V. Levy had found coliseum operations director Richard Morgan and asked him to put into effect a special security procedure they sometimes used, which was to station guards at ramp entrances and allow only ticket holders onto the plaza at the main entrance, to help eliminate the gate-crashing element. The coliseum's entry level – the concourse and plaza – is reachable only by a bridge from adjacent Riverfront Stadium, where most people park, and by ramps from street level. There were no police on the spacious plaza at 1:30. Levy suggested to Morgan that some should be there. Sixteen arrived at 3:00 p.m. and by 4:00 there were twenty-five.

December 3, 1979: Clothing, debris and bloodstains at one of the (too) few open doors of Cincinnati's Riverfront Coliseum, through which more than eight thousand Who concertgoers tried to enter

At about 6:30 p.m., Lieutenant Dale Menkhaus, who headed the twenty-five-man detail outside, decided that the eight thousand or so people who were now packed around the banks of doors were beginning to present a problem. The doors weren't scheduled to open until 7:00, but the crowd could hear the Who conducting its sound check and wanted in. It was thirty-six degrees and the wind coming off the Ohio River made it feel much colder. Menkhaus later said he told Levy and Morgan to open some doors; Levy told him the doors couldn't be opened till the sound check was over. Menkhaus was also told there weren't enough ticket takers. Morgan, like all coliseum employees, had no comment.

At 7:00 p.m., the Who finished its sound check. No one inside the coliseum knew that just outside those front doors the horror had already begun, a horror under a full moon, a horror of chilling magnitude that will probably never be fully explained.

Richard Klopp was one witness to that horror on the plaza. He saw his wife swept away from him in the crush of concertgoers trying to get inside the coliseum. He was just trying to survive himself. Klopp was six feet two inches tall and weighed over 200 pounds, but he went down; the pressure from those behind him toppled

him. He was flat on his face on the concrete, and those marching, charging feet were all around him. What Klopp felt, oddly, as he wondered whether he would live or die, was *anger* at Cincinnati's establishment, at the forces that made him get a general-admission ticket when he wanted a reserved seat, at whomever it was that wouldn't open those doors to relieve the crowd pressure. He seldom went to rock concerts anymore, but he had really wanted to see the Who and had gone to Ticketron an hour early. All tickets had been sold by the time he got to the window; he saw scalpers buying a hundred tickets each. Klopp ended up paying sixty dollars for tickets for himself and his wife.

He had gotten to the plaza at 2:40 on the afternoon of December 3 because he wanted to be sure they got good seats; he had brought a book with him to read. That book, *Structuralist Poetics* by Jonathan Culler, was still in his right hand as he lay on the concrete. Someone, miraculously, helped him to his feet and he was back in the crush, his arms pinned to his sides. At one point he was within five feet of a closed door, but he had no control over his movement. At times his feet were off the ground. Despite the cold, he was drenched in sweat. He couldn't breathe. He and everyone around him had their heads tilted straight back, their noses up to try and get some air. He noticed that an actual steam, a *vapor*, was rising off the crowd in the moonlight. He would later be angered to read that it was a "stampede," because to him it was a concentration of too many people in too small a space with nowhere to go but forward – people in the back were yelling, "One, two, three, push!" but they didn't know people in the front were falling. There was little noise. Some people tried to calm those who were panicking. Some shouted, "Stay up! Stay up or you're gone!" Some chanted, "Open the fucking doors!"

The doors were officially opened at 7:05 p.m.; according to eyewitnesses, four doors out of the sixteen were open, and two of those were closed and blocked at times by guards with billy clubs. The police force outside finally found the first body at 7:54 p.m. After the ambulances and the fire department and the fire chief and the mayor and the city safety director and the Flying Squad from the Academy of Medicine and additional police and the TV crews and everybody else got there, they finally understood that this was serious. Cincinnati proper put on its serious face. TV crews were asking onlookers if drugs and alcohol hadn't caused this "stampede."

Mayor Ken Blackwell – this was his first day on the job – was summoned from his dinner with House Speaker Tip O'Neill and said it looked to him like this awful tragedy had been caused by "festival seating." It was his decision to continue the concert, lest many thousands inside riot if the show were stopped.

Promoter Larry Magid said he first learned of the trouble at 8:45 p.m. from a coliseum employee and went backstage to tell the Who's manager, Bill Curbishly, that there were four dead, "two ODs and two crushed." According to Curbishly, the fire marshal arrived and said he thought there was a mass overdosage. He wanted to stop the concert; then he learned that the deaths were due to asphyxiation and that people were still being treated on the plaza level.

Curbishly told him it would be senseless to stop the concert, that there could be a riot and people might stampede back across the plaza. The fire marshal said, "I agree with you totally."

By the time the show was over, Curbishly knew of eleven deaths. He told the Who that something serious had happened and they should hurry their encore. After the brief encore, he took them into the tuning room and told them of the deaths. They were devastated.

"Initially, we felt stunned and empty," said Roger Daltrey three days after the concert. "We felt we couldn't go on. But you gotta. There's no point in stopping."

Lieutenant Menkhaus said sixteen doors were open and Cal Levy echoed that; Electric Factory attorney Tom Gould said nine to eleven doors were open and Roger Daltrey said three were open. Dozens of eyewitnesses told ROLLING STONE that never during the trouble were more than four doors open and that only two were open most of the time. The coliseum management still refuses to say how many tickets were sold, how many guards were on duty, how many ticket takers or ushers there were or anything else. Curbishly said Electric Factory paid $7,800 to the coliseum for ushers, ticket takers, interior security, cleanup.

Including emergency exits, there were 106 doors at the coliseum (although John Tafaro, spokesman for the coliseum, would not confirm or deny this number); why at times only two at the main entrance were open would be a point of speculation for some time.

The night of the Who concert, business continued as usual until eleven people died. Some blamed the victims for their own deaths, even though it has been proven that some of them – like David Heck, who got out of the crush and went back to try and help others – died while trying to stop the madness even as police ignored them.

Cincinnati moved quickly to blame festival seating for the tragedy, although no one explained why festival seating had been permitted for so long at the coliseum when previous concerts had proven it dangerous. No one explained why even though Ticketron claims ticket sales were limited to eight per person, scalpers were spotted leaving outlets with stacks of tickets. In the week after the concert only City Councilman and former Mayor Jerry Springer said there should have been someone at the show with the authority to open the doors when there was obviously a disaster in the offing. The *Cincinnati Enquirer*'s banner headline of December 5 read: ALL DENY BLAME FOR TRAGEDY. And that's probably where it will stand.

A team of ROLLING STONE reporters visited the coliseum and got enough "no comments" to use for ten years. The city of Cincinnati registered immediate civic outrage. No more festival seating, *probably,* said the city government. A task force was set up to find out what went wrong. Frank Wood of WEBN-FM was named to it. He said that he was not sure what the task force could do; all he knew was that he had read in the morning paper that "I'm not allowed to point a finger at anyone, and I think that's a shame." The task force had no subpoena power, and it was widely viewed in Cincinnati as window dressing.

The coroner's office said the eleven apparently died from "suffocation by asphyxiation due to compression" and "suffocation due to accidental mob stampede."

Promoters across the country blamed festival seating. Larry Magid said that he felt terrible and that he personally didn't like festival seating, but that's what the kids wanted. A kid in Cincinnati printed up a few T-shirts that read: I SURVIVED THE WHO CONCERT. ⊕

jerry springer on the who concert tragedy

CINCINNATI was an incredibly conservative city in 1979. Rock & roll was okay on the radio, but the city's institutions would say, "Please don't bring it into our community – rock means drugs and promiscuity and kids becoming anarchists" – it was put in such a political context.

When I was running for mayor in 1977, I was only thirty-three and into rock & roll. During the campaign, I said, half tongue-in-cheek, "If I'm elected, I'm going to bring rock & roll to Cincinnati." The day I was sworn in, a cartoon ran in the *Cincinnati Enquirer* picturing me as a little boy sitting in the big mayor's chair with a gavel, saying, "Awright, when can we book the Rolling Stones into Riverfront Stadium?"

We did, indeed, produce the first rock concert in Riverfront Stadium. On a nine-seat council, I cast the only vote for stadium concerts; I pushed and pushed and finally swayed the five votes necessary to pass the resolution.

The first concert took place on August 16, 1978, and featured the Eagles, Eddie Money and the Steve Miller Band. We set up showers all around the infield so that in the hot sun, people could stay cool and there'd be fewer fights. Over fifty thousand people showed up, and it went till eleven o'clock. There were no incidents; it was just a lovefest. During the Eagles' set they said, "We want to thank the mayor for bringing us here. We're going to bring him up now . . ." and I sang "Lyin' Eyes" with the Eagles! It was the single biggest thrill of my mayoralty.

On the other hand, there had been some dangerous incidents at rock shows at the Riverfront Coliseum – a smaller, indoor venue next to the stadium – where people had been running in like crazy trying to get a good seat. I remember the Led Zeppelin show in 1977, where doors had been broken and people injured. I said, "Let's give everyone assigned seats and then there's no incentive to get there early." I spoke out publicly against festival seating at indoor concerts, and there was quite a lot of debate, even a public hearing on it. The concert promoters were against it because they could sell more tickets at a better price if everyone had a chance to sit up front.

On the night of the Who concert (I was only on the city council at this time), I was at a Democratic fund-raiser with Tip O'Neill. Someone handed me a note to get down to the coliseum, that there was a major problem.

There were police, ambulances and everything. Because it was my generation, I kept wondering if *I* knew anyone among the dead. At that point, it was a human tragedy – it hadn't yet turned into a political war. By the next day, a task force was assembled, and the finger-pointing began: "They should have opened the doors. Who gave the order not to?" The promoter, the city and the police started giving statements – after talking to their lawyers to ensure they weren't admitting blame.

I believe the eleven people died for no reason. We did pass the ordinance outlawing festival seating, but it was too little, too late. I hate to think they had to die just to pass a bill. ⊕

Francisco. The Dead Kennedys' frontman pledges municipal rent rollbacks, the auction of public offices and the establishment of a Board of Bribery to set fair prices for building-code exemptions, liquor licenses and other privileges.

10 *The Rose,* a film starring Bette Midler and Kris Kristofferson that is transparently based on Janis Joplin's life, premieres in Los Angeles.

13 Rap debuts on the R&B charts with the Sugar Hill Gang's "Rapper's Delight." The project of former soul singer Sylvia Robinson, the single will sell more than two million copies and pave the way for other rap pioneers, such as Kurtis Blow, Spoonie Gee, Grandmaster Flash & the Furious Five and the Funky Four Plus One.

17 The Pittsburgh Pirates clip the Baltimore Orioles' wings in seven games to win the World Series.

20 Bob Dylan introduces his born-again Christian-rock phase, performing "Gotta Serve Somebody" on *Saturday Night Live.* His religious fervor will also surface on his *Slow Train Coming, Saved* and *Shot of Love.*

22 After much politicking and under a death threat from Khomeini, the exiled shah of Iran arrives in the U.S. for cancer surgery. Although he will later leave for Panama, this American hospitality fuels anti-U.S. sentiment in Iran.

31 The sexual-fantasy movie *10,* starring Bo Derek, and the horror flick *Halloween* are the first and second box-office draws.

1979 NOVEMBER

3 Six gunmen kill four protesters during an anti-KKK rally in Greensboro, NC. At their 1980 trial, an all-white jury will clear the six.

4 An angry mob of Iranian students storms the U.S. embassy in Teheran, demands the return of the exiled shah and takes 90 hostages. They will release all women and blacks but hold the remaining hostages for 444 days, monopolizing American attention and eventually striking a fatal blow to Carter's presidency.

29 Michael Jackson receives a gold record for "Don't Stop Till You Get Enough," the first of four Top 10 hits from his platinum LP *Off the Wall.*

two turntables & a microphone
by robert ford jr.

IN 1979 I was a *Billboard* reporter covering black music at a time when it was struggling to find its voice amid the drone of discomania. Venerable soul stars like Aretha Franklin, Diana Ross and James Brown were repeatedly resurrecting their careers, while Michael Jackson's *Off the Wall* was about to up the crossover stakes. Black music then encompassed everything from Barry White, Donna Summer and George Clinton to Teddy Pendergrass, Rick James and Prince. Over it all boomed the relentless 4/4 exhortations to dance, dance, dance. I was then a fairly conservative guy whose idea of style was a herringbone jacket, jeans and saddle shoes, and my income was low enough to make me consider working at the post office. But then something unexpected happened.

A friend from Queens named Russell Simmons had cajoled me into coming downtown to see a show at the Hotel Diplomat on Forty-third Street. There, in one of the ballrooms, he promised, I was going to see something I'd never seen before. Given my occupation, it was hard to imagine what *that* might be. I'd attended hundreds of concerts, including hip-hop shows (DJ Hollywood at the Apollo Theatre and Kool DJ Herc at Taft High School in the Bronx, to name just two), where fifty or maybe a hundred kids would be enjoying the rhythms and rhymes. But Russell was right – this one was different.

I stood among five thousand screaming kids, most of them young and black. Crushed closely together, the crowd defied every rule of prevailing party fashion, dressed in everything from elegant silk blazers (with no shirts underneath) to worn, nappy shearling. Among the young men, however, I saw the harbingers of B-boy style: Kangol caps, jogging suits and the latest sneakers.

Their eyes fixed on the stage, the revelers rocked in unison, under the spell of a solitary DJ whose only "instruments" were a microphone, a couple turntables and a stack of vinyl offering everything from James Brown funk workouts to spaghetti-Western soundtracks. These he spun with surgical precision, "scratching" or distorting the sounds by back-spinning and phasing. In between vocal tracks, while the

Along with Kurtis Blow and the Sugar Hill Gang, rap DJ Grandmaster Flash *(at right)* made records in 1979 that pointed to the future of pop music.

beat of the music continued, the DJ would grab the microphone and start shouting short, staccato bursts of rhyme:

"Grandmaster, cut faster/than any known, stone to the bone,/home grown, better leave him alone."

The lyrics – the raps – focused on putting down rival rappers (the original "Sucker MCs") or boasted about the rappers' proficiency at turning a rhyme. And the featured artists (for that's what these DJs obviously were), wielding their gift for sharp, rhythmic rhyming like weapons, turned out to be the hottest ones on the scene in 1979: Grandmaster Flash, Kurtis Blow and Eddie Cheeba.

They were unknown outside New York's tri-state area, and the genre "rap" or "hip-hop" had yet to be discovered by the record industry or a mainstream audience. But uptown, and around town, it was growing.

Rap was too spontaneous, too homegrown and too verbal to be defined by an irrefutable, written history. Geographically, it came from Harlem and the Bronx. Musically, it grew out of a singular mission to keep the party going when there were few other choices. Culturally, rap emerged during a time of economic recession, when stable urban communities were following a general downward slide. Contrary to popular belief, disco had not swept the entire nation. Disco was glamorous, and the downtown discos had become expensive, leaving uptown kids on the street. So they started creating their own entertainment, employing DJs and partying wherever they could: high school gyms, neighborhood clubs, block parties, community parks and even empty apartments.

As the parties grew and gathered larger crowds, the competition heated up among the masters of the wheels of steel and early mobile DJs experimented with new ways of working their magic. They sped up and slowed down short, rhythmic passages in obscure records that they would play over and over to the delight of the dancers, urging on the crowd with snappy patter. Soon DJs like Pete "DJ" Jones, Rip and Cliff, DJ Hollywood, Ras Maboya and Afrika Bambaataa developed huge followings based as much on their rhymes as on their mixing finesse.

I first came on the scene as an observer. My 1978 *Billboard* piece on Kool DJ Herc ("B-Beats Bombarding Bronx") and his unique way of cutting up records was one of the very first stories about rap to appear in a major white publication. I recall trying to define these new terms; I had first heard "hip-hop" in one of DJ Hollywood's raps: "A hip, a hop, a hibby, dibby hop and you don't stop."

My belief is that at the heart of hip-hop lies the essence of black expression: the beat and the word – the gift of rhythm and subtle-but-telling inflection that has always colored black speech. From the down-home drawl of Stepin Fetchit to the affected, pseudointellectual accents of black politicos like Julian Bond and Percy Sutton, we have always spoken with a certain cadence. Compact phrases like "bad mama jama" and "too through with you" can speak a world of meaning with the right rhythm, accent and tone.

It's doubtful hip-hop pioneers ever heard of, much less grooved to, the recorded sermons of master preachers like the Reverend C.L. Franklin; the good-natured, slang-happy bouncing lyrics of bandleader Louis Jordan's Forties hits ("Five Guys Named Moe") and raps ("Beware"); or Gil Scott-Heron and the Last Poets' militant spoken-word-over-percussion albums of the early and mid-Seventies. And not rap's first stars, but maybe their parents listened to popular radio DJs in the Fifties like Dr. Jive and Douglas "Jocko" Henderson, whose lightning-quick verbal acrobatics plugged such items as hair-care products:

> "If your hair is short and nappy,
> Conkoline will make you happy.
> Kings and queens may rule the world,
> but Conkoline will rule your curl."

And then there are the Jamaican toasting DJs, the mock insults and one-upmanship of the Dozens, schoolyard double-Dutch rhymes keeping time for jump-rope. Black verbal expression is so rich that rap could have come from more than a dozen sources. I believe a majority of the early rappers owe as much of their inspiration to the rapid-fire, internal rhyme schemes of Dr. Seuss's subversive kiddie books as they do to any other origin.

In 1979, rap was the right music at the right time. Its strength at the outset was that it was easy to produce, to record, to perform and to promote. By then rappers were popping up all over, working the microphones exclusively and letting the DJs handle the turntables. Kurtis Blow stood out in my mind because he was good-looking and the only Harlem rapper who would work with Russell Simmons, a middle-class black boy from Hollis, Queens. Russell, who would soon produce his little brother Joey's (a.k.a. Run) hip-hop trio Run-D.M.C., later cofounded the genre's most influential label, Def Jam, and has since become a successful Hollywood producer. He was already showing signs of becoming the P.T. Barnum of hip-hop, but under his fast-talking exterior beat the heart of a true believer who saw in rap a revolutionary black genre with the potential for mass acceptance.

The intensity and excitement of that night at the Diplomat Hotel had made me an easy mark for Russell's persuasive, persistent nagging. Before long, he had me looking at rap like a fellow entrepreneur. And there was one other thing: I was about to become a thirty-year-old, first-time father. My child's mother had recently moved in with me and my less-than-enthusiastic mother. I soon came to realize that the whopping two-dollars-an-inch raise in my freelance fee would not stretch far enough to support my new child. With the post office beckoning, I had to make a decision.

So, since there was no one else to share in Russell's dream, I – with no experience whatsoever in producing a record and no musical skills – became a record producer. I partnered with J.B. Moore, a white boy from Plandome, on Long Island's posh North Shore, who invested $10,000 in my crazy idea. The result was Kurtis Blow's "Christmas Rappin'," the first major-label rap single.

I believed in rap's potential. I knew it was edgy, new, different and challenging. But as I began to shop the tape around in hopes of having it released in time for the appropriate season, I might have given up before I started had I foreseen the industry's intensely hostile reaction to the recording. Rap was unsophisticated and raw. It did not promote melodies or singers. It was not the R&B most middle-class blacks grew up with. If anything, it seemed to exemplify everything mainstream blacks and whites wished would go away. It could be loud, arrogant, in-your-face and urban. Record company responses ranged from polite rejection to downright – and racist – hostility: "We don't put out that kind of ghetto crap."

Meanwhile, Sylvia (of Mickey and Sylvia fame) and Joe Robinson's New Jersey–based Sugarhill Records, turned out the Sugar Hill Gang's more lighthearted "Rapper's Delight." To the world below 125th Street and beyond, this happy-sounding, bouncy rap was a novelty song, a fluke. To us uptowners, it was a watered-down version of what Kurtis and Grandmaster were hitting hard with at the time. But it was big (because of rampant bootlegging we'll never know just how big) enough to get the rap ball rolling downtown and then across the nation.

So, as the door opened for rap, I got lucky.

The unlikely heroes of my first rap hit were a Greek woman named Dottie Psalidas, who was in A&R administration at Mercury Records, and the Englishman she convinced to listen to our tape. John Stainze signed our future King of Rap, and by the end of 1979 Kurtis, J.B. and I were coconspirators in rap's inexorable march toward world domination.

Rap has come a long way, evolving through many stages and growing to become the most significant musical genre to emerge from black America since jazz. In fact, rap took the sound of B-boys, the sound of New York's urban center, and helped introduce a whole street culture to the world. It's amazing to consider the global impact: Rap can now be heard in Irish pubs, French discotheques, Polish bars – all rapped by local artists in their native dialects. Even Brazilian Portuguese and South African Zulu rappers are charting locally.

Closer to home, rap's family tree is awe-inspiring; it boasts a broad spectrum of artists and subgenres whose existence not even the visionary Russell Simmons could have foreseen. Like most forms of popular music, rap can be serious and political (N.W.A), light and bubblegummy (DJ Jazzy Jeff and the Fresh Prince), macho and boastful (L.L. Cool J), cartoony and fun (Pharcyde), suggestive if not X-rated (2 Live Crew), feminine (Salt-n-Pepa), feminist (Queen Latifah), hippy (De La Soul), trippy (Digable Planets) and just plain dippy (Vanilla Ice).

Born at the same time that digital technology was becoming widely available, rap also has the distinction of bringing tape loops and sampling into the mainstream.

But like other popular musical styles, rap does not always live up to the promise of its earlier masterpieces: Kurtis Blow's "The Breaks," Grandmaster Flash and the Furious Five's "The Message," Run-D.M.C.'s "It's Like That" and Public Enemy's "Fight the Power." But when message, music and artist come together in the right way – when the beats and rhymes create the same kind of magic that I first heard back in 1979, with just two turntables and a microphone – it's simply impossible to resist.

Like anything that grows so powerful, rap lost its innocence long ago. I imagine one day a form of music as new and fresh will emerge, and I wonder whether – and hope that – it's out there now, in someone's basement in Brooklyn or in someone's dreams in China. I hope that when we do hear it, we still will have the capacity to be as surprised, as enthralled, as swept up as we were back then. The landscape has changed; it's been darkened and flattened by an increasingly corporate, tied-in, market-driven record indus-

> **I always said that hip-hop was a mutation of disco. The poor kids in the ghetto didn't have the money to pay to get into the discos, so they created their own discos in the ghetto. We had block parties, house parties and small clubs in the ghettos where we would pay two dollars to get into. It was that ideology which gave way to the creation of the B-boy. –Kurtis Blow**

try that is more inflexible than ever. In 1979 there were still places a record would be played simply because it was good; videos could be shot in a day for a few thousand dollars. We need to have conditions like those again.

After producing five albums with Kurtis Blow and a few other rap projects, I'm still a fan of rap, though coming full circle, I'm again an observer. Looking back at that time, I *still* don't know what the hell I was doing. But would I do it again? In a scratch beat. It was a great ride. Although it's hard to be optimistic, I hope that younger generations will experience the wild adrenaline rush of belonging to something so vital, so powerful, so pure, so creative and so . . . fresh.

Time moves on. As I write, that baby I worried about supporting is a nineteen-year-old Syracuse University sophomore. Although my son spent his early childhood around rap artists like L.L. Cool J and Run-D.M.C., he was never very interested in his old man's music. Recently, I was thrilled when he asked me for a copy of *The Best of Kurtis Blow*. He has finally come to appreciate my contribution to the musical revolution that began the year he was born. ⊕

contributors

Since **BILLY ALTMAN** published the first magazine to be called *Punk*, in 1973, his work has appeared in such places as the *New York Times, The New Yorker*, ROLLING STONE, *Esquire* and *People*. A longtime editor of *Creem* and editor in chief of *MTV to Go*, he also served as an assistant curator for the opening of the Rock and Roll Hall of Fame. His first book, *Laughter's Gentle Soul: The Life of Robert Benchley*, was published in 1997.

JOAN BAEZ has spent more than thirty-five years as a singer, musician, social activist and goodwill ambassador.

ALLEN BARRA has been collecting misinformation from newspapers and magazines for more than a decade. He is a regular columnist for the *Wall Street Journal* and the *New York Observer* and has been a contributor to the *Village Voice, Inside Sports, Sports Illustrated*, the *New York Times, Esquire* and *USA Today*, among others, and is often called upon to debunk myths on radio call-in shows and on television.

DEBORAH BLUM is the author of *Sex on the Brain* and *The Monkey Wars* and is a coeditor of *A Field Guide for Science Writers*. She is a professor of journalism at the University of Wisconsin at Madison. Previously, she covered science for the *Sacramento Bee* and won the Pulitzer Prize in 1992 for a series exploring the ethical dilemmas of using primates in research. Her work has been published in *Psychology Today, Discover* and Time-Life Books. She serves on the board of directors of the National Association of Science Writers.

JENNY BOYD lives in London and is a psychologist and the coauthor of *Musicians in Tune*, in which seventy-five contemporary musicians discuss the creative process. She organizes workshops in England for people in recovery and has worked in the addictions field for the last five years at treatment centers in the United States. She is currently writing her memoirs – reminiscences of a sister who married a Beatle in the Sixties and of her own two marriages to Mick Fleetwood – a journey to finding her own voice.

SUSAN BROWNMILLER, the author of *Against Our Will: Men, Women and Rape*, is writing a history of the women's liberation movement as she experienced it.

TIM CAHILL has worked for ROLLING STONE, on and off, since 1969. He is the editor at large for *Outside* magazine and the author of six books, most recently *Pass the Butterworms*. He has also written the screenplay for the Academy Award–nominated documentary *The Living Sea*, as well as the IMAX documentary *Everest*.

NIK COHN grew up in Ireland, was in London during the Sixties and has lived in America since 1975. His writings on music include *Rock Dreams* (coauthored with Guy Peellaert) and *Awopbopaloobop Alopbamboom*; his most recent books are *The Heart of the World* and *Need*, a novel.

CAROL COOPER has been writing about music professionally since 1978. Her work has appeared in *The Face*, the *Village Voice* and other New York–based publications. She has been East Coast director of black music A&R for A&M Records and national director of black music A&R for Columbia. She has returned full-time to music and arts criticism, while keeping her tiny, highly specialized Nega Fulo publishing and recording companies on the side.

STAN CORNYN was executive vice president of Warner Bros. Records during the Seventies. Also a writer, Cornyn keeps a history of the Warner music business.

ANTHONY DeCURTIS is a contributing editor at ROLLING STONE and the author of *Rocking My Life Away: Writing About Music and Other Matters*. He is

the editor of *Present Tense: Rock & Roll and Culture* and coeditor of *The* ROLLING STONE *Illustrated History of Rock & Roll* and *The* ROLLING STONE *Album Guide*.

JOE ESZTERHAS was formerly a senior editor of ROLLING STONE. He is now a screenwriter; his credits include *Music Box, Betrayed, Flashdance, Jagged Edge, Basic Instinct, Showgirls, Jade, Telling Lies in America* and, most recently, *An Alan Smithee Film: Burn Hollywood Burn*.

JIM FARBER has served as chief pop music critic for the *New York Daily News* since 1990. He wrote his first piece for a national magazine, ROLLING STONE, at age seventeen – a live review of the semiglam band Roy Wood's Wizzard. In the time since, he has written for *New York, Premiere, Harper's Bazaar* and *Entertainment Weekly*. His writing also appears in *The* ROLLING STONE *Encyclopedia of Rock & Roll* and *The* ROLLING STONE *Illustrated History of Rock & Roll*.

Former ROLLING STONE editor **TIMOTHY FERRIS** is the author of nine books, including *The Whole Shebang* and the classic *Coming of Age in the Milky Way*. He has taught in five disciplines at four universities, and is currently professor emeritus at the University of California at Berkeley.

CHET FLIPPO is Nashville bureau chief for *Billboard*. He has also been senior editor at ROLLING STONE and contributing editor to a number of magazines. He is the author of *Your Cheatin' Heart: A Biography of Hank Williams; On the Road With the Rolling Stones; Everybody Was Kung-Fu Dancing; Yesterday: A Biography of Paul McCartney; Graceland: The Living Legacy of Elvis Presley;* and *David Bowie's Serious Moonlight*.

In his time with ROLLING STONE, former senior editor **BEN FONG-TORRES** toured with, among others, the Rolling Stones, Bob Dylan, George Harrison, Wings, Linda Ronstadt, Crosby, Stills, Nash and Young, Sly and the Family Stone, the Jackson 5, Bonnie Raitt and Elton John and, to the best of his recollection, survived.

In 1979 **ROBERT FORD JR.** parlayed seven years of experience as a writer covering black music and disco at *Billboard* into producing Kurtis Blow, the first rapper signed by a major label. In addition to Blow, he produced other artists and was a vice president at Rush Productions. He also handled management for the R&B octet Hi-Five and is currently working with Medford Communications, a minority-owned public relations and media consulting firm.

DR. DONNA GAINES is a journalist, sociologist and New York State–certified social worker. Her writing has been published in ROLLING STONE, the *Village Voice, Long Island Monthly, Spin, Newsday* and *Contemporaries*, and has also appeared in scholarly collections, academic journals and underground fanzines. She is the author of *Teenage Wasteland: Suburbia's Dead End Kids* and is currently a visiting faculty member at Barnard College of Columbia University.

LEON GAST is a director/producer whose films include *Hell's Angels Forever, The Dead, Salsa* and *Our Latin Thing*. His film *When We Were Kings*, a chronicle of Muhammad Ali's defeat of George Foreman in Zaire, won an Academy Award for Best Documentary Feature in 1996.

NELSON GEORGE is the author of numerous nonfiction books, including *The Death of Rhythm and Blues*. His latest work is *Hip-Hop America*, which will be published by Viking in early 1999. He has also written several screenplays and is a consulting producer on Chris Rock's HBO shows.

MIKAL GILMORE is a ROLLING STONE contributing editor and the author of *Shot in the Heart*, which will soon become an HBO movie.

BOB GREENE is a syndicated columnist for the

Chicago Tribune and a contributing correspondent for *ABC News Nightline*. He is the author of eighteen books, including the national bestsellers *Be True to Your School; Hang Time: Days and Dreams with Michael Jordan;* and, with his sister, D.G. Fulford, *To Our Children's Children: Preserving Family Histories for Generations to Come*. For nine years his American Beat was the lead column in *Esquire*.

Keyboardist/composer **HERBIE HANCOCK**'s *Headhunters* became the top-selling jazz album in history when it was released in 1971. The winner of five Grammys and an Academy Award, Hancock continues to perform and serves as the Distinguished Artist in Residence at Jazz Aspen in Snowmass, Colorado, and as the artistic director of the Thelonious Monk Institute of Jazz at the Music Center of Los Angeles County.

DAVID HARRIS is a magazine journalist and the author of eight books. During the Vietnam War, he was student body president at Stanford University, a founder of the draft resistance movement and was imprisoned for twenty months for refusing his orders for military service.

DEBORAH HARRY is a performance artist, poet and actress, best known as the lead singer/songwriter of Blondie. Her hits with the band include "Heart of Glass," "Call Me" and "The Tide Is High"; and "In Love With Love," "French Kissing in the USA" and "I Want That Man" as a solo artist. As a featured guest singer, Deborah has collaborated with Talking Heads, Argentina's multiplatinum Los Fabulosos Cadillacs, Groove Thing and the Jazz Passengers.

ROBERT HULL has been an executive producer for Time-Life Music for ten years. Throughout the Seventies, he cut his teeth as a rock writer for *Creem*, the *Washington Post* and many long-forgotten publications and sleazy tabloids. He owes his successful career path chiefly to the influence of two remarkable gentlemen – Lester Bangs and the Mad Peck. His band, the Memphis Goons, released their debut CD, *Teenage Bar-B-Q*, in 1997 to wide critical acclaim.

Singer, songwriter and guitarist **CHRISSIE HYNDE** founded the Pretenders in 1978. She is currently at work on the band's eighth album.

Since 1984, **MARTIN JOHNSON** has covered almost every kind of music for a variety of local and national publications as well as Web sites. His work has appeared in ROLLING STONE, *Newsday, Pulse!, Vogue*, the *New York Times, New York*, the *Chicago Tribune*, the *San Francisco Weekly* and many others. He is a coauthor of *Jazz: Photographs of the Masters*. Twenty-six years ago, when he bought his first 45, his Aunt Doll said that his interest in music would lead to no good; finally he's able to admit that she was right.

HAMILTON JORDAN was campaign manager for Jimmy Carter's gubernatorial and presidential campaigns, chief aide in Carter's Georgia administration and his White House chief of staff. He is the author of *Crisis*, a bestseller about the negotiations for the release of American hostages in Iran in 1980.

ASHLEY KAHN is celebrating his tenth year as an independent journeyman, having worn the hats of journalist, columnist, editor, publicist, artist manager, music festival coordinator, tour manager, radio and video producer, youthful upstart and oldtime prattler.

LENNY KAYE is a writer, musician and record producer. He plays guitar with Patti Smith and coauthored Waylon Jennings's autobiography, *Waylon*.

MARK KEMP is vice president of music and editorial at MTV. A former editor of *Option* and former music editor of ROLLING STONE, he has written about music and other topics for a variety of publications. In 1998 he was nominated for a Grammy for his liner notes to the Phil Ochs box set *Farewells & Fantasies*.

JOE KLEIN's writing has appeared in ROLLING STONE, the *New York Times,* the *Washington Post,* the *New Republic, Life, New York* and *Newsweek.* He is a columnist at *The New Yorker* and the "anonymous" author of *Primary Colors.*

HOWARD KOHN is the author of the acclaimed *Who Killed Karen Silkwood?* and *The Last Farmer,* a family memoir that was a finalist for the Pulitzer Prize in General Nonfiction. Kohn was a senior editor and Washington bureau chief for ROLLING STONE and for the Center for Investigative Reporting. His work has appeared in the *New York Times Magazine,* the *Los Angeles Times Magazine, Reader's Digest, Esquire, Mother Jones* and other periodicals.

RICHARD MICHAEL LEVINE has written on a variety of subjects for many national magazines. In the Seventies, he wrote about religious and psychological movements for ROLLING STONE. He was the television columnist for *New Times* magazine as well as *Esquire's* media columnist and is the author of *Bad Blood: A Family Murder in Marin County.*

DAISANN McLANE is a freelance journalist based in New York. She has been a staff writer and columnist for ROLLING STONE, and her work has appeared in the *Village Voice,* the *New York Times, Vogue, Harper's Bazaar* and *Condé Nast Traveler.* She's also a regular commentator on NPR's "All Things Considered."

RUSSELL MEANS is a political activist and leader of the American Indian Movement. A full-blooded Yankton Sioux, he has played major roles in *The Last of the Mohicans, Natural Born Killers, Wagons East, Wind Runner* and *Pocahontas,* and written a best-selling autobiography, *Where White Men Fear to Tread.* He has produced television documentaries and albums of protest music, and continues to work on outreach programs on the Navajo reservation in Chinle, Arizona.

LORNE MICHAELS is the creator and producer of *Saturday Night Live.*

JOHN MILIUS is an award-winning screenwriter, producer and director who has written twenty-three feature films and directed nine. His credit or credits grace such films as *Apocalypse Now, Red Dawn, Jeremiah Johnson, Conan the Barbarian, Clear and Present Danger, Dirty Harry, Magnum Force, Rough Riders, The Wind and the Lion,* and the U.S.S. *Indianapolis* scene in *Jaws.*

GLENN O'BRIEN was editor and art director of *Interview* from 1970 to 1973 and wrote the music column Glenn O'Brien's Beat for that magazine from 1977 to 1989. He has also worked as an editor for ROLLING STONE, *Playboy* and *Spin.* O'Brien edited Madonna's book *Sex* and wrote *Madonna: The Girlie Show Book.* He currently writes two columns: the Style Guy for *Details* and AntiMatter for *Paper* magazine. A collection of his work, *Soapbox,* was published by Imschoot in 1997.

BARBARA O'DAIR is a poet and the executive editor of *Details.* Formerly the editor of *US,* she has worked as deputy music editor of ROLLING STONE and as a senior editor at *Entertainment Weekly* and the *Village Voice.* She has written for ROLLING STONE, *Spin,* the *Village Voice* and other publications. She is the editor of *The ROLLING STONE Book of Women in Rock: Trouble Girls* and the coeditor of a book of feminist essays, *Caught Looking: Women, Pornography and Censorship.*

PATRICK PACHECO survived *After Dark* magazine to become a New York–based arts reporter for the likes of *Newsday,* the *Los Angeles Times* and *Art & Antiques* magazine. He's currently writing a book about that peculiar madness known as the Broadway theater.

LAURA PALMER is a television producer and the author of several books including *Shrapnel in the Heart: Letters and Remembrances From the Vietnam Veterans Memorial.*

MARY PEACOCK has been deputy editor of *In Style* and *Mirabella,* style editor of the *Village Voice,* editor in chief of *Model* and a founding editor of *Ms.,* among other editorial jobs. She's written for many publications and is currently a contributing editor to *In Style* and a columnist for *Women's Wire* (www.womenswire.com).

GEORGE PLIMPTON is the editor of *Paris Review,* the international literary quarterly founded in 1953. He is the author of a number of books, many with a sports theme: *Paper Lion, Shadow Box, The Bogey Man,* among them. His latest book is *Truman Capote,* an oral biography published in 1997.

LLOYD PRICE is a rock & roll pioneer whose hits include "Lawdy Miss Clawdy," "Stagger Lee" and "Personality." He was inducted into the Rock and Roll Hall of Fame in 1998.

DAN RATHER, now the anchor and managing editor of *The CBS Evening News,* served as CBS News White House correspondent in the Seventies and, from 1975 to 1981, was a contributing editor of *60 Minutes.*

DAVID RITZ is a biographer (Marvin Gaye, Ray Charles, B.B. King, Smokey Robinson, Etta James, Jerry Wexler), novelist (*Blues Notes Under a Green Felt Hat*) and lyricist ("Sexual Healing"). A three-time winner of the Ralph J. Gleason Music Book Award, he received a 1992 Grammy for Best Liner Notes. He's currently collaborating with Aretha Franklin as well as the Neville Brothers on their life stories.

MICHAEL ROGERS has been a writer and editor for ROLLING STONE, *Outside* and *Newsweek.* He has written four books of fiction and nonfiction and has produced computer games, CD-ROMs, online services and Web sites. He is currently vice president of editorial research and development for *Washington Post–Newsweek Interactive Media* and is at work on his next novel.

ROBERT SANTELLI is the director of education at the Rock and Roll Hall of Fame and Museum. He has taught at Monmouth and Rutgers universities, and his writing has appeared in ROLLING STONE, *CD Review, Downbeat, Backstreets, Asbury Park Press* and *New Jersey Monthly* and on nationally syndicated radio shows. He has also written four books about rock & roll and the blues and two books about New Jersey.

HARRY SHEARER's acting credits include roles in productions ranging from *This Is Spinal Tap* and *Saturday Night Live* to *Godzilla.* He currently plays more than a dozen characters on *The Simpsons.* He has written about political conventions and the O.J. Simpson civil trial for *Slate,* and about being in *The Truman Show* for *Details.* His first book, *Man Bites Town,* teeters on the edge of out-of-printhood.

Before becoming mayor of Cincinnati, **JERRY SPRINGER** was instrumental in the passage of the Twenty-sixth Amendment, which lowered the voting age from twenty-one to eighteen. His talk show, the *Jerry Springer Show,* is currently in its seventh season.

ROGER STEFFENS is an actor, author, lecturer, archivist, broadcaster, photographer and editor who has devoted the last twenty-five years of his life to reggae music. His Reggae Archives in Los Angeles boasts the world's largest collection of Bob Marley material. He lectures internationally on Marley's life, edits *The Beat* magazine's annual Bob Marley Collectors Edition, and is cowriting Bunny Wailer's autobiography.

HUNTER S. THOMPSON is a humble man who writes for a living and spends the rest of his time bogged down in strange and crazy wars. He is the author of many violent books and brilliant political essays, which his friends and henchmen in the international media have managed for many years to pass off as Gonzo Journalism.

AL TRAUTWIG has been a broadcaster since 1979, when he started covering soccer on the radio in New York City. Since then he has worked for the USA Network, ABC Sports and News and is currently hosting coverage of the Knicks, Rangers and New York Yankees on the Madison Square Garden Network. He has covered the 1994 World Cup, Tour de France, Kentucky Derby, Indianapolis 500, U.S. Open, Ironman Triathlon and seven Olympic Games for all three networks.

PETER TRAVERS has been ROLLING STONE's film critic and senior features editor for film since 1989. He was a former chair of the New York Film Critics Circle and was the film and theater critic for *People.* Currently a regular film commentator for CNN, Travers also edited *The ROLLING STONE Film Reader.*

BILL VAN PARYS is senior editor at *Jane* magazine and a former associate editor at ROLLING STONE. He is relieved that his years of "research" have gone to good use.

PHIL WALDEN founded Capricorn Records, the premiere Southern-rock label during the Seventies, and orchestrated rock & roll fund-raisers for Jimmy Carter's presidential campaign. He relaunched the label in 1991 and continues to run it.

HARRY WEINGER is director of A&R for PolyMedia, the catalogue development division of PolyGram Records. A Grammy Award winner, he has produced dozens of funk and soul compilations for James Brown, Kool and the Gang, Parliament, Mandrill, Earth, Wind and Fire, the Ohio Players and Barry White among many others. His writing has appeared in *Vibe,* ROLLING STONE, *Billboard* and other music publications.

DAVID WEIR is the former vice president of content for *Wired Digital* and the leader of the creative team that produced *HotWired, Wired News* and *Suck.com.* He was formerly the executive vice president of KQED, Inc.; acting news director for KQED-FM; an editor of ROLLING STONE, *California* and *Mother Jones* magazines; a writer for the *San Francisco Examiner;* cofounder and executive director of the Center for Investigative Reporting; and as a consultant helped launch the online magazine *Salon.* His books include *Circle of Poison, Raising Hell* and *The Bhopal Syndrome.*

JANN S. WENNER has been the editor in chief of ROLLING STONE since he founded the magazine in 1967. The chairman of Wenner Media, he is also devoted to several causes, including the Rock and Roll Hall of Fame Foundation, of which he is vice chairman, and Cease Fire, a public-education campaign created to inform citizens about the risks associated with handguns in the home.

DAVID WILD is a senior editor at ROLLING STONE.

TOM WOLFE is the author of *The Kandy-Kolored Tangerine-Flake Streamline Baby, The Pump House Gang, The Electric Kool-Aid Acid Test, Radical Chic and Mau-Mauing the Flak Catchers, The Painted Word, The Right Stuff, From Bauhaus to Our House,* and *Bonfire of the Vanities.*

RICHARD ZACKS is the author of *History Laid Bare: Love, Sex and Perversity from the Ancient Etruscans to Warren G. Harding,* which was excerpted in *Harper's* and earned the attention of the *New York Times,* which noted that "Zacks specializes in the raunchy and perverse." He has studied Arabic, Greek, Latin, French, Italian and Hebrew and received the Phillips Classical Greek Award at the University of Michigan. His writing has appeared in the *New York Times,* the *Atlantic Monthly, Time, Life, Sports Illustrated,* the *Village Voice, TV Guide* and similarly diverse publications.

BILL ZEHME was a ROLLING STONE senior writer until 1994 and currently maintains that position at *Esquire.* He is also the author of *The ROLLING STONE Book of Comedy* and *The Way You Wear Your Hat: Frank Sinatra and the Lost Art of Livin'.*

acknowledgments

MY MOST VIVID memory of the Seventies exists mainly because I repeated it so many times: When I got home every day after grade school, I would dial 264-6149 – my mother's work number – to let her know I was okay. Then I would proceed to do whatever I wanted to for the next few hours till she got home (I still can't reveal all my activities, but generally I behaved). The latchkey kid left on her own, knowing full well that she better be good 'cause Mom would soon return, was similar to my role in putting together this book. My boss, Holly George-Warren, became a mom herself just before we began closing this book, leaving me in charge. The difference this time around is that I could never have been "good" without the help of many others. So, first off, thanks to HG-W for having confidence in me, and to Ashley Kahn, who was so dedicated to this project, he guaranteed it would be the best. Ann Abel proved that she was better than able – she was great. And two people joined this project at a crucial moment, saving the day: Alanna Stang and Helene Silverman. Putting together a book that includes the work of over sixty writers (thank you, all!) takes at least as many behind the scenes: Kathryn Adisman, Carin Companick, Trenton Daniel, Jim Duffy, Tom Gogola, Philip Higgs, Peter Kahn, Peter Keepnews, Peter Kenis (an honorary RSP staffer), Lawrence Levi, Rachel Lipton, Tracie Matthews, Angie Maximo, Lisa Miller, Matthew Morse, Tana Osa-Yande, Su Patel, Jen Reiseman, Will Rigby, Susan Rubin, John Salisbury, Laura Sandlin, Tom Soper, Kaelen Wilson-Goldie and Tricia Wygal have each inspected nearly every word and picture. Andrew B. Caploe, Mitch Goldman, Patricia Romanowski, Paul Scanlon, John Swenson and Janet Wygal provided essential editorial input. Many people at Wenner Media have helped to ensure that RSP functions properly: Stephanie Beldotti, Kent Brownridge, Alison Grochowski, David Ha, Rachel Knepfer, Hubert Kretzschmar, John Lagana, Gretchen Lutz, Mary MacDonald, Chris Raymond, Paul Rouse, Kilian Schalk, France Senoran, Richard Skanse, Brittain Stone, Rich Waltman, Lucy Ware, Jann Wenner, Fred Woodward and Tom Worley. Also deserving our gratitude are those at Little, Brown: our editor, Michael Pietsch, and David Gibbs, Susan Canavan and Bryan Quible. Others who have been generous with their time are: Kim Akhtar, Louise Allen, Carol Bernson, Marva Boea, Leonard Brady, Carol Burnham, Sarie Calkins, Woodfin Camp, Bill Clegg, Gail Colson, Tracy Columbus, Kris Dahl, Paula Donner, Tracy Halliday, Karen Howes, Ivan Lerner, Laura Levine, O.J. Lima, Bill Madison, Terry McDonell, Kim Miller, Kathy Trautwig, Julie Robinson, Sandy Sawotka, Lyle Schweitzer, Corey Seymour, Linda Shafran, Eric Simonoff, Mark Spector, Andras Szanto, Laura Thiemann, Cory Wickwire, Dianne Wisner and Soo Yuon. *Facts on File,* Joel Whitburn's *Billboard* chart books, *Chronicle of the 20th Century* and *The People's Chronology* provided information for our timeline. And at last, those close to us who've made sure we're happy are Sarah Lazin (RSP's agent), Robert Warren (father of baby Jack) and Ian Gittler (you rock!).

Shawn Dahl
Senior Editor, Rolling Stone Press
April 1998